BRUNEI

CUSTOMS, EXPORT-IMPORT REGULATIONS AND PROCEDURES HANDBOOK

VOLUME 1

STRATEGIC INFORMATION AND BASIC REGULATIONS

International Business Publications, USA
Washington DC, USA - Bandar Seri Begawan

BRUNEI

CUSTOMS, EXPORT-IMPORT REGULATIONS AND PROCEDURES HANDBOOK

VOLUME 1 STRATEGIC INFORMATION AND BASIC REGULATIONS

UPDATED ANNUALLY

We express our sincere appreciation to all government agencies and international organizations which provided information and other materials for this handbook

Cover Design: **International Business Publications, USA**

2017 Edition Updated Reprint International Business Publications, USA
ISBN 978-1-5145-1436-8

Printed in the USA

For additional analytical, business and investment opportunities information,
please contact Global Investment & Business Center, USA
at (703) 370-8082. Fax: (703) 370-8083. E-mail: ibpusa3@gmail.com
Global Business and Investment Info Databank - www.ibpus.com

BRUNEI

CUSTOMS, EXPORT-IMPORT REGULATIONS AND PROCEDURES HANDBOOK

VOLUME 1

STRATEGIC INFORMATION AND BASIC REGULATIONS

TABLE OF CONTENTS

STRATEGIC AND BUSINESS PROFILE

BRUNEI DARUSSALAM

Capital and largest city	Bandar Seri Begawan 4°53.417′N 114°56.533′E4.890283°N 114.942217°E
Official languages	Malay
Recognised	English
Other languages	• Brunei Malay • Tutong • Kedayan • Belait • Murut • Dusun • Bisaya • Melanau • Iban • Penan
Ethnic groups (2004)	• 66.3% Malays • 11.2% Chinese • 3.4% Indigenous • 19.1% other
Demonym	Bruneian
Government	Unitary Islamic absolute monarchy
- Sultan	Hassanal Bolkiah
- Crown Prince	Al-Muhtadee Billah
Legislature	Legislative Council
	Formation
- Sultanate	14th century
- British protectorate	1888
- Independence from the United Kingdom	1 January 1984
	Area
- Total	5,765 km^2 (172nd) 2,226 sq mi
- Water (%)	8.6
	Population
- Jul 2013 estimate	415,717 (175th)
- Density	67.3/km^2 (134th) 174.4/sq mi
GDP (PPP)	2012 estimate
- Total	$21.907 billion
- Per capita	$50,440
GDP (nominal)	2012 estimate
- Total	$17.092 billion
- Per capita	$39,355
HDI (2013)	▲0.855 very high · 30th
Currency	Brunei dollar (BND)
Time zone	BDT (UTC+8)

Drives on the	left
Calling code	+673
ISO 3166 code	BN
Internet TLD	.bn

Brunei officially the **Nation of Brunei, the Abode of Peace** is a sovereign state located on the north coast of the island of Borneo in Southeast Asia. Apart from its coastline with the South China Sea, it is completely surrounded by the state of Sarawak, Malaysia; and it is separated into two parts by the Sarawak district of Limbang. It is the only sovereign state completely on the island of Borneo; the remainder of the island's territory is divided between the nations of Malaysia and Indonesia. Brunei's population was 408,786 in July 2012.

At the peak of Bruneian Empire, Sultan Bolkiah (reigned 1485–1528) is alleged to have had control over the northern regions of Borneo, including modern-day Sarawak and Sabah, as well as the Sulu archipelago off the northeast tip of Borneo, Seludong (modern-day Manila), and the islands off the northwest tip of Borneo. The maritime state was visited by Spain's Magellan Expedition in 1521 and fought against Spain in 1578's Castille War.

During the 19th century the Bruneian Empire began to decline. The Sultanate ceded Sarawak to James Brooke as a reward for his aid in putting down a rebellion and named him as rajah, and it ceded Sabah to the British North Borneo Chartered Company. In 1888 Brunei became a British protectorate and was assigned a British Resident as colonial manager in 1906. After the Japanese occupation during World War II, in 1959 a new constitution was written. In 1962 a small armed rebellion against the monarchy was ended with the help of the British.

Brunei regained its independence from the United Kingdom on 1 January 1984. Economic growth during the 1990s and 2000s, averaging 56% from 1999 to 2008, has transformed Brunei into a newly industrialised country. It has developed wealth from extensive petroleum and natural gas fields. Brunei has the second-highest Human Development Index among the South East Asia nations after Singapore, and is classified as a developed country. According to the International Monetary Fund (IMF), Brunei is ranked fifth in the world by gross domestic product per capita at purchasing power parity. The IMF estimated in 2011 that Brunei was one of two countries (the other being Libya) with a public debt at 0% of the national GDP. *Forbes* also ranks Brunei as the fifth-richest nation out of 182, based on its petroleum and natural gas fields

Brunei can trace its beginnings to the 7th century, when it was a subject state of the Srivijayan empire under the name Po-ni. It later became a vassal state of Majapahit before embracing Islam in the 15th century. At the peak of its empire, the sultanate had control that extended over the coastal regions of modern-day Sarawak and Sabah, the Sulu archipelago, and the islands off the northwest tip of Borneo. The thalassocracy was visited by Ferdinand Magellan in 1521 and fought the Castille War in 1578 against Spain. Its empire began to decline with the forced ceding of Sarawak to James Brooke and the ceding of Sabah to the British North Borneo Chartered Company. After the loss of Limbang, Brunei finally became a British protectorate in 1888, receiving a resident in 1906. In the post-occupation years, it formalised a constitution and fought an armed rebellion. Brunei regained its independence from the United Kingdom on 1 January 1984. Economic growth during the 1970s and 1990s, averaging 56% from 1999 to 2008, has transformed Brunei Darussalam into a newly industrialised country.

Brunei has the second highest Human Development Index among the South East Asia nations, after Singapore and is classified as a Developed Country. According to the International Monetary Fund (IMF), Brunei is ranked 4th in the world by gross domestic product per capita at purchasing power parity.

According to legend, Brunei was founded by Awang Alak Betatar. His move from Garang [location required] to the Brunei river estuary led to the discovery of Brunei. His first exclamation upon landing on the shore, as the legend goes, was "Baru nah!" (Which in English loosely-translates as "that's it!" or "there") and thus, the name "Brunei" was derived from his words.

It was renamed "Barunai" in the 14th Century, possibly influenced by the Sanskrit word varunai (वरुण), meaning "seafarers", later to become "Brunei". The word "Borneo" is of the same origin. In the country's full name "Negara Brunei Darussalam" "Darussalam" means "Abode of Peace" in Arabic, while "Negara" means "Country" in Malay. "Negara" derives from the Sanskrit Nagara , meaning "city".

Brunei Darussalam, the host of the 1995 BIMP-EAGA EXPO is a stable and prosperous country which offers not only a well-developed infrastructure but also a strategic location within the Asean region. The country is chugging full steam ahead to diversify its economy away from an over-dependence on oil and gas, and has put in place flexible and realistic policies to facilitate foreign and local investment. The cost of utilities are the lowest in the region, while political stability, extensive economic and natural resources and a business environment attuned to the requirements of foreign investors go towards making Brunei an excellent investment choice

At present the country's economy is dominated by the oil and liquefied natural gas industries and government expenditure patterns. Brunei exports crude oil, petroleum products and LNG mainly to Japan, the United States and the Asean countries. The second most important industry is construction, a direct result of the government's investment in development and infrastructure projects. Gearing up towards putting on the mantle of a developed country in January 1996, Brunei allocated in its 1991-95 Five Year Plan a hefty B$5 billion for national development, over a billion dollars more than in the previous budget. About B$510 million was allotted for 619 projects while B$550 million or 10 percent of the development budget went to industry and commerce. Some B$100 million alone was reserved for industrial promotion and development.

STABLE, CONDUCIVE ENVIRONMENT

The oil-rich country, lying on the north-western edge of the Borneo island, has never experienced typhoons, earthquakes or severe floods. Profitable investment can be had as the country levies no personal income tax, no sales tax, payroll, manufacturing or export tax.

Competitive investment incentives are available for investors throughout the business cycle marked by the start up, growth, maturity and expansion stages. The tax advantages at start up and the on-going incentives during growth and expansion are among the most competitive around. There is no difficulty in securing approval for foreign workers, from labourers to managers. With a small labour pool of 284,500 Brunei people and Bruneians showing a marked preference for the public sector as employer, the country has had to rely on foreign workers. These make up a third of its work force.

In line with moves to promote the private sector, it is encouraging to note the contribution from the non-oil and gas sector of the economy has risen, contributing about 25 percent to GDP compared to the oil and gas sector's 46 percent. In terms of infrastructure, Brunei is ready for vigorous economy activity. At its two main ports at Muara and Kuala Belait, goods can be shipped direct to Hong Kong, Singapore and other Asian destinations. Muara, a deep-water port 29 km away from the capital of Bandar Seri Begawan, has seen continual increase in container traffic over the past two decades.

The Brunei International Airport at Bandar offers expanded passenger and cargo facilities. Its new terminal can accommodate 1.5 million passengers and 50,000 tonnes of cargo a year, which is expected to suffice till the end of the decade. A 2,000-km road network serving the whole country undergoes continual expansion. A main highway runs the entire length of its coastline, linking Muara, the port entry point at one end, and Belait, the oil-production centre, at another end.

Telecommunications-wise, Brunei has one of the best systems in the region with plans for major upgrading. Telephone availability is about one to every three people.

Two earth satellite stations provide direct telephone, telex and facsimile links to most parts of the world. Operating systems include an analogue telephone exchange, fibreoptic cable links with Singapore and Manila, a packet switching exchange for access to high-speed computer bases overseas, cellular mobile telephone and paging systems. Direct phone links are also available in the more remote parts of the country via microwave and solar-powered telephones.

PIONEER INDUSTRY INCENTIVES

Companies granted pioneer status enjoy tax holidays of up to eight years. Brunei's regulations governing foreign participation in equity are the most flexible in the region, with 100 percent foreign ownership permitted. A pioneer company is also exempt from customs duty on items to be installed in the pioneer factory and from paying import duties on raw materials not available locally or produced in Brunei for the manufacture of pioneer products.

GEOGRAPHY

Location: Southeastern Asia, bordering the South China Sea and Malaysia
Geographic coordinates: 4 30 N, 114 40 E
Map references: Southeast Asia

Area:
total: 5,770 sq km
land: 5,270 sq km
water: 500 sq km

Area—comparative: slightly smaller than Delaware

Land boundaries:
total: 381 km
border countries: Malaysia 381 km

Coastline: 161 km
Land use:
arable land: 1%
other: 12%

permanent crops: 1%
permanent pastures: 1%
forests and woodland: 85%

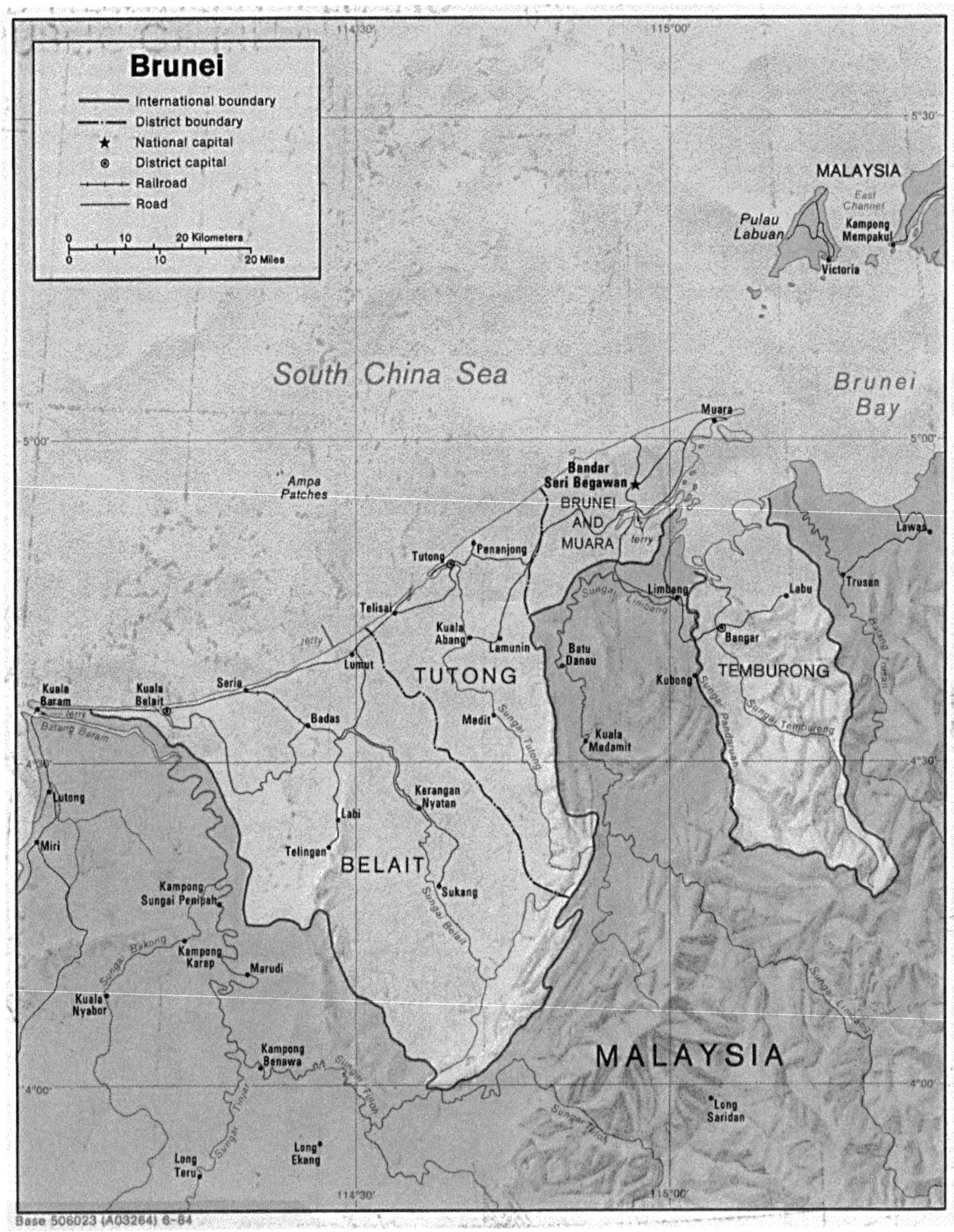
Brunei
International boundary
District boundary
National capital
District capital
Railroad
Road
0 10 20 Kilometers
0 10 20 Miles
South China Sea
MALAYSIA
Pulau Labuan
Victoria
Brunei Bay
Muara
Bandar Seri Begawan
BRUNEI AND MUARA
Tutong
Penanjong
Limbang
Labu
Trusan
Lawas
Bangar
TEMBURONG
TUTONG
BELAIT
Seria
Kuala Belait
Kuala Baram
Lumut
Badas
Labi
Telingan
Sukang
Medit
Kuala Medamit
Miri
Lutong
Marudi
Long Saridan
MALAYSIA
Base 506023 (A03264) 6-84

Irrigated land: 10 sq km
Natural hazards: typhoons, earthquakes, and severe flooding are very rare
Environment—current issues: seasonal smoke/haze resulting from forest fires in Indonesia

Environment—international agreements:
party to: Endangered Species, Law of the Sea, Ozone Layer Protection, Ship Pollution
signed, but not ratified: none of the selected agreements

Geography—note: close to vital sea lanes through South China Sea linking Indian and Pacific Oceans; two parts physically separated by Malaysia; almost an enclave of Malaysia

PEOPLE

Population: 322,982

Age structure:
0-14 years: 33% (male 54,154; female 51,766)
15-64 years: 63% (male 106,492; female 95,921)
65 years and over: 4% (male 7,945; female 6,704)

Population growth rate: 2.38%
Birth rate: 24.69 births/1,000 population
Death rate: 5.21 deaths/1,000 population
Net migration rate: 4.35 migrant(s)/1,000 population

Sex ratio:
at birth: 1.06 male(s)/female
under 15 years: 1.05 male(s)/female
15-64 years: 1.11 male(s)/female
65 years and over: 1.19 male(s)/female
total population: 1.09 male(s)/female

Infant mortality rate: 22.83 deaths/1,000 live births

Life expectancy at birth:
total population: 71.84 years
male: 70.35 years
female: 73.42 years

Total fertility rate: 3.33 children born/woman

Nationality:
noun: Bruneian(s)
adjective: Bruneian

Ethnic groups: Malay 64%, Chinese 20%, other 16%
Religions: Muslim (official) 63%, Buddhism 14%, Christian 8%, indigenous beliefs and other 15% (1981)
Languages: Malay (official), English, Chinese

Literacy:
definition: age 15 and over can read and write
total population: 88.2%
male: 92.6% *female:* 83.4%

GOVERNMENT

Country name:
conventional long form: Negara Brunei Darussalam
conventional short form: Brunei

Data code: BX
Government type: constitutional sultanate
Capital: Bandar Seri Begawan

Administrative divisions: 4 districts (daerah-daerah, singular—daerah); Belait, Brunei and Muara, Temburong, Tutong

Independence: 1 January 1984 (from UK)
National holiday: National Day, 23 February (1984)

Constitution: 29 September 1959 (some provisions suspended under a State of Emergency since December 1962, others since independence on 1 January 1984)

Legal system: based on English common law; for Muslims, Islamic Shari'a law supersedes civil law in a number of areas

Suffrage: none

Executive branch:
Brunei

Sultan	HASSANAL Bolkiah, Sir
Prime Minister	HASSANAL Bolkiah, Sir
Min. of Communications	Awang ABU BAKAR bin Apong
Min. of Culture, Youth, & Sports	MOHAMMAD bin Daud, Gen. (Ret.)
Min. of Defense	HASSANAL Bolkiah, Sir
Min. of Development	ABDULLAH bin Begawan
Min. of Education	Abdul RAHMAN bin Mohamed Taib
Min. of Energy	YAHYA bin Begawan
Min. of Finance	HASSANAL Bolkiah, Sir
Min. of Finance II	ABDUL RAHMAN bin Ibrahim
Min. of Foreign Affairs	MOHAMED Bolkiah, Prince
Min. of Foreign Affairs II	LIM Jock Seng
Min. of Health	SUYOI bin Osman
Min. of Home Affairs	ADANAN bin Begawan
Min. of Industry & Primary Resources	AHMAD bin Jumat, Dr.
Min. of Religious Affairs	MOHD ZAIN bin Serudin, Dr.
Senior Min. in the Prime Minister's Office	Al Muhtadee BILLAH, Crown Prince

Ambassador to the US	PUTEH ibni Mohammad Alam
Permanent Representative to the UN, New York	SHOFRY bin Abdul Ghafor

Legislative branch: unicameral Legislative Council or Majlis Masyuarat Megeri (a privy council that serves only in a consultative capacity; NA seats; members appointed by the monarch)
elections: last held in March 1962
note: in 1970 the Council was changed to an appointive body by decree of the monarch; an elected Legislative Council is being considered as part of constitutional reform, but elections are unlikely for several years

Judicial branch: Supreme Court, chief justice and judges are sworn in by the monarch for three-year terms

Political parties and leaders: Brunei Solidarity National Party or PPKB in Malay [Haji Mohd HATTA bin Haji Zainal Abidin, president]; the PPKB is the only legal political party in Brunei; it was registered in 1985, but became largely inactive after 1988; it has less than 200 registered party members; other parties include Brunei People's Party or PRB (banned in 1962) and Brunei National Democratic Party (registered in May 1985, deregistered by the Brunei Government in 1988)

International organization participation: APEC, ASEAN, C, CCC, ESCAP, G-77, IBRD, ICAO, ICRM, IDB, IFRCS, IMF, IMO, Inmarsat, Intelsat, Interpol, IOC, ISO (correspondent), ITU, NAM, OIC, OPCW, UN, UNCTAD, UPU, WHO, WIPO, WMO, WTrO

Diplomatic representation in the US:
chief of mission: Ambassador Pengiran Anak Dato Haji PUTEH Ibni Mohammad Alam
chancery: Watergate, Suite 300, 3rd floor, 2600 Virginia Avenue NW, Washington, DC 20037
telephone: (202) 342-0159
FAX: (202) 342-0158

Diplomatic representation from the US:
***chief of mission:* Ambassador Craig B. Allen**
embassy: Third Floor, Teck Guan Plaza, Jalan Sultan, Bandar Seri Begawan
mailing address: PSC 470 (BSB), FPO AP 96534-0001
telephone: [673] (2) 229670 *FAX:* [673] (2) 225293

Flag description: yellow with two diagonal bands of white (top, almost double width) and black starting from the upper hoist side; the national emblem in red is superimposed at the center; the emblem includes a swallow-tailed flag on top of a winged column within an upturned crescent above a scroll and flanked by two upraised hands

ECONOMY

Brunei is an energy-rich sultanate on the northern coast of Borneo in Southeast Asia. Brunei boasts a well-educated, largely English-speaking population; excellent infrastructure; and a stable government intent on attracting foreign investment. Crude oil and natural gas production account for approximately 65% of GDP and 95% of exports, with Japan as the primary export market.

Per capita GDP is among the highest in the world, and substantial income from overseas investment supplements income from domestic hydrocarbon production. Bruneian citizens pay no personal income taxes, and the government provides free medical services and free education through the university level.

The Bruneian Government wants to diversify its economy away from hydrocarbon exports to other industries such as information and communications technology and halal manufacturing, permissible under Islamic law. Brunei's trade in 2016 was set to increase following its regional economic integration in the ASEAN Economic Community, and the expected ratification of the Trans-Pacific Partnership trade agreement.

GDP (purchasing power parity):

$32.76 billion (2016 est.)
$33.17 billion (2015 est.)
$32.95 billion (2014 est.)
note: data are in 2016 dollars
country comparison to the world: 127

GDP (official exchange rate):
$11.4 billion (2016 est.)

GDP - real growth rate:
-2.5% (2016 est.)
-0.4% (2015 est.)
-2.5% (2014 est.)
country comparison to the world: 209

GDP - per capita (PPP):
$77,500 (2016 est.)
$80,600 (2015 est.)
$81,900 (2014 est.)
note: data are in 2016 dollars
country comparison to the world: 10

Gross national saving:
43.5% of GDP (2016 est.)
51.3% of GDP (2015 est.)
58.1% of GDP (2014 est.)
country comparison to the world: 6

GDP - composition, by end use:
household consumption: 22.5%
government consumption: 26.6%
investment in fixed capital: 35.3%
investment in inventories: 0%
exports of goods and services: 52.1%
imports of goods and services: -36.5% (2016 est.)

GDP - composition, by sector of origin:
agriculture: 1.2%
industry: 56.5%
services: 42.4% (2016 est.)

Agriculture - products:

rice, vegetables, fruits; chickens, water buffalo, cattle, goats, eggs

Industries:
petroleum, petroleum refining, liquefied natural gas, construction, agriculture, transportation

Industrial production growth rate:
-2.9% (2016 est.)
country comparison to the world: 179

Labor force:
203,600 (2014 est.)
country comparison to the world: 169

Labor force - by occupation:
agriculture: 4.2%
industry: 62.8%
services: 33% (2008 est.)

Unemployment rate:
6.9% (2016 est.)
9.3% (2011 est.)
country comparison to the world: 90

Budget:
revenues: $2.679 billion
expenditures: $4.561 billion (2016 est.)

Taxes and other revenues:
24% of GDP (2016 est.)
country comparison to the world: 123

Budget surplus (+) or deficit (-):
-16.8% of GDP (2016 est.)
country comparison to the world: 213

Public debt:
3.1% of GDP (2016 est.)
3% of GDP (2015 est.)
country comparison to the world: 203

Fiscal year:
1 April - 31 March

Inflation rate (consumer prices):
-0.7% (2016 est.)
-0.4% (2015 est.)
country comparison to the world: 24

Commercial bank prime lending rate:
5.5% (31 December 2016 est.)
5.5% (31 December 2015 est.)
country comparison to the world: 130

Stock of narrow money:
$3.232 billion (31 December 2016 est.)
$3.31 billion (31 December 2015 est.)
country comparison to the world: 115

Stock of broad money:
$10.08 billion (31 December 2016 est.)
$10.16 billion (31 December 2015 est.)
country comparison to the world: 105

Stock of domestic credit:
$4.066 billion (31 December 2016 est.)
$5.323 billion (31 December 2015 est.)
country comparison to the world: 131

Current account balance:
$1.091 billion (2016 est.)
$2.071 billion (2015 est.)
country comparison to the world: 41

Exports:
$5.023 billion (2016 est.)
$6.126 billion (2015 est.)
country comparison to the world: 105

Exports - commodities:
mineral fuels, organic chemicals

Exports - partners:
Japan 36.5%, South Korea 16.8%, Thailand 10.6%, India 9.8%, Malaysia 6.6%, China 4.6% (2016)

Imports:
$3.119 billion (2016 est.)
$3.216 billion (2015 est.)
country comparison to the world: 140

Imports - commodities:
machinery and mechanical appliance parts, mineral fuels, motor vehicles, electric machinery

Imports - partners:
US 28.4%, Malaysia 24%, Singapore 7.1%, Indonesia 5.7%, Japan 5.3%, China 4.9%, Australia 4.3% (2016)

Debt - external:
$0 (2014)
$0 (2013)
note: public external debt only; private external debt unavailable
country comparison to the world: 207

Exchange rates:
Bruneian dollars (BND) per US dollar -
1.3814 (2016 est.)

1.3814 (2015 est.)
1.3749 (2014 est.)
1.267 (2013 est.)
1.25 (2012 est.)

ENERGY

Electricity - production:
3.723 billion kWh (est.)
country comparison to the world: 126

Electricity - consumption:
3.391 billion kWh (est.)
country comparison to the world: 127

Electricity - exports:
0 kWh (est.)
country comparison to the world: 111

Electricity - imports:
0 kWh (est.)
country comparison to the world: 123

Electricity - installed generating capacity:
759,000 kW (est.)
country comparison to the world: 129

Electricity - from fossil fuels:
100% of total installed capacity (est.)
country comparison to the world: 9

Electricity - from nuclear fuels:
0% of total installed capacity (est.)
country comparison to the world: 57

Electricity - from hydroelectric plants:
0% of total installed capacity (2010 est.)
country comparison to the world: 161

Electricity - from other renewable sources:
0% of total installed capacity (est.)
country comparison to the world: 162

Crude oil - production:
141,000 bbl/day (est.)
country comparison to the world: 45

Crude oil - exports:
147,900 bbl/day (est.)
country comparison to the world: 35

Crude oil - imports:
0 bbl/day (est.)
country comparison to the world: 166

Crude oil - proved reserves:
1.1 billion bbl (1 January 2013 est.)
country comparison to the world: 41

Refined petroleum products - production:
13,500 bbl/day (est.)
country comparison to the world: 101

Refined petroleum products - consumption:
14,640 bbl/day (est.)
country comparison to the world: 144

Refined petroleum products - exports:
0 bbl/day (est.)
country comparison to the world: 159

Refined petroleum products - imports:
3,198 bbl/day (est.)
country comparison to the world: 169

Natural gas - production:
12.44 billion cu m (est.)
country comparison to the world: 38

Natural gas - consumption:
2.97 billion cu m (est.)
country comparison to the world: 73

Natural gas - exports:
9.42 billion cu m (est.)
country comparison to the world: 25

Natural gas - imports:
0 cu m (est.)
country comparison to the world: 167

Natural gas - proved reserves:
390.8 billion cu m (1 January 2013 est.)
country comparison to the world: 35

Carbon dioxide emissions from consumption of energy:
8.656 million Mt (2011 est.)

COMMUNCATION

Telephones - main lines in use:
70,933
country comparison to the world: 154

Telephones - mobile cellular:
469,700
country comparison to the world: 170

Telephone system:
general assessment: service throughout the country is good; international service is good to Southeast Asia, Middle East, Western Europe, and the US
domestic: every service available
international: country code - 673; landing point for the SEA-ME-WE-3 optical telecommunications submarine cable that provides links to Asia, the Middle East, and Europe; the Asia-America Gateway submarine cable network provides new links to Asia and the US; satellite earth stations - 2 Intelsat (1 Indian Ocean and 1 Pacific Ocean)

Broadcast media:
state-controlled Radio Television Brunei (RTB) operates 5 channels; 3 Malaysian TV stations are available; foreign TV broadcasts are available via satellite and cable systems; RTB operates 5 radio networks and broadcasts on multiple frequencies; British Forces Broadcast Service (BFBS) provides radio broadcasts on 2 FM stations; some radio broadcast stations from Malaysia are available via repeaters (2009)

Internet country code:
.bn

Internet hosts:
49,457
country comparison to the world: 96

Internet users:
314,900
country comparison to the world: 128

TRANSPORTATION

Railways:
total: 13 km (private line)
narrow gauge: 13 km 0.610-m gauge

Highways:
total: 1,150 km *paved:* 399 km *unpaved:* 751 km

Waterways: 209 km; navigable by craft drawing less than 1.2 m
Pipelines: crude oil 135 km; petroleum products 418 km; natural gas 920 km
Ports and harbors: Bandar Seri Begawan, Kuala Belait, Muara, Seria, Tutong
Merchant marine:
total: 7 liquefied gas tankers (1,000 GRT or over) totaling 348,476 GRT/340,635 DWT

Airports: 2

Airports—with paved runways:
total: 1
over 3,047 m: 1
Airports—with unpaved runways:
total: 1 *914 to 1,523 m:* 1 **Heliports:** 3

MILITARY

Military branches: Land Forces, Navy, Air Force, Royal Brunei Police
Military manpower—military age: 18 years of age
Military manpower—availability:
males age 15-49: 88,628
Military manpower—fit for military service:
males age 15-49: 51,270
Military manpower—reaching military age annually:
males: 3,078
Military expenditures—dollar figure: $343 million
Military expenditures—percent of GDP: 6%

TRANSNATIONAL ISSUES

Disputes—international: possibly involved in a complex dispute over the Spratly Islands with China, Malaysia, Philippines, Taiwan, and Vietnam; in 1984, Brunei established an exclusive fishing zone that encompasses Louisa Reef in the southern Spratly Islands, but has not publicly claimed the island.

IMPORTANT INFORMATION FOR UNDERSTANDING BRUNEI

PROFILE

OFFICIAL NAME: Negara Brunei Darussalam

Geography
Area: 5,765 sq. km. (2,226 sq. mi.), slightly larger than Delaware.
Cities: *Capital*--Bandar Seri Begawan.
Terrain: East--flat coastal plain rises to mountains; west--hilly lowland with a few mountain ridges.
Climate: Equatorial; high temperatures, humidity, and rainfall.

People
Nationality: *Noun and adjective*--Bruneian(s).
Population : 383,000.
Annual growth rate: 3.5%.
Ethnic groups: Malay, Chinese, other indigenous groups.
Religion: Islam.
Languages: Malay, English, Chinese; Iban and other indigenous dialects.
Education: *Years compulsory*--9. *Literacy* (2006)--94.7%.
Health: *Life expectancy (years)*--74.4 (men), 77.4 (women) yrs. *Infant mortality rate* --12.25/1,000.

Government
Type: Malay Islamic Monarchy.
Independence: January 1, 1984.
Constitution: 1959.
Branches: *Executive*--Sultan is both head of state and Prime Minister, presiding over a fourteen-member cabinet. *Legislative*--a Legislative Council has been reactivated after a 20-year suspension to play an advisory role for the Sultan. *Judicial* (based on Indian penal code and English common law)--magistrate's courts, High Court, Court of Appeals, Judicial Committee of the Privy Council (sits in London).
Subdivisions: *Four districts*--Brunei-Muara, Belait, Tutong, and Temburong.

Economy
Natural resources: Oil and natural gas.
Trade: *Exports*--oil, liquefied natural gas, petroleum products, garments. Major markets--Japan, Korea, ASEAN, U.S. *Imports*--machinery and transport equipment, manufactured goods. *Major suppliers*--ASEAN, Japan, U.S., EU.

PEOPLE

Many cultural and linguistic differences make Brunei Malays distinct from the larger Malay populations in nearby Malaysia and Indonesia, even though they are ethnically related and share the Muslim religion.
Brunei has hereditary nobility, carrying the title Pengiran. The Sultan can award to commoners the title Pehin, the equivalent of a life peerage awarded in the United Kingdom. The Sultan also can award his subjects the Dato, the equivalent of a knighthood in the United Kingdom, and Datin, the equivalent of damehood.

Bruneians adhere to the practice of using complete full names with all titles, including the title Haji (for men) or Hajah (for women) for those who have made the Haj pilgrimage to Mecca. Many

Brunei Malay women wear the tudong, a traditional head covering. Men wear the songkok, a traditional Malay cap. Men who have completed the Haj can wear a white songkok.
The requirements to attain Brunei citizenship include passing tests in Malay culture, customs, and language. Stateless permanent residents of Brunei are given International Certificates of Identity, which allow them to travel overseas. The majority of Brunei's Chinese are permanent residents, and many are stateless. An amendment to the National Registration and Immigration Act of 2002 allowed female Bruneian citizens for the first time to transfer their nationality to their children.

Oil wealth allows the Brunei Government to provide the population with one of Asia's finest health care systems. Malaria has been eradicated, and cholera is virtually nonexistent. There are five general hospitals--in Bandar Seri Begawan, Tutong, Kuala Belait, Bangar, and Seria--and there are numerous health clinics throughout the country.

Education starts with preschool, followed by 6 years of primary education and up to 7 years of secondary education. Nine years of education are mandatory. Most of Brunei's college students attend universities and other institutions abroad, but approximately 3,674 study at the University of Brunei Darussalam. Opened in 1985, the university has a faculty of more than 300 instructors and is located on a sprawling campus overlooking the South China Sea.
The official language is Malay, but English is widely understood and used in business. Other languages spoken are several Chinese dialects, Iban, and a number of native dialects. Islam is the official religion, but religious freedom is guaranteed under the constitution.

HISTORY

Historians believe there was a forerunner to the present Brunei Sultanate, which the Chinese called Po-ni. Chinese and Arabic records indicate that this ancient trading kingdom existed at the mouth of the Brunei River as early as the seventh or eighth century A.D. This early kingdom was apparently conquered by the Sumatran Hindu Empire of Srivijaya in the early ninth century, which later controlled northern Borneo and the Philippines. It was subjugated briefly by the Java-based Majapahit Empire but soon regained its independence and once again rose to prominence.

The Brunei Empire had its golden age from the 15th to the 17th centuries, when its control extended over the entire island of Borneo and north into the Philippines. Brunei was particularly powerful under the fifth sultan, Bolkiah (1473-1521), who was famed for his sea exploits and even briefly captured Manila; and under the ninth sultan, Hassan (1605-19), who fully developed an elaborate Royal Court structure, elements of which remain today.

After Sultan Hassan, Brunei entered a period of decline due to internal battles over royal succession as well as the rising influences of European colonial powers in the region that, among other things, disrupted traditional trading patterns, destroying the economic base of Brunei and many other Southeast Asian sultanates. In 1839, the English adventurer James Brooke arrived in Borneo and helped the Sultan put down a rebellion. As a reward, he became governor and later "Rajah" of Sarawak in northwest Borneo and gradually expanded the territory under his control.

Meanwhile, the British North Borneo Company was expanding its control over territory in northeast Borneo. In 1888, Brunei became a protectorate of the British Government, retaining internal independence but with British control over external affairs. In 1906, Brunei accepted a further measure of British control when executive power was transferred to a British resident, who advised the ruler on all matters except those concerning local custom and religion.

In 1959, a new constitution was written declaring Brunei a self-governing state, while its foreign affairs, security, and defense remained the responsibility of the United Kingdom. An attempt in 1962 to introduce a partially elected legislative body with limited powers was abandoned after the opposition political party, Parti Rakyat Brunei, launched an armed uprising, which the government put down with the help of British forces. In the late 1950s and early 1960s, the government also resisted pressures to join neighboring Sabah and Sarawak in the newly formed Malaysia. The Sultan eventually decided that Brunei would remain an independent state.

In 1967, Sultan Omar abdicated in favor of his eldest son, Hassanal Bolkiah, who became the 29th ruler. The former Sultan remained as Defense Minister and assumed the royal title Seri Begawan. In 1970, the national capital, Brunei Town, was renamed Bandar Seri Begawan in his honor. The Seri Begawan died in 1986.

On January 4, 1979, Brunei and the United Kingdom signed a new treaty of friendship and cooperation. On January 1, 1984, Brunei Darussalam became a fully independent state.

GOVERNMENT AND POLITICAL CONDITIONS

Under Brunei's 1959 constitution, the Sultan is the head of state with full executive authority, including emergency powers since 1962. The Sultan is assisted and advised by five councils, which he appoints. A Council of Ministers, or cabinet, which currently consists of 14 members (including the Sultan himself), assists in the administration of the government. The Sultan presides over the cabinet as Prime Minister and also holds the positions of Minister of Defense and Minister of Finance. His son, the Crown Prince, serves as Senior Minister. One of the Sultan's brothers, Prince Mohamed, serves as Minister of Foreign Affairs.

Brunei's legal system is based on English common law, with an independent judiciary, a body of written common law judgments and statutes, and legislation enacted by the sultan. The local magistrates' courts try most cases. More serious cases go before the High Court, which sits for about 2 weeks every few months. Brunei has an arrangement with the United Kingdom whereby United Kingdom judges are appointed as the judges for Brunei's High Court and Court of Appeal. Final appeal can be made to the Judicial Committee of the Privy Council in London in civil but not criminal cases. Brunei also has a separate system of Islamic courts that apply Sharia law in family and other matters involving Muslims.

The Government of Brunei assures continuing public support for the current form of government by providing economic benefits such as subsidized food, fuel, and housing; free education and medical care; and low-interest loans for government employees.

The Sultan said in a 1989 interview that he intended to proceed, with prudence, to establish more liberal institutions in the country and that he would reintroduce elections and a legislature when he "[could] see evidence of a genuine interest in politics on the part of a responsible majority of Bruneians." In 1994, a constitutional review committee submitted its findings to the Sultan, but these have not been made public. In 2004 the Sultan re-introduced an appointed Legislative Council with minimal powers. Five of the 31 seats on the Council are indirectly elected by village leaders.

Brunei's economy is almost totally supported by exports of crude oil and natural gas. The government uses its earnings in part to build up its foreign reserves, which at one time reportedly reached more than $30 billion. The country's wealth, coupled with its membership in the United Nations, Association of Southeast Asian Nations (ASEAN), the Asia Pacific Economic Cooperation (APEC) forum, and the Organization of the Islamic Conference give it an influence in the world disproportionate to its size.

Principal Government Officials

Sultan and Yang di-Pertuan, Prime Minister, Minister of Defense, and Minister of Finance--His Majesty Sultan Hassanal Bolkiah
Senior Minister--His Royal Highness Crown Prince Billah
Minister of Foreign Affairs--His Royal Highness Prince Mohamed Bolkiah

Ambassador to the United States--Pengiran Anak Dato Haji Puteh
Ambassador to the United Nations--Dr. Haji Emran bin Bahar
Brunei Darussalam maintains an embassy in the United States at 3520 International Court, NW, Washington, DC 20008; tel. 202-237-1838.

ECONOMY

Currency	Brunei dollar BND
Fixed exchange rates	1 Brunei dollar = 1 Singapore dollar
Fiscal year	1 April – 31 March (from April 2009)
Trade organisations	APEC, ASEAN, WTO. BIMP-EAGA
Statistics	
GDP	$20.38 billion PPP Rank: 123rd
GDP growth	2.8% Q1
GDP per capita	$51,600
GDP by sector	agriculture (0.7%), industry (73.3%), services (26%)
Inflation (CPI)	1.2%
Population below poverty line	1000 person
Labour force	188,800
Labour force by occupation	agriculture 4.5%, industry 63.1%, services 32.4%
Unemployment	3.7%
Main industries	petroleum, petroleum refining, liquefied natural gas, construction
Ease-of-doing-business rank	83rd
External	
Exports	$10.67 billion
Main export partners	Japan 46.5% South Korea 15.5% Australia 9.3% India 7.0% New Zealand 6.7% (est.)
Imports	$12.055 billion c.i.f.
Main import partners	Singapore 26.3% China 21.3% United Kingdom 21.3% Malaysia 11.8%
Public finances	
Public debt	$0
Revenues	$10.49 billion
Expenses	$5.427 billion
Credit rating	Not rated

Main data source: CIA World Fact Book *All values, unless otherwise stated, are in US dollars.*

Brunei is a country with a small, wealthy economy that is a mixture of foreign and domestic entrepreneurship, government regulation and welfare measures, and village tradition. It is almost totally supported by exports of crude oil and natural gas, with revenues from the petroleum sector accounting for over half of GDP. Per capita GDP is high, and substantial income from overseas investment supplements income from domestic production. The government provides for all medical services and subsidizes food and housing. The government has shown progress in its basic policy of diversifying the economy away from oil and gas. Brunei's leaders are concerned that steadily increased integration in the world economy will undermine internal social cohesion although it has taken steps to become a more prominent player by serving as chairman for the 2000 APEC (Asian Pacific Economic Cooperation) forum. Growth in 1999 was estimated at 2.5% due to higher oil prices in the second half.

Brunei is the third-largest oil producer in Southeast Asia, averaging about 180,000 barrels per day (29,000 m^3/d). It also is the fourth-largest producer of liquefied natural gas in the world.

Brunei is the fourth-largest oil producer in Southeast Asia, averaging about 219,000 barrels a day in 2006. It also is the ninth-largest exporter of liquefied natural gas in the world. Like many oil producing countries, Brunei's economy has followed the swings of the world oil market. Economic growth has averaged around 2.8% in the 2000s, heavily dependent on oil and gas production. Oil production has averaged around 200,000 barrels a day during the 2000s, while liquefied natural gas output has been slightly under or over 1,000 trillion btu/day over the same period. Brunei is estimated to have oil reserves expected to last 25 years, and enough natural gas reserves to last 40 years.

Brunei Shell Petroleum (BSP), a joint venture owned in equal shares by the Brunei Government and the Royal Dutch/Shell group of companies, is the chief oil and gas production company in Brunei. It also operates the country's only refinery. BSP and four sister companies--including the liquefied natural gas producing firm BLNG--constitute the largest employer in Brunei after the government. BSP's small refinery has a distillation capacity of 10,000 barrels per day. This satisfies domestic demand for most petroleum products.

The French oil company Total (then known as ELF Aquitaine) became active in petroleum exploration in Brunei in the 1980s. The joint venture Total E&P Borneo BV currently produces approximately 35,000 barrels per day and 13% of Brunei's natural gas.

In 2003, Malaysia disputed Brunei-awarded oil exploration concessions for offshore blocks J and K (Total and Shell respectively), which led to the Brunei licensees ceasing exploration activities. Negotiations between the two countries are continuing in order to resolve the conflict. In 2006, Brunei awarded two on-shore blocks--one to a Canadian-led and the other to a Chinese-led consortium. Australia, Indonesia, and Korea were the largest customers for Brunei's oil exports, taking over 67% of Brunei's total crude exports. Traditional customers Japan, the U.S., and China each took around 5% of total crude exports.
Almost all of Brunei's natural gas is liquefied at Brunei Shell's Liquefied Natural Gas (LNG) plant, which opened in 1972 and is one of the largest LNG plants in the world. Some 90% of Brunei's LNG produced is sold to Japan under a long-term agreement renewed in 1993.

The agreement calls for Brunei to provide over 5 million tons of LNG per year to three Japanese utilities, namely to TEPCo, Tokyo Electric Power Co. (J.TER or 5001), Tokyo Gas Co. (J.TYG or 9531) and Osaka Gas Co. (J.OSG or 9532). The Japanese company, Mitsubishi, is a joint venture partner with Shell and the Brunei Government in Brunei LNG, Brunei Coldgas, and Brunei Shell Tankers, which together produce the LNG and supply it to Japan. Since 1995, Brunei has supplied more than 700,000 tons of LNG to the Korea Gas Corporation (KOGAS) as well. In 1999, Brunei's natural gas production reached 90 cargoes per day. A small amount of natural gas is used for domestic power generation. Since 2001, Japan remains the dominant export market for natural gas. Brunei is the fourth-largest exporter of LNG in the Asia-Pacific region behind Indonesia, Malaysia, and Australia.

The government sought in the past decade to diversify the economy with limited success. Oil and gas and government spending still account for most of Brunei's economic activity. Brunei's non-petroleum industries include agriculture, forestry, fishing, aquaculture, and banking. The garment-for-export industry has been shrinking since the U.S. eliminated its garment quota system at the end of 2004. The Brunei Economic Development Board announced plans in 2003 to use proven gas reserves to establish downstream industrial projects. The government plans to build a power plant in the Sungai Liang region to power a proposed aluminum smelting plant that will depend on foreign investors. A second major project depending on foreign investment is in the planning stage: a giant container hub at the Muara Port facilities.

The government regulates the immigration of foreign labor out of concern it might disrupt Brunei's society. Work permits for foreigners are issued only for short periods and must be continually renewed. Despite these restrictions, the estimated 100,000 foreign temporary residents of Brunei make up a significant portion of the work force. The government reported a total work force of 180,400 in 2006, with a derived unemployment rate of 4.0%.

Oil and natural gas account for almost all exports. Since only a few products other than petroleum are produced locally, a wide variety of items must be imported. Nonetheless, Brunei has had a significant trade surplus in the 2000s. Official statistics show Singapore, Malaysia, Japan, the U.S., and the U.K. as the leading importers in 2005. The United States was the third-largest supplier of imports to Brunei in 2005.

Brunei's substantial foreign reserves are managed by the Brunei Investment Agency (BIA), an arm of the Ministry of Finance. BIA's guiding principle is to increase the real value of Brunei's foreign reserves while pursuing a diverse investment strategy, with holdings in the United States, Japan, Western Europe, and the Association of Southeast Asian Nations (ASEAN) countries.

The Brunei Government encourages more foreign investment. New enterprises that meet certain criteria can receive pioneer status, exempting profits from income tax for up to 5 years, depending on the amount of capital invested. The normal corporate income tax rate is 30%. There is no personal income tax or capital gains tax.

One of the government's priorities is to encourage the development of Brunei Malays as leaders of industry and commerce. There are no specific restrictions of foreign equity ownership, but local participation, both shared capital and management, is encouraged. Such participation helps when tendering for contracts with the government or Brunei Shell Petroleum.

Companies in Brunei must either be incorporated locally or registered as a branch of a foreign company and must be registered with the Registrar of Companies. Public companies must have a minimum of seven shareholders. Private companies must have a minimum of two but not more than 50 shareholders. At least half of the directors in a company must be residents of Brunei.

The government owns a cattle farm in Australia through which the country's beef supplies are processed. At 2,262 square miles, this ranch is larger than Brunei itself. Eggs and chickens are largely produced locally, but most of Brunei's other food needs must be imported. Agriculture, aquaculture, and fisheries are among the industrial sectors that the government has selected for highest priority in its efforts to diversify the economy.

Recently the government has announced plans for Brunei to become an international offshore financial center as well as a center for Islamic banking. Brunei is keen on the development of small and medium enterprises and also is investigating the possibility of establishing a "cyber park" to develop an information technology industry. Brunei has also promoted ecotourism to take advantage of the over 70% of Brunei's territory that remains primal tropical rainforest.

DEFENSE

The Sultan is both Minister of Defense and Supreme Commander of the Armed Forces (RBAF). All infantry, navy, and air combat units are made up of volunteers. There are two infantry battalions equipped with armored reconnaissance vehicles and armored personnel carriers and supported by Rapier air defense missiles and a flotilla of coastal patrol vessels armed with surface-to-surface missiles. Brunei has ordered, but not yet taken possession of, three offshore patrol vessels from the U.K.

Brunei has a defense agreement with the United Kingdom, under which a British Armed Forces Ghurka battalion (1,500 men) is permanently stationed in Seria, near the center of Brunei's oil industry. The RBAF has joint exercises, training programs, and other military cooperation with the United Kingdom and many other countries, including the United States. The U.S. and Brunei signed a memorandum of understanding (MOU) on defense cooperation in November 1994. The two countries conduct an annual military exercise called CARAT.

FOREIGN RELATIONS

Brunei joined ASEAN on January 7, 1984--one week after resuming full independence--and gives its ASEAN membership the highest priority in its foreign relations. Brunei joined the UN in September 1984. It also is a member of the Organization of the Islamic Conference (OIC) and of the Asia-Pacific Economic Cooperation (APEC) forum. Brunei hosted the APEC Economic Leaders' Meeting in November 2000 and the ASEAN Regional Forum (ARF) in July 2002.

U.S.-BRUNEI RELATIONS

Relations between the United States and Brunei date from the 1800s. On April 6, 1845, the U.S.S. Constitution visited Brunei. The two countries concluded a Treaty of Peace, Friendship, Commerce and Navigation in 1850, which remains in force today. The United States maintained a consulate in Brunei from 1865 to 1867.

The U.S. welcomed Brunei Darussalam's full independence from the United Kingdom on January 1, 1984, and opened an Embassy in Bandar Seri Begawan on that date. Brunei opened its embassy in Washington in March 1984. Brunei's armed forces engage in joint exercises, training programs, and other military cooperation with the U.S. A memorandum of understanding on defense cooperation was signed on November 29, 1994. The Sultan visited Washington in December 2002.

Principal U.S. Embassy Officials
Ambassador-- Craig Allen

Ambassador Craig Allen was sworn in as the United States ambassador to Brunei Darussalam on December 19, 2014.
Deputy Chief of Mission--John McIntyre
Management Officer--Michael Lampel

The U.S. Embassy in Bandar Seri Begawan is located on the third & fifth floors of the Teck Guan Plaza, at the corner of Jalan Sultan and Jalan MacArthur; tel: 673-2229670; fax: 673-2225293; e-mail: usembassy_bsb@state.gov

TRAVEL AND BUSINESS INFORMATION

The U.S. Department of State's Consular Information Program advises Americans traveling and residing abroad through Consular Information Sheets, Public Announcements, and Travel Warnings. **Consular Information Sheets** exist for all countries and include information on entry and exit requirements, currency regulations, health conditions, safety and security, crime, political disturbances, and the addresses of the U.S. embassies and consulates abroad. **Public Announcements** are issued to disseminate information quickly about terrorist threats and other relatively short-term conditions overseas that pose significant risks to the security of American travelers. **Travel Warnings** are issued when the State Department recommends that Americans avoid travel to a certain country because the situation is dangerous or unstable.

For the latest security information, Americans living and traveling abroad should regularly monitor the Department's Bureau of Consular Affairs Internet web site at http://www.travel.state.gov, where the current Worldwide Caution, Public Announcements, and Travel Warnings can be found. Consular Affairs Publications, which contain information on obtaining passports and planning a safe trip abroad, are also available at http://www.travel.state.gov. For additional information on international travel, see http://www.usa.gov/Citizen/Topics/Travel/International.shtml.

The Department of State encourages all U.S citizens traveling or residing abroad to register via the State Department's travel registration website or at the nearest U.S. embassy or consulate abroad. Registration will make your presence and whereabouts known in case it is necessary to contact you in an emergency and will enable you to receive up-to-date information on security conditions.

Emergency information concerning Americans traveling abroad may be obtained by calling 1-888-407-4747 toll free in the U.S. and Canada or the regular toll line 1-202-501-4444 for callers outside the U.S. and Canada.

The National Passport Information Center (NPIC) is the U.S. Department of State's single, centralized public contact center for U.S. passport information. Telephone: 1-877-4USA-PPT (1-877-487-2778). Customer service representatives and operators for TDD/TTY are available Monday-Friday, 7:00 a.m. to 12:00 midnight, Eastern Time, excluding federal holidays.

Travelers can check the latest health information with the U.S. Centers for Disease Control and Prevention in Atlanta, Georgia. A hotline at 877-FYI-TRIP (877-394-8747) and a web site at http://www.cdc.gov/travel/index.htm give the most recent health advisories, immunization recommendations or requirements, and advice on food and drinking water safety for regions and countries. A booklet entitled "Health Information for International Travel" (HHS publication number CDC-95-8280) is available from the U.S. Government Printing Office, Washington, DC 20402, tel. (202) 512-1800.

EU-BRUNEI RELATIONS

Official Name	Negara Brunei Darussalam
Population	0.38 million
Area	6000 km²
Gross Domestic Product	5 bn euros
GDP Per Capita	14.173 €
Real GDP (% growth)	3.0 %
Exports GDP %	0.85
Imports GDP %	0.27
Rate of inflation %	1.0
Exports to Brunei from EU (mn €, 2001)	108 EU imports from Brunei (mn €)
Imports to EU from Brunei (mn €, 2001)	72

Human Development Index (rank of 175°)	33
Head of State	HM Paduka Seri Baginda Sultan Haji Hassanal Bolkiah Mu'izzadddin Waddaulah (Sultan, prime minister, minister of finance and defence)

FRAMEWORK

The framework for co-operation dialogue with Brunei is the EC-ASEAN Agreement of 1980. There is no bilateral cooperation agreement.

POLITICAL CONTEXT

Brunei Darussalam became independent from the United Kingdom on 1 January 1984, and a week later joined the Association of South-East Asian Nations (ASEAN). Brunei is a constitutional monarchy with the Sultan Yang Di-Pertuan – Hassanal Bolkiah as the Head of State, Prime Minister, Defence Minister, as well as Minister for Finance. The Sultan presides over a 10-member cabinet which he appoints himself. Five councils advise the Sultan on policy matters: the Religious Council, the Privy Council, the Council of Succession, the Legislative Council and the Council of Ministers (the cabinet). Since 1962 the Sultan has ruled by decree. Thus, the system of government revolves around the Sultan as the source of executive power.

On 25 September 2004, the Legislative Council met for the first time in 20 years, with 21 members appointed by the Sultan. It passed constitutional amendments, calling for a 45-seat council with 15 elected members. In a move towards political reform an appointed parliament was revived in 2004. The constitution provides for an expanded house with up to 15 elected MPs. However, no date has been set for elections.

Brunei is a Muslim country, with a Ministry of Religious Affairs established to foster and promote Islam. Brunei continues to play a peacekeeping role in the Philippines, and is taking part in efforts to monitor peace in the Indonesian region of Aceh.

EUROPEAN COMMUNITY ASSISTANCE

By virtue of its advanced level of economic development Brunei does not benefit from bilateral development or economic projects.

EC co-operation with Brunei has for the greater part been limited to joint EC- ASEAN projects.

The EC has given financial support to the ASEAN-EC Management Centre (AEMC), located in Brunei, the contract for which has come to an end.

TRADE AND ECONOMIC

Since 1929, when oil was discovered in Brunei, the country has flourished. During 1998 and as a consequence of the Asia crisis, however, both exports and imports decreased in comparison with previous years.

- **Key role of oil and gas**: Brunei suffered little directly from the Asian financial crisis of 1997. But, in 1998, the Sultanate was hit by the sharp fall in oil sales and the bankruptcy of a locally-owned oil and gas company, resulting in a contraction in GDP of 4%.

Subsequently, economic activity recovered in step with the resumption of oil and gas extraction and, in recent years, the sharp rise in the oil price. The latest available data for GDP shows real annual growth around 3%. Oil reserves are officially estimated at 25 years, but, great hopes are placed in two new drilling concessions.

Economic structure: Almost everything the country needs is imported. Even the industrial labour force comes from abroad, mainly from India, the Philippines, Indonesia and Bangladesh as most of Brunei's citizens are employed as civil servants (60% of the population) and prefer the status related to that occupation. This also explains the apparent contradiction between the necessity to employ foreign manpower and the rising unemployment rate (officially at 4.7% but estimated at 9%).

· At the beginning of 2000, the government of the Sultanate announced an ambitious programme of **economic reforms** in order to reduce the dependence on oil and gas. Two initiatives have been taken up till know– to develop tourism and to support the creation of an off-shore financial centre in developing Islamic banking business.

· The tourism industry is, however, handicapped by the shortage of quality infrastructure, and the geographical insulation of the Sultanate.

Brunei's trade surplus fell by an estimated 74% in US dollar terms in 1999 as the price of oil and gas collapsed. A strengthening oil price and long-term contracts for natural gas, paid in US dollars, should, however, ensure that Brunei's trade position remains healthy.

At present Brunei produces oil and gas almost to the exclusion of other products. The government is trying hard, however, to develop manufactured exports, in particular cement and roofing (tiles) which are both protected sectors. The garment industry is struggling after the abolition of global quotas on the textile trade. The Sultan has announced financial reforms.

Brunei has signed a free-trade pact with New Zealand, Singapore and Chile. A Brunei Tourism Board has been set up

The domestic economy: Brunei's economic growth remains fairly sluggish, at 2.6% year on year but a recovery is likely to have taken place in the second quarter of 2005. The non-oil and gas sector is expanding more rapidly than the energy sector. High global oil prices have lifted transport prices, but overall inflation remains low.

Foreign trade and payments: High oil prices lay behind an increase in the merchandises-trade surplus in the first quarter of 2005.The oil and gas sector continues to account for the bulk of exports; garments exports were much lower than in the year-earlier period.

The investment policy in Brunei is largely open to foreign investors, as indicated by a favourable legal environment and a policy allowing full foreign ownership in a majority of economic sectors. Foreign investments have been more particularly in the last years as they are considered by the government as a key element to contribute to the targeted diversification of the country's economy.

As part of this strategy to attract foreign investments, an Economic Development Board (EDB) was created in 2001. The main sectors and projects promoted by the EDB and susceptible to attract foreign investments include port infrastructure, industry, communication (aviation hub), eco-tourism, and financial services. In parallel with the creation of the EDB, major policy changes have been made in the last years to promote foreign investments. August 2000 saw the introduction of an offshore legislation in Brunei. New laws were drafted covering international banking, insurance, offshore companies, trusts, limited partnerships and registered agents.

Changes in the legislation are too recent analyze its effects. The volume of FDI has doubled between 2001 and 2002, while the figures available until mid 2003 include that the trend is positive and that investments do not only target natural resources but also services.

BRUNEY TRADE AND CUSTOMS POLICY - STRATEGIC INFORMATION AND DEVELOPMENTS

TRADE POLICY REGIME: FRAMEWORK AND OBJECTIVES

During the period under review, new legislation in Brunei has continued to be promulgated by the Sultan as "Emergency Orders", which carry the force of law. International agreements, including WTO Agreements, once ratified by the Sultan, the Head of State and the Executive under Brunei's Constitution, must be adopted through national legislation to be enforceable in the country. A number of changes and revisions relating to WTO provisions have been made to national legislation on intellectual property rights, customs and excise, and investment, including foreign direct investment.

Regarding institutional developments, after many years without a legislature in Brunei, the Legislative Council was reconvened as a wholly appointed legislature in 2004, although no date has yet been set for a partial direct Legislative Council election. Trade policy formulation and implementation was transferred from the Ministry of Industry and Primary Resources to the Ministry of Foreign Affairs and Trade in 2005, which works in cooperation with other agencies, notably the Ministry of Finance. The institutional framework is characterized by a lack of transparency with respect to trade and trade-related policies, to the detriment of government accountability; in particular, there is no independent body to evaluate government policy and, as a consequence, to provide impetus for reform of policies that are found to be ineffective.

Brunei has intensified its participation in regional and, for the first time, bilateral trade agreements. It is active in ASEAN, the East Asia Growth Area, APEC, and the Trans-Pacific Strategic Economic Partnership Agreement, as well as in bilateral relations with the United States and Japan.

Brunei sees foreign investment as playing a key role in its economic and technological development. Seeking to promote private sector development in non-oil and gas industries, it overhauled its investment laws and established the Brunei Economic Development Board (BEDB) in 2001 to promote Brunei as an investment destination. The BEDB adopted a new approach to attracting FDI, focusing on a few large projects, including a global mega port hub and downstream manufacturing industries using natural gas. The Government expects these large-scale investment projects to improve the international image of Brunei, kick-start economic diversification, and provide significant employment opportunities for the local labour force.

TRADE POLICY OBJECTIVES AND ADMINISTRATION

OBJECTIVES

Brunei's economy remains heavily dependent on revenue from oil and gas. Small-scale manufacturers (mainly textiles and furniture) and primary production make up the rest of Brunei's merchandise economy. Brunei has a low tariff regime and imports nearly all of its major manufactured products and around 80% of its total food requirements. During the period under review, the Government has further sought to diversify the economy away from oil and gas as the primary source of revenue and economic activity by promoting private sector development in non-oil and gas industries. The Brunei Economic Development Board (BEDB) was set up in November 2001 to stimulate the growth, expansion, and development of the economy by promoting Brunei as an investment destination. In January 2003, the BEDB launched its two-pronged strategy6, through which it aims to attract US$4.5 billion in foreign direct investment and create 6,000 permanent new jobs by 2008. The BEDB also recognizes that it is imperative for Brunei to develop its small and medium enterprises (SMEs) in order to achieve sustained growth in private sector income and employment.

The Eighth National Development Plan (2001-05) continued the emphasis of the sixth and seventh plans on diversification of the economy to reduce the country's dependence on petroleum and natural gas. These plans, although far from comprehensive, have delineated proposals for government investment in infrastructure, services, and incentives, all aimed at diversifying the economy and at increasing private sector participation. In the 8th Development Plan, the Government has emphasized the need to diversify the economy through the expansion of agriculture and industry and the development of financial services, tourism, and communications technology. Brunei aims to diversify into areas like communications technology, financial services, halal (Muslim dietary law) food7, tourism and hospitality services, as well as downstream oil and gas industries like petrochemicals, oil refining, and aluminium smelting (Box I.1). Brunei would also like to turn itself into a major shipping hub. According to the authorities, the completion of the 8th Plan marked the end of the first long-term plan (1984-2005). Currently, a new, more comprehensive long-term plan is being formulated, together with supporting medium- and short-term plans. Details have not been made available.

Emphasis has been placed on the development of Brunei as a service hub for trade and tourism. Brunei sees itself as a bridge for the EAGA (East ASEAN Growth Area) member states to regional and global markets, and a gateway to EAGA markets for the rest of the world. Ports, airport facilities, and tourism services are being upgraded as part of plans to build upon Brunei's telecommunications network, both regionally and internationally.

POLICY IMPLEMENTATION

16. The Ministry of Foreign Affairs and Trade is the lead agency for trade policy formulation and implementation and is responsible for negotiating, signing, and ratifying trade treaties. The trade policy function was moved to the Ministry of Foreign Affairs (renamed the Ministry of Foreign Affairs and Trade in August 2005) from the Ministry of Industry and Primary Resources. The trade policy function is carried out in cooperation with other government agencies, including the Ministries of Finance, Industry and Primary Resources, Development, Communications, and Energy (Table II.1). In May 2005, the Sultan announced the creation of an Office of the Minister of Energy, working in conjunction with the Petroleum Unit, to improve the management of hydrocarbon resources.

MAIN TRADE-RELATED LAWS IN BRUNEI

Customs Order (2006) and related regulations Customs regulations; preferential tariffs; duty drawback; offences and penalties Valuation of Imported Goods Rules 2001 Definition of customs value consistent with WTO Customs (ASEAN Common Effective Preferential Tariffs Order) 2005; Customs (ASEAN Common Effective Preferential Tariffs) (ASEAN Integration System of Preferences) Order 2006 (not yet in force); Customs (Goods under early harvest programme) (Framework Agreement on Comprehensive Economic Cooperation between ASEAN and China) Order 2005; and Customs Agreement on Trade in Goods of the Framework Agreement on Comprehensive Economic Cooperation between ASEAN and China Order, 2006 Adoption of ASEAN trade agreements Companies Act (1957) Registration of companies; company law Securities Order (2001) Governs financial exchanges, dealers and other relevant persons providing advice in respect of managing or dealing in securities Banking Order 2006 Licensing of banks; balance sheets and information; control of banks Investment Incentives Order 2001 Investment Economic Development Board (Amendment) Order 2001 Foreign investment, economic development Income Tax Act (Amendment) Order 2001 Tax incentives Agricultural Pests and Noxious Plants Act (1962); Poisons Act; Misuse of Drugs Regulations 1984; Infectious Diseases Order 2003; and Infectious Diseases (Quarantine) Regulations 2006 Sanitary and phytosanitary regulations Public Health (Food) Regulations 2001; and Public Health (Food) Act 2002 Food labelling Halal Meat Act Regulate the supply and importation of halal meat Income Tax (Petroleum) Act Cap. 119 Corporate tax on petroleum Income Tax Act Cap. 35 Corporate tax on non-petroleum and gas companies Excise Order 2006 Excise taxes Price Control Act (1974) Price controls Copyright Order, 1999 Copyright protection Inventions Act Patents protection Trade Marks Act (2000) Trade marks Industrial Designs Order, 1999 Industrial designs Layout Designs Order, 1999 Layout designs of integrated circuits Financial Regulations, 1983 Government procurement International Banking Order, 2000; International Business Companies Order, 2000; International Takaful and Insurance Order, 2000; and Mutual Funds Order, 2001 Regulation and licensing of bodies carrying on the business of international banking Source: Government of Brunei Darussalam.

TRADE AGREEMENTS AND ARRANGEMENTS

As an original Member of the WTO, and a contracting party to the GATT since December 1993, Brunei is of the view that its economy will benefit from further multilateral trade liberalization. Brunei Darussalam is committed to applying MFN treatment to products coming from all WTO Members. At the same time, regional agreements and trade liberalization in the regional context, particularly in ASEAN (and EAGA) and APEC are considered to be important and have been pursued in the period under review to enhance access to regional markets. Brunei believes that regional and bilateral trade agreements, if consistent with WTO rules and disciplines, could contribute to multilateral trade liberalization through the WTO.

MULTILATERAL AGREEMENTS

21. Brunei is an original Member of the WTO. At the 2005 WTO Ministerial meeting, it underlined its commitment to the WTO, which it sees as one of the most important pillars of world order, and expressed the hope that the Doha negotiations could find room for the principle of fairness and for "visible development" in the sense of changes that improve day-to-day lives in the developing world. Brunei fears a situation emerging that amounts to "every country and every region for itself" which, in developing nations, could affect long-term peace, stability, and security.8

Upon accession, Brunei, as a developing country made use of transitional measures available under some of the WTO Agreements, notably Article VII of the GATT (Customs Valuation) and the Agreement on Trade-Related Aspects of Intellectual property Rights (TRIPS). According to the authorities, the Agreement on Customs Valuation was fully implemented with effect from 1 September 2001 as contained in the Customs (Valuation of Imported Goods) Rules 2001 and the Customs (Amendments) Order 2001.9

Like all Members of the WTO, Brunei is required to make regular notifications of its laws and regulations to the WTO (Table AII.1).

Brunei has not been involved in any disputes in the WTO since 2001, either directly or on a third party basis.

REGIONAL AGREEMENTS

(a) ASEAN

Brunei became a member of the Association of South-East Asian Nations (ASEAN) at independence in 1984 and attaches the highest importance to its membership. Brunei is also a member of the Brunei-Indonesia-Malaysia-Philippines-East ASEAN Growth Area (BIMP-EAGA), which seeks to promote economic growth and development in the ASEAN sub-region.

The Framework Agreement on enhancing economic cooperation, signed in 1992, established the Common Effective Preferential Tariff (CEPT) Scheme. Under the CEPT, it was agreed that tariffs on goods in the Inclusion List (i.e. subject to tariff reductions) would be reduced to 0-5% by 2002 for the founding members plus Brunei (ASEAN-6), by 2006 for Viet Nam, by 2008 for Laos and Myanmar, and by 2010 for Cambodia. Tariff reduction/elimination under the AFTA is granted on a reciprocal basis and local-content requirements apply.10 The process of reducing tariffs, which began in 1993, is almost complete for ASEAN-6 members; Brunei has reduced tariffs on 93% of tariff lines to 5% or 0% for products of ASEAN origin.11 Under the terms of AFTA, Brunei applies the two lower tiers, of 0% and 5%, to all goods imports from ASEAN members that meet the AFTA rules of origin requirements. According to the authorities, Brunei does not have any products in the temporary exclusion list.

ASEAN is also working to: remove non-tariff barriers to intra-ASEAN trade; harmonize customs nomenclature, valuation, and procedures; harmonize product standards and regulatory requirements; and improve rules of origin (ROOs) under the CEPT. With regard to the work programme on the elimination of non-tariff barriers (NTBs) by 1 January 2008 (First Package), 1 January 2009 (Second Package) and 1 January 2010 (Third Package), the authorities state that Brunei has submitted updates on its NTB list together with the relevant supporting legislation. As to the rules of origin under the CEPT, ASEAN is focussing on finalizing the product specific rules (PSRs) for products under the priority integration sectors (PIS).

The ASEAN Framework Agreement on Services, signed in 1995, guides services liberalization over and above WTO commitments, and promotes cooperation among service suppliers in ASEAN. To date, ASEAN has completed several packages of services liberalization covering construction, telecommunications, business services, financial services, air and maritime transport, and tourism. This involves preferential access for other ASEAN member states in the establishment of services entities and employment of professionals. Under the priority integration approach, tourism, healthcare, and air travel are scheduled to be liberalized by 2010. ASEAN countries are currently working on expanding negotiations to cover all sectors and modes of supply.

The ASEAN Investment Area Agreement, signed in 1998, is aimed at facilitating the free flow of direct investment, technology, and skilled professionals. The agreement covers manufacturing, agriculture, fisheries, forestry, and mining, as well as services activities related to these sectors.

The agreement is also aimed at increasing intra-ASEAN investment and FDI, promoting the economic integration of ASEAN, and jointly promoting ASEAN as an attractive region for FDI. In accordance with Articles 2(i) and 2(ii) of Schedule III of the Framework Agreement on the ASEAN Investment Area12, Brunei Darussalam is due to open all industries for investment to ASEAN investors by 2010 and to all investors by 2020; this constitutes a clear commitment to liberalizing the investment environment.

ASEAN is also seeking to enhance regional economic integration through the establishment of the ASEAN Economic Community (AEC) - a single market providing for the free flow of goods, services, skilled labour and, to some extent, capital - by 2015. Member countries have identified

11 priority sectors: agri-based products; air travel; automotive products; electronics; fisheries; healthcare; rubber-based products; information/communications technology (products and services) related to e-commerce; textiles and apparel; tourism; and wood-based products. ASEAN is currently working on legislation for the 12th priority sector, logistics. In 2003, the priority sectors accounted for more than 50% of intra-ASEAN trade. A Framework Agreement for the Integration of Priority Sectors was signed in 2004 to accelerate integration across members.

ASEAN is seeking regional trade agreements with other partners, for example China, Japan, Korea, CER members (Australia and New Zealand), and India. At the ASEAN summit in 2002, ASEAN members and China signed a framework agreement to begin negotiations in 2003 to create the world's largest FTA, with a combined market of 1.7 billion people. The ASEAN-China FTA is expected to be implemented over ten years through progressive elimination of tariffs and non-tariff barriers, and progressive liberalization of trade in services and investment. The Agreement on Trade in Goods was signed in November 2004. The first package of tariff reductions, covering 40% of tariff lines, was implemented on 1 July 2005; products covered by the "early harvest package", implemented on 1 January 2004, include live animals, meat, fish, dairy produce, other animal products, live trees, vegetables, fruit, and nuts. The ASEAN-China Services Agreement was signed in 2006 and entered into force on 1 July 2007. An ASEAN-Korea Agreement was signed in August 2006 and entered into force on 1 June 2007.

(b) BIMP-EAGA

The Brunei-Indonesia-Malaysia-Philippines East ASEAN Growth Area (BIMP-EAGA), formed in 1994, aims to increase economic cooperation, trade, investment, and tourism among participating economies in the sub-region.13 BIMP-EAGA currently has four priority areas of cooperation: transport, infrastructure, and ICT development; natural resource development; joint tourism development; and SME development. Brunei is the designated lead country in transport and oversees a number of working groups dealing with air linkages, sea linkages, and construction and construction materials and ICT.

The third BIMP-EAGA summit, held on the sidelines of the main ASEAN summit in January 2007 in the Philippines, concluded that efforts at economic integration were beginning to bear fruit and that faster growth in the region was likely over the medium term. During the summit, Brunei signed a memorandum of understanding (MoU) on air links with partner countries, which would allow fifth freedom traffic rights for passenger and cargo services in designated BIMP-EAGA points. According to the MoU, fifth freedom rights14 for both passenger and cargo services are to be available between Brunei's Bandar Seri Bagawan airport and those of Balikpapan Sepingan and Ponitanak Supadio in Indonesia, Davao and Zamboanga in the Philippines and Kota Kinabalu and Kuching in eastern Malaysia. The agreement is expected to reduce travel time in the region and boost trade and tourism links. A number of other measures were also agreed to simplify customs and immigration procedures in the region.

(c) APEC

34. Brunei is a member of the Asia-Pacific Economic Cooperation (APEC) forum, which has been instrumental in advancing regional and global trade and investment liberalization since it was founded in 1989. The 21 APEC economies collectively account for 46% of world trade and 57% of global GDP. In 2005, they undertook a review of progress towards the 1994 "Bogor Goals" of free and open trade and investment in the APEC region by 2010 for industrialized economies and by 2020 for developing countries. The review concluded that significant work was needed, including: redoubling efforts to advance the DDA negotiations; promoting high-quality FTAs; and improving the regional business environment.

Brunei has played an active role in advancing APEC's efforts to move towards the Bogor goals and to reduce the digital divide in the region with the aim of enabling individual or community-based access to Internet information and services by 2010.

To promote liberalization, each APEC member adopts a unilateral liberalization plan or Individual Action Plan (IAP). The IAPs can be implemented according to each economy's domestic policy objectives and are reviewed periodically by all APEC Members in the context of achieving the Bogor targets. The 2005 peer review of Brunei focused on a number of areas in which progress and best practices towards the achievement of the Bogor Goals were considered15: tariffs16, NTMs, services, investment, customs, IPRs, government procurement, standards and competition policy. The peer review noted that Brunei maintains low overall tariff rates and no quantitative restrictions, although non-transparent practices exist in some areas, for example quarantine and inspection. In services, the Government remains in a dominant position and maintains entry restrictions in several areas, including telecommunications. Brunei is considered to have a very progressive investment regime, which has facilitated inflows of FDI and thus national development.

(d) Trans-Pacific SEP

The Trans-Pacific Strategic Economic Partnership Agreement17 (Trans-Pacific SEP), between Brunei, Chile, New Zealand, and Singapore, was announced on 3 June 2005, on the sidelines of an APEC Ministers meeting in Korea (Box II.1). As part of the overall package, ministers also announced the conclusion of negotiations on a binding Environment Cooperation Agreement18, and a binding labour Cooperation MoU. The Agreement was first launched in October 2002 and Brunei asked to join the negotiations as a founding member before the final round in April 2005. The Agreement entered into force for Brunei on 12 July 2006, on terms that allow it to implement some of its commitments progressively by 2008.

The Trans-Pacific SEP will encourage Brunei Darussalam, Chile, Singapore, and New Zealand to pool their expertise, ideas, technology, and resources to improve their competitiveness in the global market. It will also help advance shared objectives in APEC and the WTO. Key elements comprise: a comprehensive agreement on trade in goods, whereby more than 90% of total trade among the four parties will be duty free on implementation; trade facilitation, aimed at reducing transaction costs relating to sanitary and phytosanitary measures, standards and conformance, and customs procedures; a liberalizing framework that will encourage trade in services (negotiations between Brunei and the other parties on its services specific commitments are expected to conclude in 2008); a commitment to ensure that companies from the other parties compete on an equal footing with domestic suppliers for government procurement contracts, above certain thresholds; cooperation on competition and intellectual property rights; and the provision of a framework for collaboration in strategic areas, such as innovation, and research and development.

(e) Asia Cooperation Dialogue (ACD)

Established in 2002, ACD is a forum of 30 member countries designed to consolidate Asia's competitiveness and strengths through cooperation in a number of areas, including: energy, agriculture, transport linkages, biotechnology, standards, IT development, tourism, finance, human resource development, and environmental education.19

TRANS-PACIFIC STRATEGIC ECONOMIC PARTNERSHIP

The Trans-Pacific SEP is to liberalize and facilitate trade in goods and services, improve the business environment, and promote cooperation on a broad range of economic areas of mutual interest to its parties, which have undertaken to remove all tariffs on traded goods over time. The Trans-Pacific SEP also includes broad coverage of services, which will make it easier for service providers to operate in Trans-Pacific SEP markets.

Measures relating to customs procedures, sanitary and phytosanitary procedures, technical barriers to trade, intellectual property, and competition policy are designed to reduce barriers to doing business. The agreement establishes dispute settlement mechanisms and protection to preserve governments' domestic regulatory and policy-making flexibility. It also establishes a framework for expanding the membership, through scheduled reviews and cooperation.

Goods

On entry into force, Brunei Darussalam has undertaken to ensure all tariffs currently at zero will be held at zero. Products include: dairy products, seafood products, fruit and vegetables, and meat products. Its remaining tariffs will be eliminated in three stages, in 2010 (forestry products), 2012 (some machinery) and 2015 (vehicles and vehicle parts, and remaining machinery). A short list of products (alcohol, tobacco, and firearms) is excluded, for the time being, from Brunei Darussalam's tariff elimination schedule for moral, human health, and security reasons. The list is set out in a 'side letter' to the Trans-Pacific SEP, which is available at: www.mfat.govt.nz/tradeagreements/transpacepa/transpacsepagreement.html. There are to be further discussions about how these products will be accommodated under the Trans-Pacific SEP.

Services

Under the agreed conditions for entry, Brunei Darussalam will have two years from entry into force of the Trans-Pacific SEP to negotiate its services schedule. Until it has completed these negotiations it will not benefit from the other parties' commitments in services. For temporary entry, each country has reaffirmed its commitments under the GATS relating to the movement of businesspeople. These are listed in their individual GATS schedules and set out conditions for the entry of mainly intra-corporate transferees including senior and specialized personnel.

Government procurement

The Trans-Pacific SEP applies to procurement by specific government agencies (listed in Annex

10.A of the Trans-Pacific SEP) for contracts valued above specified thresholds. Brunei has been granted a special threshold: on completion of its schedule, the provisions will apply only for tenders of goods and services above B$250,000. Brunei has been given two years in which to negotiate its government procurement schedule. Until it has completed these negotiations it will not benefit from the other parties' commitments in government procurement.

BILATERAL AGREEMENTS

In December 2002, Brunei and the United States signed a Trade and Investment Framework Agreement (TIFA) to enhance bilateral trade and investment liberalization in such areas as intellectual property, information and communication technology, biotechnology and eco-tourism, aquaculture, and halal products. It also includes consultations on the elements of a possible free-trade agreement. The TIFA was a product of the "Enterprise for ASEAN Initiative" announced by the United States in October 2002, aimed at strengthening ties between the United States and ASEAN countries.

In December 2006, Japan and Brunei announced an agreement on the principal points of a free-trade agreement to enhance cooperation in energy, human resources development, and capacity building. The Brunei-Japan Economic Partnership Agreement (BJEPA) was signed on 18 June 2007, to facilitate the free flow of goods, services, and investment. Brunei's exports to Japan consist almost entirely of oil and natural gas, while its imports from Japan are mainly cars and automotive parts. Brunei has undertaken to eliminate import tariffs on Japan's automotive products in four equal instalments from the Base Rate to free, as from the date of entry into force of this Agreement. The agreement covers trade in goods and services, customs procedures, investment, government procurement, and intellectual property protection.

According to the authorities, regular consultations between Brunei Darussalam and Pakistan are being held with the objective of further strengthening trade ties. A Brunei Darussalam-Pakistan Joint Study Group, initiated in 2005, held its first meeting in November 2006 in Pakistan, and subsequently in August 2007 in Brunei Darussalam.

FOREIGN INVESTMENT REGIME

43. The authorities state that foreign investment is open except in restricted sectors in which the Government is the major provider of services, such as the mass media, telecommunications, posts, energy and utilities. Other restricted activities are banking, arms and ammunition, retail businesses, petrol stations, and manufacture and sales of liquor. According to the type of industry and particular situation, full, majority or minority foreign ownership is allowed. Only activities relating to national food security and those based on local natural resources require local participation. Brunei does not restrict the repatriation of capital and there are no restrictions on the remittance of profits (e.g. dividends) or royalties from investments. Brunei allows recruitment of foreign workers ranging from labourers to executive managers in areas in which the supply of local workers is insufficient.

LEGISLATIVE AND INSTITUTIONAL FRAMEWORK AND INVESTMENT PROCEDURES

44. The basic legislation on investment, the Investment Incentives Order 2001, replaced the Investment Incentives Act (chapter 97), and the authority to administer the legislation was transferred from the Ministry of Finance to the Ministry of Industry and Primary Resources. Its main objectives are to promote the diversification of Brunei's economic activities by providing tax-based incentives to promoted activities; and to encourage investment and reinvestment activities to upgrade technology, undertake research and development, increase production capacities. Foreigners may be allowed to hold up to 100% of the equity in certain industries and activities in which the Government wishes to encourage investment (Table AII.2). Foreign nationals are generally not permitted to own land (of which 95% is estimated to be owned by the State), but may lease land for industrial purposes, agriculture, forestry, and aquaculture on a long-term basis.20

The Government of Brunei has established several agencies to promote foreign direct investment (FDI), which it hopes will become an important driver of growth in the local economy. The Ministry of Foreign Affairs and Trade is involved with national agencies, including MIPR and JPKE, in formulating national investment policies and monitoring developments nationally and regionally with a view to improving the investment climate of Brunei. The Brunei International Financial Centre (BIFC), under the Ministry of Finance, also aims to attract investment to the financial sector. In addition, the Brunei Industrial Development Authority (BINA), under the Ministry of

Industry & Primary Resources, coordinates all industrial development activities and liaises with other agencies to expedite applications for those requiring Government facilities and assistance. The BINA has developed several industrial parks near the Muara Port and in other parts of Brunei, with infrastructure to facilitate small and medium-sized enterprises.

Other significant legislation on domestic and foreign investment is the Economic Development Board (Amendment) Order 2001, which restructured the EDB as an autonomous statutory body tasked with promoting inward and outward investment. The Brunei Economic Development Board (BEDB), formed in 2001, aims to attract FDI and promote joint ventures so as to further diversify Brunei's economy and create employment opportunities for its people (Box II.2). The BEDB coordinates with relevant ministries and agencies to maximize the benefits generated by both local and foreign direct investment. The BEDB proposed a five-year US$4.5 billion infrastructure development strategy in January 2003, which could offer foreign firms significant technical, construction, and expansion opportunities. Specifically, the plans include a US$3 billion industrial site at Sungai Liang and a US$1.5 billion Mega port at Pulau Muara. The proposed industrial site includes a US$400 million power plant, relying on the Sultanate's natural gas resources, an aluminium smelter and downstream projects, as well as a port, free-trade zone, and supporting infrastructure. The Government of Brunei is in various stages of negotiation with investors on those projects.21

Additionally, the BEDB announced significant incentives and loans to encourage other investment projects from abroad. International consultancies have confirmed the growth potential for hospitality and tourism, focusing on eco-tourism, sports and medical tourism; financial services, aiming at high-end, niche investment management services and asset fund management; transportation and logistics primarily focusing on aircraft maintenance services; and business services, concentrating on software development and business process outsourcing.

The Ministry of Industry and Primary Resources is the main coordinating agency for investment and industrial development in the primary sector, manufacturing, and tourism. The Ministry encourages and helps local and foreign investors to participate in ventures to produce goods and services for export and local markets and to satisfy national food security and employment needs. The Ministry is aware of the importance of a clear timeframe and decision making process with respect to investment approvals.22

The Brunei Economic Development Board's (BEDB) economic diversification strategy is designed to create long-term business and employment opportunities for Bruneians. It is currently focusing on developing downstream oil and gas industries, particularly on its Sungai Liang Industrial Park (SPARK) and planning the development of a globally competitive port on Pulau Muara Besar, supported by an export processing zone for logistics, distribution and light to medium manufacturing industries. In addition to industrial site development, in 2003 the BEDB sponsored a study to identify industry clusters with the potential for growth. Subsequently, four industry clusters were prioritized: transportation and logistics; business services; financial services; and hospitality and tourism. The BEDB collaborates with various lead agencies to develop these clusters.

The BEDB's main objectives are to: stimulate the growth and development of the economy by promoting Brunei Darussalam as an investment destination; develop plans to attract foreign and local investment in industries and skill-intensive services that enjoy good export-market prospects; promote and assist in the development of industrial activities; encourage foreign and local industries to invest in new technology, automation, training, research, and product development activities; and support the development of local entrepreneurs and SMEs.

The general criteria for evaluation of investment projects are: sustainability, prospects of industrial spin-off and businesses opportunities for domestic SMEs, potential to create employment opportunities and fit with the national economic development plan. In keeping with its efforts to ensure real and sustainable benefits are derived from investments, investors enter into a Cooperation Agreement with the BEDB. In signing the agreement, the BEDB helps the investor in securing incentives, utilities, and infrastructure. The investor commits to agreed quantifiable and qualitative undertakings on a best endeavours basis in such areas as employment, transfer of technology, local participation, promotion of local SMEs, spin-offs, and community development.

INCENTIVES

49. In January 2001, the Sultan issued the Investment Incentives Order 2001 and the Income Tax Act (Amendment) Order 2001, which contained reforms designed to stimulate investment. The first made application for tax incentives simpler for corporations and the second broadened the tax incentives. The Investment Incentives Order 2001 provides for a number of incentives, mainly in the form of tax exemptions for companies that have been granted "Pioneer Status" and for the expansion of established enterprises. Administration of the legislation is under the Minister of Industry and Primary Resources. Longer corporate tax relief periods are provided to promote the establishment of industries; the emphasis is on pioneer enterprises, including high-technology industries, export-oriented manufacturing and services, research and development, transhipment, and activities that support the introduction of new technology into Brunei Darussalam. Any limited company with a Pioneer Status Certificate will be granted an exemption from corporate income tax (normally levied at a rate of 30%), for between two and five years depending on the level of investment on capital assets. The exemption begins on the first day of production and may be extended to 20 years. Pioneer Status companies are also exempted from customs duty on plant, machinery, and equipment for their premises, and on raw materials that are not available in Brunei and are to be used in the production of the pioneer products. Tax incentives are also provided for the expansion of an enterprise already established in Brunei.

BILATERAL INVESTMENT TREATIES AND DOUBLE TAXATION AGREEMENTS

50. During the period under review, Brunei has concluded bilateral investment treaties with France, Bahrain, India, and Iran; they will be signed once approval by the Government is obtained. Double taxation agreements (DTAs) have been signed with China, Singapore, and Laos; a number of other DTAs have been concluded (with Thailand, Pakistan, Oman, Viet Nam, and the Philippines) and await signature pending approval.

AID FOR TRADE

Brunei continues to face significant human resource and capacity challenges that limit its responsiveness at the multilateral level and affect the pace of implementation of its WTO obligations. New obligations for implementation arising out of the DDA may further challenge already stretched resources. Support from the international community could assist Brunei in achieving greater integration into the multilateral trading system. Two prominent areas in this regard are standards/SPS measures and intellectual property protection. Brunei could benefit from technical assistance to help develop its resources and establish appropriate standard institutions. Officials involved in the development of national standards, for example, could benefit from improved training, monitoring, and surveillance capacity, and performance in the area of notifications in both TBT and SPS matters. On TRIPS, while Brunei has enacted much of the legislation necessary to be fully compliant with the Agreement, lack of administrative capacity in a number of IPR-related areas is a major obstacle to implementation. Additional training on TRIPS and on the administration of IP legislation, including the development bodies to deal with IPR issues, and enforcement issues would be beneficial.

In 1962, the then Sultan annulled legislative election results after the Brunei People's Party (BPP) won all 10 elected seats in the 21-member council. The BPP then mounted an anti-monarchist insurgency that was put down by British troops. The Sultan invoked constitutionally granted emergency powers, which remain in force, and began ruling by decree. The Brunei National Solidarity Party is now one of only three legal political organization in the country. In 1993, the Mukim (district) and Kampong (village) Consultative Councils were established in order for the people to air their views and concerns to the Government through locally elected village officials.

MEASURES DIRECTLY AFFECTING IMPORTS

CUSTOMS PROCEDURES

During the period under review, Brunei Customs has introduced a several improvements in its procedures, in line with APEC trade facilitation guidelines as outlined in Table III.1. Brunei has amended legislation and streamlined administrative practices in order to, inter alia: harmonize its tariff nomenclature; make customs-related information more readily available to traders and the public; align its laws with the WTO agreements on customs valuation and intellectual property protection; improve its appeal procedures and advance tariff classification ruling systems; provide facilities for temporary importation; introduce risk-management techniques; introduce the green channel/red channel mechanism for cargo into the Customs Order 2006; raise the level of integrity in customs administration; and enhance computerization by adopting the UN/EDIFACT1 standard and reducing the requirement for paper documents. Also, Brunei is working with other ASEAN members to develop and put into operation by 2008 its national single window to facilitate customs documentation procedures, cargo release, and clearance.2

According to the authorities, several phases of the e-government initiative have been completed and others are in progress. The aim of the initiative is to provide an infrastructure using IT as a platform for paperless transactions. The Customs and Excise Department now accepts declarations using electronic media and is participating in the ASEAN single window project.

All imports into Brunei must be accompanied by: a bill of lading/delivery order or airway bill; packing list; commercial invoice, and at least three copies of the customs declaration form, which must include the number and description of packages; marks and numbers of individual packages; detailed description of the goods being imported; gross and net weights or quantities of packages; value (f.o.b. and c.i.f.); place of shipment and destination; and country of origin. The invoice must be signed by the exporter or seller. If applicable, an exemption of duty determination issued by the Economic Development Board and a certificate of origin may be requested.

Brunei Darussalam Customs continues to update information on Customs website, which will include Customs laws, tariff and procedures, currently available to the public. Announcement of changes with regard to customs procedures is made through customs circulars and briefings to importers and forwarders. A hotline was also provided to enable the public to lodge any complaint related to illegal activities or contraband to Customs.

-In 2004, some of the information related to customs procedures made available through the ASEAN customs website (http://www.asean.or.id/economic/customs/info_ brunei.htm). Legislation and most of the procedures available on a hard copy. Alignment with UN/EDIFACT International Standards for Electronic Commerce/Paperless Trading

-Brunei Darussalam introduced computerization and information system known as Customs Information Control System (CCIS). The main function of the system is the processing of customs import/export declarations at the major entry points/customs office. By 2001, the network system of the CCIS expanded to nearly all customs entry points.

-Finalizing the Department's IS/IT Plan 2004-2009 for the implementation of e-Government, which include the following:

-Submission of importer/exporter data (customs declaration) electronically;

-Submission of manifest information electronically;

-Exchange of information electronically with other government agencies;

-Online payment; and

-Development of web-services portal (i.e. online application for permits, drawbacks, registrations etc.).

-Implementation of Clear Appeals Provisions

The appeal provision is contained in the Brunei Darussalam Customs Act 1984, in which any person aggrieved by Controller's decision except specifically provided that such decision is at the absolute discretion of the Controller, may appeal therefrom to the Minister of Finance whose decision shall be final.

-Brunei Darussalam will review its current appeal provision in order to conform to the international practice.

-Alignment with WTO Valuation Agreement

Brunei Darussalam implemented the WTO Valuation Agreement in September 2001 after the five-year delay permitted by the WTO.

The Customs (Amendment) Order, 2001 came into force on 1 September 2001 and inserted a new definition of customs value into Customs Act and provided for the keeping of business record. The audit and examination of records, conditions for entry into buildings, the retention of documents obtained during a search and seized documents subjects to court order and proceedings. At the same time the Customs (Valuation of Imported Goods) Rules, 2001 took effect. These Rules applied the WTO Valuation Agreement as the method for valuing imported goods (on the c.i.f. basis).

Provision of Temporary Importation Facilities (APEC economies will provide facilities for temporary importation, by taking such action as acceding, where appropriate, to the Customs Convention on the A.T.A. Carnet for the Temporary Admission of Goods (the A.T.A. Convention))

Brunei Customs is in the process of updating the current facilitation to align with the international practices on temporary importation. Efforts have also been made to study A.T.A. Carnet and Temporary Import Provisions and the legal aspects from the member APEC economies.

Goods for trade sample, exhibition and demonstration are allowed for temporary importation without payment of duty on condition that they are to be re-exported within six months from the date of importation and they must be covered by a Customs Import Declaration. If the goods are not re-exported after the expiry date of the permission granted, duty will become payable. A security deposit is required to cover the potential customs duty on the goods temporarily imported.

Brunei Darussalam received technical assistance on ACR in June 2000 by experts from Korea and New Zealand. The Committee on Customs Procedures is in the process of drafting legislation. Standard application forms for customs ruling on customs tariff and classification will be introduced for use by applicants requesting tariff and classification.

The Customs Matters Section is responsible for the determination of customs tariff and classification and it is subject to request. Under the provisions of the Customs Act 1984, Brunei Customs Administration provides facilitation upon request either by writing or phone for the determination of tariff and classification.

Implementation of Harmonized System Convention

Brunei Customs Administration implemented HS 2002 version. In 1996, the HS Committee was set up to incorporate current version with the national tariff into the HS version 2002. Brunei Darussalam is not a contracting party to the HS Convention.

In line with the commitment to ASEAN on the HS Convention, Brunei Customs Administration is incorporating the HS version 2002 to ASEAN Harmonized Tariff Nomenclature (AHTN 2004).

Adoption of Systematic Risk Management Techniques (to allow customs administrations to facilitate trade and travel while maintaining high-level border control)

All cargoes are subject to customs examination ranging from 10% to 100%. Passengers and their belonging are subject to random inspection (10% to 100% is still applied in the course of conducting the examination).

Brunei Darussalam Customs is in the process of studying the Risk Management Techniques through training and seminar attended by officer internals or overseas. An Ad Hoc Committee has been set up to study legal aspects and requirements of Risk Management Techniques.

Brunei Darussalam introduced Red and Green Channels at the International Airport.

INTEGRITY

Brunei Darussalam customs officers are subject to the Public Service Commission Act to uphold integrity among public servants (including customs officers) "11 Principal Work Ethic" introduced by the Public Service Department and "Code of Conduct and Rules of Ethics" introduced to customs officers and customs personal.

A Discipline Committee has been set up with the objectives among others, to deal with integrity of customs officials and penalties for non-compliance.

a APEC economies have agreed to facilitate trade in the Asia-Pacific region by: (a) Simplifying and harmonizing customs procedures; (b) Encouraging the use of technologies and e-commerce as productivity tools in keeping with developments of the new economy; and (c) Enhancing cross-border cooperation in the movement of goods and services to counter terrorism.

mporters must register with the port of entry. Import permits are required for some products, including plants, animals, birds, fish, salt, sugar, rice, drugs, gambling machines, and used motor vehicle. These are available from the relevant government ministries and departments. In some cases, including for plants, animals and animal products, birds, and fish, import licences must be accompanied by sanitary or phytosanitary certificates from the exporting country. All other goods, unless prohibited, can be imported under open general licences.

Customs decisions may be appealed under section 153 of the Customs Order 2006. Authority for all customs decisions lies with the Controller of Customs; unless it is specifically stated that such decisions may only be made at the absolute discretion of the Controller, appeals may be made to the Minister, whose decision is final.

Brunei notified the WTO in 1995 that it has no laws pertaining to pre-shipment inspection. To date, no companies have provided pre-shipment inspection services in Brunei.

CUSTOMS VALUATION AND RULES OF ORIGIN

(a) Customs valuation

15. Brunei made use of the transitional measure under Article VII of the GATT 1994, which gave developing countries the right to delay application of this Article. At the end of the transition period, Brunei informed the WTO that the legislation on customs valuation had been gazetted and implemented and, with effect from 1 September 2001, the Customs and Excise Department would officially apply the Customs Valuation Code as contained in the Customs (Valuation of Imported Goods) Rules 2001 and amendments made to the Customs Act (Cap. 36) as contained in the Customs Order 2006.3

(b) Rules of origin

According to the authorities, there are no laws, regulations or administrative rulings on non-preferential rules of origin. Preferential rules of origin are applied under various preferential trading arrangements, notably ASEAN, the Trans-Pacific SEP and the Brunei-Japan EPA.

Under the ASEAN CEPT local-content requirement a product is considered as originating from an ASEAN member country if at least 40% of the f.o.b. price of the finished good originates from any member country. The requirement refers to both single country and cumulative ASEAN content. There are also alternative substantial transformation rules, including: process criterion for textiles and textile products; change in chapter for wheat flour; change of tariff sub-heading for wood-based products; change in tariff classification for certain aluminium products. Tariff preferences under the CEPT scheme depend on certain conditions: the product must be in the CEPT inclusion list of both the importing and exporting countries and must have a CEPT tariff of 20% or below; and the product must meet the local-content requirement of 40% or alternative substantial transformation rules.

Under the Trans-Pacific SEP, the rules of origin take into account where the goods are produced and what materials are used in their production, to ensure that only goods originating in the territory of one of the three other parties are entitled to preferential tariff treatment. Generally, the product-specific rules on eligible goods require substantial transformation in the territory of one of the parties, be i.e. a change in tariff classification (CTC) between the imported or non-originating materials and the end product. The CTC based on the HS classification requires the product to have a different HS chapter, 4-digit or 6-digit HS heading or subheading from the non-originating materials used in its production. For a limited range of products regional-value content (RVC) is required, based on the transaction value of the good; depending on the product-specific rules, minimum local-value content must be either 45% or 50% (for textiles, apparel and footwear). For imports into Brunei under the Trans-Pacific SEP, it appears that traders may opt for the rules of origin established under the AFTA.

APPLIED TARIFF

(a) Structure of the MFN tariff

19. Brunei adopted the Harmonized Description and Coding System (HS) in 1992 although it is not a contracting party to the Convention. Import duties are assessed on the basis of c.i.f. value. In 2001, at the beginning of the review period, Brunei's applied MFN tariff was based on the 9digit HS 96 nomenclature, consisting of 6,503 tariff lines ranging from 0% to 200%. The 2004, 2006, and 2007 tariff schedules are based on the 8-digit HS02 nomenclature consisting of 10,689 tariff lines, ranging from 0% to 30%. According to the authorities, this change in nomenclature has not resulted in any tariff rates exceeding bindings. Around 98.8% of the tariff is subject to ad valorem rates while 131 lines carry specific rates.

As information was not available on ad valorem equivalents for the specific rates, the 131 lines, which cover mainly cigarettes, alcoholic beverages, coffee, tea, petroleum oils, and lubricants, are not included in the tariff analysis in this report. Ad valorem equivalents of specific rates tend to be high and are often used to conceal high rates of tariff. According to the authorities, the preference for specific rates for these products is based on their high rates of smuggling; the specific rate is also considered to be administratively simpler for collecting duty. Although the customs tariff is levied on a relatively small number of tariff lines, it accounted for around 3.6% of total tax revenue in 20064, from 4% in 2001. For most of the tariff lines with specific rates, the authorities indicated that there are no or very few imports; this may be because they are prohibitively high in ad valorem terms.

In 2007, the simple average MFN tariff was 4.8%5, zero for agricultural products (both HS 124 and under the WTO definition of agriculture) and 5.4% for industrial/non-agricultural products. Tariff rates range from zero for several agricultural products to 30% for hair preparations and fireworks (6 lines in all in the 30% band). In general, basic foodstuffs and goods for industrial use are exempted from import duties as are computers and related products. There are six tariff bands: duty free, 5%, 10%, 15%, 20% and 30% (Chart III.1). The majority of tariff lines (68.1%) are zero rated while 20.4% are subject to rates of 20%, including wood and wood products, boilers, machinery and mechanical appliances, electrical machinery and appliances, vehicles and vehicle parts (except for heavy vehicles, which are taxed at 15%) and precision instruments and apparatus (Table AIII.1). A significant number of tariff lines entail peaks; over 21% of tariff lines exceed three times the simple average MFN tariff, and 20.4% exceed 15% (Table III.2).

Although the overall average applied MFN tariff is low, escalation is particularly pronounced in wood and furniture, fabricated metal products and machinery and chemicals, providing relatively higher effective protection to these industries (Chart III.2). In the case of wood and furniture, the tariff on unprocessed and semi-processed products is considerably higher than for finished products; this de-escalation provides higher protection for producers of raw material and semi-processed goods in Brunei.

a Based on 2007 tariff schedule. Implementation of the U.R. was reached in 1995. Calculations on bound averages are based on 9,924 bound tariff lines (representing 92.8% of total lines).

b Domestic tariff peaks are defined as those exceeding three times the overall simple average applied rate.

c International tariff peaks are defined as those exceeding 15%.

d Negligible. Only one tariff line is bound at zero.

e Nuisance rates are those greater than zero, but less than or equal to 2%.

Note: Excludes specific rates. The 2000 tariff schedule is based on 9-digit HS96 nomenclature consisting of 6,503 tariff lines (ranging from 0% to 200%); the 2004, 2006, and 2007 tariff schedules are based on 8-digit HS02 nomenclature consisting of 10,689 tariff lines (ranging from 0% to 30%).

Source: WTO calculations, based on data provided by the authorities of Brunei Darussalam.

(b) Preferential tariffs

Under the Customs Law, customs duties on imports or exports may be changed by order of the Sultan, and subsequently published in the Government Gazette. Brunei has adopted ASEAN trade agreements, which have been incorporated into the following laws: preferential rates applying to imports from other ASEAN countries are contained in the Customs (ASEAN Common Effective Preferential Tariffs) (ASEAN Integration System of Preferences) Order 2006, and the Customs (ASEAN Common Effective Preferential Tariff) Order 2005, which was deemed to commence at the beginning of 2004 and repeals the Customs (ASEAN Common Effective Preferential Tariff) Order of 1999. Regarding the related agreement on the ASEAN-China FTA, Brunei introduced the Customs (Goods under the Early Harvest Programme) (Framework Agreement on Comprehensive Economic Cooperation between ASEAN and China) Order 2005.

ASEAN

As a member of ASEAN, Brunei participates in the CEPT scheme, which came into effect in 1993. ASEAN agreed to reduce tariffs to 0-5% over 15 years: it is committed to eliminating all tariffs in the Inclusion List6 (IL) by 2010 for the ASEAN-6 (Brunei, Indonesia, Malaysia, Philippines, Singapore, and Thailand) and by 2015 for the new ASEAN countries (Cambodia, Laos, Myanmar, and Viet Nam). For the ASEAN-6, 99.7% of tariff lines in the IL are currently at 05%; 65% of items in the list are at zero. In Brunei's case, over 71% of tariff lines are duty free and nearly 22% are at 5% (Chart III.3). The exception to the programme of reducing most tariffs to the 0-5% range appears to be transport equipment, for which the average rate was 13.9% in 2006, well above the target range. In addition, tea, coffee, alcoholic products, and tobacco, which are excluded from CEPT reductions, carry specific rates of duty and are not included in the CEPT analysis presented here. Brunei's CEPT tariff contains 10,689 lines at the HS nine-digit level of which 99.3% have ad valorem rates; under 1% of lines, mainly relating to coffee, tea, tobacco, alcohol, petroleum products and matches, carry specific rates of duty. Overall, the CEPT tariff rate is half of the average applied MFN rate (Chart III.4). The simple average rate accorded to other ASEAN members under the CEPT was 2.4% in 2006, down from 2.6 % in 2004. Differences between average applied MFN and CEPT tariffs are mainly (by HS section) in plastic and rubber products, hides and skins, wood and wood articles, footwear and headgear, machinery, transport equipment, and precision instruments.

Other preferential agreements

Under the Trans-Pacific SEP duties are to be eliminated on the majority of tariff lines upon entry into force of the agreement. Brunei will bind its current MFN applied zero rates at zero and eliminate tariffs on other products by 2015, except for a short list of products, such as alcohol, tobacco and firearms, that it seeks to exempt on moral, human health, and security grounds.

Upon the full implementation of the Brunei-Japan Economic Partnership Agreement (expected in 2007), Brunei will eliminate tariffs on a range of products, including automobiles and auto parts, which are currently set at 20%. Also, the EPA entails tariff exemption for Japanese-made electronic and electrical appliances within five years of EPA approval.

TARIFF BINDINGS

28. Brunei has bound 92.8% of tariff lines. A high percentage of lines are bound in most HS sections, the exceptions being prepared foods (04) at 88.7%, mineral products (05) at 93.4% and transport equipment (17) at 36%, (Chart III.5). Brunei did not sign the WTO Agreement on Information Technology Products. In 2008, Brunei's overall bound rate was 25.8% (24.8% in 2000), 23.4% for agriculture, and 26.2% for industrial products. In agriculture, tariff peak rates of 50% are found mainly in animal products, diary products, coffee and tea, and fruit and

vegetables; for non-agricultural products bound rates of 40% and above are mainly in chemicals, leather products, wood and pulp, transport equipment, and electric machinery.

Although a high share of the tariff is bound, there remains a significant difference between the overall bound average of 25.8% and Brunei's 2007 applied MFN tariff of 4.8% (Table AIII.1). The difference is even greater in agriculture where the bound average tariff is 23.4% compared with an MFN average of zero. The gap imparts uncertainty to traders and economic agents operating in Brunei by providing the Government with scope to raise tariff rates of products within their corresponding bound rates, although the authorities have stated that applied rates have not been raised during the review period. Regarding agricultural products, the authorities maintain that the difference is necessary to address food security concerns and that it would consult with, and notify, all affected parties in advance, should tariffs be raised.

Other charges affecting imports

Brunei's legislation on excise taxes is contained in the Excise Order 2006 (repealing the Excise Act), which allows the Minister of Finance to impose and revoke excise taxes on any goods deemed appropriate. Currently, it appears that excise taxes are levied on locally produced Samsoo (including medicated Samsoo liquor) at the rate of B$5 per gallon (equal to 0.4546 decalitres, or B$11 per decalitre). In comparison, imports of Samsoo face customs duties at rates of B$90 per decalitre for bottled Samsoo not exceeding 40% alcoholic strength by volume, and B$120 for other kinds of Samsoo.

Contingency measures

31. Brunei informed the WTO Secretariat in 1996/97 that it does not have legislation or regulations on dumping, or relevant to the Agreement on Subsidies and Countervailing Measures

or those governing safeguard measures. It appears that no anti-dumping, countervailing or safeguard measures are currently in force or have been taken in the period under review.

IMPORT PROHIBITIONS, RESTRICTIONS, AND LICENSING

Brunei continues to maintain non-tariff measures (NTMs) in the form of various import limitations, which are deemed necessary to protect health, safety, security, the environment, and religion or to discharge Brunei's obligations under international agreements. In general, the NTMs are in the form of prohibitions, restrictions, and licensing, and they do not appear to have declined significantly since 2001.

(a) Import prohibitions

33. Import prohibitions are maintained on a limited number of products, including opium, indecent and obscene printed matter, firecrackers, vaccines from Chinese Taipei, cough mixture containing codine, Java sparrows and turtle eggs, arms and ammunition, and alcoholic beverages, including spirits and liquors (Table III.3). The prohibitions are maintained for security, health, protection of wild life, and moral reasons. In addition, imports and manufacture of alcohol and alcohol products are restricted for religious reasons under the Customs (Prohibitions and Restriction of Imports and Exports) Amended Order 1990. Imports of alcoholic beverages have been prohibited since 1991 although non-Muslims are allowed to import 2 litres of alcohol and limited quantities of beer duty free. Local distillation of alcohol is governed by the Excise Act. The temporary import ban on cement in order to protect the sole (state-owned) domestic supplier was lifted in February 2005.

(b) Import restrictions and licensing

Brunei maintains import restrictions, mainly for health, sanitary and phytosanitary, and moral reasons, on, inter alia, plants and animals, poisons, radioactive material, and alcohol (Table III.4). All imported eggs must be marked with the word "imported" on the shell, to identify the source of supply, thereby preventing illegal cross-border movements of eggs and to ensure conformity with the sanitary and food safety requirements of the Veterinary Authority and the Ministry of Health. Imports of salt, sugar, and rice paddy are restricted to maintain security of domestic supply and for price stability, and to ensure long-term sustainable supplies and market stability. Imports of used motor vehicles of five years and older are restricted for road safety reasons. Import permits for salt, sugar, and rice paddy may be obtained from the Department of Information Technology and State Stores; import permits for used vehicles are issued by the Land Transport Department. In all cases, the importer must also submit the import permit to the Royal Department of Customs to obtain an approval permit (AP).

A number of products, including telecommunications equipment, medical products, live plants and animals, mineral water, and used cars over five years old, require an import licence (Table AIII.2). In general, according to the authorities, the main distinction between restricted and licensed imports is that restricted imports require the import and approval permits, while licensed imports require only a licence from the relevant government agency. The procedure for obtaining permission is the same for restricted and licensed imports.

Import licences may be granted to persons domiciled and working in Brunei who have a business licence. No specific documents are required to apply for a permit or a licence, although for some products prescribed forms may be required from the relevant authority, including Customs. The primary purpose for requiring licences for these products, according to Brunei's notification to the WTO (which dates back to 1997), is to safeguard health, national security, and morals, although in the course of this Review, the authorities stated that domestic food security is also an objective.7 Licences, which must be obtained prior to importation, are issued every six months and are valid for six months; once issued, a licence may not be transferred to another importer.

STANDARDS AND SANITARY AND PHYTOSANITARY MEASURES

(a) Standards

There is no national body for setting standards in Brunei.8 The Construction Planning and Research Unit (CPRU), based in the Ministry of Development, is the focal point and coordinator for standards and conformity assessment activities. The unit's main functions are to: promote construction quality through conformity assessment (e.g. ISO 900, ISO/IEC 17025), certification of personnel and materials, and training; develop guidance documents and national standards (including adoption of international standards where appropriate) for the construction industry; maintain a library of standards and appropriate technical bulletins to serve industry in general; and to act as the national focal point for safety, standards, and conformity assessment activities.9 All standards are voluntary.

National standards, which are prepared by technical committees, are submitted for approval to the Standards Committee, which is chaired by the Minister of Development or the Permanent Secretary in the Ministry. Technical committees currently exist for the construction sector only (for timber, roads, iron and steel, concrete, locally manufactured building products, such as bricks and cement, and quality management systems). A new Technical Committee for food-related standards was set up recently and a standard on halal food was published in August 2007;

another ten are being drafted. According to the authorities, it is the policy of the Technical Committees to adopt international standards, where relevant; also the alignment of national standards with existing relevant international standards is being reviewed in line with the ISO/IEC Guide 25. Following examination by the Standards Committee, a standard is sent for comment to the Standards Secretariat at the CPRU, and for public comment (the period for comment is usually six weeks); any comments are forwarded to the Technical Committees (Chart III.6). To maintain transparency, the Ministry of Development publishes a directory of certified products, companies, and accredited laboratories.10

There are currently 42 voluntary, mainly construction-related standards in Brunei Darussalam (Piawaian Brunei Darussalam or PBDs); 37 are directly adopted from international standards. They cover use of the metric system in construction, quality management, steel reinforcement, cement, concrete, timber, and roads. In addition, guidance documents (GDs) and guidance specifications (GSs) in these areas have been published by the technical committees; at present, there are 22 GDs, and 8 GSs. Standards for electrical and electronic goods, gas appliances, and fire equipment are currently voluntary and are based on ISO or IEC standards (for electrical/electronic products), where international equivalents exist.11 The authorities note that Brunei has completed the alignment of its standards with international standards in four priority areas: electrical/electronic appliances; rubber products; food labelling; and machinery.

Other than setting standards for construction in Brunei, the CPRU also monitors testing and conformity carried out by six testing laboratories associated with the construction industry in Brunei, and manages regional proficiency testing programmes e.g. APLAC. The laboratories are accredited by, and registered with, the Ministry of Development. There are also two accredited laboratories for products related to oil and gas and a calibration laboratory related to defence. Brunei signed a Letter of Understanding with the Singapore Accreditation Council (SAC) in April 2001 for technical cooperation in the area of accreditation, including the use of SAC accreditation of laboratories, certification bodies, and inspection bodies. To date, two laboratories have been accredited by the SAC. Brunei maintains that it has reviewed the laboratory accreditation scheme to ensure that it meets ISO/IEC Guide 58. In addition, Brunei's accredited commercial laboratories have increased their scope of testing and calibration services for the construction sector.

Brunei has little industry other than petroleum and construction; petroleum is dominated by multinational companies with their own testing facilities and standards. Other industries tend to rely on third-party certification in conformity assessment. However, the national Standards and Accreditation centre (NSAC) under the Ministry of Industry and Primary Resources, formed in 2006, is moving towards centralising standards by acting as a quality and accreditation centre for local food and handicraft products. Brunei has no national measurement and metrology centre; the administration of weights and measures for commercial activities is carried out by the Weights and Measures Department. However, the NSAC is working to establish a calibration laboratory that complies with the international measurements system, under the Bureau International des Poids et Mesures, and has proposed the establishment of a national metrology laboratory under the budget of the next national development plan. Measurement and metrology facilities in Singapore (PSB) and Malaysia (SIRIM) are used frequently by Brunei's laboratories in their calibration activities Currently, laboratory accreditation for the construction sector is covered by the Ministry of Development Laboratory Accreditation Scheme; all other sectors are covered by the Brunei-Singapore SAC MoU on accreditation.

Brunei is a member of several international and regional standard-setting fora, including the ISO, Pacific Area Standards Congress, Codex, the ASEAN Consultative Committee on Standards and Quality, the ASEM Trade facilitation Action Plan on Standards and Quality, the ASEM Trade Facilitation Action Plan, the APEC Sub-Committee on Standards and Conformance, and the Asia-

Pacific Laboratory Accreditation Cooperation scheme.12 It was admitted to the IEC Affiliate Member programme in 2001. Brunei participates in the APEC E/E MRA (since 2003) and in May 2004 signed the TEL MRA with Singapore in telecommunications; the scope of these MRAs concerns acceptance of test and certification. To reduce business compliance costs, Brunei unilaterally accepts certificates of conformity from such recognized bodies, and therefore does not require re-certification or testing.

(b) Sanitary and phytosanitary measures

Brunei's national notification authority for sanitary and phytosanitary measures is the Department of Agriculture in the Ministry of Industry and Primary Resources. SPS measures are implemented by: the Department of Agriculture for plants and plant products, live animals, and eggs and other fresh animal (non-halal) products; the Ministry of Religious Affairs for halal meat products; the Fisheries Department for fish and fisheries products, and the Forestry Department for forestry products.

Plant regulations

Phytosanitary regulations are implemented by the Plant Quarantine Unit of the Department of Agriculture, under the Agricultural Pests and Noxious Plants Act, revised in 1984. Under the Act, imports of all plants and plant materials require import permits, issued by the Department of

Agriculture, and phytosanitary certificates, issued by the legal issuing authority in the country of origin, certifying the phytosanitary status of the plants.13 Imports of a number of plants and materials from specific regions or countries may be prohibited to prevent entry of dangerous pests and diseases. All plant imports are subject to inspection by the Department of Agriculture on arrival in Brunei. Imports of soil (including attached to plant roots), are prohibited. Phytosanitary certificates for exports of agricultural materials may be obtained from the Department of Agriculture.

Animal regulations

The Quarantine and Prevention of Disease (Animals) Regulations allow for the prohibition of import, detention of animals for treatment and examination, and for the investigation of imported products. Imports and exports of animals or their products must be declared at the port of entry or exit for quarantine inspection and must be accompanied by an import permit issued by the Department of Agriculture and a veterinary health certificate issued by a veterinarian authorized in the country concerned within seven days before departure; exports of live animals and poultry must be accompanied by a veterinary health certificate. When a certificate is required for exports of products derived from animals, an Animal Health Certificate may be obtained from the Contagious Veterinary Office.14 Following the outbreak of avian flu in several countries, the Brunei Government imposed an import ban on all types of poultry products from countries affected by, or suspected of having, avian flu outbreaks.15

Halal

Imports of beef and poultry are subject to import restrictions under the Second Schedule of the Customs (Prohibition and Restriction on Imports and Exports) Order, unless they have been slaughtered in a foreign abattoir approved in writing by the Minister of Religious Affairs. The Government maintains a list of approved abattoirs from which meat or poultry may be imported by holders of halal import permits issued under the Halal Meat Act (chapter 183) and the Halal Certificate and Halal Label Order 2005. Under the Halal Meat Act, the Board for Issuing Halal Import Permits grants the permit if the slaughterhouse is already on a list approved by the Majlis

Ugama Islam16; for slaughterhouses not on the list, an inspection committee, including representatives from the Ministry of Religious Affairs, the Majlis, the Ministry of Health, and the Department of Agriculture is required to inspect and approve the abattoir. The Board forwards the application to the Majlis who makes the final decision on issuing the import permit.17 Authorized officers from the Ministry of Health and the Agriculture Department examine all imports of halal meat and certify it fit for human consumption. Currently, halal meat and poultry can be imported only from Malaysia and Australia. Brunei imports live cattle from its state-owned cattle farm located in Northern Australia for slaughter at local abattoirs.

Other regulations

Other sanitary and health restrictions are maintained under the Poisons Act and the Misuse of Drugs Regulations, which are enforced by the Pharmaceutical Enforcement Services, in the Ministry of Health. This includes regulation of all imports and exports of pharmaceuticals, chemicals, agri-chemicals, pesticides, etc. in collaboration with Customs. Regular inspections are also conducted on pharmaceutical wholesalers, clinics, and retailers in Brunei. Imported veterinary pharmaceuticals, animal vaccines, and agri-chemicals are controlled by the Department of Agriculture through the Ministry of Health under the Poisons Act. The Drug Quality Control Service also inspects all drugs, both locally produced and imported, to ensure quality.

The Department of Health Services under the Ministry of Health ensures food imported and distributed in Brunei is safe. Food importers are required to comply with the Public Health Order (Food) 1998, Public Health (Food) (Amendment) Order 2002 and its Regulations 2000, which protect consumers from dangerous adulterated or poor quality foods. Food importers are required to submit the customs declaration form together with relevant documents (including health certificates) to the Food safety and Quality Control Division, Department of Health Services, for endorsement.

(c) Labelling and marking

Brunei's legislation on food labelling requirements is contained in the Public Health (Food) Order, 1998, which came into force in January 2001. Labels for food products must contain the following information either in Malay or English: name of food, list of ingredients, net/drained content, name and address of manufacturer, packer, wholesaler, importer and distributor, the country of origin, lot identification, date and storage instructions, and instructions and date for use. Where a suitable common name for the food product is not available, a description to indicate the nature of the food is required. All imports of meat and products containing meat must conform to labelling requirements approved by the Board for Issuing Halal Import Permits.18 For food with animal or alcohol content, the origin of the animal or alcohol product must also be indicated. In addition, the contents of all meat products should be clearly mentioned on the label.

Since 1 January 2002, 25 categories of food and beverage products require date marking and must be registered with the Food Safety and Quality Control Division before importation into Brunei. The products include cream, milk and milk products, pasteurised fruit and vegetable juice, soya bean curd, chilled food, sauces, peanut butter, flour and flour products, egg products, raisins and sultanas, chocolate, edible fats and oils, food additives, margarine, meat products, and nutrient supplements.

Labelling requirements on imported tobacco are set out in the Tobacco (Labelling) Regulations, 2007 and the Tobacco Order, 2005 (S/49/05). Labels must include a printed health warning in English on one surface and in Malay on the other surface, and conform to the specifications set out in the specific schedules in the Tobacco (Labelling) regulations, 2007.

52. Brunei does not have any labelling requirements for genetically modified foods.

GOVERNMENT PROCUREMENT

(a) Overview

The Government, through its public works department and individual ministries, is the major source of contracts in the country.19 Government construction activities play a major part in the construction industry and in the economy as a whole; the level of government spending has a direct impact on the country's economic climate. According to figures supplied by the authorities, goods and services procured by the Government were valued at B$780 million in 2006, down from over B$1.1 billion in 2005, accounting for 4% and over 7% of GDP, respectively (Table III.5). Although foreign suppliers can participate in government tenders, most retain a local agent to represent them in Brunei, as corporate relationships with the Government are of great importance. Teamed with a good local agent with the appropriate connections and knowledge of local business practices, foreign suppliers have a better chance of winning contracts.

The main legislation with regard to government procurement is contained in the Financial Regulations 1983 (paragraphs 327-340), which aims to maintain equity, integrity, and efficiency in the tendering process. Relevant circulars include the Ministry of Finance Circular Letter 3/2004 (of 24 October 2004). The State Tender Board is responsible for awarding contracts/projects/services above B$250,000 (tenders considered by the State Tender Board are approved by the Minister of Finance) and the Mini Tender Board of each Ministry is responsible for awarding contracts/projects/services of B$250,000 and below. The Ministry/Department submitting the tender recommendations must prepare a detailed report on its evaluation process, a description of the evaluation, and a comparison of prices of all the bids received. The name of the recommended bidder, it's tender price and deadline for completion of the project or delivery date are recorded in the minutes of Boards' meetings; recommendations are audited by the Auditor General. The notification timeframe from receiving tender recommendations to award of contracts is approximately a month.

Information on government procurement opportunities above B$25,000 is published in the Government newsletter and other local newspapers not less than two weeks from the date of issue. If the goods or services are not available locally, foreign companies will be invited to submit bids, with prior approval from the State Tender Board or Mini Tender Board depending on the value.

Brunei is not a signatory to the WTO Government Procurement Agreement; the authorities state that further study is needed before the Government can make a decision. Coverage under the Trans-Pacific SEP Agreement is extensive.20 Brunei has been given two years (from July 2006) to negotiate its government procurement schedule. Owing to its small size, procurement by Brunei's Mini Tender Board will be exempted from coverage.

(b) Tendering procedures

57. According to the Brunei Darussalam authorities, tenders are awarded to bids that represent the best value for money: criteria include the price offered, compliance with tender specifications, quality of goods and services, timelines in delivery, reliability, and after sales service. Procurement procedures depend on the estimated value of the procurement: for goods or services up to B$2,000, procurement may be carried out directly by the Department; for goods or services between B$2,000 and B$25,000 at least three quotations must be obtained from qualified suppliers; procurement exceeding B$25,000 should be made by open tender.

Selective and invited tender, and waiver of tender procedures may only be used by the Mini Tender Boards. Under Open Tendering, invitations are widely published in order to obtain a reasonable and competitive price. Under Invited Tendering invitations to tender are published, and selected companies are invited to tender. Approval is required from the relevant Tender Board. Selective Tendering is used for procurement of specialized supplies or services, whereby only certain companies are capable of delivering the supplies or services required. Approval is required from the relevant Board. For urgently needed supplies or services, software licence renewal, specialized products, or specialized work or national security concerns, Normal tender procedures are waived. No detailed data were available from the authorities concerning the breakdown of procurement contracts awarded and their values by tender method.

Tender notices are published in the Pelita Brunei at least two weeks before the closing date of a tender. The tenders submitted by suppliers are recorded and witnessed by an elected quorum appointed by the Sultan, and submitted to the relevant government agencies for evaluation. Evaluated tenders are submitted to the Mini or the State Tender Board for approval.

The bid evaluation criteria are applied differently by different Ministries/Departments depending on the nature of projects: they may involve financial capability, technical capability, past performance, and track records of potential bidders. These criteria are specified in the tender document. Tender documents should include: pertinent instruction to bidders, such as forms that need to be submitted; specifications; tender document fees; validity of tender; terms of acceptance or rejection; criteria for consideration; tenderer's responsibilities; terms and conditions of the contract.

IMPORT-RELATED OPERATIONS OF STATE ENTERPRISES

Brunei has not notified any state-trading enterprises to the WTO. Certain products subject to import restrictions and licensing, such as rice and sugar, are imported directly by the Government through the Department of Information Technology and State Stores, in the Ministry of Finance. In particular, the Department imports much of Brunei's rice through BruSiam Food Alliance, a joint venture between the governments of Brunei and Thailand. The Department also issues import permits for other restricted products, such as salt.

Other state-trading companies, according to the authorities, are Royal Brunei Catering Sdn Bhd; Mulaut Abbatoir Sdn Bhd; Royal Brunei Airlines Group of Companies and its subsidiaries; the DST Group of Companies, and the Royal Brunei Technical Services (RBTS) Sdn Bhd. The RBTS is the authorized agent of the Government for certain equipment for the use of the Royal Brunei Air Force, Police Force, and other lawfully established security forces of the Government.

MEASURES DIRECTLY AFFECTING EXPORTS

PROCEDURES

63. There have been no substantial changes in export procedures during the review period. Exporters must be registered with the Ministry of Industry and Primary Resources and the Royal Customs and Excise Department. Documentation requirements include an export declaration for customs, invoice, packing list, and certificate of origin. An SPS certificate, an export licence, and other documents are required for restricted exports, under the Quarantine and Prevention of Disease (Animals) Regulations and the Agricultural Pests and Noxious Plants Act (chapter 43). As in the case of imports, appeals against Customs decisions may be made to the Minister, under section 153 of the Customs Order 2006; the Minister's decision is final.

EXPORT PROHIBITIONS, RESTRICTIONS, AND LICENSING

Export prohibitions remain in place for prawn refuse and copra cake, and exports of timber, oil palm, rice, and sugar are still restricted (Table III.6). Consumer prices for rice and sugar are subject to ceilings, and export restrictions appear to be intended to ensure adequate domestic supply. Export licences are required for cigarettes, diesel, gasoline, kerosene, and salt. The authorities state that, in general, there is no distinction between restricted and licensed exports. Licences may be obtained upon fulfilment of certain requirements including local content, and packaging and labelling requirements.

Provisions for duty drawback are made under Part X of the Customs Order 200621 (as amended in 2006). Nine-tenths of the import duty paid is reimbursed on goods re-exported without transformation within 12 months of duty payment, for import consignments of not less than B$500 in value.

Imported inputs used in the manufacture of exports may also be eligible for drawback under certain conditions, including that the manufactured premises are approved by the Controller of

Customs and that re-export is within 12 months of payment of the import duty.22 Drawback is also permitted for personal effects and other goods imported by visitors for their personal use in Brunei and for trade samples, if the goods are re-exported within three months of importation.

(b) Other tax concessions and subsidies

Brunei has no other explicit tax concessions or subsidies for exports, but tax rebates may be available under the pioneer status programme for investment in industries with favourable export prospects.

(c) Export-processing zones

69. The Muara EPZ, situated outside Brunei's main port (the Muara Port) was developed mainly to promote and develop Brunei as a regional trade hub, and especially to promote the BIMPEAGA region. In 2004, the Brunei Economic Development Board (BEDB) proposed a new deepwater port at Pulau Muara Besar (PMB) in association with a new EPZ, to develop the PMB into a transhipment port for a wide range of manufacturing goods for re-export. The EPZ would play a crucial role in supporting the operation and profitability of the port by attracting foreign investment, and stimulating export-oriented growth and industrial development. It should also create jobs.

EXPORT OPERATIONS OF STATE ENTERPRISES

70. No information was available to the Secretariat on exports by state enterprises. Petroleum and natural gas are exported by Brunei Shell Marketing, jointly owned by the Government of Brunei and Brunei Shell Petroleum. It is not clear which companies are involved in the export of restricted items, including timber, oil palm, rice and sugar, cigarettes, and salt.

MEASURES AFFECTING PRODUCTION AND TRADE

LEGAL FRAMEWORK FOR BUSINESSES

71. All companies intending to do business in Brunei must be registered with the Registrar of Business Names or Registrar of Companies, both based in the office of the Attorney General of Brunei. Certain types of business must obtain special approval and a licence before commencement of business activities: such controls are deemed necessary to safeguard the public, for health, environmental, security or moral interests. Banks, finance companies, insurance agencies, money changers, travel agencies, private schools, tuition classes, and securities and investment companies require approval from the relevant government regulatory authorities.

A business may be established as a sole proprietorship, partnership, company, or branch of foreign company. Foreign individuals may hold equity in partnerships but may not register as sole proprietorships. Companies formed as partnerships or proprietorships are not subject to corporate tax in Brunei, which is normally 30%. Foreign companies are required to register under section 299 of the Companies Act.

Companies may incorporate in Brunei under the Companies Act (Cap 39), as (either private or public): companies limited by shares; companies limited by guarantee; companies limited by both shares and guarantees; or unlimited companies. At least half the directors of a company incorporated in Brunei must be either nationals of Brunei or ordinarily resident in Brunei.

Registration of the company by the Registrar may take place after the compliance conditions imposed by the Government have been fulfilled. Registration fees are graduated depending on the authorized share capital of the company. Under the Companies Act, there is no restriction on the ownership in the equity of a company, although some form of local participation is required in industries based on local resources and related to national food security.

A foreign company that does not incorporate as a local company, must register as a branch of the foreign company as provided under Part IX of the Companies Act. The branch must have a registered office in Brunei and appoint a local authorized person.

CORPORATE GOVERNANCE

The main regulations concerning corporate governance in Brunei Darussalam are in the Companies Act and the Securities Order 2001, which was enacted to manage and regulate financial exchanges, dealers and other persons who provide advice in respect of dealings in securities. "Securities" has been broadly defined to encompass most forms of financial instruments as well as dealings in currencies and commodities. Brunei does not have its own tradeable stock exchange, and there is no specialized corporate governance code or takeover code.

Since its enactment in 1956, the Brunei Companies Act has undergone minor additions. Shareholders retain the right to appoint or remove directors from the board of directors. However, only executive directors can control day-to-day operations. Directors have a duty to act in good faith as well as to perform to the best of their abilities when discharging their fiduciary duties to the company.

INCENTIVES

(a) Tax regime

77. There are no export, sales, payroll or manufacturing taxes, and sole proprietorships and partnership businesses are not subject to income tax. Brunei has no personal income tax. Only companies are subject to income tax, which is levied at rates of 55% for petroleum companies under the Income Tax (Petroleum) Act, 1963 as amended, 55% for natural gas companies, and 30% for all other companies.23 Companies are subject to tax on: gains or profits from any trade, business or vocation; dividends received from companies not previously assessed for tax in Brunei; interest, rents, royalties, premiums, and any other profits arising from properties. There is no capitals gains tax, unless the gains are considered as part of the operational income from normal trading activities. Petroleum and natural gas companies pay tax on a quarterly basis, while all other companies pay taxes annually. Other taxes include stamp duty on documents, a withholding tax of 20% on interest paid to non-residents, a 3% estate duty for estates valued at over B$2 million (of persons deceased on or after 15 December 1988), and a building tax with rates varying up to 12% of the value of the building.

(b) Tax incentives

In order to attract investment to targeted sectors, the Government provides a number of tax incentives (Table AIII.3). At the start of the period under review, the Government enacted the Investment Incentives Order 2001 and Pioneer Status and Income tax Relief in June 2001. The new law and regulations replace the Investment Incentives Act (chapter 97) with the stated objectives of: promoting the diversification of economic activities by providing tax incentives to promoted activities; and encouraging investment and reinvestment activities to upgrade technology, undertake research and development, increase production capacities, and expand market coverage. The authority to administer the new legislation was transferred to the Minister of Industry and Primary Resources.

The new law provides guidelines in granting pioneer status to industries and tax relief for foreign and local investment, as well as extending the tax relief period. The investment incentives include exemption from payment of corporate tax for up to 5 years for companies that invest B$500,000 to B$2.5 million in approved ventures; up to 8 years for investing more than B$2.5 million, and up to 11 years if the venture is located in a high-tech industrial park.

The legislation also specifies that to encourage the development of new service activities not yet established on a commercial scale, companies may be classified as pioneer service companies if they are engaged in any qualifying activity including: any engineering or technical services including laboratory, consultancy and R&D activities; computer-related services; industrial design development; leisure and recreational services; publishing; educational services; medical services; services related to agricultural technology and the provision of warehousing facilities, financial and business services. The incentives include a full corporate tax holiday of up to 8 years (extendable up to 11 years), with carry-forward of losses.

Investment incentives in the form of tax concessions continue to be granted to enterprises or industries approved by the Government under the Investment Incentives Order 2001. According to the authorities, tax concessions play a vital role in the pace and direction of Brunei's industrial development: they are used to promote new investment in preferred industries and services and to encourage existing companies to upgrade through modernization and automation and through the introduction of new products and services. However, in the absence of any available studies by the authorities to evaluate the effectiveness of these tax incentives in achieving their industrial development objectives and in relation to tax revenues forgone, the cost-effectiveness of these measures is questionable. Brunei's economic development might be better served by a more broadly-based corporate income tax system involving fewer incentives, but with a tax rate substantially lower than the 30% currently levied. This would bring it more into line with the tax rates in several of Brunei's neighbours (possibly complemented by a personal income tax levied at a similarly low rate). Such a tax would be more neutral, and thus less distorting, as far as private investment decisions are concerned.

OTHER ASSISTANCE

(a) Subsidies

As noted in the previous report, Brunei notified the Secretariat in 1997 that it maintains no subsidies that are notifiable pursuant to Article XVI:1 of GATT 1994, or Article 25 of the Agreement on Subsidies and Countervailing Measures.24 Subsidies, nevertheless, appear to be provided for agricultural inputs and for water, energy, and telecommunications services. In addition, housing, education, and medical care are provided free of charge. Government employees also have access to low-interest or interest-free loans for the purchase of cars and houses.

(b) Price controls

Under the Price Control Act (chapter 142), administered by the Economic Planning and Development Department in the Prime Minister's Office, maximum prices for selected goods may be fixed by the Price Controller, for consumer protection purposes. The goods are within the category of basic necessities: motor vehicles, infant milk powder, and cigarettes. The Act covers several aspects of market activity, such as control of movement, export/import of specified goods, refusal to sell goods, prohibition against selling greater quantities of a controlled article than required for "ordinary use", hoarding, and display of prices on goods.

Internal distribution controls are maintained by the Department of Information Technology and State Stores in the Ministry of Finance on items subject to import and export restrictions, for example, rice and sugar.

(c) Assistance under the East ASEAN Growth Area

The Government of Brunei also provides assistance in the form of tax exemptions for companies investing in the BIMP-EAGA, as well as tariff exemptions on imports of all raw materials and capital goods. The main activities appear to include production of halal meat, shrimp and fisheries cultivation, bio-pharmaceuticals, high-value-added forestry products, and tourism activities such as diving and eco-resorts.

(d) Assistance for small and medium-sized enterprises

As part of its efforts to increase private sector participation in the economy, the Government has continued to encourage the development of small and medium-sized enterprises (SMEs), which make up 98% of enterprises in the country and account for 58% of Brunei's total employment in the private sector. Financial assistance for SMEs consists of the Enterprise Facilitation Scheme (EFS), a financing scheme developed by the Enterprise Development Centre in the MIPR, and the Micro-credit Financing Scheme (MFS); the EFS and MFS provide maximum loans per enterprise of B$1.5 million and B$30,000, respectively. Under the EFS, priority is given to enterprises operating in industrial sites, agricultural development sites, and fisheries development sites as well as operators of tourism activities in Brunei. Both schemes are financed by the Government through the Industrial Development Fund, managed jointly with two appointed local banks responsible for the administration of the fund. The loans are at a favourable rate of interest of 4%, repayable over seven years for EFS projects and four years for MFS loans. At end-March 2007, total EFS applications covered 75 enterprises (with a loan value of B$21.4 million) and MFS loans amounted to B$7 million disbursed to 369 micro-enterprises.25

MIPR runs a number of courses in business management, an area that has been identified as one of the causes of SME failure. Training covers accounting and finance, business management, marketing, quality and standards, and new technologies. Nevertheless, the Government continues to be concerned about the number of SME bankruptcies. According to the Economist Intelligence Unit, in 2006 there were 114 bankruptcies, up from only three in 1996.26 The Government also set up the SME Innovation Centre in 2006 to help SMEs in the information and communications business. The Centre is managed in partnership with Sun Microsystems and Malaysian Incubation specialist SKALI (main providers of Java and Open Source technology) and aims to provide a supportive environment for promising Brunei ICT businesses.

The Government is taking a "proactive" approach to diversifying the country's sources of economic growth and creating opportunities for SMEs. As noted in the previous chapter, the Brunei Economic Development Board (BEDB), formed in 2001, aims to attract FDI and promote joint ventures - targeting US$4.5 billion in new investment and at least 6,000 new permanent jobs by 2008. BEDB has a two-prong strategy: to develop a number of industry clusters, including tourism, transportation and logistics, and financial services; and to develop a port and industrial complex at Pulau Muara Besar as well as develop oil and gas-related downstream activities at Sungai Liang27, with proposals including urea and ammonia plants, a methanol plant28, an aluminium smelter, and a tyre recycling facility. The BEDB considers that projects around the world similar to the Sungai Liang Industrial Park have shown that a number of "spin-off" opportunities can be derived from the production of methanol and ammonia/urea. In addition, the BEDB anticipates that 6,000 construction workers will be required for the construction of the petrochemical projects. This would create opportunities for the local construction industry for around two years and for support and service industries in catering for the worker population at the Sungai Liang site.

THE PUBLIC SECTOR AND PRIVATE INVESTMENT

(a) The public sector

The Government is the largest employer in Brunei. It has large shareholdings in key companies, including a 50% share in Brunei Shell Petroleum Company Limited (BSP), which is owned jointly with Royal Dutch Shell and is the main producer of petroleum and natural gas in Brunei. The state-owned Petroleum Brunei, which took over the roles of the Brunei Oil and Gas Authority and the Petroleum Unit, in 2002, is responsible for managing Brunei's assets in its joint oil and gas ventures and for regulating the country's petroleum industry. The Government also has a 50% share in Brunei LNG. Public sector monopolies also appear to exist in key infrastructure sectors, including electricity, and water.

The Government also plays a major role in the economy through its holding company Semaun Holdings Sendirian Berhad. Semaun Holdings was incorporated as a private limited company under the Companies Act in 1994 and it serves as an investment and trading arm of the Ministry of Industry and Primary Resources in enhancing economic diversification programmes in Brunei. Its Board of Directors is almost entirely composed of government representatives, including from the Ministries of Industry and Primary Resources, Communications, Finance, and the Bank Islam of Brunei. According to the authorities, the company's mission is to spearhead industrial and commercial development through direct investment in key industrial sectors and thereby accelerate industrial and commercial development in Brunei as well as generate opportunities for active participation of Brunei citizens.

Semaun Holdings focuses on: integrated poultry projects; commercial mushroom production; food manufacturing and processing; computer software development; design of electronic components; technology park development, including commercial ventures into biotechnology; high-tech manufacturing, including downstream activities from oil and gas and packaging projects; and value-added services in tourism and related services, packaging support services and information communication technology. The company, along with its subsidiary and joint-venture companies, appears to dominate domestic manufacturing. Little information is available, however, on its contribution to GDP, or annual accounts, suggesting a lack of transparency and public accountability.

Semaun Holdings Sdn Bhd has established six joint-venture companies under partnership with SemaunPrim Sdn Bhd, its subsidiary in the fisheries industry29: Seiwa Sdn Bhd; Semaun Seafood Sdn Bhd; Semaun Aquaculture Sdn Bhd; Semaun Marine Resources Sdn Bhd; and AquaMas Farm Services Sdn Bhd. In addition, it has formed Mahkota Crystal Sdn Bhd a joint-venture company directly in partnership with Semaun Holdings and acquired equity shareholdings in OakTree Holding Ltd and Falcon Cross (B) Sdn Bhd, two Semaun linked companies.

(b) Corporatization and privatization

Efforts to reduce the scope of direct government involvement in the economy began under the Sixth National Development Plan and continued under the Seventh and Eighth National Development Plans. The various plans have been aimed at promoting diversification and strengthening economic growth, but progress has been slow. Under the Eighth Plan (2001-05), the Government pushed for economic diversification by: strengthening the private sector by encouraging FDI and corporatization, commercialization of government agencies and activities, and enhancing SME capabilities; and by improving the legal and administrative system and procedures relating to investment, the business climate, and land ownership policies. In this regard there have been a number of important legislative improvements including the Economic Development Board Act (chapter 104), the Industrial Coordination Order 2001, and the Investment Incentives Order 2004, which were introduced at the start of the Eighth Plan. Overall, the Government has encouraged the private sector to play a leading role in economic growth and diversification, while increasingly restricting its own activities to investment in infrastructure facilities. The Eighth Plan recommended boosting annual government expenditure to B$7.3 billion (B$7.2 billion under the previous Plan). However, it appears that only a small part of the money allocated was disbursed. In 200330, for example, only 26% of allocated funds were spent and in some sectors the proportion was much lower (only 2% in information technology). Persistent underspending, even in areas such as public housing, makes the realization of government plans difficult.

The authorities state that during the 8th NDP a total of B$1.8 billion was spent, which constituted about 25% of the overall planned budget. This is considered to be low, mainly due to delays in the pre-contract stages (appointment of consultants, preparation of documents, assessment of tenders, securing bankers' guarantees), and in implementation.

The authorities indicated in 2001 that government agencies in the pipeline for corporatization, commercialization or privatization, included the Department of Telecommunications, part of Electrical Services, the Postal Department, the Department of Information Technology and State Stores, the Meragang Hatchery section of the Department of Fisheries, and the Employees Provident Fund.

Subsequent efforts to reduce public sector involvement in the economy included "corporatization" of public sector companies, contracting out public sector services to the private sector, and privatization of some public sector services. Privatization, however, has been piecemeal and ad hoc. So far, the Government has incorporated the Employees Trust Fund as an autonomous board; also, a decision was reached to establish the Housing Development Department as a board and in April 2006, the Government announced the corporatization of the Telecommunications Department. JTB's functions were split between two successor organizations, TelBru, responsible for delivering telecom services, and AiTi, responsible for regulating the local ICT industry; in addition, the Government partially privatized certain services, such as internet access and mobile telephony in 2006.

COMPETITION POLICY

96. According to Brunei's APEC Individual Action Plan, it has no specific legislation on competition policy but is considering competition policies in line with APEC principles. So far, competition regulations exist only in the telecommunications sector under AiTi, the telecoms

regulator. Under the Trans-Pacific SEP Agreement, owing to its small size, Brunei was granted flexibility to apply the commitments in the competition chapter on a best endeavours basis; if, however, Brunei establishes a competition law or competition authority, the provisions of the competition chapter will fully apply.31

INTELLECTUAL PROPERTY RIGHTS

(a) Overview

Brunei is a party to the Convention Establishing the World Intellectual Property Rights Organization (since 1994). It acceded to the Berne Convention for the Protection of Literary and Artistic Works on 30 August 2006. Brunei has not joined the Paris Convention for the Protection of Intellectual Property. Brunei has notified several of its intellectual property laws to the WTO and, as a developing country Member, made use of the transitional period available to it until 1 January 2000. Brunei's national legislation on intellectual property rights was reviewed by the WTO Council for TRIPS in November 2001. The authorities state that enforcement procedures and remedies are available under the various laws, as well as under the common law, to enable effective action against infringement.

The IP Section of the Registries Division of the Attorney General's Chambers32 (under the Prime Minister's Office) is responsible for all matters concerning intellectual property including formulating and reviewing intellectual property policies, drafting relevant legislation, registration and administration under the respective intellectual property legislation and promoting awareness and disseminating information on intellectual property in the country. The Head of Registries, who is also Assistant Solicitor General, is responsible for administering the Division. The Royal Brunei Police Force is responsible for general enforcement and investigation of criminal offences under the relevant laws, while the Royal Customs and Excise Department enforces border control measures. The Criminal Justice Division of the Attorney General's Chambers initiates prosecution of IPR cases. The Division does not have a public awareness programme as it lacks capacity in implementing such a programme. Public outreach is limited to talks and lectures on the importance of IPR protection for local businesses, SMEs, and business students. The IP Section would benefit from appropriate technical assistance in this area as public awareness on IP in the country is considered generally low.

At the regional level, Brunei participates in the work of ASEAN on intellectual property cooperation, including measures to strengthen and enhance intellectual property rights protection, enforcement, administration, and legislation in ASEAN member countries.33 Brunei also participates in the EC-ASEAN Intellectual Property Rights Cooperation Project (ECAP II). ECAP II's main objectives are to foster trade, investment, and technical exchanges between Europe and ASEAN member countries and to foster intra-ASEAN trade and investment.

The intellectual property chapter of the Trans-Pacific SEP seeks to provide an enhanced standard of IP protection beyond that under the TRIPS Agreement. The three salient features of the IP chapter are: Brunei (and Chile and Singapore) is considering accession to the WIPO Copyright Treaty and the WIPO Performances and Phonograms Treaty, which address copyrighted works in a digital environment; they acknowledge their consensus on specific IP principles between the rights holders and the legitimate interests of users; and acknowledge that geographical indications will be protected in the respective jurisdictions according to the terms and conditions of their respective domestic laws.

(b) Trade marks

The Trade Marks Act (Cap. 98) and Trade Marks Rules of 2000 cover the registration of trade marks in Brunei Darussalam and entered into force on 1 June 2000. Prior to this, the repealed Act was based on the English Trade Marks Act of 1938 with some modifications to suit local conditions. The law provided for the registration of trade marks in respect of goods but not services. In line with the TRIPS Agreement, the current Act caters for applications for goods and services, and geographical indications, and incorporates border control measures. A trade mark must be visually perceptible, capable of being represented graphically (thus smell and scent marks are excluded) and capable of distinguishing goods and services of one undertaking from those of others. In addition, the proposed trade mark must satisfy the formalities and substantive requirements set out in the Act and Rules that govern the registration procedures. After an application has been accepted for registration, it is published in the Government gazette (for a period of two months). If there is no opposition, a certificate of registration is issued to the applicant. Once registered, a trade mark is protected for ten years, renewable upon payment of a fee.

Any person (individual, partnership or company), whether local or foreign, claiming ownership of a trade mark used or proposed to be used by him in Brunei Darussalam may apply for registration of the trade mark. Under the Act, a foreign applicant must provide an address in Brunei Darussalam for all related correspondence from the Registrar.

To register a trade mark, an applicant must file Form TM1 together with the fee of B$150. Foreign applications account for 99% of all applications received (Table III.7).

Amendments to the Trade Marks Rules, expected to take effect by end 2007, include revision of the fee structure and electronic filing of trade mark applications. In line with the e-Government initiative, the Registry of Trade Marks is in the process of automating its business processes under the e-Registry Project; the project is expected to be completed by end 2007 and will enable online filing of trade mark applications and statutory documents.

Brunei provides protection for geographical indications under the Trade Marks Act (chapter 98).

(c) Patents

106. Under the Inventions Act (chapter 72), patents granted in the United Kingdom, Singapore, and Malaysia, may be re-registered in Brunei within three years from the date of grant. These privileges will cease once the Patents Order comes into force. Patent registration is administered by the Registry of Patents under the auspices of the Attorney General's Chambers; applications may be made by any persons. There is no independent system of examination for patentability; substantive examination is done by the patent office that granted the patent. The patent re-registrations received by the Registry are from foreign applicants; patent applications and grants (all from non-residents) averaged around 30 annually between 2001 and 2006.

At the time of the previous Review, the Patents Order 1999 was expected to be implemented in 2001 to replace the Inventions Act, 1984, essentially a re-registration system for patents granted in the United Kingdom, Malaysia, and Singapore. However, according to the authorities, the Order was published in the Government Gazette but has yet to be implemented. The new patent regulations, submitted to WIPO in 2006 for comments and recommendations, are based on Singapore's Patent Act, and will provide for an independent system based on examination only. Due to lack of qualified persons and expertise, substantive examination for patentability will be conducted abroad under a referral arrangement with foreign patent offices.

The Order provides for patent protection for 20 years from the date of filing, for any product or process that is considered to be novel, involves an inventive step, and is industrially applicable. Pharmaceutical and agricultural products and processes are protected under the new law. The Order will not include protection for plant varieties; the authorities are currently looking into the possibility of a sui generis system of protection for plant varieties, given the lack of expertise in the area.

The Order also provides for compulsory licensing under Sections 55 to 57 if, after three years from the date of grant or four years from the date of filing, the market for the patented invention is not being supplied by the patent holder on reasonable terms or if the patent is not being adequately worked. Compulsory licensing may be granted by the High Court or an intermediary court; under this provision they are non-exclusive, and may only be used predominantly in Brunei and for the purpose for which they were authorized. The patent holder must be paid adequate remuneration, as agreed between the licensee and patent holder or as determined by the Court.

In determining whether it is appropriate to grant a compulsory licence, the court takes into account: the nature of the invention, the time that has elapsed after the grant of the patent, measures already taken by the proprietor to make use of the invention, the ability of the potential compulsory licensee to work the invention to the public advantage, and investment and other risks involved for the applicant.

Non-exclusive use for the services of the Government of Brunei of any patented invention is also provided for under the Order and may only occur if the Government has taken all reasonable steps to obtain the consent of the patent holder to use the patented product. Under the Inventions Act, which is to be replaced by the Emergency (Patents) Order, there is no provision for the granting of compulsory licences. The exclusive rights to the invention can only cease if the Sultan declares in a public statement in Bandar Seri Begawan that the exclusive right, or the way in which it is exercised, is detrimental to Brunei Darussalam or prejudicial to the public.

There are no provisions on parallel imports in the IP laws currently in force. The Inventions Act (chapter 72) does not prohibit parallel importation, and the Patents Order does not give the patent holder an opportunity to interfere with a parallel trader.34

(d) Copyright and related rights

The Copyright Order 1999, entered into force on 1 May 2000.35 It protects literary, dramatic, musical, and artistic works, including computer programs, as well as sound recordings, films, broadcasts, and cable programmes. It also provides for the protection of performers' rights and any other rights granted to other persons under an exclusive recording contract. Data compilations, including databases, whether in machine-readable or other form, which are original by reason of selection or the arrangement of contents, are protected under the Order, as are producers of phonograms and broadcasting organizations, provided they meet the conditions of

authorship described under section II of the Order. The Order provides copyright protection for the creator's life plus 50 years for works; 50 years from the date that the work was made or recorded for computer-generated works, sound recordings or films; and 50 years from the date of broadcast or performance for broadcasters and performers. Copyright for published works is granted for 25 years from the year of the first publication. Foreign works are protected in Brunei under the Order by virtue of an international convention or agreement to which Brunei is a party. Thus, as a Member of the WTO, Brunei provides copyright protection to works from all the other WTO Members. Under the Order, copyright owners have exclusive rights to reproduce, adapt, issue, perform, broadcast or otherwise communicate the work to the public.36 Any infringement of these rights may be actionable by the copyright holder or the licensee and remedies may be sought through a local court of law.

The Copyright Order is being amended; the amendments will include higher penalties for offences under the Order; entry without warrant by police officers; arrest without warrant by police officers; and power to stop and search vehicles.37

(e) Other industrial property rights

The Industrial Designs Order and Rules, which came into force on 1 June 2000, are based on the Hong Kong industrial designs law. The Order provides for registration of new industrial designs for the visual appearance of products. The Registry administers a registration system based on formalities examination only and does not conduct prior art searches. To be registered, an industrial design must be new at the filing date of the application. An industrial design is new if it has not been registered, published, used or sold in Brunei Darussalam or elsewhere before the date on which the application for registration was lodged. Once accepted for registration, industrial designs are published in the Government gazette and a certificate of registration is issued to the applicant. Registration is for five years, extendable for two periods of five years each, subject to payment of a renewal fee. Protection for textile designs, including textile and plastic pieces of goods, handkerchiefs, shawls, and other similar articles that the Registrar may include, is limited under the Order to features of pattern and ornaments.

The Layout Designs Order 1999 protects the exclusive rights of the rights holder, with the exception of copying for private, research, or teaching purposes. Protection is from the day on which the layout design was created, for 10 years from the date of commercial exploitation, if it was commercially exploited within 5 years of creation, or for 15 years in all other cases. Only layout designs created after 1 May 2000 are protected. As with industrial designs, non-exclusive use by the Government for security and defence purposes is permitted, provided the right holder is remunerated. Infringement issues may be addressed in the national courts, including through injunctions, and damages.

(f) Trade secrets

117. There is no specific law on trade secrets; according to the authorities, protection is accorded under the common law. Article 39.3 of the TRIPS Agreement obliges Members, when requiring the submission of undisclosed test or other data (as a condition for the marketing of pharmaceutical or agricultural chemical products), to protect such data against unfair commercial use and disclosure. According to the Brunei authorities, the marketing of pharmaceutical or agricultural chemical products in Brunei is not currently subject to an approvals procedure requiring the disclosure of undisclosed test or other data. The Ministry of Health is in the process of drafting legislation that will regulate the disclosure of information on medical products and cosmetics.

(g) Enforcement and penalties

The legislation on intellectual property rights also provides for penalties for infringement of rights.38 The powers of the police however, dependent the complainant or right holder reporting an infringement of specific products and supplying sufficient information and proof. According to the authorities, the main impediments to effective enforcement of IP rights include: the reluctance of rights holders to use border enforcement measures; lack of technical assistance and training for customs and police officers; absence of rights holders; and the frequent lack of documentation from complainants to show they own the rights or that they act on behalf of the rights holder.

Resources and manpower are limited, and success is highly dependant on the commitment and support of rights holders to protect their own rights. Police officers from the Commercial Crime Unit and Attorney General's Chambers officers have been trained in general IPR enforcement, for example to detect counterfeit hard goods, and are trying to improve enforcement capabilities.

Border enforcement measures for infringements are undertaken by the Brunei Darussalam Customs Department. Statutory authority for border enforcement is expressly provided for under the Copyright Order 1999, which enables copyright holders to give notice to the Controller of Customs if they suspect that infringing copies are crossing the border. The authorities state that no such notice has been received and therefore no seizures have been made. Border enforcement measures do not appear to be well received by rights holders, despite advice from the authorities as to the effectiveness of this method.39 However, the Customs Department can on their own initiative, under different grounds and laws, seize certain articles detriment to public health and safety, providing they have information to show that there exists a potential danger to the public or individuals.

The authorities did not provide statistics on the number of trade mark and copyright infringement complaints received during the period under review. However, the authorities have indicated that in the case of copyright infringement, the majority of complaints were withdrawn on the basis of an agreement with the alleged infringer.

Trade marks and copyright legislation has been tested in Court and is deemed by the authorities sufficient to give protection to rights holders. The authorities also state that in ordinary criminal cases the courts in Brunei Darussalam have handled cases expeditiously. Delays are attributed due to the unavailability of the complainant rights holder and necessary documents.

Under the Emergency (Copyright) Order 199940, copyright infringements are actionable by the copyright holder, or in the event of a licence, the exclusive licensee. The production, import, sale, rental or distribution of copyright-infringing goods on a commercial scale is considered a criminal offence under the new legislation. Remedies include damages, injunction, and the right to seize infringing copies. Seizure can be made when a reasonable complaint has been laid with supporting evidence. Most complainants are based outside of Brunei Darussalam.

Penalties for infringement include imprisonment for up to two years, a fine or both; the size of the fine and the period of imprisonment is at the discretion of the Intermediate and High Courts, which have jurisdiction in cases of infringement of intellectual property rights.41 According to the authorities, there have been four prosecutions for offences under the Copyright Order, with the courts imposing fines in all four cases ranging from B$2,000 to B$12,000. The prosecutions were instigated by complaints made to the police by the copyright owners/exclusive licensee.

Once the Patents Order has been implemented a patent holder will be able to bring civil proceedings against an alleged infringer in any national court of law. Available remedies include injunctions, orders to deliver or destroy the infringing product or the means of its production, damages, and accounts of profits. Under certain circumstances, including falsely representing a product, criminal penalties may apply.

Wilful counterfeiting of trade marks is a criminal offence under the Trade Marks Act (chapter 98) 199942, and may result in fines of up to B$100,000 or up to ten years imprisonment or both. Furthermore, seized counterfeit goods may be forfeited, destroyed or otherwise disposed of.

CUSTOMS ORGANIZATION AND EXPOR-IMPORT REGULATIONS

CUSTOMS DEPARTMENT

The Royal Customs and Excise Department previously known as Customs and Bea Department is one of the oldest government department. It was established in April 1906 and now it was already over 90 years.

The Royal Customs and Excise Department is under the Ministry of Finance since 1984.

Early April 1998, the Headquarters of Royal Customs and Excise Department have moved to its new building as the address below:-

Headquarters of Royal Customs and Excise Department Jalan Menteri Besar Berakas BB 3910 Negara Brunei Darussalam.

SECTIONS

Administration Section

Responsible for general administration in accordance with "General Orders" and government circulars.

Responsible for the financiali management and administration (Annual Departmental Budget) and government properties as in the Finance Regulations and government circulars.

Research and Human Resource Development Section.

Public Relation.

Customs Matters Sections

i. To handle all application regarading customs procedures as follows:-

o Approval Permits

o Refund/Drawback /Deposit

o Exemption of Duty

o Classification of Goods

o Classification/Evaluation and Assessment

o Processing the import and export application

ii. Coordinating the implementation of government gazette regarding the customs affairs

iii. As a coordinator in updating the Customs legislation concerning with Customs procedure, Classification of Goods Systems(HS) and GATT Valuation system.

International Section

i. Responsible for the customs affairs in the International organisations such as:

ASEAN -Association of South East Asian Nations APEC -Asia-Pacific Economic Cooperation WCO -World Customs Organisation ASEM -Asia Europe Meeting

FUNCTIONS AND RESPONSIBILITIES

This department have four main function and responsibilities:-

1. To implement collection of the country revenue by levying toxes on certain imported goods.

o The main revenue of Customs is from the Customs import duty. Goods tariff duty are base on the Customs Import Duties Order 1973, which came into force on 15th January 1973 together with Customs Act Section 36 and Excise Act Section 37 (Amendment) 1984. In these order, the export duty have been revoked.

2. To enforced customs legislation and regulations.

o Customs Officers at, Customs check point, periodically makes "random check" inspection to every passenger, vehicle and goods which are comes in and out from this country. If there is any suspicion 100% inspection will be carried out.

o Some arrests have been made as a result of investigation and observation by the officers from time to time.

o The Public also play an important role in giving the information to this department in order to detect any activities against Customs legislation and regulation.

o The department have attended some training, seminar and meeting to cooperate with other Customs Administrations of ASEAN, APEC and WCO in exchanging the information related to enfoce customs legislation and regulations.

3. As a coordinating agency to other department in controlling the prohibited and restricted goods.

o To assist various government departments in controlling the prohibited and restricted goods for the benefits and sovereignity of the country.

o Approval of licence or permit must be obtained before Approval Permit is issued to bring in and out controlled and restricted goods.

GOODS NEED LICENCE/APPROVAL PERMIT

Barangan	Memerlukan lisen / surat kebenaran daripada
Plants, Crops and life animals	• Agriculture Department

Firearms,Explosives	• Royal Brunei Police Force
Printed Media	• Royal Brunei Police Force • Ministry of Religious Affair • Ministry of Home Affair
Woods	• Forestry Department
Rice, Sugar and Salt	• Information Technology and State Store Department
Used Vehicle	• Land Transport Department • Royal Customs and Excise Department
Telephone equipment & Radio	• Telecommunications Department
Antiques & Prehistorical materials made and found in Brunei	• Museums Department
Medicine including poison	• Ministry of Health
Fresh, cool, and frozen chicken & beef	• Ministry of Religious Affair • Ministry of Health • Agriculture Department

To facilitate the industries in order to encourage the flow of business activities and develop the country economy.

Facilities for the Exemption of Import Customs Duty for equipment, tools/machineries or special parts itself specific for industry under section 15(B), 18(B), 47(A),56(A) and 57(B) First Schedule Customs Import Duties Order 1973.

Facilitate the temporary import for specimen of goods, exhibition and demonstration.

Give services and facilitation for importing goods via this country to neighbouring countries.

STRATEGY AND PROGRAMS

CUSTOMS STRATEGY

There are some amendments to the Customs Import Duty Order according to the country's economy policy and the development of International Trades.

Among the amendments are as follows:-

I. Amendment on 1st December 1994. The increase of tobacco/cigarette duty from ($.00 - $10.00 per Ib) to ($30.00 - $100 per Kgm)

II. Amendment on 2nd February 1995. The increase of vehicle duty from 20% to 40%-200% according to vehicles category.

III. Amendment on 1st April 1995. Decrease in tax for domestic goods e.g. perfumes decrease (from 30% to 5%) and the tax tariff of furniture, aircondition,TV & Radio decrease from 20% to 5%.

IV. Amendment on 14th October 1996. Elimination of tax on textiles and clothes.

PROGRAMS

i. Implementation of GATT Valuation System in the year 2000. The objectives to implement GATT Valuation System are as follows:- a) To ensure that the valuation price is according to the procedure fixed by WTO and moreover,

the most important is the countryís commitment to APEC in which GATT Valuation is one of the agenda. b) To prevent or avoid under or over valuation. c) To increase the revenue. d) To create Level Compliances among large number of importers and customs agents.

ii) Implementation of GATT Valuation programmes a) To form a commitee on GATT Valuation. b) Sending senior officers to attend seminar, workshop and course overseas in order to upgrade

their knowledges especially about the law and regulation of GATT Valuation. c) "Awareness Programme" for all levels of customs officers. iii) The implementation of "computerised permit module" in early 1999. This include the process of applying the Appproval Permit, Import Permit and Exempted Permit into the CCIS System.

Objective to implement "Permit" module

a) To update the control on the prohibited and restricted goods. b) To upgrade the efficency in processing the application.

TARIFF LIBERALISATION INITIATIVE

BRUNEI DARUSSALAM'S APPROACH TO TARIFFS IN 2008

Section	Improvements Implemented Since Last IAP	Current Tariff Arrangements	Further Improvements Planned
Bound Tariffs	Brunei Darussalam reduced the bound tariff of 80% of its total tariff lines to 8% between 1997-2000	7,999 of Brunei Darussalam's 10,702 tariff lines (74.7%) are bound at 0 %. Of the 10,702 tariff lines, 8,313 tariff lines are industrial products while 1,216 tariff lines are agricultural products. Brunei Darussalam will bind 82% of total tariff lines at 5%* within the ten year period beginning in 2001 to 2010. Contact: Abd Wahab Yusof Assistant Trade Officer Ministry of Foreign Affairs and Trade Tel: 673-2-383374 Fax: 673-2-384099 e-mail: wahab.yusof@mfa.gov.bn	Brunei Darussalam will bound 82% of the total tariff lines at 5%* in ten years period (2001-2010). Brunei Darussalam will progressively reduce bound tariff to zero between 20102020.* *These do not include those items which are not bound under Brunei Darussalam's

			WTO commitments which falls under Article XX.
Applied Tariffs	The Department of Royal Customs and Excise implemented the ASEAN Harmonised Tariff Nomenclature. 2004/HS 2002 version The Ministry of Finance had converted all of Brunei Darussalam's specific tariff (87 tariff lines) to ad valorem. http://www.customs.gov.bn / Contact: Haji Asmayuddin Hj Hamid International Section Royal Customs and Excise Department Tel:673-2-382477 Fax: 673-2-382666	Brunei Darussalam's import tariffs are generally low and about 74.7% are already at zero tariff while rates between 5% to 30% apply to some goods The tariff of products under the EVSL sectors ranges from 0-20%. Most of these import tariff are kept because of moral/ religious reasons (toys and food and food product sector) http://www.apectariff.org/ Contact: Abd Wahab Yusof Assistant Trade Officer Ministry of Foreign Affairs and Trade Tel: 673-2-383374 Fax: 673-2-384099 e-mail: wahab.yusof@mfa.gov.bn	Brunei Darussalam will continue to review its tariff policy in view of reducing them on an MFN basis.

Section	Improvements Implemented Since Last IAP e-mail: jked@brunet.bn	Current Tariff Arrangements	Further Improvements Planned
Tariff Quotas		Brunei Darussalam does not impose any tariff quotas.	
Tariff Preferences	As of 1st January 2000,Brunei Darussalam has included a total of 6,276 tariff lines or about 96% out of total tariff lines into the CEPT scheme and almost 98% are now in with tariff rates between 0-5%.	As a member of ASEAN, Brunei Darussalam is committed to the programme of tariff reductions under the Common Effective Preferential Tariff Scheme (CEPT Scheme) for the ASEAN Free Trade Area (AFTA). Under the Scheme, the tariff of all products will be reduced to 0-5% by 2002. Tariffs on all products in the Inclusion List would be scheduled to be eliminated by 2010. http://www.asean.or.id/ Contact: Abd Wahab Yusof Assistant Trade Officer Ministry of Foreign Affairs and Trade Tel: 673-2-383374 Fax: 673-2-384099 e-mail: wahab.yusof@mfa.gov.bn	Brunei Darussalam will continue to implement its AFTA commitment to reach the goal of 100% tariff lines between 0-5% by 2002. Brunei Darussalam will also implement its commitment under the Trans-Pacific Strategic Economic Partnership agreement with Chile, Singapore and New Zealand

Transparency of Tariff Regime, including Implementation of APEC Leaders' Transparency Standards on Market Access'	Updated the Brunei Darussalam's Tariff data in the APEC Tariff Database. http://www.apectariff.org/	Brunei Darussalam continues to update its tariff data in a timely manner. Contact: Ms Johariah Wahab Deputy Director Ministry of Foreign Affairs and Trade Tel: 673-2-383374 Fax: 673-2-384099 e-mail: johariah.wahab@mfa.gov.bn	The Royal Customs Department is currently putting all information related to tariff on its website. http://www.customs.gov.bn/
		Ibrahim Abd Rahman Superintendent of Customs Customs Services and Technique Royal Customs & Excise Department Tel: 673 - 2 - 382333 Fax: 673 - 2 - 382666 E-mail: ibrahim.rahman@customs.mof.gov.bn info@customs.gov.bn	

IMPROVEMENTS IN BRUNEI DARUSSALAM'S APPROACH TO TARIFF MEASURES

Section	Position at Base Year (1996)	Cumulative Improvements Implemented to Date
Bound Tariffs	As of January 1996, 4,311 of Brunei Darussalam's 6,545 tariff lines (66%) were bound at 20% of which 3,447 tariff lines are industrial products and the rest agricultural products	Brunei Darussalam reduce the bound rate of 80% of the total tariff lines from 10% to 8% between 1997 to 2000.
Applied Tariffs	As of January 1996, about 79% of Brunei Darussalam's total tariff lines are already at zero tariff while rates between 5% to 30% apply to some goods. However, import tariffs on motor vehicles are in the range of 40% to 200%. As of January 1996, the import tariff of products under the EVSL sectors ranges from 0-20%.	The Ministry of Finance reduced import tariff on 688 items on an MFN basis in 1995 as part of its Osaka Initial Actions. Tariff on electrical home appliances, gems and jewellery and furniture were reduced to 5%, while tariff on computers and related products were abolished. (1996 IAP). The Ministry of Finance eliminated import tariff on 910 items (textile and clothing) in April 1996. (1996 IAP). The Ministry of Finance eliminated import tariff on 30 items (computerrelated products) in April 1999. (1999 IAP). The Ministry of Finance is converting all specific tariff (87 tariff lines) to ad valorem and itemise the tariffs at the 9-digit level. (1998 IAP) The Department of Royal Customs and Excise implemented the Harmonised Tariff Nomenclature. (1999 IAP)
Tariff Quotas	Brunei Darussalam does not impose any tariff quotas.	

Tariff Preferences	As a member of ASEAN, Brunei Darussalam is committed to the programme of tariff reductions under the Common Effective Preferential Tariff Scheme (CEPT Scheme) for the ASEAN Free Trade Area (AFTA).	Under the Scheme, the tariff of all products will be reduced to 0-5% by 2002. Brunei Darussalam has included a total of 6,276 tariff lines or about 96% out of total tariff lines into the CEPT scheme and almost 98% are with tariff rates between 05%. (1999 IAP).

Section	Position at Base Year (1996)	Cumulative Improvements Implemented to Date
	As of January 1996 (2 years after the implementation phase started), Brunei Darussalam has included a total of 6,078 tariff lines or about 93.6% of the total tariff lines into the CEPT scheme and almost 92% are with tariff between 0-5 %.	
Transparency of Tariff Regime including Implementation of APEC Leaders' Transparency Standards on Market Access, '		Brunei Darussalam participate actively in the development of the APEC computerised tariff database development and update its tariff data on a timely manner. (1997,1998 and 1999 IAP).

IMPORTANT REGULATIONS

IMPORT REGULATIONS BY BRUNEI DARUSSALAM CUSTOMS

Imports

The following goods may be imported into Brunei by travellers aged over 17 years without incurring customs duty: 200 cigarettes or 225g tobacco products; 1l bottle of spirits or 1l bottle of wine (by non-Muslims for personal consumption only, provided declared at customs upon arrival); 1.1l of perfume and 0.8l of eau de toile

EXPORT REGULATIONS BY BRUNEI DARUSSALAM CUSTOMS

Customs Regulations: Brunei customs authorities may enforce strict regulations concerning temporary importation into or export of items such as firearms, religious materials, antiquities, medications, business equipment, currency restrictions, ivory and alcohol. For non-Muslims, limited amounts of alcohol for personal consumption are permitted. It is advisable to contact the Embassy of Brunei in Washington, D.C. for specific information regarding customs requirements. In many countries around the world, counterfeit and pirated goods are widely available. Transactions involving such products are illegal and bringing them back to the United States may result in forfeitures and/or fines

OTHER BRUNEI DARUSSALAM CUSTOMS INFORMATION

There is a slight risk of malaria in border areas. No prophylaxis is recommended.

Food drink: All water should be regarded as being potentially contaminated. Water used for drinking, brushing teeth or making ice should have first been boiled or sterilised. Milk is unpasteurised and should be boiled. Powdered or tinned milk is available and advised, but should be reconstituted with pure water. Avoid all dairy products. Only eat well-cooked meat and fish, preferably served hot. Pork, salad and mayonnaise may carry increased risk. Vegetables should be cooked and fruit peeled.

Other risks: Amoebic and bacillary dysentery and hepatitis A and E may occur. Hepatitis B is highly endemic in the region. Dengue fever and Japanese encephalitis occur occasionally. Epidemics of Avian influenza (bird flu) were reported in early 2004 in flocks of poultry in parts of Asia, and human cases were confirmed. In recent months, Asia has seen a resurgence in such cases and visitors to Asia should still be mindful of prolonged exposure to poultry or the consumption of poultry that has not been cooked to a high internal temperature.

Health care: Medical insurance is advised. Medical facilities are of a high standard. The health administration of Brunei reserves the right to vaccinate arrivals not in possession of required certificates and to take any other action deemed necessary to ensure arrivals present no health risk.

Immigration Violations: Americans in Brunei are subject to the laws of the country and may be arrested for violation of the new immigration regulations, or any other law. In such cases, the Embassy will provide consular services to American citizens arrested in Brunei, in accordance with international law and U.S. regulations. However, the Embassy may not intervene in local judicial matters. Americans should be aware that the new immigration law is more stringent and less flexible than the previous one, with harsher penalties.

The Embassy strongly recommends that U.S. citizens on contract in Brunei be fully aware of their immigration status and of crucial dates regarding contract extensions and renewals, and have their employment documents in order. It would be wise to apply the same approach to any personal and domestic staff they may have hired, to ensure that they, too, do not run afoul of Brunei immigration regulations.

TRADE REGULATIONS AND STANDARDS

IMPORT TARIFFS

Brunei generally has very low tariffs. In 2005, the average tariff rate for most favored nations was 2%. The Asia Pacific Economic Cooperation (APEC) online database lists 932 tariff rates for Brunei: http://www.apectariff.org/tdb.cgi/ff3235/apeccgi.cgi?BN.

In general, basic foodstuffs and goods for industrial use are exempted from import duties. Since November 2001, the import duty on cars is 20% for all types except for heavy vehicles, which are taxed at 15%. There is no tax on computers and peripherals. Other consumer products such as perfume, cosmetics, clothes, carpets, shoes, jewelry, office equipment, telephones, television sets, lamps, cameras, etc., are taxed at 5 percent. The Association of Southeast Asian Nations (ASEAN) online data on tariff and duty rates for Brunei: http://www.aseansec.org/14270.htm.

TRADE BARRIERS

The World Trade Organization has made available its analysis of Brunei's trade policies online: http://www.wto.org/english/tratop_e/tpr_e/tp165_e.htm.

IMPORT REQUIREMENTS AND DOCUMENTATION

The Department of Health Services under the Ministry of Health ensures food imported and distributed in Brunei is safe. Food importers are required to comply with the Public Health Order (Food), 1998, Public Health (Food) (Amendment) Order 2002 and its Regulations 2000. The legislation protects consumers from foods dangerous to health, fraud, adulteration and use of low quality food ingredients. Food importers are required to comply with the provisions of the said food legislations and import requirements. A customs declaration form together with the relevant documents (including health certificates), are required to be submitted to the Food Safety and Quality Control Division, Department of Health Services for endorsement. A health endorsement on Custom Declaration Forms is required.

The following items are required from all suppliers:

A Hazard Analysis Critical Control Point (HACCP) certificate or an equivalent.

Samples of all items to be imported to Brunei. The Ministry of Health will accept sample of empty packages with the expiry dates printed on but not stuck on as labels.

A list of all the ingredients and additives used categorized into natural, synthetic plant or animal and where a vegetable oil is used, the type used (e.g. canola, corn or etc).

Address on the package must be the same as the address on the HACCP or equivalent certificates.

All certificates must be current and valid and if no validity dates are shown, than the certificate is good for one year from the date of issue.

All products must not contain alcohol or any derivative from slaughtered animals.

Processed food imports must be registered and must identify additives' origin under Regulation 9, Public Health (Food) Regulation, 2000.

Further information can be obtained from the Food Safety and Quality Control Division, Department of Health Services, Ministry of Health. The telephone contact is 673-2331100, Fax: 673-2331107 or website at www.moh.gov.bn.

Importers must register with the port of entry. Imports require original commercial inventory (Proforma No. 7 is not accepted), a packing list, a customs clearance and, if applicable, an exemption of duty documentation, issued by the Economic Planning & Development at the Prime Minister's Office. The website is at http://www.depd.gov.bn/.

LABELING AND MARKING REQUIREMENTS

The print for the expiry dates must not be less than three millimeter in height. Information on food label is required to be labeled in a prominent and conspicuous position on the package.

Importation of food products (25 categories that require date markings) including food supplements are subject to "set requirements" as outlined by the Public Health (Food) Regulation 2000 and are required to registered with the Food Quality and Safety Control Division, Environmental Health Services, Department of Health Services. Health supplements that contain ingredients which can be used therapeutically or contain any medical claims are required to be referred to the Department of Pharmaceutical Services, Ministry of Health for clearance.

Food labeling including the name and address of the local importer or distributor or agents are among the requirements set in the Public Health (Food) Regulations 2000.

Further information can be obtained from:

The Food Quality and Safety Division Environmental Health Services Department of Health Services Ministry of Health Tel: 673-2331106 / 7 / 9 Fax: 673-2331107 www.moh.gov.bn

PROHIBITED AND RESTRICTED IMPORTS

Importers for "halal" meat / products need approval from the Ministry of Religious Affairs before they can import from a particular country. Once approved, two Religious Affairs officers will go to the particular country to check on the slaughtering procedure. The importers have to pay for the trip. So far, Australia, Malaysia and India are accredited to supply halal beef.

The Halal Certificate and Halal Label Order 2005 covers the issuance of Halal Certificate and Halal Labels on processed food, separation of food storage and business premises such as restaurants and others.

Importation of alcoholic beverages has been prohibited since 1991. Importers should also note that Muslim restaurants and stores will only accept meat that the Brunei Islamic Committee Council has accorded special recognition as "Halal". Currently, Halal meat and poultry can be imported only from Malaysia, Australia and India. Brunei imports live cattle from the state owned cattle farm located in Northern Australia. Then the imported cows are slaughtered at local abattoirs.

As for poultry, Brunei claims to be 90% self sufficient from the poultry production for the local requirements. Control of the ritual and religious slaughter of live poultry is carried out by mandating the use of state licensed abattoirs. Imports of frozen poultry and poultry parts, frozen beef and mutton are currently severely restricted due to the near impossibility of complying with Brunei's halal requirements. Brunei does not allow the electronic stunning of animals and birds prior to slaughter. In addition, the country does not allow the mechanical slaughter of animals and birds. Every animal or bird must be hand slaughtered.

Pork is consumed only by non-Muslims. There is no production of pork in Brunei. Brunei imports fresh and frozen pork from neighboring Malaysian state of Sarawak.

The contact for Halal issue:

The Secretary Board for Issuing Halal Import Permits Ministry of Religious Affairs Jalan Elizabeth II Bandar Seri Begawan BS8510 Brunei Darussalam Tel: 673-2242565 / 6 Fax: 673-2223106 Website: http://www.religiousaffairs.gov.bn/index.php?ch=bm_service&pg=bm_service_halhar

CUSTOMS REGULATIONS AND CONTACT INFORMATION

Royal Customs and Excise Department Customs Building Jalan Mentai Besar Bandar Seri Begawan BB 3910 Tel: (673) 2382-333 Fax: (673) 2382-666 Website: http://www.customs.gov.bn/

CUSTOMS STANDARDS

The construction industry in Brunei uses metric system. Further information on Piawaian (Standards) Brunei Darussalam (PBD) can be obtained from http://www.mod.gov.bn/cpru_web/PBD3_pbdseries.htm.

STANDARDS ORGANIZATIONS

The Ministry of Development prefers ISO 9000 for contracting jobs. At least 10 Brunei-based companies have been awarded ISO 9001.

CONFORMITY ASSESSMENT

Conformity Assessment Procedure is available at http://www.mod.gov.bn/cpru_web/PBD4_conformity.htm.

CONTACTS

Construction Planning and Research Unit, Ministry of Development, Bandar Seri Begawan BB3150, Tel: 673-2383222, Fax: 673-2381541 or e-mail: modcpru@brunet.bn.

TRADE AGREEMENTS

Brunei is a member of the ASEAN, APEC, WTO, BIMP-EAGA (Brunei Darussalam, Indonesia, Malaysia & the Philippines-East Asean Growth Area) and the Multilateral Agreement on the Liberalization of International Air Transportation (MALIAT). In addition trade liberalization regimes under ASEAN, Brunei is party to a multilateral free trade agreement with Singapore, New Zealand and Chile known as Trans-Pacific Strategic Economic Partnership Agreement (TPSEP).

TRADE POLICIES BY SECTOR

Through its many development plans, the Government has sought to diversify Brunei's economy and create sustainable employment in the non-oil private sector.1 The Plans have delineated proposals for government investment in infrastructure, development of services, and incentives, all aimed at diversifying the economy and increasing private sector participation. In the 8th Plan covering 2001-052, the Government emphasized the need to move the economy away from oil and gas as the primary source of economic activity (and revenue) through the expansion of agriculture and industry and the development of certain industries with the potential to achieve growth. In 2001, the Government identified four priority areas: business services; financial services; hospitality and tourism; and transport and logistics.

However, during the period under review, Brunei's economy has become even more heavily dependent on the oil and gas sector, which in 2006 accounted for well over two thirds of current GDP. Despite the Government's emphasis on diversification, the non-oil and gas manufacturing sector remains weak and underdeveloped, and has shrunk from 3% to 1% of current GDP since

2002 (Table I.1). Therefore, it would appear that, overall, Brunei's diversification policy has met with little success.

A strong government presence continues in several key sectors of the economy, such as oil and gas, telecommunications, transport, and energy generation and distribution, often in the form of a state-owned monopolies, which can act unencumbered by any competition law. The resulting lack of competition may have affected prices and the cost of doing business in Brunei, although relevant data are not available. The very small size of the domestic market seems to discourage local and foreign participation in the economy and hampers the ability of non-oil and gas industries to achieve economies of scale and thus to compete against imports as well as in export markets. The only other major source of export revenue has been the garment industry, which was established to take advantage of the international quota system under the MFA, but following the expiry of the MFA at the beginning of January 2005, exports have declined strongly.

Government figures show continual growth in the labour force, which reached over 180,000 in 2006, up from around 154,000 in 2001 (Table I.3). Of those in employment in 2006, over 43,000 or approximately 25% were employed in the government sector (not including members of the security forces), making the Government by far the largest employer.

The private sector remains highly dependent on immigrant labour, primarily from the ASEAN countries, but also from India, Bangladesh, and Pakistan. According to the Government, there were 74,046 foreign workers (temporary residents) in the private sector in Brunei in 2005 (although this figure did not cover maids, drivers, and private gardeners, who are thought to number around 22,000). In 2004, foreign workers accounted for over 80% of the workforce in manufacturing and construction, and between 60% and 70% in personal services, retailing, hotels and restaurants, and agriculture.

Brunei Malays (bumiputera or "sons of the soil"), who constitute the majority of the population, generally aspire to work in the civil service, in state-owned Brunei Shell Petroleum (BSP), Royal Brunei Airlines, or in more prestigious jobs in the private sector, such as in the banking sector, avoiding the construction industry, agriculture, and other sectors regarded as having low status. In 2004, the Government set up a careers centre with the aim of finding private sector jobs for Bruneians entering the market.

AGRICULTURE, FORESTRY, AND FISHING

Agriculture and forestry were the basis of Brunei's economy before the discovery of petroleum in the late 1920s. Sixty years ago more than 50% of the population was employed in the primary sector; that share has now fallen to under 3% (of which more than two thirds are foreign workers or temporary residents).

(i) Agriculture

8. Farming has become a part-time business for most rural families, owing to the availability of more lucrative forms of employment. Brunei's agriculture sector is very small, accounting for under 1% of nominal GDP in 2006; Brunei imports more than 80% of its food requirements.

(a) National Development Plan

9. Government policy is to reduce Brunei's dependence on food imports and to attain greater self-sufficiency in agriculture. The enhancement of long-term food security has been a key objective

of the National Development Plans both for food security reasons and to diversify production and exports.3 Generally, the Plans have sought to: boost domestic production of rice, vegetables, poultry, and livestock; develop the agri-food industry; produce high-value-added products using new techniques; and conserve and protect the country's biological diversity.

Foreign investment in agriculture and food processing is encouraged, although it appears that a minimum of 30% participation by local producers is required. The Eighth Plan (2001-05) allocated B$90.5 million (or 1.2% of overall expenditure) for the development of agriculture. There are a number of measures to assist local producers, including subsidized infrastructure facilities such as roads, irrigation, and electricity, as well as inputs such as seeds, fertilizer, vaccines for livestock, and farming equipment; financial and technical assistance is also provided for local producers. Brunei has not notified its Aggregate Measurement of Support (AMS) to the WTO since 1995.

The 8th Plan also called for increasing self-sufficiency in vegetables, poultry, livestock, and rice. A goal was set to increase rice production to 1,300 tonnes (3% of local needs) by 2006, when production reached 895 tonnes (Table IV.1). The Government encouraged the planting of rice through various schemes such as price support and the provision of improved infrastructure, irrigation, and drainage facilities.4 With smallholding rice production declining, the Government has initiated a pilot large-scale rice mechanization project aimed at increasing output. It is hoped that once fully mechanized, 30% of Brunei's rice needs will be met by domestic production. Despite such efforts, however, there has not been much investment in agriculture in recent years. According to the authorities, the lack of interest appears to be due mainly to better employment opportunities in other sectors, notably the public sector, as well as unstable prices, limited marketing outlets, and lack of access to start-up funds.

The plan for the development of the poultry industry aimed to encourage the development of small and medium-scale enterprises linked to processing and marketing centres, such as the Mulaut Abattoir, which act as market outlets for poultry producers. The programme emphasized the participation of private enterprise in the development of the industry; government involvement was limited to the provision of basic infrastructure and production-support services. As a result, according to the authorities, Brunei is almost self-sufficient in the production of eggs and poultry.

The plan for vegetable production was oriented towards the development of high-value products and higher technology farming, such as protected cultivation. Under the Eighth Plan, the production target for vegetables was 12,700 tonnes (94% of local requirements) and in 2004 vegetable production was estimated at over 11,000 tonnes (Table IV.1). Under the Department of Agriculture's long-term strategic plan, the production target for vegetables is 58,000 tonnes by 2023. The 8th Plan also envisaged the development of small fruit plantations (mainly bananas and coconuts), which could support the development of large-scale plantations in the future. The aim was to increase production to 8,000 tonnes and the level of self-sufficiency to 47% by 2005, in which year production exceeded 5,200 tonnes. Brunei envisages production on fruit farms to increase to 24,000 tonnes by 2023 and the level of self-sufficiency to 50% by 2012. Local production of livestock is low and live cattle are imported for slaughter from a cattle ranch in Australia owned by the Government of Brunei. For religious reasons, the rearing of pigs has been banned since 1993.

(b) Import measures

14. The current MFN tariff is virtually zero for agriculture and fishing (Table AIII.1). Tea and coffee are subject to specific import duties for which ad valorem equivalents are not available and are hence not included in this overall tariff average. However, the bound tariff in agriculture is

considerably higher than the applied rate, giving the Government scope to raise the applied rates of agricultural products within their bindings. The authorities argue that the difference between the bound and applied rates enables the Government to address domestic food security concerns more effectively by ensuring a meaningful domestic supply and reliable imports from MFN sources. They also believe that the bound tariff enables domestic institutions and enforcement agencies to adapt and adjust their capacity requirements to suit the varying needs for sanitary and phytosanitary requirements when the need arises.

Although there are few tariff restrictions, some agricultural products, i.e. rice, sugar, and salt, are subject to import restrictions. Most of Brunei's rice is imported directly by the Department of Information Technology and State Stores under a government-to-government contract, from Thailand. The Government, through the Information Technology and State Stores department, which is under the Ministry of Finance maintains a minimum level of rice and sugar stocks on food security grounds.

Imports of beef and poultry are subject to a "food balancing" requirement, whereby the volume of required imports is determined on the basis of local demand for the products and local production. Imported eggs must be stamped accordingly, in order to distinguish them from locally produced eggs. Export restrictions are maintained on rice and sugar. In addition to import and export restrictions, all agricultural products are subject to sanitary and phytosanitary measures, and random checks may be carried out at the border or in Brunei. Imports of all meat and poultry products are subject to Halal requirements and may only be sourced from government-approved abattoirs.

(ii) Forestry

Forestry is not economically significant in Brunei, but is important for the conservation of soils, water, wildlife, and the environment. Primary (60%) and secondary (16%) rain forest covers around 76% of Brunei's total land area. The Forestry Act of Brunei (revised in 1984) provides the legal framework for the protection and conservation of forestry resources, and the National Forest Policy (NFP), issued in 1989, guides and governs forestry activities in accordance with international sustainable forest management obligations and standards. Logging and other forestry activities are limited in large part due to Brunei's emphasis on sustainable use of natural resources and the preservation of biological diversity.

Timber is logged mainly for local consumption; Brunei maintains restrictions on imports and exports of timber to ensure local supply and for environmental reasons. The Department of Forestry in the Ministry of Industry and Primary Resources, the principle regulator in the sector, oversees the Reduced Cut Policy (introduced in 1990), which limits the production of round timber to 100,000 m3 per year, which accounts for over 50% of domestic demand; the rest has to be imported. However, illegal logging appears to be increasing, especially near the Malaysian border. Brunei also uses its forests to develop eco-tourism.

(iii) Fishing

19. The Brunei Fisheries Act (1982) delimits a maritime area of about 38,600 sq km extending to about 200 nautical miles (370 km) from the coast. Fish is an important part of the local diet. Brunei's catch in 2006 was nearly 17,000 tonnes of fresh fish, more than two thirds of which was caught by small-scale fishermen. Brunei has set a goal for the industry of 20,000 tonnes per year on a sustainable basis and has targeted the aquaculture industry, which produced 540 tonnes in 2006 (Table IV.1), for development.5 In 2005, the fisheries sector was worth an estimated B$100 million and the Government believes that the industry has the potential for B$400 million in

annual production by 2023. Nevertheless, although the sultanate has more than 100 kilometres of coastline, and 85% of its population live on the seaboard, Brunei still has to import around 40% of its fish and related products.

To increase fish production, the Government encouraged the establishment of a small, modern, offshore fishing industry to meet projected demand and, under the Eighth Plan, B$90 million was allocated for the continued development the fisheries sector. The Government has emphasized the sustainable exploitation of fisheries resources; the current permitted exploitation level is self-imposed at the estimated maximum economic yield, and is managed through the number of fishing licences issued for each fishing method.6 Other than providing facilities for aquaculture and overall basic infrastructure, the Government also seeks joint ventures with foreign enterprises to obtain finance and expertise in expanding both the annual catch and processing activities.

Brunei's relatively clean environment and freedom from extreme climate-related phenomena is conducive to the development of aquaculture. Once identified, potential areas are upgraded with basic infrastructure such as access to roads, water and power supplies, and telephone lines.

OIL AND GAS SECTOR

The export of oil and gas has dominated Brunei's economy since the 1930s and the oil and gas sector accounts for over two thirds of nominal GDP and generates more than 90% of total export earnings and government revenues. Wealth from oil and gas provides Brunei's small population with a relatively high standard of living compared with its ASEAN neighbours.

(i) Production and trade

Brunei is the fourth-largest oil producer in South East Asia and is the ninth-largest exporter of liquefied natural gas in the world. Brunei's economy has followed the swings of the world oil market; economic growth has averaged around 2.6% in the 2000s, heavily dependent on oil and gas production. Oil production averaged slightly over 200,000 barrels a day during the period under review. The output target is flexible, however, and production in 2006 was 219,000 barrels per day, up from average annual production of 201,000 b/d in 2005 and 206,000 b/d in 2004 (Table IV.2); this allowed Brunei to take advantage of the high oil prices in 2006, which rose to US$69.4/b up from US$57.7/b in 2005 and US$41.7/b a year earlier.

In 2006, Brunei consumed an estimated 13,000 barrels/day of oil; most crude oil production is exported to other countries in the region. Oil exports of 206,000 b/d were recorded in 2006, up from 193,000 b/d in 2005. Despite Brunei's status as a net exporter of oil, it imports about half of the refined petroleum products it consumes, as has limited domestic refining capacity.

In 2006, Brunei produced over 1,200 million standard cubic feet (MMscf) of natural gas per day (Table IV.2), which translated into a liquefied natural gas output that has fluctuated at around 1,000 trillion btu (British thermal units) per day during review period.

Brunei's wealth is based on its hydrocarbon reserves, which were at 1.1 billion barrels of mainly low-sulphur oil in January 2007.7 According to two reports, Brunei's oil reserves are expected to last 25 years or only another 10 years, at current rates of extraction.8 Brunei's gas reserves have been estimated at 390 billion cu metres, and are expected to last another 40 years. The Government aims to conserve resources and continue exploration to open new fields; in early 2006, a consortium led by Canada's Loon Energy was awarded a 2,253 sq km oil exploration block. A 3,011 sq km block covering most of Brunei's Belait district was also awarded to a consortium led by the UK-registered Valiant International Petroleum.

However, the development of offshore areas is hampered by a territorial dispute with Malaysia. In 2003, Malaysia disputed Brunei-awarded oil exploration concessions for offshore

blocks J and K (Total and Shell, respectively), which led to a moratorium on exploration activities in the areas.9 Negotiations in order to resolve the conflict are continuing.

28. According to export figures for the first half of 2006, Indonesia, Australia, and Korea took about 67% of Brunei's total crude exports; traditional customers Japan, the United States, and China each took between 5% and 8% (Table IV.3). Brunei is one of the world's largest producers of liquefied natural gas (LNG), the bulk of which (over 5 million tonnes) is purchased by three Japanese utility companies under a long-term contract signed in 1972 and extended for 20 years in 1993. The Japanese company Mitsubishi is a joint venture partner with Shell and the Brunei Government in Brunei LNG Sdn Bhd, Brunei gas Carriers Sdn Bhd, and Brunei Shell Tankers Sdn Bhd, which produce the LNG. The second largest market is South Korea10, which accounts for around 10% of total LNG exports.

(ii) Oil and gas industry

Brunei's oil industry is largely dominated by Brunei Shell Petroleum (BSP), a joint venture owned in equal shares by the Brunei Government and the Asiatic Petroleum Company Ltd. BSP had a monopoly on all upstream and downstream activities until 1999, when the Government awarded some exploration blocks to other companies, notably Total E&P Borneo BV11, which started production from offshore Block B.

BSP is the leading oil and gas production company in Brunei and operates the only refinery, which meets domestic demand for most petroleum products. BSP, BLNG, Brunei Shell marketing Company Sdn Bhd (BSM) and BST together constitute the largest employer in Brunei after the Government (Table IV.4) with some 4,000 personnel, of which 90% are Bruneians.12

a End-user prices of petroleum products (gasoline, diesel, kerosene and bottled LPG) have been regulated since 1978 under Price Stabilization Agreement signed by the Government and BSM, under which the Government subsidizes end-user prices if the price of crude rises above a certain level.

Natural gas is also used domestically for petroleum operators' own-use, power generation, liquefied petroleum gas (LPG) used domestically, and as a reserve for industrial purposes. Approximately 90% of Brunei's natural gas is exported as LNG by BLNG. Petroleum products for local consumption are marketed solely by BSM, jointly owned by the Government of Brunei and Shell Overseas Holdings Ltd. Retail/end-user prices of gasoline, diesel, kerosene, and bottled LPG have been regulated since 1978, under a Price Stabilization Agreement (PSA) between the Government and BSM, under which the Government subsidizes prices if the price of crude oil rises above a certain level. According to the authorities, the subsidization costs over B$200 million per year.

The Government encourages diversification, including downstream activities related to the petroleum and natural gas sector. At present, around 93% of Brunei's petroleum and 90% of its natural gas output is exported as crude oil and LNG, respectively. The remaining crude oil output is refined for domestic use. Brunei's only refinery, located in Seria, has a capacity of 10,000 bpd for its crude distillation unit and 6,000 bpd for its reformer unit. The main products include unleaded gasoline, gasoil, Jet A1 fuel, and kerosene.

The Government is keen to encourage investment in downstream activities and has set aside a trillion cubic feet of gas for industrial use. In 2006, an MoU was signed for the Gas Sales and Supply Agreement between BSP Co. Sdn Bhd and a consortium comprising Itochu, Mitsubishi Gas Corporation and Petroleum Brunei; a marketing agreement was also signed for the methanol plant located at the Sungai Liang Industrial Complex.

Under the Income Tax (Petroleum) Act, Cap. 119 (Laws of Brunei revised edition, 1984), Brunei levies a corporate tax on petroleum and gas operations at a rate of 55%. Royalties and petroleum income tax are payable on both concessions and production sharing agreements.

(iii) Policy

In 2002, the Government established the Brunei's first national oil company, the Brunei National Petroleum Company Sdn Bhd, also known as Petroleum Brunei. Petroleum Brunei is responsible for managing assets in designated areas (Blocks J, K, L and M). It has chosen to award private companies the exploration rights for the blocks it controls. Despite efforts to introduce competition, BSP is likely to remain the dominant oil producer by virtue of its control of Brunei's major oil and natural gas fields. In 2003, BSP signed an extension of the petroleum mining agreements with the Government for a further 19 years until the end of 2022.13

The Petroleum Unit, established in 1982 under the Prime Minister's Department, is the principal regulator of the petroleum and gas sector in Brunei. The Petroleum Unit reports to the Minister of Energy, whose portfolio was created in May 2005. The Unit's responsibilities include: overseeing the exploitation of Brunei's petroleum and gas reserves, and promoting the development of downstream industries; fixing crude oil prices; and ensuring compliance with internationally acceptable technical, accounting, health and safety, and environmental standards.

Under the Petroleum Mining Act (Chapter 44 of the Laws of Brunei, revised edition 2002), investors, including foreign investors, may apply for petroleum mining agreements in respect of state land, whether onshore or offshore; the applications are considered by the Sultan of Brunei in Council.

NON-OIL AND -GAS INDUSTRY

38. Apart from the energy and construction sectors, Brunei's industrial base remains limited. Foreign capital and technology have been deterred by the small domestic market; a poorly developed local private sector; high wage costs; a shortage of skilled labour; slow bureaucratic procedures and lack of transparency; an unwillingness on the part of the Government to underwrite risk-taking ventures; and the ban on foreigners owning land.

(i) Manufacturing

39. Non-oil and gas manufacturing accounted for a mere 1.1% of nominal GDP in 2006, down from 3.2% in 2002. However, the sector accounted for 13% of employment in 2005 (latest figure), indicating that labour productivity in manufacturing is less than one tenth of that in the rest of the economy; statistics on productivity trends in the manufacturing (or any other), sector were not available from the Brunei authorities. The main large-scale industries are cement production, garment making, and production of pre-cast concrete structures.

Other industries include building material products; electronic and electrical products, such as cables, switchboard, and assembly appliances; mineral water; canned food; dairy products; silica sands products; and publishing and printing. In November 2006, a local firm (Berjaya Majmur) began construction work on an animal feed manufacturing plant in Muara, which is expected to commence production in 2007. The plant will have sufficient capacity to supply Brunei's animal feed needs; in 2004, 34,000 tonnes of animal feed were imported.

Ready-made garments constitute the third biggest export after crude oil and liquefied natural gas. The garment industry was established to take advantage of the international quota system agreed under the terms of the Multi-Fibre Agreement (MFA). The industry benefited from a quota arrangement with the United States but this expired at the end of 2004 leading to a 25% fall in earnings from garment exports in 2005. Figures supplied by the authorities for the first half of 2006 show garment export earnings of just B$100.3 million, down from B$303.4 million in 2005 as a whole. In view of the increasing competition from China and India, the future of the garment industry in Brunei has become more uncertain. The industry has been encouraged to upgrade through the adoption of modern machinery and more efficient production methods.

Fish processing has been the fastest growing sector in recent years. Production has risen from 479 tonnes in 2004 to 867 tonnes in 2006 (Table IV.1). As part of the industrial development programme, a number of industrial estates have been established, including a 40 ha site near Bandar Seri Begawan and the Beribi Light Industrial Complex, which comprises, inter alia, textiles, food, and electrical manufacturers.

(a) Industrial development policy

Manufacturing has continued to be encouraged in order to reduce Brunei's dependence on its petroleum resources, and a number of incentives are used to encourage investment in priority sectors identified by the Government. The incentives include financial assistance to local companies and tax breaks for all investors (Chapter III); in addition, the Government provides free or subsidized infrastructure and inputs. In priority sectors in which private investment is not forthcoming, the Government invests directly, mainly through its holding company Semaun Holdings,14 which is especially active in trading and commercial ventures in the food, manufacturing, and service sectors.

The Government's industrial development policy is managed by the Brunei Industrial Development Authority (BINA)15, a department of the Ministry of Industry and Primary Resources. BINA's main role is to facilitate industrial development, manage Brunei's industrial sites and advise investors wishing to make use of these sites. There appear to be nine industrial sites covering around 300 hectares, which provide basic infrastructure such as roads, drainage and sewerage facilities, electricity, telecommunications, and water. The Government also takes a direct stake in industrial sectors in the economy through its holding company Semaun Holdings Sendirian Berhad. Investment by Semaun Holdings may take the form of joint ventures with local or foreign companies, or direct investment in the desired sectors.

(b) BEDB

The Brunei Economic Development Board (BEDB) was formed in November 2001 to stimulate the growth, expansion, and development of the economy by promoting Brunei as an investment destination. In January 2003, the BEDB launched a two-pronged strategy through which it aimed to attract US$4.5 billion in foreign direct investment and create 7,700 new jobs by 2008.

The first prong involves the development of the Sungai Liang area outside of Bandar Seri Begawan into an advanced industrial site for petrochemical and manufacturing industries that can capitalize on Brunei's proven gas reserves. In September 2004, the BEDB announced it had entered into final negotiations to establish a US$720 million ammonia/urea plant and US$350 million methanol plant.16 The Government has approved the methanol plant and is in the final stages of considering the proposed ammonia urea plant. If the project proceeds, the plant would be the largest urea manufacturing operation in Asia, with a capacity to manufacture 1.2 million tonnes of urea per year. The second prong involves the construction of a deep water port facility at Pulau Muara Besar (section (iv)(b)).

46. The BEDB recognizes that Brunei must develop its SMEs in order to achieve sustained growth. In the long term, the Government's emphasis is to support and develop the private sector, and it has continued to implement a spending package to stimulate the economy in the short term. A number of industrial parks are being developed to cater for services and manufacturing activities; specific industries targeted for these sites include steel, dairy products, glass, pre-cast concrete, and light-weight aggregate production.

(ii) Construction

47. The construction sector's share of current GDP contracted from 3.7% in 2002 to 2.9% in 2006. The industry was badly damaged by the 1998 collapse of the Amadeo conglomerate, which had spent lavishly on construction projects. The Government has announced a number of projects aimed at bolstering the industry, including the construction of the 271 ha industrial park at Sungai Liang, beginning in 200717; but a real estate glut in the capital has to some extent offset these efforts.

(iii) Electricity

48. The electric supply industry in Brunei Darussalam is governed by the Electricity Act 1973 and Electricity Act (Amendment) Order, 2002. The Department of Electrical Services (DES), under the Prime Minister's Office, is responsible for the generation, transmission, and distribution of electricity. Other than DES, electricity is also generated by an independent power utility, the Berakas Power Company (BPC). The two power utilities operate independently with their own transmission and distribution networks, which are not interconnected.18 About 99% of electricity uses natural gas as the main fuel while the remaining 1% is generated by diesel fuel. Electrical energy demand increased by about 1.2% in 2006. Big power consumers such as BSP and BLNG also have their own power generating facilities: BSP has an installed capacity of about 30 MW powered by gas and BLNG has steam turbine generators with an installed capacity of about 40 MW.

SERVICES

(i) Overview

The share of private sector services (excluding construction and utilities) in current GDP fell from 22% in 2002 to just 15% in 2006. The leading services sectors are finance and business services, the wholesale and retail trade and transport and communications (Table I.1). Recognizing the importance of services for economic growth, the Government aims to transform Brunei into a service hub for trade and tourism (SHuTT). The SHuTT programme would promote trade, travel, business, and communications in and through Brunei. The programme was intended to further develop Brunei's infrastructure, including upgrading facilities at Brunei International Airport; expanding Muara Port, Brunei's main port, and increasing capacity in the telecommunications services network to increase penetration rates, as well as expanding coverage by the domestic and international postal services.

In May 2005, Brunei made a conditional initial offer under the GATS in the framework of the on-going services negotiations in the DDA.19 The offer covers 5 out of the 12 services in the WTO Secretariat classification20: business services (professional and computer and related services), communication services (telecoms), financial services (insurance), tourism and travel-related services, and transport services (air transport). Overall, the offer is similar to its commitments undertaken in the Uruguay Round. For example, commercial presence is unbound except for existing companies where half the board members of a public company and half the directors of a private company must be nationals or residents of Brunei; and all companies incorporated outside Brunei must have one or more local agents. The movement of natural persons (mode 4) is unbound with respect to both market access and national treatment, with the exception of temporary intra-corporate transfers at the level of management, executives and specialists.

In its Article II (MFN) exemptions, future liberalization with regard to foreign equity participation is subject to discretionary changes and dependent on Brunei's development requirements. Brunei also has a preference for recruiting labour from traditional sources of supply to ensure social cohesion in the country. Sector-specific MFN exemptions are also proposed to be maintained for legal services, radio and television services, financial services, reinsurance and retrocession, and banking and other financial services. The authorities have indicated that they intend to revise their offer at an appropriate time in the DDA negotiations.

(ii) Financial services

(a) Overview

At end 2006, there were eight banks in Brunei (six branches of foreign banks, one local conventional bank and one local Islamic bank), and 33 non-banking financial institutions, comprising: one Islamic trust fund; three international insurance companies; three finance companies (two local and one foreign); the Employees Trust Fund (ETF)21, and 25 money changers and 19 remittance companies. In February 2006, the Finance Ministry approved the merger of the Islamic Bank of Brunei (IBB) and the state-owned Islamic Development Bank of Brunei (IDBB) to create the Sultanate's largest bank, the Islamic Bank of Brunei Darussalam (IBBD). The Government is promoting Islamic banking as a niche area. In addition, the Islamic Trust Fund (Perbadanan Tabung Amanah Islam Brunei) provides savings and investment facilities under Islamic principles.22 The three finance companies in Brunei provide mainly hire-purchase financing for cars and other consumer durables, and mortgages.

The development of a Brunei capital market is in an infant stage. Brunei does not have its own tradeable stock exchange. The Securities Order 2001 regulates financial exchanges, dealers, and other persons providing advice in respect of dealings in securities. The Order confers on the regulating authority extensive powers in monitoring all records maintained for securities dealing. The Securities (Amendment) Order 2005 contains additional provisions with respect to unlicensed persons purporting to act as investment advisers as well as representatives of dealers who are not resident in Brunei.

Brunei does not have a central bank. The Ministry of Finance, through the Treasury, the Brunei Currency and Monetary Board, the Brunei Investment Agency, and the Financial Institutions Division (FID), exercises most of the functions of a central bank. The FID, the regulator and supervisor of the financial industry, publishes guidelines on minimum paid-up capital, cash balances, and capital adequacy ratios. In July 2000, Brunei opened the Brunei International Financial Centre (BIFC), an offshore financial centre that has since attracted more than 8,000 international firms, licensed under the International Business Companies Order 2000. Brunei has updated its legislative and regulatory framework to attract investors to the BIFC.

55. Since the establishment of the BIFC, Brunei has dual jurisdiction whereby the international legislation offers "offshore" facilities alongside the usual range of "domestic" legislation. The FID and the BIFC are responsible for regulation, supervision, and the financial stability of the financial sector. The supervisory authorities have institutional units dealing with: banking, insurance, finance companies, money changers and money remittance, and securities, and there is a Financial Intelligence Unit. The authorities perform both off-site and on-site inspection of domestic banks and have implemented Basel I since 1998. Officials are currently working on building the infrastructure required for the implementation for Basel II.

(b) Banking

In 2006, more than half of banking assets were held by three banks: Citibank, Standard Chartered Bank (SCB), and Hongkong and Shanghai Banking Corporation (HSBC). Commercial bank assets increased from B$11.4 billion in 2001 (or 114% of nominal GDP) to B$14.9 billion in June 2007. Total loans made by Brunei's commercial banks increased from B$4.25 billion in 2001 to B$5.64 billion in June 2007, an increase of 32%. Personal loans accounted for over two thirds of commercial bank lending during 2001-05, followed by general commerce (around 11%), construction (10%) and transportation (4%). Mortgages accounted for between 10% and 15% of total personal loans, and other personal loans made up between 50% and 60% of all loans in the same period. Commercial banks tend to have limited scope for providing mortgages as the Government provides loans without interest to civil servants for purchasing housing and automobiles.

Given the level of personal lending, the Ministry of Finance issued a personal loan capping directive in May 2005 to the Brunei Association of Banks (BAB). The objectives of the directive are to: reduce the level of personal debt and promote a savings culture. The directive outlines more stringent guidelines on the granting of personal loans and issuance of credit cards. It also requires the banks to set their own prime lending rate, which was previously set by the BAB.

Regulatory framework for prudential supervision

According to the IMF, at the start of the review period the regulatory requirements, limited to minimum paid-up capital and a 6% reserve requirement at the BCMB, were minimal and appropriate standards for accounting, valuation, and loan classification and provisioning, single borrower limits, and capital adequacy requirements were necessary. It also recommended "systematizing" reporting requirements for domestic and foreign banks and regular monitoring basic financial soundness indicators.23 The level of non-performing loans was relatively high and warranted close monitoring as did the rise in consumer loans

The Banking Order, 2006 has most of the provisions for effective banking supervision recommended by Basle Committee through the 25 Core Principles for Effective Banking Supervision. These include requirements on capital adequacy, off-site surveillance, on-site examinations, borrowing limits, major acquisitions or investments by banks, transfer of a bank's shares, scope and frequency of reporting, confidentiality of supervisory information, and disclosure. Banks use the risk-weighted assets to calculate the capital adequacy ratio, and comply with the minimum requirement of 10% (section 11 of Banking Order, 2006). Since June 2006, all banks send monthly reports to FID on the core set of financial soundness indicators, which include capital adequacy, asset quality, earnings and profitability, liquidity, and sensitivity to market risk.

During the review period, there appears to have been considerable strengthening of financial sector supervision and regulation, including efforts to enhance monitoring of financial soundness indicators. In particular, the enactment of the new Banking, Finance Company, Insurance and Securities Amendment Orders brings the regulatory framework more in line with international standards. The Banking Order 2006, which amended the Banking Act, paved the way for on-site inspection, increased capital requirements of local Brunei incorporated banks to not less than B$100 million, and tightened provisions affecting financial leasing, money transmission services, means of payment such as credit cards, guarantees, foreign exchange dealings, financial futures, and participation in share issues. The Finance Companies Act (Amendment) Order 200624 increased the capital requirement for local Brunei finance companies to not less than B$25 million; it also provides for new forms of business, including Islamic financing business.25 Also, the authorities issued guidelines in 2005 to reduce risks associated with the rapid rise in personal loans.

Islamic banking

The Government has continued to encourage Islamic banking, which (as of June 2007), account for 38% of commercial banks' assets. Legislation is in place to support banks operating under these principles, including taking a share of profits from the firms they fund rather than charging interest.26 Prudential regulations for Islamic banks are, in general, more stringent than for commercial banks. In addition to minimum cash balances, the Islamic Banking Act (Cap. 168) requires regular reporting of audited statements and monthly balance sheets to the Minister of Finance, through the FID; banks are also obliged to furnish any additional data as requested by the Minister. Foreign-owned or controlled companies may not be granted Islamic banking licences.27 According to the authorities there are plans to harmonize Islamic and conventional banking regulations by 2007; the new Islamic banking Order 2007 is in its final stage of drafting.

As part of its diversification programme, and to support the development of Islamic financing, the Syariah Financial Supervisory Board was established in January 2006 to regulate Islamic financial institutions. The Government also floated its first non-interest-bearing Islamic bond in 2006. In April 2006, the Government launched the first Islamic money market programme, worth B$150 million, which is a three-month paper based on the Al-Ijarah concept.28

Brunei International Financial Centre (BIFC)

The Government established the Brunei International Financial Centre (BIFC) in 2000 to diversify financial services in Brunei and to establish Brunei as an off-shore banking and trading centre for the region offering both conventional and Islamic financial services. The legislation to accompany the formation of the BIFC, sought to introduce measures against money laundering activities and to bring Brunei's standards up to international standards, thereby improving transparency and attracting companies to the BIFC. At end of June 2007, six banks and seven investment advisors had obtained a licence and begun operations (Box IV.1). The legislation in force also caters for Islamic financial services, which have been attracting growing interest from the international market.

BIFC

Brunei International Financial Centre (BIFC), a multi-disciplinary unit within the Ministry of Finance, was established in 2000 to help Brunei become a financial hub in the region, especially in banking, finance, securities, and insurance.

BIFC has registered more than 7,000 international business companies, licensed 10 registered agents under the Registered Agents and Trustees Licensing Order 2000; 6 banks under the International Banking Order 2000; 3 licences under the International Insurance and Takaful

Order, 2002; 25 licences under the Mutual Funds Order, 2001; and 7 investment advisers licensed under the Securities Order, 2001.

A comprehensive set of legislation covering financial activities associated with BIFC was enacted from 2000 to 2002, including Islamic finance. BIFC has a policy of reviewing the legislation and making amendments when required in order to reflect current practices and ensure that stringent international standards are met. There are ten statutes in effect, which include the Money Laundering Order, Criminal Conduct (Recovery of Proceeds) Order, International Limited Partnerships Order, International Banking Order, Registered Agents and Trustees Licensing Order, International Trusts Order, International Business Companies Order, Mutual Funds Order, Securities Order and International Insurance and Takaful Order. The Sultan of Brunei Darussalam had consented to the introduction and amendment of several laws, namely the Insurance Order 2006, the Banking Order 2006, the Hire Purchase Order 2006 and Finance Companies Amendment Order 2006, all of which came into effect in March 2006.

The launch of the nation's first Islamic Bond, the Short Term Government Sukuk Al-Ijarah programme in 2006, has paved the way for the development of a wider range of Islamic financial instruments and products that comply with Syariah principles. As of September 2007, the issuance of the Short-term Sukuk Al-Ijarah securities reached B$925 million.

The recent formation of a Syariah Financial Supervisory Board pursuant to the Syariah Financial Supervisory Board Order, 2006, will further boost Islamic finance in Brunei. The Syariah Financial Supervisory Board is the authority for regulating Islamic banking, takaful, Islamic financial business, Islamic development financial business and any other business, which is based on Syariah principles.

(c) Insurance

At the end of 2006, there were 21 active insurance companies: 12 locally incorporated29, 6 branches of foreign companies, and 3 foreign underwriting companies represented by locally incorporated firms. Gross premiums for all general insurance companies totalled B$147.9 million (up from B$51 million in 2001): general premiums accounted for B$81.6 million, motor insurance for 63%, fire insurance for 14%, and workmen's compensation for 7%. In general business, takaful operators were heavily concentrated in motor insurance, and dominated the market with 51% of total general premiums. In life business, conventional insurers remain the biggest market players as products offered are more extensive compared with takaful.

In addition to the Motor Vehicles (Third-Party Risks) Act, recent specific legislation relating to the insurance industry, the Insurance Order 2006, which raised the paid-up capital of Brunei insurance companies. It also provides for tighter regulations on the establishment and maintenance of insurance funds; the allocation of surplus; the form, investment, and situation of assets; the restrictions on payment of dividends; and the requirements of disclosure of interests by directors.

The main elements of supervision include a security deposit with the Government of B$1 million for insurers underwriting motor insurance, and for licensed life and/or general insurers under the Insurance Order 2006; minimum paid-up capital of B$8 million; a solvency margin for general insurers of 20% of net premium income (NPI) of the previous year; and guidelines for the appointment of foreign employees and motor insurance agents. Additionally, all insurance and takaful companies are required to provide their audited annual accounts, ASEAN unified statistics, and quarterly data on premiums collected, to the FID.

Supervision, which has been provided by the Financial Institutions Division (FID) in the Ministry of Finance, since 1993, was based on moral suasion, and regular contacts with the General Insurance Association of Brunei, which represents general insurance companies. However, since the introduction of the Insurance Order 2006, the Permanent Secretary at the Ministry of Finance was granted extensive powers to govern the insurance industry, including the power to inspect and investigate the affairs of insurers, to approve the appointment of as well as to disqualify the principal officer and director. A standardized application form, available from FID, requires applicants to disclose details of the share of equity; management structure; proposed operational and internal control of the company; projected financial highlights of the company including the authorized capital; and, for foreign companies, prior approval from the regulatory authorities of the country in which the company originates. No new insurance companies were registered during the period under review.

GATS commitments were made for direct insurance (life and non-life), reinsurance and retrocession, insurance and intermediation (broking and agency services) and auxiliary services (consultancy, actuarial risk assessment, risk management, and maritime loss adjusting). In general, Brunei's schedule reflects current requirements and restrictions, including commercial presence only through companies registered in Brunei for direct insurance; and purchase of compulsory insurance for motor third-party liability and workmen's compensation only from insurance companies established in Brunei. The initial offer tabled in 2005 does not appear to go beyond current commitments.

(iii) Telecommunications

69. Brunei, as a small wealthy nation in South East Asia, has endeavoured to ensure up-to-date telecommunication services to its population; the target of 100% digitalization was achieved in 1995. Telecommunications throughout Brunei are of a high standard and the country ranks well in Asia in terms of penetration and infrastructure. Brunei has a telephone household penetration rate of 100% and there has been significant growth of cellular subscribers. Mobile penetration had reached 74% by October 2006 (up from 32% at end 2001) (Table IV.6). There is a nationwide broadband network (RaGAM 21), at the core of which is a high-speed switching ATM-based network. There has also been significant investment in a rural telecoms network, which allows all rural and remote areas access to telephone and the Internet.

(a) Industry developments

70. Brunei's telecommunications industry has recently shifted from a monopoly in fixed-line and mobile telephony to a state of oligopoly, with the eventual goal, according to the Brunei authorities, of creating a competitive environment where home-grown companies would be challenged to rise to global standards and even break into international markets. Currently, TelBru, the successor to the Government Telecoms Department, has a monopoly over the fixed-line network; B-mobile has a monopoly over the provision of 3G telephony, and the DST Group has a monopoly over the provision of GSM telephony. According to the authorities, there is some competition in mobile telephony with the entry of B-mobile into the market in 2005, and in the dialup internet access segment with TelBru and DST Group in competition. The authorities point out that TelBru, DST and B-mobile are corporate entities and, although the eventual controlling parties are the Government or linked to the Government, the general perception is that they are quasi private-sector companies.

There are three telecommunications infrastructure providers: TelBru Bhd, which provides basic telephony and a range of value-added services such as leased-line services, dial-up internet, ADSL broadband, VoIP, ATM lines and pre-paid calling cards; the DST Group Sdn Bhd, a private company based in Brunei, which operates a GSM mobile network and provides some value-added services, VoIP, leased-line, and a dial-up internet; and B-mobile Communications Sdn Bhd (a joint venture between TelBru Bhd and QAF Comserve), which operates a 3G mobile network and provides VoIP, and internet access via 3G. The three companies are locally owned and controlled and, according to the authorities, there is currently no significant foreign participation. AiTi's published licensing framework excludes companies that are majority-owned or controlled by foreign parties from being licensed to operate in Brunei.

(b) Regulatory developments

Under the Telecommunications Act of 1952, the Government was the exclusive provider of telecommunications services. Jabatan Telekom Brunei/Telecommunications Department (JTB) was established as a government department in 1952 to provide telecom services and to act as the regulatory body for telecommunications. At the start of the current review period, the Government began restructuring the telecom industry through corporatization (and eventual privatization). JTB was to be corporatized and transformed into a government-administered private company as part of the larger programme to corporatize a number of government services. Telekom Brunei Bhd (TelBru) was established in June 2002, under the Telecommunication Successor Company Order 2001, as the designated telecom successor company, which would take over JTB's service operations. That Order, together with the Telecommunications Order 2001 and the AiTi Order 2001, enabled the repeal of the 1952 Act and, as from entry into force in 2006, provide the legal basis for the restructured telecom sector (Box IV.2).30

Key dates in regulation of telecoms, 2001-06

2001: The Government of Brunei Darussalam commenced a restructuring of the ICT industry; three new pieces of legislation were enacted.

-The Telecommunication Successor Company Order, 2001 transfers all property, rights and liabilities belonging to JTB to Telekom Brunei Limited (TelBru) whereby TelBru assumed the role of service provider in place of the JTB. (JTB to undergo the process of corporatization.)

-The AiTi Order, 2001 establishes the Authority for Info-communications Technology Industry of Brunei Darussalam (AiTi) as an independent statutory body to regulate the local ICT industry. This Order took effect on 1 January 2003.

-The Telecommunications Order, 2001 confers upon AiTi the exclusive privilege to operate and provide telecommunication systems and services in Brunei Darussalam and allows AiTi to grant licences for the same.

B-mobile created as a joint venture between TelBru and QAF Comserve. Granted a licence to operate a W-CDMA network and begins operations as the competitor to incumbent mobile operator DST (and incumbent fixed-line operator TelBru)

The Telecommunication Order entered into force, giving AiTi full power to grant licences; Telecoms Act 1952 repealed.

Government telecommunications department (JTB) corporatized as TelBru. a public limited company registered under the Brunei Darussalam Companies Act and 100% owned by the Government of Brunei Darussalam.

Following lengthy delays, JTB was corporatized in April 2006 and its duties shared between TelBru and the Authority for Info-Communications Technology Industry (AiTi)31, which was established in January 2003 to administer the regulatory function and the development of the info-communication industry in Brunei. Thus, TelBru assumed responsibility for the supply of telecom services in Brunei, while AiTi was charged with regulating and developing the industry and is answerable to the Minister of Communications. AiTi issues licences to operators and manages the radio communications spectrum. AiTi's licensing regime is technologically neutral, with no distinction drawn on the basis of the technology used. It has a two-tier licensing structure: InTi (Infrastructure Provider for the Telecommunication Industry) whereby licensees own infrastructure, and SeTi (Service Provider for the Telecommunication Industry) whereby licensees repackage and resell retail services to consumers or corporate customers through wholesale arrangements with InTi licensees. With regard to fixed-line telephony, the licensing framework published by AiTi mandates a certain level of local loop unbundling (LLU); the lack of de facto LLU and competition in this segment is one of AiTi's key issues.

Brunei Darussalam does not have provisions on competition in its legislation applicable to the telecom sector. Hence, to allow AiTi to monitor and curb anti-competitive behaviour, the licensing framework provides obligations for licensees in relation to competitive behaviour, and powers for the regulator to take action against undesirable or unfair practices. Existing licences, under the Telecommunications Act, are deemed to have been issued by AiTi by virtue of the Telecommunications Order. AiTi is of the view that for the sake of consistency of industry practices, and to create a "baseline" for all industry discussions, existing licensees should be migrated to the new licensing framework, which, among other things, mandates interconnection between fixed network suppliers and other service providers, local loop unbundling, specific clauses regarding anti-competitive behaviour and infrastructure-sharing to foster competition.32

Under the new licences, licensees are required to shift towards alignment with AiTi's and the Ministry of Communications' vision for the industry's future, for example mandating interconnectivity, accounting separation, and USP fund payments.33 There is no specific regulation on price/tariff regulation, but AiTi has the power to give regulatory directions to licensees in the public interest and to ensure fair and efficient market conduct. Under this framework, AiTi may issue a Directive to regulate prices and tariffs.

In its initial GATS offer of 2005, Brunei made offers in local, international, and mobile telephone services and stated that in its eventual commitments JTB's (now TelBru's) monopoly over voice telephone services will be maintained for ten years after its privatization and subject to

a Government review to allow new suppliers into the market. Similarly, for mobile telecom services, the Government has indicated that it will consider issuing new licences to mobile telecommunications providers (employing other than AMPS and GSM technology) in 2010 if public interest and economic conditions would justify this.

(iv) Transport

(a) Air transport services

Brunei's main airport is Brunei International Airport (BIA) at Bandar Seri Begawan; it has the capacity to handle around 1.5 million passengers and 50,000 tonnes of cargo a year. Five airlines link Brunei to 21 cities in 12 countries.34 In 2006, there were 11.9 thousand aircraft movements at BIA: total passenger throughput (inbound, outbound, and transit) was more than 1.4 million up from 1.28 million in 2001; and cargo throughput was 22.7 million tonnes (23.3 million tonnes in 2001).

Brunei International Airport is owned by the Government of Brunei and managed by the Department of Civil Aviation in the Ministry of Communications. In view of its geographical location, Brunei also hopes to establish an air cargo transhipment centre and to establish the airport as a regional refuelling centre by offering attractive fuel prices and liberalizing the supply of fuel. All air cargo transhipment activities are carried out by Royal Brunei Airlines (RBA), although the Government is seeking offers to establish, operate, and manage an air cargo centre for transhipment and distribution.

The national carrier, RBA, is a corporation founded in November 1974, and wholly owned by the Government of Brunei. The airline currently serves 21 destinations in Europe, the Middle East, Asia, and Australia, including several short-haul destinations in Malaysia and Indonesia. Code-sharing agreements are in place between RBA and a number of regional airlines. RBA has yet to record a profit in its three decade long history.35 Ground-handling services, for passengers and cargo, are provided by RBA, whilst airline catering facilities are supplied by Royal Brunei Catering. The authorities state that consideration would be given to additional companies applying to provide ground-handling services.

Brunei maintains a liberal air service policy: a reciprocal "open skies" policy has been adopted in order to attract more foreign airlines to operate into Brunei. As part of this effort, bilateral open skies agreements have been signed with New Zealand, Singapore, the United States, and the United Arab Emirates. The agreements allow designated airlines to provide air services between the two countries with rights to pick up passengers at intermediate stops or in third countries with no limitation on frequency, capacity, and aircraft type. Brunei also signed the world's first multilateral open skies agreement with Chile, New Zealand, Singapore, the United States, Samoa, Cook Islands, and Tonga in 2001.

Local airlines require an operating permit or aircraft operating certificate from the Department of Civil Aviation. Regarding the system of allocating landing slots at Brunei International Airport, landing charges are based on the aircraft's maximum weight at take-off, and there are no differences in charges between peak and off-peak hours. Government employees are encouraged to travel with Royal Brunei Airlines on official trips.

Brunei has included in its 2005 GATS offer a commitment for rental of aircraft with crew. Market access through cross-border supply is subject to certification and approval from the authorities and infrastructure capacity; commercial presence is allowed only through a representative office with a permanent address in Brunei, or through a general sales agent, which must be a Bruneian-controlled company. Market access for personnel is unbound except for the requirement of a general sales agent in Brunei, who is in turn subject to a local availability test and the designation of a specified number of local trainees.36

(b) Maritime transport services

Overall, most of Brunei's international waterborne trade is carried by foreign vessels; only eight vessels fly the Brunei flag. According to the Brunei Marine Department, at end 2006, 69 vessels were registered in Brunei, eight of which were owned by the Government. Total gross registered tonnage under the Brunei flag was 472,454 tonnes. Eight LNG vessels trade internationally, in particular transporting gas to Japan; foreign-owned vessels are used to transport crude oil on a charter basis. Brunei imports most of its commodities, which are carried by foreign vessels operating through Muara port. Brunei has three passenger vessels plying between Muara in Brunei and Labuan (in Malaysia); it also provides car ferry services between Muara and Menumbok in Sabah, Malaysia.

The main port is Muara, 29 km from the capital.37 More than 90% of Brunei's imports and exports (except oil and gas) are channelled through Muara. Under a 25-year agreement38, the Port of Singapore Authority, in a joint venture with a local company, manages the container terminal at Muara. Muara Port has gone through extensive improvements since 1973, increasing the wharf size and overall storage space. It covers a total of 24 hectares, and has two main terminals; one is a conventional terminal and the other a container terminal. Muara Port is connected to 16 ports and receives more than 1,000 calls per year. The conventional terminal consists of a multi-purpose berth for conventional cargo carriers and roll-on/roll-off car carriers, with a total berth length of 611 metres. An additional berth is available for smaller crafts. According to the authorities, Muara Container Terminal aspires to be a regional transhipment hub to serve the developing economies of the East ASEAN Growth Area comprising 50 million population in Brunei Darussalam, Indonesia, Malaysia, and the Philippines (BIMP-EAGA).

Since 2004, annual cargo going through Muara Port has exceeded 100,000 TEUs (twentyfoot equivalent units) (Table IV.7); existing capacity is 350,000 TEUs a year. According to the authorities, vessel productivity, turnaround time, and berth throughput are closely monitored by the Ports Department with the aid of modern computer equipment to ensure that accepted performance indicator targets are maintained.

However, Muara Port is considered to have reached its physical limit for expansion. The Government plans to develop Pulau Muara Besar (PMB), an island opposite the existing port, to accommodate a new container terminal, a cruise-line terminal, and an oil tanker jetty and refinery, as well as an export processing zone. The development of PMB is part of the BEDB's on-going strategy, together with the development of the Sungai Liang Industrial Park, to diversify Brunei's economy. In 2006, the BEDB planned to establish a consortium with the Brunei Government to fund, design, develop, and operate the proposed PMB project by 2009. The main competitive advantage of the project is deep water. As container ships get rapidly larger, they require deeper waters: future generation vessels, with a capacity of 12,500 TEU or more, need ports with a minimum of 16 m of water; PMB's natural seascape would keep dredging expenses relatively low, giving it a long-term cost advantage. In addition, the Government considers that PMB only needs to attract a small part of the rapidly growing transhipment trade for the port development to be viable.

Policy

The maritime transport sector is regulated by the Marine Department in the Ministry of Communications. The Marine Department is responsible for the safety and security of ships, the protection of the marine environment, and for all ships registered in Brunei, trading domestically or internationally. Merchant shipping is subject to the Merchant Shipping Act, 1984 and a number of orders and regulations.40 The Act establishes rules, inter alia, for registering ships under the Brunei flag, licensing ships operating in Brunei waters, and maritime safety. All Brunei ships must be registered under the Brunei flag unless exempt.41 According to the authorities, Brunei encourages the registration of ships under the Brunei flag, subject to the rules and regulations of the Merchant Shipping Act. They also state that the Department is upgrading institutional capacity to ensure maritime safety and sustainable development.

All ships operating in Brunei waters, either wholly owned by Brunei nationals or by a corporation established in Brunei, must be registered with or licensed by the Registrar of Brunei Ships in the Marine Department. Under the Merchant Shipping (Registration of Ships) Regulations 2006, applications must be accompanied by, inter alia, a declaration of ownership, technical details of the vessel, as well as details of the manager, who must be resident in Brunei, and an agent.

Port services are regulated by the Ports Department, while the navigation of vessels entering Muara Port is under the purview of the Marine Department, both in the Ministry of Communications. The Ports Department manages: Muara Port, Kuala Belait Port, and Bangar Wharf. Some operations, including stevedoring, shore crane services, and cargo handling forklift services, appear to be provided by the private sector. Towage and tug boat services, previously provided by the Marine Department, were handed over to the Ports Department in April 2007.

Brunei made no commitments under the GATS with respect to maritime services; nor has it included the sector in its 2005 GATS offer in the DDA negotiations.

(v) Tourism

Tourism has been identified as a major contributor to exports in the service sector with the potential to play an important role in Brunei's economic diversification plans. However, the tourism industry in Brunei remains relatively undeveloped, with around 200,000 foreign tourists in 2007 (Table IV.8). At the beginning of the review period, Brunei designated the year 2001 as "Visit Brunei Year" but tourist arrivals fell that year by 20% partly as a result of a global tourism slowdown after the 11 September terrorist attacks in the United States. Tourism dropped again in early 2004 following the regional outbreak of SARS.

Around 70% of tourists come from other ASEAN and Asian countries, in particular Malaysia, China, and Singapore. In addition, a much larger number of same-day visitors from Malaysia enter Brunei through land-entry points. The Government's objective is to increase international tourist arrivals as well as the average length of stay and expenditure. In order to reach a target of 250,000 tourists by 2010, additional facilities, including accommodation, transport and communication, and banking services, need to be further developed.

A study in 2006 found that the wider travel and tourism economy accounted for 11% of all activity and 13% of total employment in Brunei Darussalam in 2005; residential and business travel, especially travel abroad, are significant items of spending on travel and tourism; spending by foreign visitors accounts for over a third of all service export earnings, but most visits are brief and are mainly to friends and relations rather than for business or leisure purposes; and Brunei has the potential to raise foreign visitor spending significantly. Growth over the decade is forecast to raise travel and tourism's contribution to GDP to over 13.5%, increasing employment to almost 35,000 from 21,000 in 2005.42

Tourism promotion is carried out by the Tourism Development Division in the Ministry of Industry and Primary Resources, acting under the advice of the Brunei Tourism Board. The Ministry and the Board intend to develop Brunei as a unique tourism destination in South East Asia while taking into consideration the traditional and cultural values of Brunei and the sustainability of its environment. Tourism planning focuses on the economic and social benefits for Brunei, while preventing an erosion of Brunei's socio-cultural and religious values, and ensuring conservation of the environment. Particular activities that are targeted include niche markets such as eco-tourism, adventure and cultural tourism, theme parks, and cruising targeting mature, well-travelled, tranquillity-seeking visitors from the region and beyond.

The Tourism Development Division is also responsible for regulating tourism services and issuing licences for tourism services providers. Travel agencies are regulated and licensed by the Economic Development Board in the Ministry of Finance, under the Travel Agents Act (Chapter 103). Licences issued for travel agencies are usually valid for a year and expire at the end of the calendar year; they are not transferable.43

Brunei made no commitments under the GATS in tourism services.

TARIFF CLASSIFICATIONS AND VALUATION IN COMMODITY TAXATION

Customs tariff in Brunei Darussalam is based on the Brunei Darussalam Trade Classification. The Brunei Darussalam Trade Classification, which incorporates the Brunei Darussalam Customs Tariff, is set out in accordance with the new Standard International Trade Classification which is produced by the Statistical Commission of the United Nations Economic and Social Council and recommended for use in 1960. This new Standard International Trade Classification is a combination of two systems, that of the Standard International Trade Classification already in existence prior to 1960 which follows generally the degree of manufacture of the commodities enumerated, and that of the Brussels Tariff Nomenclature, a standard system of nomenclature for tariff purposes adopted by a considerable number of countries since 1959. The new Standard International Trade Classification combines the two systems to preserve the accurate identification achieved by the Brussels system with the Standard International Trade Classification of commodities.

TARIFF MEASURES

Structure of the tariff schedule

Brunei applies a nine-digit tariff nomenclature based on the Harmonized Commodity Description and Coding System. The tariff schedule has one column of duty rates.

Tariff publications

Current information on customs related matters is available from the Royal Customs and Excise Department, Jalan Mentarei Besar, Berakas BB 3910, Negara Brunei Darussalam.

Tariff rates

DECREED CUSTOMS EVALUATION

24 Used motor vehicles may only be imported subject to customs valuation.

QUANTITY CONTROL MEASURES

Non-automatic licensing

Licensing under the authority of Royal Customs and Excise Department, Jalan Menteri Besar, Berakas BB 3910, Negara Brunei Darussalam

61.6 Most items may be imported under Open General Licence. However, for environmental,
61.7 health, safety, security or religious reasons, the Royal Customs and Excise Department has introduced the Approval Permit System. This system is applicable for the importation of certain restricted items, under the provisions of the Customs (Prohibition and Restriction on Imports and Exports) (Amendment) Order, 1994 & 1995 - Section 28 Customs Enactment, 1984. In addition, approval of licence or permit must be obtained from other competent departments before the Approval Permit is issued to import controlled and restricted goods, i.e.: plants, crops and live animals (from the Agriculture Department), firearms and explosives (from the Royal Brunei Police Force), printed media (from the Royal Brunei Police Force, the Ministry of Religious Affair, the Ministry of Home Affair), woods (from the Forestry Department), rice, sugar, and salt (from the Information Technology and State Store Department), used Vehicles (from the Land Transport or the Royal Customs and Excise Department), telephone equipment and radio (from the Telecommunications Department), medicine including poison (from the Ministry of Health), and fresh, cool and frozen chicken and beef (from the Ministry of Religious Affair, the Ministry of Health, the Agriculture Department).

Prohibition

63.1 Indecent and obscene articles or prints, articles bearing the imprint or reproduction of
63.7 any currency, bank notes or coins, knives, and video games are absolutely prohibited. There is a short list of prohibited items including dangerous drugs such as opium, heroin, morphine, and psychotropic substances, mescaline, barbiturates, and amobarbital.

TECHNICAL MESURES

Technical regulations

Standards and technical regulations are the responsibility of: Ministry of Development, Old Airport, Bandar Seri Begawan 1190, Negara Brunei Darussalam.

81.1 Phytosanitary certificates from the Department of Agriculture are required for imported plants and plant materials. No soil may be attached.

81.5 Motor vehicles, agricultural products, pharmaceuticals, and drug related products may be imported subject to certificate of origin requirements. In conformity with the Emergency (Halal Meat) Order, 1998, "halal" imported meat must originate from facilities which have been approved by Brunei authorities as "halal". Health certificates are required for beef and poultry. Inedible tallow must be accompanied by a sterilization certificate. Imports of live animals and animals products must be covered by veterinary certificates. Inspection requirements are set on such imports as motor vehicles, pharmaceuticals, beef, plant and plant materials. Inspection is conducted by various government departments controlling the restricted goods including the Transport Department, the Health Department, and the Department of Agriculture, respectively.

CUSTOMS TARIFF AND DUTY RATES

NO	COMMODITIES	DUTY RATE
1	LIVE ANIMALS; ANIMAL PRODUCT:-	NIL

2	VEGETABLE PRODUCTS:-	
	A. Coffee, whether or not roasted or decaffeinated; coffee husk and skins; coffee substitutes containing in any proportion:-	
	(1) Coffee not roasted –	B$ 110.00 per tonne
	(2) Coffee roasted –	B$ 220.00 per tonne
	(3) Other-	NIL
	B. Tea, whether or not flavoured -	B$ 220.00 per tonne
	C. Other -	NIL
3	ANIMAL OR VEGETABLE FATS AND OIL AND THEIR CLEAVAGE PRODUCTS; PREPARED EDIBLE FATS; ANIMAL OR VEGETABLE WAXES:	NIL
4	PREPARED FOODSTUFFS; BEVERAGES, SPIRITS AND VINEGAR, TOBACCO AND MANUFACTURED TOBACCO SUBSTITUTES:-	

A. Extracts, essences or concentrates of coffee, tea or mate and preparations with a basis of these product or with a basis of coffee, tea or mate; roasted chicory and other roasted coffee substitutes, and extracts, essences and concentrates thereof	
(1) Extracts, essences and concentrates, of coffee, tea or mate and preparations with a basis of these extracts, essences or concentrates or with a basis of coffee, tea or mate -	5%
(2) Roasted chicory and other roasted coffee substitutes, and extracts, essences and concentrates thereof -	NIL
B. Beverages, spirit and vinegers	
(1) Beer made from malt -	B$ 30.00 per dal
(2) Wine of fresh grapes including fortified wines; grape must other than grape must of fruit juices:	
(i) Sparkling wine -	B$120.00 per dal
(ii) Still wine and grape must: of an alcoholic strength by volume not exceeding 15% vol -	B$ 55.00 per dal
(iii) Still wine and grape must: of an alcoholic strength by volume exceeding 15% vol -	B$ 90.00 per dal
(3) Vermouths and other wine of fresh grapes flavoured with plants or aromatic substances	
(i) Of an alcoholic strength by volume not exceeding 15% vol -	B$ 55.00 per dal
(ii) Of an alcoholic strength by volume exceeding 15% vol -	B$ 90.00 per dal

(4) Other fermented beverages (for example, cider, perry and mead); mixtures of fermented beverages and mixtures of fermented beverages and non alcoholic beverages, not elsewhere specified or incleded

(i) Cider and perry -	B$ 30.00 per dal
(ii) Sake or toddy -	B$ 90.00 per dal
(iii) Other -	B$ 30.00 per dal

(5) Undenatured ethyl alcohol of an alcoholic strength by volume of 80% vol or higher; ethyl alcohol and other spirits, denatured, of any strength

(i) Undenatured ethyl alcohol of an alcoholic strength by volume of 80% vol or higher	B$250.00 per proof dal
(ii) Ethyl alcohol and other spirits, denatured of any strength -	NIL

(6) Undenatured ethyl alcohol of an alcoholic strength by volume of less than 80% vol, spirits, liqueurs and other spirituous beverages for example brandy, whiskies, rum and tafia, gin and geneva, vodka, liqueurs and cordials	B$250.00 per proof dal

(7) Arrack, pineapple spirit and samsu (including medicated samsu):

(i) Of an alcoholic strength not exceeding 40% vol -	B$ 90.00 per dal
(ii) Other -	B$120.00 per proof dal

C. Tobacco and manufactured tobacco substitute

(1) Unmanufactured tobacco; tobacco refuse -	B$ 30.00 per kg

(2) Cigars, cheroots, cigarillos and cigarettes, of tobacco or of tobacco substitutes.

(i) Cigars, cheroots and cigarillos, containing tobacco -	B$100.00 per kg
(ii) Cigarettes containing tobacco -	B$ 60.00 per kg
(iii) Other -	NIL

(3) Other manufacture tobacco and manufacture tobacco substitutes

(i) Tobacco extracts, essences and manufactured tobacco substitutes -	NIL
(ii) Other -	B$ 60.00 per kg

D. Other –	NIL

5 MINERAL PRODUCTS:-

A. Mineral fuels, mineral oils and products of their distillation; bituminous substances; mineral waxes

(1) Motor spirit, aviation spirit and similar light oil; distilled fuel (diesel or gas oils suitable for use in internal commbustion engines) –	B$ 0.22 per dal
(2) Lubricating oil -	B$ 0.44 per dal
(3) Lubricating grease –	B$ 0.11 per kg
(4) Other -	NIL
B. Other -	NIL

6 PRODUCTS OF THE CHEMICAL OR ALLIED INDUSTRIES:-

A. Essential oils and resinoids; perfumery, cosmetic or other toilet preparations

(1) preparations for use on the hair;

(i) Shampoos -	5%
(ii) Other -	30%

(2) Other perfumery, cosmetic and toilet preparation

(i) Dentifrices, including denture cleaners, fixative pastes and powders -	NIL
(ii) Prepared incense; perfumed joss sticks and joss paper -	NIL
(iii) Other -	5%

B. Soap, organic surface-active agents, washing preparations, lubricating preparations, artificial waxes, prepared waxes, polishing or scouring preparations, candles and similar articles, medelling pastes, “dental waxes” and dental preparations with a basis of plaster

(1) Soap; organic surface-active products and preparations for use as soap, in the form of bars, cakes or moulded pieces or shapes, whether or not combined with soap -	5%

(2) Organic surface-active agents; surface active preparation and washing preparation, whether or not containing soap; scouring powder and similar preparations

(i) Organic surface-active agents -	NIL
(ii) Other -	5%

(3) Lubricating preparation and preparations of a kind used for oil or

grease treatment of textile, leather, or other materials other those item number 5A and 5B	
(i) Liquid -	B$ 0.44 per dal
(ii) Other -	B$ 0.11 per kg
D. Explosives; pyrotechnic products; matches; pyrophoric alloys; certain combustible preparations	
(1) Fireworks -	30%
(2) Matches (excluding Bengal Matches):	
(i) In packings of less than 25 matches per container -	B$ 0.50 per 100 containers
(ii) In packings of 25 or more but less than 50 matches per container -	B$ 1.00 per 100 containers
(iii) In packings of 50 or more but less than 100 matches per container -	B$ 2.00 per 100 containers
(iv) Other -	B$ 1.00 per 5,000 containers
(4) Other	NIL
D. Photographic or cinematographic goods	
(1) Photographic plates and film of any material including sensitized paper, paperboard and cloth; chemical products in a form suitable for use in photography:	
(i) X – ray plates and film -	NIL
(ii) Exposed, whether or not developed -	NIL
(iii) Other -	5%
E. Other -	NIL
7 PLASTICS AND ARTICLES THEREOF: RUBBER AND ARTICLES THEREOF:	
A. Plastics and articles thereof	
(1) Magnetic tapes webs for sound recording -	20%
(2) Spools, cops, bobbins, and similar support.	
(i) for sewing machines -	10%
(ii) or cinematographic and photographic -	20%

(iii) other -	NIL
(3) Other -	NIL
B. Rubbers and articles thereof	
(1) Rubber tyres, tyre cases, interchangeable tyre treads, inner tubes and tyre flaps, for wheels of all kinds:	
(i) For earth-moving equipment -	15%
(ii) For use on the vehicles -	20%
(iii) Other -	NIL
(2) Other articles of vulcanized rubber other than hard rubber	
(i) Mats -	10%
(ii) Parts and accessories of vehicles -	20%
(iii) Other -	NIL
(3) Other -	NIL
8 RAW HIDES AND SKINS, LEATHER, FURSKINS AND ARTICLES THEREOF; SADDLERY AND HARNESS; TRAVEL GOODS, HAND BAGS AND SIMILAR CONTAINERS; ARTICLES OR ANIMAL GUT (OTHER THAN SILK-WORM GUT):-	
A. Articles of leather, saddlery and harness; travel goods, handbags and similar containers; articles of animal gut (other than silk worm gut); furskins and artificial fur; manufactures thereof.	
(1) Articles of leather or of composition leather; or of furskin or artificial fur;	
(i) Articles of apparel and clothing accessories, of leather or of composition leather; or of furskin or artificial fur -	10%
(ii) Boot laces; mats of leather or of composition leather	10%
(iii) Other articles of furskin or of artificial fur -	10%
(iv) Other -	NIL
(2) Other -	NIL
9 WOOD AND ARTICLES OF WOOD; WOOD CHARCOAL; CORK AND ARTICLES OF CORK; MANUFACTURES OF STRAW, OF ESPARTO OR OF OTHER PLAITING MATERIALS; BASKETWARE AND WICKERWORK:-	
A. Wood and articles of wood; wood charcoal	

	(1) Wood in the rough, roughly squared, sawn lengthwise, sliced or peeled; wood blocks, staves, poles, stakes, hoopwood and the like; wooden sticks, drawn wood, match splints, wooden pegs or pins; wood shavings, chipwood, wood wool and wood flour; wood planed, tongued, grooved and the like; wood parquets or wood block flooring; veneer sheets and sheets for plywood, plywood, blockboard, laminboard, battenboard and similar laminated wood products; cellular wood panels, whether or not faced with base metal; improved wood, in sheets, blocks or the like; reconstituted wood in sheets, blocks or the like	20%
	(2) Other -	NIL
	B. Other -	NIL
10	PULP OF WOOD OR OF OTHER FIBROUS CELLULOSIC MATERIAL; RECOVERED (WASTE AND SCRAP) PAPER OR PAPERBOARD; PAPER AND PAPERBOARD AND ARTICLE THEREOF -	NIL
11	TEXTILE AND TEXTILE ARTICLES:-	
	A. Carpets and other textile floor covering -	5%
	B. Impregnated, coated, covered or laminated textilemfabrics; textiles articles of a kind suitable for industrial use	
	(1) Tyre cord fabric of high tenacity yarn of nylon or other polymides, polyesters or viscose or reyon -	10%
	(2) Textile fabrics impregnated, coated, covered or laminated with plastic, other than those item 11 B (1) -	10%
	(3) Linoleum whether or not cut to shape; floor covering consisting of a coating or covering applied on a textile backing, whether or not cut to shape -	10%
	(4) Rubberised textile fabrics other than those item 11 B (1).	
	(i) Adhesive tape of a width not exceeding 20cm.-	NIL
	(ii) Other -	10%
	C. Other made up textile articles; sets; worn clothing and worn textile articles; rags;	
	(1) Blankets and traveling rug; linens; curtains and interior blinds or bed valances; bedspread and other furnishing articles (other than item No. 20); floor-cloths, dish-cloths, dusters and similar cleaning cloths; rags -	5%
	(2) Worn clothing and worn textile articles; mosquito nets; sack and bags used for the packing of goods -	NIL
	(3) Tarpaulins, sails for boats, sail boards or landcraft, awnings and sunblinds; tents	

and camping goods

(i) tarpaulins, awnings and sunblinds, tents, sails of, synthetic fibres -	NIL
(ii) tarpaulins, awnings and sunblinds, tents, sails, of other than synthetic fibres -	5%
(iii) other -	5%
(4) Other -	NIL
D. Other -	NIL

12 FOOTWEAR, HEADGEAR, UMBRELLAS, SUN UMBRELLAS, WALKINGSTICK, SEAT-STICK, WHIPS, RIDING-CROPS AND PARTS THEREOF; PREPARED FEATHERS AND ARTICLES MADE THEREWITH

A. Footwear; gaiters and the like; part of such articles footwear.

(1) Incorporating a protective metal toe-cap -	10%
(2) Other footwear -	5%
(3) Parts:	
(i) of metal -	NIL
(ii) other -	5%
B. Headgear and parts thereof -	10%
C. Umbrellas and sun-umbrellas (including working-stick umbrellas, garden umbrellas and similar umbrellas) and part thereof -	10%
D. Other -	NIL

13 ARTICLES OF STONE, PLASTER, CEMENT, ASBESTOS, MICA OR SIMILAR MATERIALS; CERAMIC PRODUCTS; GLASS AND GLASSWARE

A. Glass and glassware

(1) Safety glass, consisting of toughened (tampered) or laminated glass

(i) For vehicles -	20%
(ii) Earth moving machineries -	15%
(iii) Other -	NIL
(2) Rear-view mirror for vehicles -	20%
(3) Clock or watch glasses -	10%

(4) Other - NIL

B. Other - NIL

14 NATURAL OR CULTURED PEARLS, PRECIOUS OR SEMIPRECIOUS STONES, PRECIOUS METALS, METALS CLAD WITH PRECIOUS METAL, AND ARTICLES THEREOF; IMITATION JEWELLERY; COIN

A. Pearls, precious and semi-precious stones; articles of jewellery and parts thereof, of precious metal or rolled precious metal; articles of goldsmith' or silversmith' ware and parts thereof, of precious metal or rolled precious metal; articles consisting of, or incorporating pearls, precious or semi-precious stone; imitation jewellery; articles of personal adornment of any material - 5%

B. Other - NIL

15 BASE METALS AND ARTICLES OF BASE METAL

A. Articles of iron or steel

(1) Spring and leaf for springs, of iron or steel

(i) for Vehicle - 20%
(ii) for earth moving - 15%
(iii) other - NIL

(2) Other - NIL

B. Other - NIL

16 MACHINERY AND MECHANICAL APPLIANCES; ELECTRICAL EQUIPMENT; PART THEREOF; SOUND RECORDER AND REPRODUCERS, TELEVISION IMAGE AND SOUND RECORDERS AND REPRODUCERS, AND PARTS AND ACCESSORIES OF SUCH ARTICLES.

A. Nuclear reactors, boilers, machinery and mechanical appliances; part thereof

(1) Nuclear reactors; fuel elements (cartridge), non-irradiated, for nuclear reactors; machinery and apparatus for isotopic separation - NIL

(2) Central heating boilers; auxiliary plant (for example, economizers, super heaters, soot removers, gas removers); condenser for steam or other vapour power unit; producer gas or water gas or acetylene generators, with or without their purifiers; steam turbines and other vapour turbines - NIL

(3) Spark-ignition reciprocating or rotary internal combustion piston engines;

compression-ignition internal combustion piston engines (diesel or semi-diesel) and part thereof	
(i) Engines of a kind used for the propulsion of vehicles of item No. 17A of this tariff	20%
(ii) For earth moving machinery -	15%
(iii) Other -	NIL
(4) Hydraulic turbines, water wheels, and regulators; turbo-jets, turbo-propellers and other gas turbines; other engines and motors and parts thereof -	NIL
(5) Air or vacuum pumps, air or other gas compressors and fans; ventilating or recycling hoods incorporating a fan, whether or not fitted with filters -	
(i) hand or foot-operated air pumps -	NIL
(ii) compressors of a kind used in refrigerating equipment -	5%
(iii) air compressors mounted on a wheel chasis for towing -	NIL
(iv) other, electrically operated -	5%
(v) other -	NIL
(6) Air conditioning machines and parts thereof -	5%
(7) Industrial or laboratory furnaces and ovens, including incinerators, non electric; furnace burners for liquid fuel, for pulverized solid fuel or for gas; mechanical stokers, mechanical grates, mechanical ash discharges and similar appliances -	NIL
(8) Refrigerators, freezes and other refrigerating equipment other than those item A (6) of this heading and parts thereof -	5%
(9) Calendering or other rolling machines and cylinders and part thereof -	NIL

(10) Dish washing machines; household or laudry-type washing machines, including machines which both wash and dry and part thereof -	5%
(11) Pulley tackle and hoists other than skip hoists; winches and capstans; jacks	
(i) jack used in tipping mechanisms for lorries -	20%
(ii) electrically operated -	20%
(iii) other -	NIL
(12) Ship's derricks; cranes, including cable cranes; mobile lifting frames, straddle carriers and works trucks fitted eith crane or lifting or handling equipment; fork-lift trucks; other lifting, handling, loading or unloading machinery (e.g. lifts, escalators, conveyors, teleferics) -	NIL
(13) Excavating, leveling, tamping, boring and extracting machinery, stationery or mobile, for earth, minerals or ores (for example, mechanical shovels, coal-cutter, excavators, scrapers, levelers, bull-dozers and road rollers); pile drivers and pile extractors and parts thereof -	NIL

(14) Agricultural, horticultural or forestry machinery for soil preparation or cultivation; lawn or sport-ground rollers; harvesting or threshing machinery, including straw of fodder balers; grass or hay mowers - NIL

(15) Sewing machines and parts thereof, other than book-sewing machines; furniture, bases and covers specially designed for sewing machines; sewing machine needles - 5%

(16) Converters, ladles, ingot moulds and casting machines, of a kind used in metallurgy or in metal foundries; metal-rolling mills and rolls therefore - NIL

(17) Tools for working in the hand, pneumatic hydraulic or with self-contained non-electric motor; machinery and apparatus, brazing or welding, whether or not capable of cutting; gas operated surface tempering machines and appliance and parts thereof - NIL

(18) Typewriters; word processing machines; calculating machines and pocket-size data recording; accounting, postage-frankling, ticket-issuing machines and similar machines, incorporating a calculating device; cash registers; automatic data processing macines and unit thereof; magnetic or optical readers - NIL

(19) Other office machines (for example, hectograph or stencil duplicating machines, addressing machines, automatic banknote dispensers, coin sorting machines, coin-counting or wrapping machines, pencil-sharpening machines, perforating or stapling machines) electrically operated and parts thereof - 5%

(20) Automatic goods-vending machines (for example, postage stamp, cigarette, food or beverage machine), includinf money changing machines - 5%

(21) Transmission shafts (including cam shafts and crank shafts) and cranks; bearing housings and plain shaft bearings; gears and gearing ball or roller screws; gear boxes and other speed changers, including torque converters; flywheels and pulleys, including pulley blocks; clutches and shaft couplings (including universal joints).

(i) gears and gearing, other than toothed wheels, chain sprockets and other transmission elements presented separately; ball or roller screws; gear boxes and other speed changers, including torque converters - NIL

(ii) flywheels and pulleys, including pulley blocks - NIL

(iii) clutches and shaft couplings (including universal joints) - NIL

(iv) other for motor vehicle engine - 20%

(v) other for earth moving machinery engines - 15%

(vi) other - NIL

(22) Electrically operated of addressing and address plate embossing, sorting or folding or inserting or opening or closing or sealing mail or affixing or canceling postage stamps 15%

(23) Other - 20%

B. Electrical machinery and equipment and parts thereof; sound recorders and reproducers, television image and sound recorders and reproducers, and parts and accessories of such articles

(1) Electro-mechanical tools for working in the hand, with self-contained electric motor and parts thereof -	NIL
(2) Electro-mechanical domestic appliances; shavers, hair clippers and hair-removing appliances, with self-contained electric motors and parts thereof -	5%
(3) Electric instantaneous or storage water heaters and immersion heaters; electric space heating apparatus and soil heating apparatus; electro-thermic hair-dressing apparatus (e.g. hair dryers, hair curlers, curling tong heaters) and hand dryers; electric smoothing irons; other electro-thermic appliance of a kind used for domestic purposes; electri heating resistors other than item no. 17 of this section -	5%
(4) Electrical apparatus for line telephony or line telegraphy, including line telephone sets with cordless handsets and telecommunication apparatus for carrier-current line systems or for digital line systems; videophones and parts thereof -	5%
(5) Microphones and stands therefore; loudspeakers, whether or not mounted in the enclosures; headphones, earphones and combined microphone/speaker sets; audio-frequecy electric amplifiers electric sound amplifier sets and parts thereof -	5%
(6) Turntables (record-decks), record-players, cassette-players and other sound reproducing apparatus, not incorporating a sound recording device and parts thereof -	5%
(7) Magnetic tape recordersand other sound recording apparatus, whether or not incorporating a sound reproducing device; video recording or reproducing apparatus, parts and accessories -	5%
(8) Prepared unrecorded media for sound recording or similar recording of other phenomena -	NIL
(9) Records, tapes and other recorded media for sound or other similarly recorded phenomena, including matrices abd masters for the production of records	
(i) gramophone records -	5%
(ii) cards incorporating magnetic stripe -	NIL
(iii) other for used in computer -	NIL
(iv) other -	5%
(10) Transmission apparatus for radio-telephony, radio broadcasting or television, whether or not incorporation reception apparatus or sound recording or reproducing apparatus; television cameras; still image video cameras and other video camera recorders and parts thereof -	5%
(11) Radar apparatus, radio navigational aid apparatus and radio remote control apparatus and parts thereof	

(i) radio remote control apparatus - 5%
(ii) other - NIL

(12) Reception apparatus for radio-telephony, radio telegraphy or radio broadcasting, whether or not combined, in the same housing, with sound recording or reproducing apparatus or a clock and parts thereof - 5%

(13) Reception apparatus for television, whether or not incorporating radio-broadcast receivers or sound or video recording or reproducing apparatus; video monitors and video projectors and parts thereof - 5%

(14) Electric signaling, safety or traffic control equipment for railways, tramways, roads, inland waterways, parking facilities, port installation or airfield - NIL

(15) Diodes, transistors and similar semi-conductor devices; photosensitive semi-conductor devices, including photovoltaic cells; light emitting diodes; mounted piezo-electric crystal; electronic integrated circuits and microassemblies.

(i) Parts - 20%
(ii) Other - NIL

(16) Winding wire; electric insulators of any material - NIL

(17) Carbon electrodes, carbon brushes, lamp carbons, battery carbons and other articles of graphite or other carbon, with or without metal, of a kind used for electrical purposes - 20%

(18) Waste and scrap of primary cells/batteries and electric accumulators; spent primary cells/batteries and spent electric accumulators NIL

(19) Other 20%

17 VEHICLES, AIRCRAFT, VESSELS AND ASSOCIATED TRANSPORT EQUIPMENT

A. Vehicles other than railway or tramway rolling-stock and parts and accessories thereof

(1) Road tractor for semi-trailer - 20%
(2) Motor vehicles for the transport of ten or more persons, including the driver - 20%
(3) Vehicles special designed for traveling on snow, golf cars, and semi vehicles - 20%
(4) Motorcars and other motor vehicles principally designed for the transport of person less than 10 persons including driver:

(i) with spark-ignition internal combustion piston engine

(a) of a cylinder capacity not exceeding 1000 cc 20%

(b) of a cylinder capacity exceeding 1000 cc but not exceeding 2000 cc -	20%
(c) of a cylinder capacity exceeding 2000 cc but not exceeding 3000 cc -	20%
(d) of a cylinder capacity exceeding 3000 cc but not exceeding 4000 cc -	20%
(e) of a cylinder capacity exceeding 4000 cc -	20%
(ii) with compression-ignition internal combustion piston engine (diesel or semi-diesel):	
(a) of a cylinder capacity not exceeding 2000 cc	20%
(b) of a cylinder capacity exceeding 2000 cc but	20%

not exceeding 4000 cc -	
(c) of a cylinder capacity exceeding 4000 cc	20%
(iii) other -	20%
(5) Motor vehicles for the transport of goods -	20%
(6) Special purpose motor vehicles (for example breakdown, crane, concrete mixer lorries and etc)	
(i) fire fighting vehicles, street cleansing vehicles including cessfiat empties, mobile radiological unit and mobile clinics and spraying lorries of all kinds -	NIL
(ii) other -	20%
(7) Chassis fitted with engines; bodies (including cap); part and accessories except safety seat belts of motor vehicle -	20%
(8) Motorcycles, bicycle and other cycles -	20%
(9) Works truck, self propelled, not fitted with lifting or handling equipment, of the type used in factories, warehouses, dock areas or airports for short distance transport of goods; tractors of the type used on railway station platforms; tanks and other armoured fighting vehicles, motorist, whether or not fitted with weapons, and part of such vehicles -	NIL
(10) Trailers and semi-trailers; other vehicles; not mechanically propelled; part thereof	
(i) trailers and semi trailers of the caravan type, for housing or camping -	20%
(ii) other trailer or semi-trailers for the transport of goods -	20%
(iii) self-loading or self-unloading trailers and semitrailers for agricultural purposes; agriculture wagons, carts and trailers; wheel barrows, suck trucks and hand trolleys and similar hand propelled vehicles of a kind used in factories or workshop -	20%
(iv) other trailers and semi-trailers -	NIL
(v) invalid carriages, whether or not motorized or otherwise mechanically propelled; baby carriages and part thereof -	NIL
(10) Other -	20%
B. Aircraft, spacecraft and parts thereof; ships, boats and floating structures -	NIL

18 OPTICAL, PHOTOGRAPHIC, CINEMATOGRAPHIC, MEASURING, CHECKING, PRECESSION, MEDICAL OR SURGICAL INSTRUMENTS AND APPARATUS; CLOCKS AND WATCHES; MUSICAL INSTRUMENT; PARTS AND ACCESSORIES

THEREOF.

A. Optical, photographic, cinematographic, measuring, checking, precession, medical or surgical instruments and apparatus; parts and accessories thereof

(1) Photographic (other than cinematographic) cameras; photographic flashlight apparatus and flash bulb other than item 16B; parts and accessories of the foregoing articles:	
(i) Cameras of a kind used for preparing printing plates or cylinders -	NIL
(ii) cameras specialized for medical used; surveys cameras; lithographic process cameras and part and accessories thereof -	NIL
(iii) other -	5%
(2) Cinematographic camera, projectors, sound recorder and reproducers; any combination of these articles; parts and accessories -	20%
(3) Image projectors (other than cinematographic projectors); photographic (except cinematographic) enlargers and reducers; parts and accessories thereof -	20%
(4) Apparatus and equipment of a kind used in photographic or cinematographic laboratories, not elsewhere specified; photocopying apparatus (contact type); spools or reels, for film; screen for projectors; parts of the foregoing articles:	
(i) photocopying apparatus -	NIL
(ii) Other -	20%
(5) Spectacles, goggles and the like, corrective, protective or other; frames and mountings for spectacles, goggles or the like; binoculars, monoculars, other optical telescopea and mountings therefore; other astronomical instruments and mounting therefore, but not including instruments for radio astronomy, accessories and parts thereof	NIL
(6) Microscopes other than optical microscopes; diffraction apparatus; compound optical microscopes, including thoses for microphotography, micro-cinematography or microprojection; liquid crystal devices not constituting articles provided for more specifically in other item; laser other than laser diodes; other optical appliances and instruments -	NIL
(7) Direction finding compasses, other navigational instruments and appliances and parts thereof	
(i) instruments and appliances for aeronautical or space navigation (other than compasses) -	10%
(ii) other -	NIL

	(8) Surveying (including photogrammetrical survying), hydrographic, oceanographic, hydrological, meteorological or geophysical instruments and appliances, excluding compasses; rangefingers -	20%
	(9) Other instruments and apparatus not elsewhere specified, electrically operated and parts thereof -	20%
	(10) Other -	NIL
	B. Clocks and watches and parts thereof -	5%
	C. Musical instrument; parts and accessories of such articles	
	(1) Musical boxes; decoy calls of all kinds; call horns and other mouth blown sound signaling instrument and parts thereof –	NIL
	(2) Other -	10%
19	ARM AND AMMUNITION; PART AND ACCESSORIES THEREOF: --	NIL
20	MISCELLANEOUS MANUFACTURED ARTICLES:-	
	A. Furniture; bedding, mattress, mattress support, cushions and similar stuff furnishings; lamps and lighting fittings, not elsewhere specified or included; illuminated signs, illuminated name-plates and the like; prefabricated building.	
	(1) Seats other than item (2) of this heading whether or not convertible into beds and part thereof	
	(i) seats of a kind used for aircraft -	NIL
	(ii) other -	5%
	(2) Medical, surgical, dental or veterinary furniture (e.g. operating or examination tables, hospital beds with mechanical fittings, dentists' chairs); barbers' chairs and similar chairs, having rotating as well as both reclining and elevating movements; other furniture and parts there of	
	(i) baby walkers -	NIL
	(ii) other -	5%
	(3) Mattress supports; articles of bedding and similar furnishing fitted with springs stuffed or internally fitted with any material or expanded -	5%
	(4) Lamp and lighting fittings; including search light and sportlight and parts thereof, not elsewhere specified or included; illuminated signs, illuminated name-plates and the like, having a permanently fixed light source, and part thereof not elsewhere specified or included -	

(i) Non-electrical lamps and lighting fittings	NIL
(ii) Warning signs to protect the public for danger or to protect property, street names plates, road and traffic sign) and parts	NIL
(iii) Prefabricated building -	NIL
(iv) Other -	5%

B. Toys, games and sport requisites; part and accessories and thereof

(1) Articles for funfare, table or parlour games, including pintable, billiards, special table for casino games and automatic bowling alley equipment:

(i) Video games of a king used with a television receiver; articles and accessories for billiard; other games, coin – or disc – operated other than bowling alley equipment -	5%
(ii) Playing cards -	10%
(iii) Bowling alley equipment -	NIL
(iv) Other -	10%
(2) Festive, carnival or other entertainment articles, including conjuring tricks and novelty jokes -	10%
(3) Articles and equipment for table tennis -	5%
(4) Puzzles of all kind -	5%
(5) Roundabouts, swings, shooting galleries and other fair ground amusement; traveling circuses, traveling menageries and traveling theatres -	Constituent articles dutiable according to kind
(6) Other -	NIL

C. Other miscellaneous manufactured articles:

(1) Cigarette lighters and other lighters, whether or not mechanical or electrical, and parts thereof other than flints and wicks -	10%
(2) Smoking pipes (including pipe bowls) and cigar or cigarette holders, and parts thereof -	10%
(3) Hair slides, decorative hairpins -	10%
(4) Other -	NIL

21 Works of arts, collertors, pieces and antiques:-

A. Antiques of and age exceeding one hundred years -	Constituent articles dutiable according to kind
B. Other -	NIL

As this list not an authoritative tariff yet to provide background information of the Brunei Darussalam Customs tariff, if there is any doubt in regard to dutiability of the goods please refer to Customs Officer on duty at the address below;

Customs Services and Technique Section
Royal Customs & Excise
Department
Ministry of Finance
BB3910 Jalan Menteri Besar, Berakas
Brunei Darussalam.
Tel: +673-2382333
Fax: +673–2382666
e-mail: jked@brunet.bn

TAXATION

Brunei Darussalam has no personal income tax. There are no export, sales, payroll or manufacturing taxes. In fact Brunei Darussalam has the least taxes compared to other countries in the region. Sole proprietorship and partnership businesses are not subject to income tax. Only companies are subject to income tax and it is one of the lowest in the region.

Moreover tax advantages at start-up and ongoing incentives throughout growth and expansion offer investors profitable conditions that are comparable if not better than those offered by other countries in the region.

COMPANY TAXATION

Companies are subject to tax on the following types of income:-

*Gains of profits from any trade, business or vocation;

*Dividends received from companies not previously assessed for tax in Brunei Darussalam;

*Interest and discounts; and

*Rents, royalties, premiums, and any other profits arising from properties.

There is no capital gains tax. However, where the Collector of Income Tax can establish that the gains form part of the normal trading activities, they become taxable as revenue gains.

(a) Scope of Income Tax

A company resident in Brunei Darussalam is liable to income tax on its income derived from or accrued in Brunei Darussalam or received from overseas. A non-resident company is only taxed on its income arising in Brunei Darussalam.

(b) Concept of Residence

A company, whether incorporated locally or overseas, is considered as resident in Brunei Darussalam for tax purposes if the control and management of its business is exercised in Brunei Darussalam The control and management of a company is normally regarded as resident in Brunei Darussalam if, among other things, its Directors' meetings are held in Brunei Darussalam.

The profits of a company are subject to tax at the rate of 30%. Tax concession may be available. The profit or loss of a company as per its accounts is adjusted for income tax purposes to take into account certain allowable expenses, certain expenses prohibited from deduction, wear and tear allowances and any losses brought forward from previous years, in order to arrive at taxable profits.

TREATMENT OF DIVIDENDS

Dividends accruing in, derived from, or received in Brunei Darussalam by a corporation are included in taxable income, apart from dividends received from a corporation taxable in Brunei Darussalam which are excluded. No tax is deducted at source on dividends paid by a Brunei Darussalam corporation.

Dividends received in Brunei Darussalam from United Kingdom or Commonwealth countries are grossed up in the tax computation and credit is claimed against the Brunei Darussalam tax liability for tax suffered either under the double tax treaty with the United Kingdom or the provision for Commonwealth tax relief. Any other dividends are included net in the tax computation and no foreign tax is available. Brunei Darussalam does not impose any withholding tax on dividends.

ALLOWABLE DEDUCTIONS

All expenses wholly or exclusively incurred in the production of taxable income are allowable as deductions for tax purposes. These deductions include:-

*Interest on borrowed money used in acquiring income;

*Rent on land and buildings used in the trade or business;

*Costs of repair or premises, plant and machinery;

*Bad debts and specific doubtful debts, with any subsequent recovery being treated as income when received; and

* Employer's contributions to approved pensions or provident funds.

DISALLOWABLE DEDUCTIONS

Expenses not allowed as deductions for tax purposes include:

*Expenses not wholly or exclusively incurred in acquiring income;

*Domestic private expenses;

*Any capital withdrawal or any sum used as capital;

*Any capital used in improvements apart from replanting of plantations;

*Any sum recoverable under an insurance or indemnity contract;

*Rent or repair expenses not incurred in the earning of income;

*Any income tax paid in Brunei Darussalam or in other countries; and

*Payments to any unapproved pension or provident funds.

Donations are not allowable but claimable if they are made to approved institutions.

ALLOWANCES FOR CAPITAL EXPENDITURE

Depreciation is not allowable expense and is replaced by capital allowances for qualifying expenditure. The tax payer is entitled to claim wear and tear allowances calculated as follows-

(a)Industrial Buildings

An initial allowance of 100% is given in the year of expenditure, and an annual allowance of 2% of the qualifying expenditure is provided on a straight-line basis until the total expenditure is written off.

(b)Machinery and Plant

An initial allowance of 20% of the cost is given in the year of expenditure together with annual allowances calculated on the reducing value of the assets. The rates prescribed by the Collector of Income Tax range from 3% to 25%, depending on the nature of the asset. Balancing allowances or charges are made on disposal of the industrial building machinery or plant.

These adjustments cover the shortfall or excess of the tax written down value as compared to the sale proceeds. Any balancing charge is limited to tax allowances previously granted, and any surplus is considered a capital gain and therefore does not become part of chargeable income.

Unabsorbed capital allowances can be carried forward indefinitely but must be set off against income from the same trade.

LOSS CARRYOVERS

Losses incurred by a company can be carried forward for six years for set-off against future income, and can be carried back one year. There is no requirement regarding continuity of ownership of the company, and also the loss set-off is not restricted to the same trade.

FOREIGN TAX RELIEF

A double taxation agreement exists with the United Kingdom and provides proportionate relief from Brunei Darussalam income tax upon any part of the income which has been or is liable to be charged with United Kingdom income tax. Tax credits are only available for resident companies.

Unilateral relief may be obtained on income arising from Commonwealth countries that provide reciprocal relief. However, the maximum relief cannot exceed half the Brunei Darussalam rate. This relief applies to both resident and non-resident companies.

STAMP DUTY

Stamp duties are levied on a variety of documents. Certain types of documents attract an ad valorem duty, whereas with other documents the duty varies with the nature of the documents.

PETROLEUM TAXES

Special Legislation exists in respect of income tax from petroleum operations which is taxable under the Income Tax (Petroleum) Act 1963 as amended.

WITHHOLDING TAXES

Interest paid to non-resident companies under a charge, debenture or in the respect of a loan, is subject to withholding tax of 20%. There are no other withholding taxes.

ESTATE DUTY

Estate duty is levied on an estate of over B$2 million at 3% flat rate for a person who died on or after 15th December 1988.

IMPORT DUTY

In general, basic foodstuffs and goods for industrial use are exempted from import duties. Electrical equipment and appliances, timber products, photographic materials and equipment, furniture, motor vehicles and spare parts attract duties of 20%, while cosmetics and perfumes are subject to 30% duty.

In addition, cigarettes are dutiable items.

TARIFF MEASURES

STRUCTURE OF THE TARIFF SCHEDULE

Brunei applies a nine-digit tariff nomenclature based on the Harmonized Commodity Description and Coding System. The tariff schedule has one column of duty rates.

TARIFF PUBLICATIONS

Current information on customs related matters is available from the Royal Customs and Excise Department, Jalan Menteri Besar, Berakas BB 3910, Negara Brunei Darussalam.

TARIFF RATES

11 Statutory Custom Duties

All dutiable goods imported into Negara Brunei Darussalam are subject to customs duties in accordance with the schedule of the Customs Duty Order 1973. Duties are assessed either on specific or ad valorem basis. Some 70 percent of items including basic foodstuffs, and goods for industrial use are zero rated. Most other goods are subject to rates of 10%, 20% or 30%. A 10% rate applies to gold jewellery. Timber, electrical equipment and appliances, photographic materials, furniture, and public transport type motor vehicles and spare parts are dutiable at 20%. A rate of 30% is set on cosmetics and perfumes. Motor vehicles including station wagons and racing cars are subject to rates of 40%, 60%, 80%, 100% or 200% depending on engine size. Specific duties apply to cigarettes and alcoholic

12 MFN Duties

A commercial and economic agreement was signed between the Brunei and the European Union providing for MFN tariff treatment.

Temporary reduced duties

The Industrial Incentive Act of 1975 provides for tax advantages in four industrial categories: industries related to national food security, local market industries, industries based on local resources, and export market industries. In addition, companies granted pioneer status, and established companies planning expansion are eligible for exemption from import duties.

REGIONAL AND SUB-REGIONAL AGREEMENTS

The Association of South-East Asean Nations (ASEAN) decided in 1992 to establish an ASEAN Free-Trade Area (AFTA) by the year 2008, later brought forward to 2003 for the six original founding members of ASEAN: Brunei Darussalam, Indonesia, Malaysia, the Philippines, Singapore, and Thailand. Vietnam joined in 1995, Laos and Myanmar in 1997, and Cambodia in April 1999. In December 1998, the ASEAN members decided to accelerate the completion of the ASEAN Free-Trade Area. In this regard, the six original founding members would advance their tariff reductions to 05% from 2003 to 2002. In May 2000, Malaysia received approval from its ASEAN partners for an extension of its commitments under AFTA to reduce tariffs in the automobile sector and selected agricultural products until 2005. Vietnam would implement its tariff reductions to 0-5% by 2003, and Laos and Myanmar by 2005.

In the year 2015, final reductions will be achieved by these four countries. Since 1 of January 2003, the ASEAN countries have announced the abolishment of tariffs on 60 per cent of traded goods and the introduction of a 5% on import tariffs within its six original members, i.e. Brunei Darussalam, Indonesia, Malaysia, the Philippines, Singapore, and Thailand. Products affected essentially by this measure are electronic products, machinery items and petrochemicals. And goods excluded from the tariff reduction agreements are goods of key industries in some of the member countries; for example, the Philippines and Indonesia will delay the 5% cap on sugar and petroleum, and Malaysia will shelve the cap on car imports until 2005. As for Cambodia, Myanmar, Lao People's Democratic Republic and Vietnam, the four ASEAN's latecomers, will introduce the 5% tariff cap only in 2010.

ASEAN member states decided, in December 1998, to expand access to the 1996 Basic Agreement on the ASEAN Industrial Cooperation (AICO) Scheme, which promotes joint manufacturing industrial activities between ASEAN-based companies. AICO provides tariff preferences on inputs sourced in the region.

The eight ASEAN summit was held in Phnom Penh, Cambodia, from 4 to 6 November 2002. During this meeting, several free trade plans were developed involving 14 Asian countries, i.e. the 10 ASEAN members such as Brunei Darussalam, Cambodia, Indonesia, Lao PDR, Malaysia, Myanmar, the Philippines, Singapore, Thailand, and Vietnam with China, India, Japan and the Republic of Korea. The objectives of these free-trade plans are to quicken the pace of trade liberalization and foster multilateralism in the region

At the 19th ASEAN summit held from 6 to 8 October 2003 in Bali (Indonesia) members reinforced regional integration and fostered economic cooperation, signing a strategic partnership with China, a framework for economic comprehensive partnership with Japan, and a framework agreement for economic cooperation with India.

Brunei is a participant in the East Pacific Economic Cooperation (APEC) forum, formed in 1989. The objective of the agreement is to implement free trade among the member countries by the year 2020, with advanced industrialized countries realizing the goal by the year 2010. Individual action plans for each member country were established to outline a path to the goal. Brunei has pledged to reduce tariffs on 688 items as part of its APEC Commitment. On 10 November 2000, APEC leaders agreed to EVSL (early voluntary sectoral liberalization) in 15 sectors, that is liberalization before the agreed goals of 2010 or 2020, respectively.

The 15 sectors comprise automotive products, chemicals, civil aircraft, energy, environmental goods and services; fish and fish products, food, forest products, gems and jewellery, medical equipment and instruments, natural and synthetic rubber, oilseeds and oilseed products, toys; also mutual recognition agreement for telecommunication products. Of these 15 sectors, nine were to be accelerated under the ATL initiative (ATL) namely: chemicals, energy, environmental goods and services, fish and fish products, forest products, gems and jewellery, medical equipment and instruments and toys, as well as the mutual recognition agreement for telecommunications products.

BIMP-EAGA, the East ASEAN Growth Area established in March 1994 by Brunei Darussalam, Indonesia, Malaysia and the Philippines is also, the largest growth area in Asia and aims at developing trade opportunities through the pooling of common and complementary resources and encouraging the free movement of resources across borders.

19.3 Bilateral agreements

A new trade initiative between the ASEAN and the U.S.A. has been set up as the Enterprise for Asean Initiative (EAI), which objectives aim at developing the Southeast Asian Region, and enhance close U.S. ties with ASEAN. The EAI offers bilateral free trade agreements (FTAs) between the United States and individual ASEAN countries, by determining jointly the launching of FTA negotiations. ASEAN members and China leaders decided in Brunei on November 2001 to work on creating a free trade area within the next ten years.

ASEM or the Asia-Europe Meeting, held its first summit meeting in 1996, in Thailand with seven members of ASEAN of which Brunei Darussalam, together with the European Commission and the 15 members of the European Union, Japan, China and Korea; ASEM objectives aim at reducing non-tariff barriers.

At their third meeting in Seoul, Korea, in October 2000, members reiterated their commitment to trade liberalization.

TREATI, or Trans-Regional EU-ASEAN Trade Action Plan, was launched on 9 July 2003 by the European Commission with the objective of boosting trade between the two regions. This action aims at enhancing relations with ASEAN members.

PARA-TARIFF MEASURES

Excise taxes

Excise taxes legislation lays in the Excise Act amended of 1984, and are levied as follows: B$5 per gallon on locally produced Samsoo and medicated Samsoo.

Decreed customs valuation

Used motor vehicles may only be imported subject to customs valuation.

PRICE CONTROL MEASURES

31.9 Administrative pricing n.e.s.

Imported rice and sugar under monopoly by the Department of Information Technology and State Stores, are subject to maximum retail prices.

Under the Price Control Act and the Emergency Price Control Act Amendment Order of 1999, administered by the Economic Planning and Development Department in the Ministry of Finance, administrative pricing is set on the following items: rice, sugar, motor vehicles, petroleum products, cigarettes, infant milk, milo bread, coffee, and tea.

FINANCE MEASURES

Finance measures n.e.s.

Duty drawback provisions under Part X of the Customs Law Amendment of 1984, allows repayment of import duties paid when goods are re-exported unprocessed within 12 months period and payment for each consignment should not be less than B$100.

AUTOMATIC LICENSING MEASURES

Import monitoring

Import monitoring of beef and poultry in order to protect local market supplies.

QUANTITY CONTROL MEASURES

Non-automatic licensing

Licensing under the authority of Royal Customs and Excise Department, Jalan Menteri Besar, Berakas BB 3910, Negara Brunei Darussalam

61.4 Barter or counter trade

The Department of Information Technology and State Stores, Ministry of

Finance subject to licensing the importation of sugar and salt, rice paddy and the products thereof, separated, skimmed or filled milk; equally licensing for converted timber, timber, classes 1A, 1B, 1C, Nibong, Rotans, by the Forestry Department, Ministry of Industry and Primary Resources.

61.6 Licence combined with or replaced by special import authorization

Registration requirement for all importers with the Government in order to be eligible for conducting the clearance of imported goods from Customs Control.

Most items may be imported under Open General Licence. However, for environmental, health, safety, security or religious reasons, the Royal Customs and Excise Department has introduced the Approval Permit System. This system is applicable for the importation of certain restricted items, under the provisions of the Customs (Prohibition and Restriction on Imports and Exports) (Amendment) Order, 1994 & 1995 -Section 28 Customs Enactment, 1984.

61.7 Prior authorization for sensitive product categories

In addition, approval of licence or permit must be obtained from other competent departments before the Approval Permit is issued to import controlled and restricted goods.

Import restrictions apply as well to petrol, kerosene, cigarettes, spirits and liquors, firecrackers, and items bearing the imprint of state emblems.

61.71 To protect human health

Import of Persian glue is subject to licensing by the Ministry of Health, the same requirement applies to meat, meat products and edible offal, including poultry meat and its products; the medical Department and the Ministry of Health require license for deleterious drugs, any kind of chemical substances, agricultural chemicals, poisons, antiseras and vaccines.

61.72 To protect animal health and life

Import permit issued by the Agriculture Department, Ministry of Industry and Primary Resources is required for eggs for hatching purposes and fresh eggs unless such eggs are clearly stamped "imported" with non-erasable ink or similar substance, and for live cattle, and any other animals, poultry and birds, including from Sabah and Sarawak; any live insects, invertebrate animals in any stage of their life cycles.

61.73 To protect plant

Import permit requirement issued by the Agriculture Department, Ministry of Industry and Primary Resources for any living plant or planting material, including from Sabah and Sarawak, and seeds for germinating, and commercial shipments of fruit and vegetables.

61.75 To protect wildlife

The Department of Museums controls the import of Rhinoceros horn and all other parts of, or products derived from the carcass of a rhinoceros. The Department of Fisheries, Ministry of Industry and Primary resources subjects to licensing in order to regulate and to ensure adequate protection of marine resources, fish and any other marine products except those listed under CITES, prawn, crab, cuttlefish and any kind of crustaceans and molluscs, Piranha and Arawana, and fishing equipment.

61.76 To control drug abuse

Poisons and deleterious drugs are under the administration or Narcotics Control Bureau.

61.77 To ensure human safety

Import restrictions of motor vehicles of five years and more, including motorcars, motorcycles, lorries, omnibuses, tractors and trailers, for road and safety reasons. The permit is issued by the Land Transport Department. Further the importer must also submit the import permit to the Royal Department of Customs to obtain an admission permit (AP) in order to import. Imports of any radio-active materials under the control of the Ministry of Health.

61.78 To ensure national security

Royal Brunei Police Force, Ministry of Religious Affairs, Ministry of Home Affairs, subject to licensing, importation of printed media, radio communication apparatus and dealers, radar apparatus-remote control such as for motor car, racing car and boat, wireless telephone, walkie talkie, pagers, mobile radio transmitters, amateur and hand transceiver, radio transmitter and transmitter receiver,maritime radio communications apparatus for use in coastal and shipping communication, aeronautical communications apparatus for use in aircraft and aviation, telecommunications fixed line set dealers such as domestic telephone sets, arms, explosives, and fireworks/crackers. Publications and printed materials and recorded media including cassette, videos, CD, LD etc...

61.9 Non-automatic licensing n.e.s.

The Ministry of Home Affairs subjects to licensing the import of pin tables, fruit machines, slot machines and any other machines of like nature whether involving an element of chance or not, Poh Ka, Poh Kah or Poh Kau, Liow Ko, and Ch'ow Ko.

Religious reasons restrict the import and manufacture of alcohol and alcohol products under the Customs Prohibitions and Restriction of Imports and Exports Amended Order of 1990, effective since 1 of December 1990, which subjects imports of alcohol to a licence issued by the Controller.

The Ministry of Religious Affairs, Ministry of Health, and Department of Agriculture, and Ministry of Industry and Primary Resources, restrict the importation of beef and poultry including the carcass of the animal or any part thereof, the meat whether frozen, chilled or fresh, bones, hide, skin, hooves, horns, offal or any other part of the animal or any portion thereof, unless it has been slaughtered in an abattoir approved in writing by the Minister of Religious Affairs; the same Ministry subjects to licensing meat, meat products and edible offal, including poultry meat and its products.

Antiques and articles of a historical nature made or discovered in Brunei Darussalam, and wild life, are controlled by Brunei Museums. The import of natural mineral water requires a permit issued by Brunei Industrial Development Authority (Bina).

Prohibitions

63.1 Total prohibition

Indecent and obscene articles or prints, articles bearing the imprint or reproduction of any currency, bank notes or coins, knives, and video games are absolutely prohibited.

63.4 Temporary prohibition

Temporary ban on import of cement, in order to protect the state-owned sole domestic supplier.

63.71 To protect human health

Import ban is set on the following goods: opium and Chandu, the "Salk" polio vaccine, and vaccines of Chinese Taipei origin, and cough mixture containing codine.

Imported cigarettes are prohibited unless with health warning written on the packages approved by the Ministry of Health.

Due to the risk of transmission of the Avian Influenza virus to humans through consumption of infected poultry products, a ban is set on the importation of all types of poultry products including those live and frozen and all types of poultry eggs from all countries affected by and suspected of having cases of Avian Influenza.

With the incidence of Bovine Spongiform Encephalopaty and the outbreak of Foot-and-Mouth diseases, in Europe including the United Kingdom, an import ban has been set since 4 of March 2001, on all types of meat, including those chilled and frozen, their by-products such as sausage, meat extract and canned meat. Import ban is set also on milk and other dairy products such as pasteurised milk, cheese, butter, ice-cream, yoghurt, powdered milk and baby formulation from the U.K. produced on 1 February 2001.

63.72 To protect animal health and life

Import prohibition on pigs bred from Thailand, in order to prevent the introduction of animal diseases into Brunei Darussalam.

With the incidence of Bovine Spongiform Encephalopaty and the outbreak of Foot-and-Mouth diseases, in Europe including the United Kingdom, an import ban has been set since 4 of March 2001, on all types of meat, including those chilled and frozen, their by-products such as sausage, meat extract and canned meat. Import ban is set also on milk and other dairy products such as pasteurised milk, cheese, butter, ice-cream, yoghurt, powdered milk and baby formulation from the U.K. produced on 1 February 2001.

With the outbreaks of the Avian Influenza virus in several countries, and with the view of avoiding the transmission of the disease to animals, effective from 28 January 2004, an import ban is set on all types of poultry products, including those live and frozen and all types of poultry eggs from all countries affected by and suspected of having cases of Avian Influenza.

63.73 To protect plant health

Imports of a number of plants from specific regions or countries, soil itself or attached to plant roots are prohibited.

63.75 To protect wildlife

Import prohibition of Java Sparrows and turtle egg.

63.76 To control drug abuse

There is a short list of prohibited items including dangerous drugs such as opium, heroin, morphine, and psychotropic substances, mescaline, barbiturates, and amobarbital.

63.77 To ensure human safety

Fire crackers known as "double bangers" are banned at importation.

63.78 To ensure national security

All prohibitions under any order under the Sedition Enactment (cap.24) or the Undesirable publications Enactment (cap.25) arms and ammunitions, and fabrics of tissues consisting of any fibre whatsoever and of any other article whatsoever which fibre or tissue or other articles bear the imprint of any currency note, bank note or coins which are or have not at any time been issued or current, in any other country whatsoever, are prohibited imports as broadcasting equipment.

63.9 Prohibitions n.e.s.

Import prohibitions on pens, pencils and other articles resembling syringes, and on alcoholic beverages including spirit and liquors.

MONOPOLISTIC MEASURES

Single channel for imports

71.1 State trading administration

Import monopoly of rice bought mostly from Thailand by the Department of Information Technology, and State Stores in the Ministry of Finance under a government to government contract. Sugar is also subject to import monopoly.

TECHNICAL MEASURES

Technical regulations

Standards and technical regulations are the responsibility of: Ministry of Development, Old Airport, Bandar Seri Begawan 1190, Negara Brunei Darussalam

As there is no national body for elaborating standards, the Construction Planning and Research Unit (CPRU) in the Ministry of Development stands for a focal point for standards and conformity assessment activities. Yet Brunei is a member of the following international and regional standard setting fora which include ISO, WHO, Codex, the ASEAN, ACCSQ (consultative committee on Standards and Quality), the ASEM Trade Facilitation Action Plan, the APEC Sub-Committee on Standards and Conformance, and the Asia-Pacific Laboratory Accreditation Cooperation Scheme.

81.1 Product characteristics requirements

Motor vehicles, agricultural products, pharmaceuticals, and drug related products may be imported subject to certificate of origin requirements.

In conformity with the Emergency (Halal Meat) Order, 1998, "halal" imported meat must originate from facilities which have been approved by Brunei authorities as "halal".

81.12 To protect animal health and life

Health certificates are required for beef and poultry. Inedible tallow must be accompanied by a sterilization certificate. Imports of live animals and animals products must be covered by veterinary

certificates. Imported eggs must be identified with the imprint "imported" on the shell of the egg, in order to track out the source of supply and prevent illegal cross

bordering movements of eggs of unknown sanitary status and to ensure conformity with veterinary and sanitary requirements.

Under Regulations ruling the Quarantine and Prevention of Animal Diseases, all import of dogs, cats and related species must be accompanied by a veterinary health certificate and a certificate from the Veterinary authority of the exporting country stating that the country is free from rabies for a period of six months prior to exportation.

81.13 To protect plant health

Phytosanitary certificates from the Department of Agriculture are required for imported plants and plant materials. No soil may be attached.

The Plant Quarantine Unit of the Department of Agriculture in the Ministry of Industry and Primary Resources, Under the Agricultural Pests and Noxious Plants Act, 1962, is responsible for implementing phytosanitary regulations. Phytosanitary certificates must accompany imports of plants.

81.3 Labelling requirements

81.4 Packaging requirements

Legislation on food labelling requirements is contained in the Emergency Public Food Order of 1998, in force since January 2001. Labels must be written in Malay or English and must contain the following information: name of food, list of ingredients, net/drained content details of the manufacturer, importer; the country of origin, lot identification, the best before date, storage and use instructions etc. Imports of meats and products containing meat must conform to labelling requirements approved by the Board for Issuing Halal Import Permits. As for food with animal or alcohol content, the origin of both animal or alcohol must also be indicated; imported eggs must be clearly marked "imported" to distinguish them from locally produced eggs.

81.5 Testing, inspection and quarantine requirements

Inspection requirements are set on such imports as motor vehicles, pharmaceuticals, beef, plant and plant materials. Inspection is conducted by various government departments controlling the restricted goods including the Transport Department, the Health Department, and the Department of Agriculture, respectively.

Random samples analysis of imported Mineral water, conducted by the Ministry of Health.

Imported live animals are subject to veterinary inspection at the border, with the exception of those imported from Australia, Ireland, New Zealand, Sabah, Sarawak, Singapore, the United Kingdom; for other countries that are free from rabies, animals may be subject to quarantine for six months upon arrival. Inspection of imported and locally produced drugs by the Drug Quality Control Service, to ensure quality.

IMPORTANT LAWS AND REGULATIONS

BRUNEI CUSTOMS ACT

An Act to amend and consolidate the law relating to customs and the importation and exportation of goods and to provide for the recording of statistics thereof

Commencement: 1st January 1955 [GN 10/55]

PART I PRELIMINARY

This Act may be cited as the Customs Act. Short title.

(1) In this Act — Interpretation.

"agent" in relation to a vessel, includes chinchew [S 23/89] and comprador;

"aircraft" includes any kind of craft which may be used for the conveyance of passengers or goods by air;

"the Controller" means the Controller of Customs;

"customs airport" means any place which has been prescribed as a customs airport;

"customs duty" means any import duty, export duty, surtax, surcharge or cess, imposed by or under this Act;

"customs' laws" includes any enactment relating to customs, importation or exportation which has effect in Brunei Darussalam;

*NOTE — Not in operation on the first revision date, the minor amendments effected by the Ports Enactment 1981 have been included.

"customs port" means any port within the meaning of the Ports Act prescribed to be a customs port;

"customs warehouse" means a warehouse or other place established by the Minister of Finance with the approval of His Majesty the Sultan and Yang Di-Pertuan under section 57 for the deposit of dutiable goods;

"denatured" means effectually rendered unfit for human consumption to the satisfaction of the Controller;

"dutiable goods" means all goods subject to the payment of customs duty;

"export" means to take or cause to be taken out of Brunei Darussalam, by land, sea or air to place any goods in a vessel, conveyance or aircraft for the purpose of such goods being taken out of Brunei Darussalam by land sea or air:

Provided that goods *bona fide* in transit, including goods which have been transhipped, shall not, for the purpose of levy of customs duties, be deemed to be exported unless they are or become uncustomed goods;

"exporter" includes any person by whom any goods (including goods transferred from an importing aircraft or ship) are exported from Brunei Darussalam or supplied for use as aircraft's or ship's stores, and also the owner, or any person acting on his behalf, and any person who for customs purposes signs any document relating to goods exported or intended for exportation or supplied or intended for supply as aircraft's or ship's stores as aforesaid;

"goods" includes animals, birds, fish, plants and all kinds of moveable property;

"hover" in the case of a vessel in territorial waters means to linger without apparent lawful purpose, whether such vessel be moving or not moving;

"import" means to bring or cause to be brought into Brunei Darussalam by land, sea or air;

Provided that goods *bona fide* in transit, including goods for transhipment, shall not, for the purpose of levy of customs duties, be deemed to be imported unless they are or become uncustomed goods;

"importer" includes and applies to any owner or other person for the time being possessed of or beneficially interested in any goods at and from the time of importation thereof until such goods are duly removed from customs control;

"inland custom station" means a place prescribed for the collection duties under paragraph (7) of section 133 and in relation to any prescribed route under paragraph (5) of section 133 means a place so prescribed for that route;

"in transit" means taken or sent from any country and brought into Brunei Darussalam by land, sea or air (whether or not landed or transhipped in Brunei Darussalam) for the sole purpose of being carried to another country either by the same or another conveyance;

"legal landing place" means any place for the landing and shipping of goods within the limits of a post defined under the Ports Act and any other place which has been prescribed as a legal place for the landing and shipping of goods;

"licensed warehouse" means a warehouse or other place licensed for the warehousing of dutiable goods under section 58;

"liquor" includes all liquids containing more than 2 per centum or pure alcohol by weight but does not include denatured spirits;

"local craft" means any junk, *tongkang*, *perahu*, *kumpit* or other similar type of vessel, and any steam or motor vessel under 15 net registered tons;

"master" means any person (except a pilot or harbour master) having for the time being control or charge of a vessel;

"the Minister" means the Minister responsible for finance;

"officer of customs" means —

(a) the Controller;

(b) any Deputy Controller, Senior Superintendent, Superintendent, Assistant Superintendent or Supervisor of Customs;

(c) any member of the Department of Trade and Customs authorised under the hand of the Controller to act as such;

(d) the persons authorised by section 5 to exercise the powers of senior officers of customs or of officers of customs and any person appointed by His Majesty to act as an officer of customs;

"owner" in respect of a ship includes every person acting as agent for the owner or who receives freight or other charges payable in respect of the ship;

"owner" in respect of goods includes any person (other than an officer of customs acting in his official capacity) being or holding himself out to be the owner, importer, exporter, consignee, agent or person in possession of, or beneficially interested in, or having any control of, or power of disposition over, the goods;

"petroleum" includes the liquids commonly known by the name of rock oil, Rangoon oil, Burma oil, kerosene and kerosene substitutes, paraffin oil, petrol, gasoline, benzol, benzoline, benzine, naphtha, and any like inflammable liquid, whether a natural product or one that is made form petroleum, coal, schist, shale or any other bitumious substance, or from any products therof;

"pilot of an aircraft" means every person having or taking command or charge of an aircraft;

"Ports Department warehouse" means a Government warehouse controller and managed by the Controller of Ports under the Ports Act;

"preferential tariff" means the tariff of the different rates of duty imposed by order of Minister of Finance with the approval of His Majesty the Sultan and Yang Di-Pertuan under subsection (2) of section 8;

"preventive vessel" means any vessel employed for the prevention of smuggling or for any other purpose relating to the customs;

"prohibited goods" means goods the import or export of which is prohibited, either absolutely or conditionally by an order under section 28 or by any other written law for the time being in force in Brunei Darussalam;

"proper officer of customs" means any officer of customs acting in the fulfilment of his duties under this Act, whether such duties are assigned to him specially or generally, or expressly or by implication;

"sea" includes inland water;

Provided that His Majesty in Council may from time to time by order in the *Gazette* amend such Schedule;

"senior officer of customs" means any officer included in paragraphs *(a)* and *(b)* of the definition of officer of customs and also any other officer of customs authorised by this Act or under the hand of the Controller to act as a senior officer of customs;

"sufferance wharf" means any place other than an approved place of loading or unloading at which the senior officer of customs may, in his discretion, and under such conditions and in such manner as he may direct, either generally or in any particular case, allow any goods to be loaded or unloaded;

"uncustomed goods" means goods in respect of which a breach of the provisions of this Act or of any subsidiary legislation made thereunder has been committed;

"value" in relation to imported goods means the price which an importer would give for the goods on a purchase in the open market if the goods were delivered to him at the place of payment of duty and if freight, insurance, commission and all other costs, charges and expenses (except any customs duties) incidental to the purchase and delivery at such place had been paid;

"vessel" includes any ship or boat or any other description of vessel used in navigation;

"warehouse" means a place for the deposit of goods under customs control.

(2) For the purposes of this Act, goods shall be deemed to be under customs control whilst they are deposited or held in any Ports Department warehouse, customs or licensed warehouse, post office, or in any vessel, conveyance, aircraft or place from which they may not be removed except with the permission of the proper officer of customs.

PART II ADMINISTRATION AND POWERS OF OFFICERS

3. (1) The Controller shall be the chief officer of customs and shall have the superintendence of all matters relating to the customs, subject to the direction and control of the Minister.

(2) Deputy Controllers, Senior Superintendents, Superintendents, Assistant Superintendents and Supervisors of Customs shall be subject to the general direction and supervision of the Controller, and, subject thereto, shall have and exercise all powers conferred on the Controller by or under this Act, other than those conferred by section 20.

All officers of customs shall be deemed to be public servants within the meaning of the Penal Code.

For the purposes of this Act, subject to the general direction and supervision of the Controller, and all police officers not below the rank of Inspector shall have and may exercise all the powers by this Act conferred on senior officers of customs, and all police officers below the rank of Inspector shall have and may exercise all the powers by this Act conferred on officers of customs.

(1) Every officer of customs other than a senior officer of customs when acting against any person under this Act shall, if not in uniform, on demand declare his office and produce to the person against whom he is acting such authority card as the Controller or, in the case of a police officer, the chief police officer, may direct to be carried by such officers.

(2) It shall not be an offence for any person to refuse to comply with any request, demand or order made by any officer of customs acting or purporting to act under this Act if such officer being an officer other than a senior officer of customs is not in uniform and refuses to declare his office and produce his authority card, on demand being made by such person.

Administration.
Officers of customs to be public servants.
Powers of Police Officers.
Authority cards to be produced.
Persons employed on customs duty to be deemed proper officers for such service.
Power of Minister of Finance to fix customs duties by orders.

7. Every person employed on any duty or service relating to the customs by the orders or with the concurrence of the Controller (whether previously or subsequently expressed) shall be deemed to be the proper officer for that duty or service; and every act required by law at any time to be done by, or with any particular officer nominated for such purpose, if done by or with any person appointed by the Controller to act for such particular officer, shall be deemed to be done by or with such particular officer.

PART III LEVYING OF CUSTOMS DUTIES

8. (1) Minister of Finance with the approval of His Majesty the Sultan and Yang Di-Pertuan may, from time to time, by order signified in the *Gazette*, fix the customs duties to be levied on any goods imported into or exported from Brunei Darussalam and to be paid by the importer or exporter, as the case may be.

(2) Any such order may impose different rates of import duty upon goods which are shown to the satisfaction of the Controller —

(a) to have been consigned from a part of the prescribed countries and either —

(i) to be the produce of the prescribed countries; or

(ii) to have been manufactured in the prescribed countries;

(such duties to be distinguished in the order as duties imposed under the preferential tariff), and

(b) upon goods not shown to the satisfaction of the Controller to have been so consigned and produced or manufactured (such duties to be distinguished as duties imposed under the General Tariff).

(3) Notwithstanding the provisions of subsection (2) no goods shall be admitted under the preferential tariff unless the importer shall comply with any regulations made under this Act in that behalf.

(4) Without prejudice to any other remedy, any customs duty payable under Act may be recovered as a civil debt due to the Government.

(5) For the purpose of this section the expression [S 23/89] "prescribed countries" means the countries which have been specified as prescribed countries by order made under this section.

9. The Controller may, from time to time, by notification in Power to fix value.

the *Gazette*, fix, for the purpose of the levy and payment of customs duties, the value of any dutiable goods.

10. (1) The proper officer of customs may value, weigh, Valuation by proper officer measure or otherwise examine, or may cause to be valued, of customs.

weighed, measured or otherwise examined any dutiable or uncustomed goods for the purpose of ascertaining the duty leviable thereon.

(2) When a value, weight or quantity of any goods has been assessed by the proper officer of customs, such value, weight or quantity shall be presumed to be correct until the contrary is proved.

11. (1) The Minister may, by order, exempt, subject to such conditions as he may deem fit to impose, any class or description of goods or persons from the payment of the whole or any part of any customs duty which may be payable. [S 184/64]

(2) The Minister may in any particular case —

Re-imposition of duty.

(a) exempt any person from the payment of the whole or any part of the customs duties which may be payable by such person on any goods; or

(b) may direct the refund to any person of the whole or any part of the customs duties which have been paid by such person on any goods, and in granting such exemption or directing such refund the Minister may impose such conditions as he may deem fit.

(3) Any goods in respect of which an exemption from the payment of customs duties has been granted under the provisions of subsection (1) or (2) shall be deemed to be dutiable goods until the conditions, if any, subject to which the exemption from duty was granted are fulfilled and shall be liable to all other charges, not being customs duties, to which they would be subject if no such exemption had been granted.

12. (1) If any goods on which customs duty has not been paid by reason of an exemption granted under section 11, cease to comply with the conditions subject to which such exemption was granted or cease to be kept or used by the person or for the purposes qualifying them for such exemption, such goods shall, upon such cesser, become liable to the customs duty to which they would have been liable if they had not been the subject of an exemption, and the person to whom such exemption was granted and any person found in possession of such goods shall be jointly and severally liable to pay such customs duty:

Provided that if the Controller is satisfied that at the time when any such goods become liable to customs duty the value thereof is less than the value at the time when exemption was granted he shall fix the value thereof as at the time when such goods become liable to customs duty and duty shall be paid accordingly.

(2) If any goods, which are liable to customs duty under subsection (1) and on which such duty has not been paid, are found in the possession or on the premises of any person other than the

person authorised to possess them under the terms of such exemption, such goods shall, until the contrary is proved, be deemed to be uncustomed goods within the meaning of this Act.

13. It shall be lawful for the Controller, if it is proved to his satisfaction that any money has been overpaid as customs duties or as warehouse rent or as any other charge under this Act, to order the refund, of the money so overpaid:

Provided that no such refund shall be allowed unless a claim in respect thereof is made within one year after the overpayment was made.

14. Whenever —

(a) through inadvertence, error, collusion, misconstruction on the part of any officer of customs, or through misstatement as to value, quantity or description by any person, or for any other reason, the whole or any part of any customs duties or other moneys payable under this Act have not been paid; or

(b) the whole or any part of such customs duties or other moneys, after having been paid, have been, owing to any cause, erroneously refunded, the person liable to pay such customs duties or other moneys or the person to whom such refund has erroneously been made, as the case may be, shall pay the deficiency or repay the amount paid to him in excess, on demand being made within 12 months from the date on which customs duty was payable or deficient customs duty was paid or the refund was made, as the case may be, and without prejudice to any other remedy for the recovery of the amount due, any dutiable goods belonging to such person which may be in any customs or licensed warehouse may be detained until such customs duty or deficiency be paid or the refund be paid, as the case may be.

15. Where any goods, whether made or produced within Brunei Darussalam or not, being of a class or description liable to any import duty are re-imported into Brunei Darussalam after exportation therefrom, and it is shown to the satisfaction of the senior officer of customs that any duty chargeable in respect of the goods prior to their exportation was duly paid, either prior to exportation or at any subsequent time, and either that no drawback of any such duty was allowed on exportation, or that any drawback so allowed has been repaid, and

(a) if it is further shown as aforesaid that the goods have not been subjected to any process abroad, the goods shall be exempt from any such duty when the same are re-imported into Brunei Darussalam, unless the rate of duty chargeable on goods of the same class or description at the time when the same are imported into Brunei Darussalam shall exceed the rate paid on the said goods as import duty on first importation, in which case such goods shall be chargeable with duty at a rate equal to the difference between the rate at which the duty previously paid was calculated and the rate in force at the date when such goods are re-imported into Brunei Darussalam;

(b) if the goods at the time when the same are re-imported into Brunei Darussalam are of a class or description liable to an import duty *ad valorem* and it is further shown as aforesaid that the goods have been subjected to a process of repair, renovation or improvement abroad, but that their form or character has not been changed, such goods shall be chargeable with duty as if the amount of the increase in the value of the goods attributable to the process were the whole value thereof and where any sum has been contracted to be paid for the execution of the process, the sum shall be *prima facie* evidence of the that amount, but without prejudice to the powers of the proper officer of customs as to the ascertainment of the value of the goods for the purpose of assessing duty thereon *ad valorem*:

Provided that if the rate of duty chargeable on goods of the same class or description at the time when the same are re-imported into Brunei Darussalam shall exceed the rate paid on the said goods on first importation, then in such case, in addition to the *ad valorem* import duty chargeable hereunder according to the amount of the increase in the value of the goods attributable to the process, such goods shall be chargeable with additional duty calculated in the manner set out in paragraph *(a)*, as if such goods had not been subjected to any process or repair, renovation or improvement abroad.

16. (1) If any dutiable goods which have been imported are, by unavoidable accident, lost, damaged or destroyed at any time after their arrival within Brunei Darussalam, and before removal from customs control, the Controller may remit the whole or any part of the customs duty payable thereon.

(2) After removal of any goods from customs control no abatement of customs duties shall be allowed on any such goods —

(a) on account of damage; or *(b)* on account of any claim to pay duty at a preferential rate, unless notice in writing of such claim has been given at or before the time of such removal.

(3) After removal of any goods from customs control no abatement of export duty shall be allowed on any such goods on account of damage, theft or loss.

17. The rate of import duty and the valuation (if any) applicable to any goods shall be —

(a) in the case of goods lawfully imported —

(i) if such goods (other than petroleum in a licensed warehouse) are warehoused the rate and valuation in force on the day on which the removal of the goods is authorised by the proper officer of customs;

(ii) if such goods consist of petroleum which is in a licensed warehouse, the rate in force on the day on which such petroleum is removed from such warehouse;

Remission of import duty on goods lost, damaged or destroyed before or after removal from customs control.

Calculation of import duty.

(iii) if such goods are imported by post, the rate and valuation in force on the day on which duty is assessed by the proper officer of customs; and

(iv) in any other case, the rate and valuation in force on the day on which such goods are released by the proper officer of customs;

(b) in the case of uncustomed goods, the rate and valuation in force on the day on which such goods became uncustomed goods, if known, or the rate and valuation in force on the day of seizure, whichever is the higher.

18. The rate of export duty and the valuation (if any) applicable to any goods shall be —

(a) in the case of goods lawfully exported, the rate and valuation in force on the day on which a receipt is issued for the payment of duty:

Provided that when payment of duty in arrears has been permitted under the provisions of section 73 the rate and valuation shall be the rate and valuation in force on the day on which the goods are released by the proper officer of customs, or, as the case may be, by an officer appointed under any law for the time being in force in Brunei Darussalam relating to the collection of export duties on goods exported from Brunei Darussalam;

(b) in the case of uncustomed goods, the rate and valuation in force on the day on which such goods became uncustomed goods, if known, or the rate and valuation in force on the day of seizure, whichever is the higher.

19. Whenever by virtue of an order made under subsection

and (1) of section 8 a customs duty is fixed on any goods which exportation previously were not dutiable goods or any customs duty on when duty is goods is abolished or when the importation or exportation of any imposed or repealed.

goods is prohibited or any such prohibition abolished by an order made under section 28 and it becomes necessary for the purpose of this Act to determine the time at which an importation or exportation of any goods made and completed shall be deemed to have had effect, such importation or exportation shall, notwithstanding anything in this Act contained, be deemed to be —

(a) in the case of importation by sea, the time at which the vessel importing such goods had actually come within the limits of the customs port to which such goods are consigned;

(b) in the case of importation by land, the time at which such goods come within Brunei Darussalam;

(c) in the case of importation by air, the time at which the aircraft lands at a customs airport;

(d) in the case of exportation by sea, the time at which shipment of such goods on board the vessel by which they were exported commenced;

(e) in the case of exportation by land, the time at which such goods leave Brunei Darussalam;

(f) in the case of exportation by air, the time at which the aircraft leaves a customs airport;

20. If any question arises as to whether any particular goods are or are not included in a class of goods appearing in an order made under subsection (1) of section 8, such question shall be decided by the Controller.

PART IV IMPORTATION AND EXPORTATION

21. (1) No goods imported by sea shall be landed —

Questions in respect of goods deemed to be dutiable.
Time and place of landing goods inwardly.

Places of landing of goods imported by air.
Time and place imported by land.
Time and place of loading goods for export by sea.

(a) except at a legal landing place or sufferance wharf;

(b) until permission to do so has been received from the proper officer of customs; and,

(c) except on such days and during such times as may be prescribed, unless permission to land goods on other days and during other times has been granted by the proper officer of customs.

(2) Except with the permission of the proper officer of customs, no such goods —

(a) after having been landed or unshipped shall be transhipped; or

(b) after having been put into any boat or craft to be landed shall be removed into any other boat or craft previously to their being landed.

(3) The foregoing provisions of this section shall not apply to fresh fish, whether packed with ice or not, which is landed from any vessel licensed for the purpose of fishing under any written law for the time being in force in Brunei Darussalam or Sarawak or Sabah.

No goods imported by air shall be landed except at a customs airport.

No goods imported by land shall be imported except at a prescribed place of import and where a route has been prescribed by such route and on the days and during the times prescribed for such importation unless permission to import goods on other days and during other times has been granted by the proper officer of customs.

No goods shall be loaded, or water-borne to be loaded for exportation by sea —

(a) except at a legal landing place or sufferance wharf;

(b) except on such days and during such times as may be prescribed, unless permission to load goods on other days and during other times has been granted by the proper officer of customs.

No goods shall be exported by land except at a prescribed place of export and, where a route has been prescribed, by such route and on such days and during such time as may be prescribed unless permission to export goods on other days and during other times has been granted by the proper officer of customs.

No goods shall be exported by air except at a customs airport.

The Controller may exempt any person from all or any of the provisions of sections 21, 22, 23, 24, 25, and 26 on such conditions as he may deem fit to impose.

Minister of Finance with the approval of His Majesty the Sultan and Yang Di-Pertuan may, by order provide for —

prohibiting the importation into, or the exportation from, Brunei Darussalam or any part thereof, either absolutely or conditionally, or from or to any specified country, territory or place outside Brunei Darussalam, or the removal from one place to another place in Brunei Darussalam of any goods or class of goods; and

prohibiting the importation into, or the exportation from, Brunei Darussalam or any part thereof, or removal from one place to another place in Brunei Darussalam of any goods or class of goods, except at specified ports or places.

The Controller may, at his discretion, either generally or in a particular case or in respect of a particular area, require security to be given by any person moving dutiable goods within

Time and place of export by land.

Exportation by air.

Arriving vessels, unless exempted to produce last clearance.

No vessel, unless exempted to sail without clearance.

Brunei Darussalam and where any such security has been required to be given no person shall move such goods unless such security has been given. Such security shall not exceed the amount of duty leviable on such goods.

PART V CLEARANCE

The master or the agent of every vessel arriving at any customs port and not being a vessel to which the exemption under section 36 applies shall produce to the proper officer of customs on arrival the clearance, or other document which it is usual to grant, granted at the last port of call whether such place be situate within or without Brunei Darussalam, and the proper officer of customs may retain the same and the master or the agent of any vessel who fails to comply with the provisions of this section shall be guilty of an offence.

(1) No vessel whether laden or in ballast, not being a vessel to which the exemption under section 36 applies, shall depart from any port in Brunei Darussalam until a clearance has been granted by a proper officer of customs.

(2) Such officer shall not issue a clearance for any vessel until the master of such vessel has declared to that officer the name of the Nation or State to which he claims that she belongs and that officer shall thereupon inscribe that name on the clearance.

(3) If any such vessel shall leave or attempt to leave any port without a clearance the master of the vessel and also the owner and any person who sends or attempts to send the vessel to sea, if that owner or person is party or privy to the offence, shall be guilty of an offence against this Act, and the vessel if she has not left the territorial waters of Brunei Darussalam, may be detained.

(4) Clearances shall be in the form prescribed.

32. (1) If the master of any vessel shall obtain a clearance and shall not sail within 48 hours thereafter, he shall report to the proper officer of customs his reason for not sailing, and if so required obtain a fresh clearance.

(2) If the master of any vessel shall fail to comply with the provisions of this section he shall be guilty of an offence against this Act, and the vessel may be detained.

33. The master or agent of any vessel shall, at the time applying for clearance —

(a) unless exempted by the senior officer of customs, deliver to the proper officer of customs a list of all goods, dutiable on export, for delivery at another port in Brunei Darussalam;

(b) answer to the proper officer of customs such questions concerning the departure and destination of the vessel as are demanded of him.

The proper officer of customs shall endorse upon the clearance granted the list of goods submitted under the provisions of section 33, or at his discretion shall firmly attach the list submitted to the clearance.

The proper officer of customs may refuse to grant clearance to any vessel until —

the provisions of section 33 shall have been complied with;

the provisions of section 53 concerning local craft shall have complied with; and

all charges and penalties due by such vessel or by the owner or master thereof and all duties payable in respect of any goods shipped therein shall have been duly paid, or their payment secured by such guarantee or by deposit at such rate as the proper officer of customs directs; or the agent (if any) of the vessel shall have delivered to the proper officer of customs a declaration in writing to the effect that he will be liable for all such charges and penalties as aforesaid, and shall have furnished security for the discharge of the same if so required.

Vessels **36.** (1) The provisions of this Part shall not apply to vessels of the following classes, namely—from requiring clearance.

(a) vessels other than vessels propelled by mechanical power engaged solely in fishing and licensed for the purpose of fishing under any written law for the time being in force in Brunei Darussalam or Sabah or Sarawak;

(b) vessels whose movements are confined to navigable rivers upstream of a customs station situated at or near the mouth of such river;

(c) privately owned pleasure vessels not plying for hire and not carrying cargo;

(d) vessels of a class in respect of which an order under subsection (2) is in force.

(2) The Minister may, be order, exempt either absolutely or conditionally, any class of vessels from the operation of this Part.

Application **37.** The provisions of this Part shall apply, with such

to aircraft.

modifications and adaptations as may be necessary, in respect of aircraft arriving at, or departing from, any customs airport.

PART VI GENERAL PROVISIONS AFFECTING VESSELS IN TERRITORIAL WATERS

Vessels in **38.** (1) The master of any vessel in territorial waters shall territorial obey any signal made to him from a preventive or police vessel waters.

or any instructions given by an officer of customs or police officer in uniform from any other vessel or any place requiring him to stop or to heave to or to perform any other act.

(2) The master of any vessel found without lawful excuse in territorial waters or without a clearance for a customs port in Brunei Darussalam, or carrying cargo or passengers or both without a proper manifest of such, or found to have passed the customs port named in the papers of such vessel without haying made entry and declared at such port, shall be liable on conviction before a magistrate to a fine of $8,000 and to imprisonment for a term of 12 months.

(3) Any vessel found in the circumstances described in subsection (2) shall be liable to seizure by any officer of customs or police officer and shall be escorted to a convenient port in Brunei Darussalam and may there be detained by such officer of customs or police officer for a period not exceeding 14 days.

(4) Upon an application by the Solicitor General or any senior officer of customs or police officer in any proceedings commenced against the master of such vessel, or if no such proceedings are commenced then upon notice of such application being served on the master, owner or agent or affixed in some prominent place on such vessel, the provisions of subsections (1) and (2) of section 357 of the Criminal Procedure Code shall apply to such vessel and to its cargo and to everything on such vessel as if it were produced before the Court as having been used in the commission of an offence and any magistrate may make any orders for custody, sale, destruction or confiscation authorised under such subsections.

(5) An appeal shall lie from any order of a magistrate under subsection (4) at the instance of the master, owner or agent of such vessel as if from a conviction by such magistrate

(6) Nothing contained in subsections (2) and (3) shall apply to —

(a) any vessel the master of which satisfies the magistrate that its entry into the waters of Brunei Darussalam was due to circumstances beyond his control and that its entry and the reason therefore was at the first possible opportunity reported to the nearest customs or police authority and that after such entry no person on board or connected with the vessel has done any act contrary to any written law; or

(b) any local craft if the person in charge thereof of can shew to the satisfaction of a senior officer of customs or magistrate that he has come from a place of departure from which it is unusual to grant or carry clearances or manifests.

39. (1) If any vessel hovers within territorial waters and on examinations is found to be conveying goods dutiable on import or goods of a class the importation of which is prohibited, the master and every member of the crew of such vessel shall be presumed, until the contrary is proved, to have imported uncustomed or prohibited goods, as the case may be.

(2) If any vessel hovers within territorial waters and on examination is found not to be carrying of the goods referred to in subsection (1), such vessel shall be presumed, until the contrary is proved, to be hovering for the purpose of receiving dutiable goods upon which export duty has not been paid or prohibited goods exported contrary to a prohibition and the master and every member of the crew of such vessel shall be guilty of an offence against this act.

If goods, other than *bona fide* ship's stores, are found by a proper officer of customs in any vessel in territorial waters and such goods are not correctly accounted for in the manifest or other documents which ought to be aboard such vessel, then such goods shall be deemed to be uncustomed goods and shall be liable to seizure.

If in any vessel in territorial waters the quantity of any goods entered in the manifest or other documents which ought to be aboard such vessel, is found by a proper officer of customs to be short, and the deficiency is not accounted for to the satisfaction of such officer, then such goods shall be deemed to have been illegally landed in Brunei Darussalam.

When in exercise of the powers conferred by this Act, a proper officer of customs boards any vessel, the master of such vessel shall provide such officer with suitable shelter and accommodation on the vessel remains in territorial waters.

(1) When in exercise of the powers conferred by this Act, a proper officer of customs boards any vessel, he shall have free access to every part of the vessel, and shall have the power to fasten down hatchways or entrances to holds, to mark any goods before landing, and to lock-up, seal, mark or otherwise secure any goods, including ship's stores, on board such vessel; and no hatchway or entrance, after having been fastened down by such officer, shall be opened, and no lock, seal or mark shall be opened, broken or altered without the consent of the proper officer of customs while the vessel is within the limits of the customs port or before any goods are delivered to be landed.

(2) Ship's stores on board a vessel may be used on such vessel without payment of import duty to such an extent and under such conditions as the Controller may, in his absolute discretion, permit.

44. (1) No dutiable or prohibited goods shall be carried in any local craft except with the permission of the Controller and subject to such conditions as the Controller may impose.

(2) Such permission may be granted either generally, by notification in the *Gazette*, in respect of all local craft or any class or classes of local craft, or specially, in writing under the hand of the Controller or an officer authorised by him in that behalf, in respect of a particular local craft.

(3) This section shall not apply to any local craft lawfully engaged in transporting cargo from or to a vessel to or from a legal landing place.

45. After the arrival of any vessel within territorial waters —

(a) bulk shall not be broken;

(b) no alteration shall be made in the stowage of the cargo so as to facilitate the unloading of any part of the cargo, before the permission to land goods required by paragraph *(b)* of subsection (1) of section 21 has been received by the master of such vessel; and

(c) no package shall at any time be opened on board such vessel, without proper cause shown to a senior officer of customs.

46. The provisions of this Part shall apply, with such modifications and adaptations, as may be necessary, in respect of aircraft arriving at, or departing from, any customs airport.

PART VII MANIFESTS

47. (1) Save as provided in subsection (3), the master or agent of every vessel, other than a local craft, arriving in any customs port, shall, within 24 hours after the arrival and before any cargo is unshipped, present to the proper officer of customs at the customs office a true inward manifest of the vessel, substantially in the prescribed form, certified by such master or agent, together with a duplicate copy thereof, containing all particulars as to marks, numbers and contents of each package intended to be landed at the customs port, together with the names of shippers and consignees of the same, if known to him, and the proper officer of customs may, at his discretion, demand, in addition, a complete manifest of the whole cargo of the vessel and a complete list of stores on board such vessel.

(2) A separate transhipment manifest shall be presented in duplicate in the prescribed form in respect of goods to be transhipped at the customs port.

(3) Where it is shown to the satisfaction of the proper officer of customs that it is not practicable to present an inward manifest or a transhipment manifest within a reasonable time after the arrival of a vessel the proper officer of customs may permit cargo to be landed or transhipped prior to presentation of the manifest, but no cargo so landed shall, except with the permission of the proper officer of customs, be delivered to the

importer or consignee or his agent until such time as the manifest has been presented to, and scrutinised by, the proper officer of customs.

In any case in which such master or agent is unable to ascertain the particulars of any inward or transhipment cargo or the names of the consignees thereof, he shall sign the declaration, endorsed upon the prescribed form, that he has exercised due diligence to ascertain the particulars of such cargo and the names of the consignees and shall therein enumerate the packages in respect of which his information is defective.

The master of every local craft, whether carrying cargo or not, arriving in any customs port shall attend in person at the customs office and make a written or oral declaration in the prescribed form or manner of all the cargo to be landed from his vessel.

(1) On completion of the discharge of cargo or within 2 months of such discharge or within such further period as the proper officer of customs may allow, the master or agent of the vessel shall present to the proper officer of customs a certified statement in duplicate of the outturn of such

cargo and shall enumerate therein any alteration in the manifest due to short shipment, short landing, over landing or any other cause.

(2) If any goods entered in the manifest of any vessel are not accounted for to the satisfaction of the proper officer of customs within 2 months of the presentation of such statement or within such further period as such officer may allow, the master or the agent of the vessel shall be liable to pay to such officer on demand a sum not exceeding $100, and in addition, in the case of dutiable goods, the agent shall be liable to pay to such officer on demand the amount of duty leviable thereon or, when the correct duty cannot be assessed, and amount not exceeding $1,000.

(3) If the person liable to the penalties laid down in subsection (2) refuses or fails to pay the penalties demanded of him the senior officer of customs may sue for and recovery such penalties in a Court of a Magistrate.

Provision for cases where all particulars are not known.
Person in charge of local craft to make declaration on arrival.
Correction to be made on completion of discharge and liability of master.

Pilot or agent of arriving aircraft to present inward manifest.
Outward manifest of vessel to be presented.
Person in charge of local craft to make declaration before departure.

Pilot of departing aircraft to present outward manifest.

The pilot or agent of every aircraft arriving at a customs airport shall, before any cargo is delivered, present to the proper officer of customs at the customs office a true inward manifest of the aircraft, substantially in the prescribed form, certified by such pilot or agent, together with a duplicate copy thereof, containing all particulars as to marks, numbers and contents of each package consigned to such customs airport, together with the names of consignors and consignees if known to him, and the proper officer of customs may, at his discretion, demand, in addition, a complete manifest of the whole cargo of the aircraft and a complete list of stores on the aircraft.

The owner or agent of any vessel, other than a local craft, leaving any customs port shall, within 2 days of the departure of such vessel, present to the proper officer of customs at the customs office a true outward manifest of the vessel, substantially in the prescribed form, certified by such owner or agent, together with a duplicate copy thereof, containing all particulars as to marks, numbers and contents of each package shipped at the customs port and the names of the shippers and consignees of the same.

The master of any local craft, whether carrying cargo or not, leaving any customs port shall, before the departure of such vessel, attend in person at the customs office, and make a written or oral declaration in the prescribed form or manner of all cargo shipped on board his vessel and the port or ports of destination of such cargo, and if no cargo is being carried he shall make a declaration accordingly:

Provided that in the case of a local craft which in the circumstances mentioned in, and under the provisions of, section 55 is deemed to leave such customs port, no declaration shall be required if the proper officer of customs is satisfied that declaration has already been made at a customs port further upstream.

The pilot or agent to any aircraft leaving any customs airport shall, before the departure of such aircraft, present to the proper officer of customs at the customs office a true outward manifest of the aircraft, substantially in the prescribed form, certified by such pilot or agent, together with a duplicate copy thereof, containing all particulars as to marks, numbers and contents of each package loaded at such customs airport and the name of the consignors and consignees of the same.

Every local craft proceeding up or down a navigable river, at or near the mouth of which there is a customs port, shall stop at such port and shall, for the purposes of this Part, be deemed to arrive at or leave, as the case may be, such customs port.

The provisions of this Part shall not apply to any vessel to which the exemption referred to in section 36 applies or to any aircraft not engaged in carrying goods.

PART VIII WAREHOUSING

The Minister with the approval of His Majesty the Sultan and Yang Di-Pertuan may by order signified in the *Gazette* establish and maintain customs warehouses, wherein dutiable goods may be deposited and kept without payment of duty, at any customs port, customs airport, place of import or export or at any inland customs station and may prescribe the amount to be paid as warehouse rent on goods deposited in such warehouses and remit any amount payable as rent.

(1) The Controller may, at his absolute discretion, on payment of such fees as may be fixed by him in each case, grant a licence to any person, hereinafter in this section referred to as the licensee, for warehousing goods liable to customs duties in a place or places specified in such licence.

(2) Any such licence shall be for such period and subject to such conditions as the Controller in each case may specify in the licence and may at any time be withdrawn by the Controller in his absolute discretion.

(3) A senior officer of customs, or any officer of customs deputed by him for the purpose, shall at all times have access to any licensed warehouse.

Local craft arriving at or leaving certain navigable rivers.
Saving in respect of exempted vessels and certain aircraft.
The Minister may establish customs warehouse.
[S 24/85]

Licensed warehouse.

All goods to be deposited in a warehouse on arrival.

(4) If it appears at any time that in any licensed warehouse there is a deficiency in the quantity of dutiable goods which ought to be found therein, the licensee of such warehouse shall, in the absence of proof to the contrary, be presumed to have illegally removed such goods and shall, without prejudice to any proceedings under this Act, be liable to pay to the proper officer of customs the duty leviable on the goods found deficient:

Provided that if it is shown to the satisfaction of the Controller that such deficiency has been caused by unavoidable leakage, breakage or other accident, the Controller may remit the whole or any part of the customs duty leviable on the goods found deficient.

59. (1) Subject to the provisions of section 66, all goods imported into Brunei Darussalam shall, on first arrival or landing, be deposited by the importer or his agent in a Ports Department, customs or licensed warehouse or in a warehouse approved by the Controller.

Provided that, subject to such conditions as the Controller may impose either generally, by order or in any special case —

(a) the Controller, if satisfied that on account of the weight, quantity or bulk or any such goods or for any other reason it is not practicable to deposit such goods in a warehouse, may exempt such goods from being so deposited and such goods whilst kept in any other place shall be deemed to be under customs control;

(b) such goods on first landing at a customs airport where there is no warehouse may be dealt with as the Controller may direct; and

(c) where the bill of lading, invoice or other document concerning any goods landed at a customs port or customs airport show them to be consigned to any person at any place in Brunei Darussalam where there is a senior officer of customs then a senior officer of customs at such customs port or customs airport may in his discretion permit such goods to be forwarded to that place in which event such goods shall be deemed for the purposes of this Part to have first arrived on reaching such place and shall for the purposes of Part IX not be deemed to have been imported or landed until their arrival at such place.

(2) No goods deposited in a warehouse or exempted form being deposited, under subsection (1), shall be removed from such warehouse or from any place except with the permission of the proper officer of customs.

(3) Dutiable goods deposited in a warehouse not being a customs or licensed warehouse, shall be removed therefrom within 10 days or such extended time as the senior officer of customs may allow, of their being so deposited and if the goods are not so removed, the proper officer of customs may remove them to a Ports Department or customs warehouse at the expense of the owner of such goods.

(4) The provision of this section shall not apply—

(a) to goods imported by post;

(b) to goods imported by land or by sea at places of import where there is no customs warehouse;

(c) to passengers baggage, containing personal effects only.

60. (1) A warehouse deposit receipt shall be issued by the proper office of customs for all dutiable goods deposited in a customs warehouse;

Provided that in the case of dutiable goods imported by land no such receipt shall be issued except at the request of the importer or his agent.

(2) Where the warehouse deposit receipt is lost, a copy of such receipt duly certified by the proper office of customs shall be supplied to the owner of the dutiable goods or his agent on delivery of an indemnity bond approved by a senior officer of customs and delivered to him at the customs office, securing the Government against any claim for loss owing to wrong delivery of the goods deposited.

(3) The holder or endorsee in due course of a warehouse deposit receipt or a certified copy thereof granted under the provision of subsection (2) shall be deemed, for the purpose of this Act, to be the owner of the goods deposited, and delivery to the holder or endorsee or the agent of the holder or endorsee of such warehouse deposit receipt or certified copy thereof shall be a good and lawful delivery.

A senior officer of customs may, at any time, direct that any goods or package lodged in any Ports Department, customs or licensed warehouse shall be opened, weighed or otherwise examined, and after such goods or package has been so opened or examined, may cause the same to be sealed or marked in such manner as he sees fit.

(1) The proper officer of customs may detain in a customs warehouse any goods if he is in doubt whether such goods are dutiable or not.

(2) In every such case the proper officer of customs shall forthwith make a report to a senior officer of customs, who shall, without undue delay, decide whether such goods are dutiable or not.

(3)

If any such goods are found not to be dutiable, no warehouse rent, handling or other charges shall be payable in respect thereof.

(4)

The proper officer of customs, in his discretion and subject to such conditions as he may think fit, may permit the deposit of non-dutiable goods in a customs warehouse.

63. The Government shall not be liable to make good any loss sustained in respect of any goods by fire, theft, damage or other cause while such goods are in any customs warehouse or in the lawful custody or control of any officer of customs, unless such loss is caused by the wilful neglect, or default of an officer of customs or of a person employed by the Government in connection with the customs.

No officer of customs or other person employed by the Government in connection with the customs shall be liable to make good any loss sustained in respect of any goods by fire, theft, damage or other cause while such goods are in any customs warehouse or in the lawful custody or control of such officer or any other officer of customs or person employed in connection with customs unless such loss is caused by his wilful neglect, or default.

The owner of any goods deposited in a customs warehouse or his agent shall pay to the proper officer of customs the warehouse rent at the prescribed rates which may be due in respect of such goods.

Such rent shall be payable at the end of each month whether or not a demand in respect thereof is made and if not so paid may be recovered as a civil debt due to the Government.

No goods of an inflammable nature or of such a nature as to be likely to cause detriment to other goods shall be deposited in any customs warehouse without the sanction of a senior officer of customs, and if any such goods are landed lawfully outside the limits of a port declared under the Ports Act they may be deposited, at the expense and risk of the importer thereof, in any place but are such limits as aforesaid that a senior officer of customs may deem fit, and whilst so deposited such goods shall be deemed to be in a customs warehouse, and unless within a period of 14 days they have been duly cleared or warehoused in some approved warehouse, shall at the expiration of that period, be liable to be dealt with in the same manner as goods of a similar nature actually deposited in a customs warehouse. Such goods shall be chargeable with such expenses for securing, watching and guarding the same until sold, cleared or warehoused as aforesaid, as the senior officer of customs may deem fit.

(1) Goods of a perishable nature deposited in a customs warehouse shall be cleared forthwith, and if not so cleared a senior officer of customs may sell such goods.

(2) Goods of an inflammable nature deposited in a customs warehouse shall be cleared within 14 days of the date of deposit.

(3) Goods not of a perishable or inflammable nature deposited in a customs warehouse shall be cleared within 6 months of the date of deposit: Provided that a senior officer of customs may permit any goods to remain deposited for such further periods of not less than one month at a time and not exceeding 12 months in the aggregate as he may in his discretion think fit.

(4) If any goods are not cleared within the time specified in subsection (2) or (3) or if any warehouse rent in respect of any goods is not duly paid in the manner provided by section 65, a senior officer of customs may, after giving not less than 14 days notice in writing to the owner (if the name and address of such owner are known to him), or after due notice in the *Gazette* (if the name and address of such owner are not known to him), sell such goods by auction.

(5) The proceeds of the sale of any such goods shall be applied to the payment of any customs duties, warehouse rent, port dues and rates and other charges which may be due in respect of such goods or of any other goods deposited by the owner of such goods, and the surplus, if any, shall be paid to the owner of such goods, and if the owner cannot be found within 2 months of the sale, such surplus shall be paid to general revenue of Brunei Darussalam.

(6) If at the sale of any goods no sufficient bid is forthcoming to defray the customs duties, warehouse rent, port dues and rates and other charges which are due in respect of such goods, and goods shall be forfeited to Government and shall be disposed of in such manner as the Controller may direct.

(7) Every auction sale under this section shall be conducted by or in the presence of a senior officer of customs.

68. No dutiable goods shall be removed from Ports Department customs control except—

(a) after payment of the import duty payable thereon;

(b) if such goods are in a Ports Department or customs or licensed warehouse, under such conditions as the Controller may impose, for deposit in another customs or licensed warehouse; or

(c) under such conditions as the Controller may impose, for re-export from Brunei Darussalam;

and in no case shall any goods be removed from a customs warehouse until all warehouse rent and other charges due in respect thereof have been paid:

Provided that petroleum in a licensed warehouse may be removed therefrom before payment of the import duty if security has been lodged to the satisfaction of the Controller by which payment of duty is guaranteed within such time as the Controller may allow.

> Goods arriving in Brunei Darussalam for transhipment and landed at a customs port to await the arrival of the vessel to which they are intended to be transhipped shall, if they are dutiable on import or on export or prohibited to be imported or exported, or belong to a class of such goods, be deposited in a Ports Department, customs or licensed warehouse or in a warehouse approved by the Controller and shall be liable to warehouse rent at the appropriate prescribed rates applicable to such goods under the Ports Acts or this Act, or, if such rates are not prescribed, at the appropriate prescribed rates applicable under the Ports Act or this Act, to goods warehouse prior to export:
>
> Provided that the Controller may exempt any particular goods from the operation of this section.

(1) All necessary operations relating to the loading, shipping, unloading, unshipping, landing, carrying, weighing, opening, unpacking, repacking, bulking, sorting and marking of goods, including passenger's baggage, whether warehoused or not, shall be performed by or at the expense of the owner, importer, exporter, consignor, consignee or agent as the case may be:

Provided that outside the limits of a port declared under the

Ports Act the proper officer of customs may, at his discretion, direct that any such operations shall be performed by officers of customs or other persons under his control, and in any such case such operation shall be performed at the expense of the owner, importer, exporter, consignor, consignee or agent as the case may be.

(2) The Minister may prescribe the charges to be paid for operations performed under this section by officers of customs or other persons under the control of the proper officer of customs and may remit any charge due.

PART IX DECLARATION OF GOODS

A — Dutiable goods

Declaration of dutiable goods imported.

71. (1) Every importer of dutiable goods, warehoused under the provisions of section 59 or exempted from being warehoused by virtue of paragraph *(a)* of the proviso to subsection (1) of section 59 shall, before removal of such goods or any part thereof from customs control or if such goods are not removed within a period of 10 days from the date on which they were landed, within such period, make personally or by his agent to the proper officer of customs at such warehouse, a declaration, substantially in the prescribed form of the goods imported, and in any particular case the proper officer of customs may, by notice in writing, require the importer either personally or by his agent to submit such declaration within 3 days of the receipt of such notice, and the importer shall be required to comply with such notice if it is within his power to do so:

Provided that in the case of goods imported by land such declaration shall be made on arrival at the inland customs station on the prescribed route within such time after arrival in Brunei Darussalam of such goods as may be prescribed.

(2) Every importer of dutiable goods exempted from being warehoused under the provisions of subsection (1) of section 59 shall, upon arrival of such goods at a place of import, make personally or by his agent to the proper officer of customs at such place of import, a declaration, in such manner or in such form as may be prescribed, of the goods imported, and shall pay the duties and other charges leviable thereon.

(3) The addressee of any dutiable goods imported by post shall, on demand by the proper officer of customs, make personally or by his agent to such officer a declaration, substantially in the prescribed form, of the goods imported.

72. (1) The declaration referred to in section 71 shall give a full and true account of the number and description of packages and of the description, weight, measure or quantity, and value of all such dutiable goods, and of the country of origin of such goods:

Provided that if it is shown to the satisfaction of the proper officer of customs that such goods are urgently required for home consumption and that it is not within the power of the importer to furnish all the details required, such officer may, at his discretion, release the goods on payment of such duty as he may estimate to be leviable thereon, together with a deposit of such amount as such officer may determine not exceeding such estimated duty and on an undertaking being given by the importer or his agent to furnish a correct declaration within 2 months or such further period as the proper officer of customs may allow.

(2) On the submission of a correct declaration the proper amount of duty and otehr charges leviable shall be assessed and any money paid and deposited in excess of such amount shall be returned to the importer or his agent and in default of such submission within the aforesaid period the deposit shall be forfeited and paid into the general revenue of Brunei Darussalam.

73. (1) Every exporter of dutiable goods shall —

(a) personally or by his agent make a declaration in the prescribed form, of the goods to be exported. Such declaration shall be made to the proper officer of customs specified in subsection (2);

(b) produced such goods to such proper officer of customs; and

(c) pay the export duty and any other charges leviable thereon to such proper officer of customs:

Provided that, the Controller may permit the export of any goods without prior payment of duty —

(a) if it is shown to his satisfaction that unnecessary delay will be occasioned in ascertaining the net weight of the goods before the export thereof is permitted; and

(b) if security has been given to his satisfaction for the payment of duty within such time as he may determine.

(2) The declaration referred to in paragraph *(a)* of subsection (1) shall be made at the time and to the officer of customs hereunder specified, that is to say —

(a) if export is to be by sea, before such goods are shipped, or water-borne to be shipped, to the proper officer of customs at the customs port of shipment;

(b) if goods are exported by land, before export, to the proper officer of customs at the inland customs station on the prescribed route; or

(c) if goods are to be exported by air, before export, to the proper officer of customs at the customs airport.

(3) The declaration referred to in paragraph *(a)* of subsection (1) shall give a full and true account of the number and description of packages and of the description, weight, measure or quantity, and value of all such dutiable goods, and the country of origin of such goods.

B — Non-dutiable goods

74. (1) When any goods which are not dutiable on import are imported by sea or air, the importer thereof shall, before taking delivery of such goods and in any case not later than 10 days after the arrival of the vessel or aircraft in which such goods are imported, make personally or by his agent to the proper officer of customs at the customs port at which such goods are landed, or at the customs airport at which such goods are imported, a declaration substantially in the prescribed form, giving particular of the goods imported.

(2) No owner, master or agent of any vessel, and no pilot or agent of any aircraft arriving at any customs port or airport shall deliver any inward cargo consisting of goods which are not dutiable until he has been authorised to do so by the proper officer of customs to whom the declaration referred to in subsection (1) has been made.

When any goods which are not dutiable on import are imported by land, the importer thereof shall within 48 hours of the arrival of such goods at the inland customs station on the prescribed route make personally or by his agent to the proper officer of customs at the such inland customs station a written or verbal declaration substantially in the prescribed form, giving particulars of the goods imported, and shall not proceed till this has been done.

(1) When any goods which are not dutiable on export are exported by sea or air the exporter thereof shall, before such goods are shipped or waterborne to be shipped or loaded into aircraft, make personally or by his agent to the proper officer of customs at the customs port at which such goods are to be shipped or at the customs airport at which such goods are to be loaded, a declaration substantially in the prescribed form, giving particulars of the goods to be exported.

(2) No owner, master or agent of any vessel, and no pilot or agent of any aircraft shall allow any goods which are not dutiable on export to be shipped or loaded until he has been authorised by the proper officer of customs to do so.

When any goods which are not dutiable on export are exported by land, the exporter thereof shall make personally or by his agent to the proper officer of customs at the inland customs station on the prescribed route a declaration, substantially in the prescribed form, giving particulars of the goods to be exported, and shall not proceed till this has been done.

The declarations referred to in section 74, 75, 76 and 77 shall give a full and true account of the particulars for which provision is made in the respective prescribed forms:

Provided that, if, in the case of imported goods, any of the particulars required be unknown to the importer thereof, delivery of such goods may be given on a written undertaking of the importer or his agent to furnish the necessary information to the proper officer of customs, within 10 days of such undertaking or such further period as the proper officer of customs may allow and if the importer or his agent fails to furnish the information as required by the undertaking he shall be deemed to have failed to make the required declaration.

C — General Provision

79. The provisions of this Part shall not apply—

(a) to accompanies passengers' baggage or personal effects;

(b) to fresh fish locally taken; and

(c) except as provided by subsection (3) of section 71, to any goods sent by post.

Nothing in this Part contained shall release any person from any obligation imposed by or under any written law for the time being in force in Brunei Darussalam regulating the movement of any special goods or currency.

(1) No person shall act as agent for transacting business relating to the import or export of any goods or luggage or the entry or clearance of any vessel, except with the permission of a senior officer of customs.

(2) When any person applies to a senior officer of customs for permission to act as agent on behalf of another person, such officer may require the applicant to produce a written authority from the person on whose behalf he is to act and in default of the production of such authority such officer may refuse such permission.

(3) Before granting such permission, a senior officer of customs may require such agent to give such security as he may consider adequate for the faithful and incorrupt conduct of such agent and of his clerks acting for him both as regards the customs and his employers.

(4) A senior officer of customs may suspend or cancel any permission granted under this section, if the agent commits any breach of this Act or of any regulation made hereunder or if he fails to comply with any direction given by an officer of customs with regard to the business transacted by the agent.

(5) Any person aggrieved by the decision of a senior officer of customs in respect of any of the following matters, that is to say —

(a) refusal to grant permission;

(b) the nature or the amount of security required from the agent;

(c) suspension or cancellation of the permission, may, within one month from the date on which the decision is notified to him, appeal to the Controller, whose decision shall be final.

(6) Any person who acts as agent when permission has not been granted to him under this section or while such permission is cancelled or suspended, or who makes or causes to be made a declaration of any goods without being duly authorised for that purpose by the proprietor or consignee of such goods shall be guilty of an offence: Penalty, a fine of $4,000.

(7) The clerk or servant of any person or firm who deposits with a senior officer of customs a signed authority authorising him so to do may transact business generally at any customs office on behalf of such person or firm:

Provided that a senior officer of customs may refuse to transact business with such clerk or servant unless such person or a member of such firm identifies such clerk or servant to such officer as empowered to transact such business.

Notwithstanding anything contained in section 81 the person in charge of any goods imported or exported by land, who makes the declaration required by this Part shall be deemed to be the agent of the importer or exporter, as the case may be.

Every declaration required to be made under this Act shall be in duplicate or in such other number of copies, as the person, to whom such declaration is required to be made, may direct.

PART X DRAWBACK

84. (1) When any goods, other than goods affected by section 86, upon which import duty has been paid are reexported, nine-tenths of the duties calculated in accordance with the provisions of subsection (2) may be repaid as drawback, if —

(a) the goods are identified to the satisfaction of a senior officer of customs at the customs port or customs airport at which such goods are shipped or loaded for reexport, or at the place of re-export;

(b) the drawback claimed in respect of any one consignment of re-exported goods is not less than $100;

(c) the goods are re-exported within 12 months of the date upon which the duty was paid;

(d) payment of drawback upon goods of a class to which the goods to be re-exported belong has not been prohibited by regulations made under this Act;

(e) written notice has been given to a senior officer of customs at or before the time of re-export that a claim for drawback will be made, and such claim is made and established to the satisfaction of a senior officer of customs within 3 months of the date of reexport; and

(f) except as provided by section 87, the goods have not been used after importation.

(2) The amount of drawback allowed shall be calculated at the rate of the customs duty levied at the time of import.

Every person claiming drawback on any goods reexported shall, personally or by his agent, make to a senior officer of customs a declaration, substantially in the prescribed form, that such goods have actually been re-exported and have not been relanded and are not intended to be relanded at any customs port, customs airport or place in Brunei Darussalam or within any port of Brunei Darussalam, where goods of a like description are liable to import duty.

The Controller may, at his discretion, allow drawback of import duty on goods which suffer deterioration or damage and are destroyed in the presence of a senior officer of customs, if the conditions set out in section 84 in respect of re-exported goods are fulfilled in respect of such destroyed goods, and the provision of section 84 and 85 shall, with such modifications as the circumstances of the case may require, apply to such destroyed goods.

When any personal effects or other goods which have been imported by visitors to Brunei Darussalam for their personal use, or samples imported by commercial travellers, or trade samples or such other goods as may be prescribed, on which import customs duty has been paid are re-exported within 3 months from the date of importation or within such further period as the Controller may, either generally or in any special case allow, the Controller may allow a drawback of such import duty.

The Controller may, in any case, at his discretion and subject to such restriction as he may deem fit to impose, allow any goods, which on the exportation thereof have been declared as trade samples, to be re-imported free of duty.

Where any goods are prescribed to be goods in respect of which drawback may be allowed on re-export as part or ingredient of any goods manufactured in Brunei Darussalam and such prescribed goods are so re-exported by the manufacturer as part or ingredient of any goods manufactured in Brunei Darussalam, then, if import duty has been paid on such prescribed goods the Controller may, on such re-export, allow to the manufacturer a drawback of the duty so paid at such rates as may be prescribed, if —

(a) the goods exported have been manufactured on premises approved by the Controller;

(b) provision to the satisfaction of the Controller has been made for the control and supervision on such premises of the deposit and issue for use of the prescribed goods;

(c) such books of account are kept as the Controller may require for the purpose of ascertaining the quantity of the prescribed goods used in such manufacture;

(d) such prescribed goods have been imported by the manufacturer; and

(e) such prescribed goods are re-exported within 12 months of the date upon which import duty was paid.

PART XI MISCELLANEOUS

On demand of the proper officer of customs the importer or exporter of any goods or his agent shall produce to such officer all invoices, bill of landing, certificates of origin or of analysis and any other documents, which such officer may require to test the accuracy of any declaration made by such importer or exporter to any officer of customs.

Every person required by the officer of customs to give information on any subject into which it is such officer's duty to enquire under this Act and which it is in such person's power to give shall be legally bound to give such information.

Every notice or document, required by this Act or by any regulation made hereunder, to be served on any person may be served personally upon such person or may be served by sending such notice or document to him by registered post at his usual or last known place of abode, and in the latter case shall, except for the notice referred to in subsection (4) of section 67, be deemed to have been served on him at the time at which it would have been delivered to him in the ordinary course of the post.

(1) Notwithstanding anything in this Act contained, every passenger or other person arriving in or leaving Brunei Darussalam shall declare all dutiable or prohibited goods in his possession, either on his person or in any baggage or in any vehicle, to the proper officer of customs, and if he fails so to do such goods shall be deemed to be uncustomed goods.

The proper officer of customs may take samples.

Packing of dutiable goods.

Addition or deduction of new or altered import duties in the case of contract.

(2) The baggage of passengers may be examined and delivered in such manner as the Controller may direct, and it shall be the duty of the person in charge of such baggage to produce, open, unpack and repack such baggage.

94. (1) The proper officer of customs may at any time, if his duty requires, take samples of any goods to ascertain whether they are goods of a description liable to any customs duty, or to ascertain the customs duty payable on such goods or for such other purposes as the proper officer of customs may deem necessary, and such samples may be disposed of in such manner as the Controller shall direct.

(2) No payment shall be made for the cost of any sample taken but the proper officer of customs shall, on demand, give a receipt for any such sample.

No dutiable goods shall be packed in any manner calculated to deceive an officer of customs so that a proper account of such goods may not be taken.

(1) Where any new import duty is imposed or where any such duty is increased. and any goods in respect of which the duty is payable are delivered after the day on which the new or increased duty takes effect, in pursuance of a contract made before that day, the seller of the goods may, in the absence of agreement to the contrary, recover from the purchaser of the goods as an addition to the contract price, a sum equal to any amount paid by him in respect of the goods on account of the new duty or increase of duty, as the case may be.

(2) Where any import duty is cancelled or decreased and any goods affected by the duty are delivered after the day on which the duty is cancelled or the decrease in the duty takes effect, in pursuance of a contract made before that day, the purchaser of the goods, in the absence of agreement to the contrary, may if the seller of the goods has had in respect of those goods the benefit of the cancellation or decrease of the duty, deduct from the contract price a sum equal to the amount of the duty or decrease of duty, as the case may be.

PART XII SEARCH, SEIZURE AND ARREST

97. (1) Whenever it appears to any magistrate, upon written information upon oath, and after any enquiry which he may think necessary, that there is reasonable cause to believe that in any dwelling house, shop, or other building or place, there are concealed or deposited any prohibited or uncustomed goods or goods liable to forfeiture under this Act or under any regulation made hereunder, or as to which any offence under this Act or such regulation has been committed, or any books or documents relating to any such goods such magistrate may issue a warrant authorising any officer of customs named therein, by day or night and with or without assistance—

(a) to enter such dwelling-house, shop, or other building or place and there to search for and seize and goods reasonably suspected of being prohibited or uncustomed goods, or goods liable to forfeiture under this Act or any regulation made hereunder, or as to which any offence under this Act or such regulation is suspended to have been committed, and any books or documents which may reasonably be believed to contain information as to any offence under this Act or any regulation made thereunder.

(b) to arrest any person or persons being in such dwelling-house, shop, building or place, in whose possession such goods as aforesaid may be found, or whom such officer may reasonably suspect to have concealed or deposited such goods.

(2) Such officer may if it is necessary so to do—

(a) break open any outer or inner door of such dwelling-house, shop, or other building or place and enter thereunto;

(b) forcibly entry such place and every part thereof;

(c) remove by force any obstruction to such entry, search, seizure and removal as he is empowered to effect;

(d) detain every person found in such place until such place has been searched.

Whenever it appears to any senior officer of customs that there is reasonable cause to belief that in dwelling-house, shop, or other building or place there are concealed or deposited any prohibited or uncustomed goods or goods liable to forfeiture under this Act or any regulation made thereunder or as to which an offence under this Act or such regulation has been committed, and if he has reasonable grounds for believing that by reason of the delay in obtaining a search warrant such goods are likely to be removed, such officer may exercise in, upon and in respect of such dwelling-house, shop, or other building or place all the powers mentioned in section 97 in as full and ample a manner as if he were authorised so to do by a warrant issued under that section.

(1) A proper officer of customs may —

(a) go on board any vessel or aircraft in any customs port or customs airport or place or within territorial waters;

(b) require the master of such vessel or the pilot of such aircraft to give such information relating to the vessel or aircraft, cargo, stores, crew, passengers or voyage as he may deem necessary;

(c) rummage and search all parts of such vessel or aircraft for prohibited or uncustomed goods;

(d) examine all goods on board and all goods then being loaded or unloaded;

(e) demand all documents which ought to be on board such vessel or aircraft; and

(f) require all or any such documents to be brought to him for inspection;

and the master of any vessel and the pilot of any aircraft refusing to allow such officer to board or search such vessel or aircraft, or refusing to give such information or to produce such documents on demand shall be guilty of an offence against this Act.

(2) If any place, box or chest on board such vessel or aircraft is locked and the key withheld, such officer may break open any such place, box or chest.

(3) If any goods be found concealed on board any vessel or aircraft, they shall be deemed to be uncustomed goods.

Every senior officer of customs shall be entitled to exercise in and upon and in respect of any vessel, aircraft, landing place or wharf all the powers mentioned in section 97 in as full and ample a manner as if he were authorised so to do by a warrant issued under that section.

(1) The person in charge or in control of any vehicle arriving at a prescribed place of import and export shall, on arrival at such place, produce his vehicle to the proper officer of customs, and shall, if so required, move his vehicle to another place for examination, and shall not proceed until permission to do so has been given by the proper officer of customs.

(2) Any officer of customs may stop and examine any vehicle for the purpose of ascertaining whether any uncustomed or prohibited goods are contained therein, and the person in control or in charge of such vehicle shall, if required so to do by such officer, stop such vehicle and allow such officer to examine the same.

102. Any proper officer of customs may examine any goods in the course of being imported or exported or intended to be imported or exported and may for the purposes of such examination bring the same to a customs office and may open any package or receptacle.

103. Any person landing, or being about to land, or having persons arriving in recently landed, from any vessel or aircraft, or leaving any Brunei vessel or aircraft in territorial waters, whether for the purpose of landing or otherwise, or entering or having recently entered Brunei Darussalam by land shall, on demand by any proper officer of customs either permit has person, goods and baggage to be searched by such officer, or together with such goods and baggage accompany such officer to a customs office of police station and there permit his person, goods and baggage to be searched by an officer of customs:

Provided that —

(a) any person who requests that his person be searched in the presence of a senior officer of customs shall not be searched except in the presence of and under the supervision of such officer, but such person may be detained until the arrival of such officer, or taken to any customs office or police station where such officer may be found;

(b) the goods and baggage of any person who requests to be present when they are searched and so present himself within a reasonable time shall not be searched except in his presence;

(c) no female shall be searched except by a female.

104. (1) All goods in respect of which there has been, or subject of an there is, reasonable cause to suspect that there has been offence. committed any offence against this Act or any regulation made hereunder, or any breach of any of the provisions of this Act or of any regulation made hereunder or of any restriction or condition subject to or upon which any licence or permit has been granted, together with any receptacle, package, conveyance, vessel not exceeding 200 tons nett registered tonnage, or aircraft, in which the same may have been found or which has been used in connection with such offence or breach, and any books or documents which may reasonably be believed to have a bearing on the case, may be seized by any officer of customs in any place either on land or in territorial waters.

(2) All such goods and such receptacles, packages, conveyances, vessels or aircraft shall, as soon as conveniently may be, be delivered into the care of a proper officer of customs whose duty it is to receive the same.

(3) Whenever any goods, conveyances, vessels or aircraft are seized under this Act, the seizing officer shall forthwith give notice in writing of such seizure and the grounds thereof to the owner of such goods, if known, either by either by delivering such notice to him personally or by post at his place of abode; if known:

Provided that such notice shall not be required to be given where such seizure is made on the person, or in the presence of the offender or the owner or his agent, or in the case of a vessel or an aircraft, in the presence of the master or pilot, as the case may be.

(4) The provisions of this section relating to the seizure of goods shall apply to all the contents of any package or receptacle in which the same are found and to any article used to conceal the same.

(5) The provisions of this section relating to the seizure of any vessel or aircraft shall apply also to the tackle, equipment and furnishing of such vessel or aircraft.

(6) The provisions of this section relating to the seizure of conveyances shall apply to all equipment thereof and to any animal by which the same is drawn.

(7) Any goods of a perishable nature or any animal seized under the provisions of this section may be sold forthwith and the proceeds of sale held to abide the result of any prosecution or claim.

105. When any conveyance, vessel or aircraft has been seized under this Act, a senior officer of customs may, at his discretion, temporarily return such conveyance, vessel or aircraft to the owner of the same on security being furnished to the satisfaction of such officer that the conveyance, vessel or aircraft shall be surrendered to him on demand.

Powers of **106.** (1) Any officer of customs may arrest without warrant —

(a) any person found committing or attempting to commit, or employing or aiding any person to commit, or abetting the commission of, an offence against this Act or any regulation made hereunder;

(b) any person whom he may reasonably suspect to have in his possession any uncustomed or prohibited goods or any goods liable to seizure under this Act;

(c) any person against whom a reasonable suspicion exists that he has been guilty of an offence against this Act or any regulation made hereunder, and may search or cause to be searched, any person so arrested:

Provided that no female shall be searched except by a female.

(2) Every person so arrested shall be taken to a police station.

(3) If any person liable to arrest under this Act is not arrested at the time of committing the offence for which he is so liable, or after arrest makes his escape, he may at any time afterwards be arrested and be dealt with as if he had been arrested at the time of committing such offence.

PART XIII PROVISIONS AS TO TRIALS AND PROCEEDINGS

Who may **107.** Prosecutions in respect of offences committed under this Act or any regulation made hereunder may be conducted by a senior officer of customs specially authorised in writing in that behalf by the Controller.

Notwithstanding the provisions of any written law to the contrary, a Court of a Magistrate shall have jurisdiction to try any offence under this Act and to award the full punishment for any offence.

If in any prosecution in respect of any good seized for non-payment of duties or for any other cause of forfeiture or for the recovery of any penalty or penalties or for the condemnation or forfeiture of any vessels or goods or for any offence under this Act, any dispute arises whether the customs duties have been paid in respect of such goods, or whether the same have been lawfully imported or exported or lawfully landed or loaded, or concerning the place whence such goods were brought or where such goods were loaded, then and in every such case the burden of proof thereof shall lie on the defendant in such prosecution.

When any goods suspended of being prohibited or uncustomed or otherwise liable to seizure have been seized, it shall be sufficient to open, examine, and if necessary test the contents of 10 per centum only of each description of package or receptacle in which such goods are contained and the Court shall presume that the goods contained in the unopened packages or receptacles are of the same nature, quantity and quality as those found in the similar packages or receptacles which have been opened.

(1) In any prosecution for a breach of a provision of this Act or of any regulation made hereunder, a certificate of analysis purporting to be under the hand of an analyst shall, on

production thereof by the prosecutor, be sufficient evidence of the facts stated therein unless the defendant requires that the analyst be called as a witness, in which case he shall give notice thereof to the prosecutor not less than 7 clear day before the day on which the summons is returnable.

(2) In like manner a certificate of analysis purporting to be under the hand of an analyst shall, on production thereof by the defendant, be sufficient evidence of the facts stated therein, unless the prosecutor requires that the analyst be called as a witness.

Court of a Magistrate to have full jurisdiction.
Burden of proof.
Proportional examination or testing of goods seized to be accepted by courts.
Evidence of analysis may be given in writing.
Proof as to registration or licensing of vessels in Brunei Darussalam.

(3) A copy of the certificate referred to in subsection

(1)or (2) shall be sent to the defendant or the prosecutor as the case may be at least 7 clear days before the day fixed for the hearing, and if it is not so sent the Court may adjourn the hearing on such terms as it may think proper.

(4) Analysts are by this Act bound to state the truth in certificates of analysis under their hands.

(5) In this section the word “analyst” includes —

(a) any person employed for the time being wholly or partly on analytical work in any department of the Government;

(b) any chemist employed by the Governments of Brunei Darussalam, Malaysia and Singapore: Provided that no such chemist shall, without his consent, be called as a witness in connection with any report signed by him;

(c) any other person to whom this section may be declared by the Minister, by notification in the *Gazette*, to apply.

(6) If an analyst is called by the defendant as provided by subsection (1), he shall be called at the expense of the defendant unless the Court otherwise directs.

(7) If in any trial or proceeding under this Act it is necessary to determine the alcoholic content of any liquor, the certificate of a senior officer of customs as to such alcoholic contents shall be accepted as if such officer were an analyst and in any such case the provisions of subsections (1), (4) and (6) shall apply in the same manner and to the same extent as if such officer were an analyst.

112. Where in any prosecution under this Act it is relevant to ascertain particulars as to the registration or licensing of any vessels registered or licensed in any port of Brunei Darussalam, a certificate purporting to be signed by the officer responsible under any written law for the time being in force in Brunei Darussalam for such registration or licensing shall be *prima facie* evidence as to all particulars cencerning such registration or licensing contained therein, and the burden of proving the incorrectness of any particular stated in such certificate shall be on the person denying the same.

113. Notwithstanding the provisions of the Criminal Procedure Code the period of imprisonment imposed by any Court in respect of the non-payment of any fine under this Act, or in respect of the default of a sufficient distress to satisfy any such fine, shall be such period as in the opinion of the Court will satisfy the justice of the case, but shall not exceed in any case the maximum fixed by the followed scale:

Where the fine The period may extend to
does not exceed $100 2 months
exceeds $100 but does not exceed $1,000 4 months
exceeds $1,000 but does not exceed $5,000 6 months
with 2 additional months for every $1,000 after the first $5,000 of the fine until a maximum period of 3 years is reached.

On any trial before any Court and in any proceeding on appeal to any Superior Court, relating to the seizure of goods subject to forfeiture under this Act, the Court shall proceed to such trial or hear such appeal on the merits of the case only, without enquiring into the manner or form of making any seizure, except insofar as the manner and form of seizure may be evidence on such merits.

(1) Except as hereinafter provided, no witness in any civil or criminal proceeding shall be obliged or permitted to disclose the name or address of an informer or the substance of the information received from him or to state any matter which might lead to his discovery.

Imprisonment for non payment of fine.
Manner of seizure no to be enquired into on trial or on appeal.
Protection of informers from discovery.
Goods liable to seizure liable to forfeiture.
Court to order disposal of goods seized.

Goods seized in respect of which there is no prosecution, deemed to be forfeited if not claimed within one month.

(2) If any books, documents or papers which are in evidence or liable to inspection in any civil or criminal proceeding whatsoever contain any entry in which any informer is named or described or which might lead to his discovery, the Court shall cause all such passages to be concealed from view or to be obliterated so far only as may be necessary to protect the informer from discovery.

(3) If on the trial for any offence against this Act or any regulation made thereunder the Court after full enquiry into the case believes that the informer wilfully made in his complaint a material statement which he knew or believed to be false or did not believe to be true, or if in any other proceeding the Court is of opinion that justice cannot be fully done between the parties thereto without the discovery of the informer, it shall be lawful for the Court to require the production of the original complaint, if in writing, and permit enquiry, and require full disclosure, concerning the informer.

All goods liable to seizure under the provision of this Act shall be liable to forfeiture.

Any order for the forfeiture or for the release of anything liable to forfeiture under the provisions of this Act shall be made by the Court before which the prosecution with regard thereto has been held, and an order for the forfeiture of goods shall be made if it is proved to the satisfaction of the Court that an offence against this Act or any regulation made thereunder had been committed and that the goods were the subject matter of or were used in the commission of the offence notwithstanding that no person may have been convicted of such offence.

(1) If there be no prosecution with regard to any goods seized under this Act such goods shall be taken and deemed to be forfeited at the expiration of one calendar month from the date of seizure unless a claim thereto is made before that date in the manner hereinafter set forth.

(2) Any person asserting that he is the owner of such goods and that they are not liable to forfeiture may personally or by his agent authorised in writing give written notice to a senior officer of customs that he claims the same.

(3) On receipt of such notice the senior officer of customs shall refer the claim to the Controller who may direct that such goods be released or may direct such senior officer of customs, by information in the prescribed form, to refer the matter to a Magistrate for his decision.

(4) The Magistrate shall issue a summons requiring the person asserting that he is the owner of the goods and the person from whom they were seized to appear before him, and upon their appearance or default to appear, due service of such summons being proved, the Magistrate shall proceed to the examination of the matter and on proof that an offence against this Act or any regulation made hereunder has been committed and that such goods were the subject matter, or were used in the commission, of such offence shall order the same to be forfeited, or may in the absence of such proof order their release.

(5) In any proceedings under subsection (4) the provisions of section 109 shall apply to the person asserting that he is the owner o f the goods and to the person from whom they were seized as if such owner or person had been the defendant in a prosecution under this Act.

The Minister may order any goods seized under this Act, whether forfeited or not, to be delivered to the owner or other person entitled thereto, upon such terms and conditions as he may deem fit.

Nothing in this Act contained shall be deemed to prevent the prosecution, conviction and punishment of any person according to the provisions of any other written law for the time being in force in Brunei Darussalam, but so that no person shall be punished more than once for the same offence.

(1) Any senior officer of customs may compound any offence, which is prescribed to be a compoundable offence, by accepting from the person reasonably suspected of having committed such offence a sum of money not exceeding $500.

Goods seized may be delivered to owner or other person.
Conviction under other law.
Compounding of offences.

Power of senior officer of customs to purchase goods in certain cases.

(2) In like manner the proper officer of customs, not being a senior officer of customs, may compound any offence which is prescribed to be compoundable by such officer, by accepting from the person reasonably suspected of having committed such offence a sum of money not exceeding $20.

(3) On the payment of such sum of money the person reasonably suspected of having committed an offence, if us custody shall be discharged, any properties seized shall be released and without prejudice to civil proceedings for the recovery of any duty which has not been paid not further proceedings shall be taken against such person or property in respect of such offence.

122. (1) Notwithstanding any provisions in this Act or in any regulations made hereunder relating to penalties which may be imposed for any offence committed, if, upon the examination of any imported goods which are chargeable with duty upon the value thereof, it appears to a senior officer of customs that the value of such goods as declared by the importer and according to which duty has been or is sought to be paid is not the value thereof, if shall be lawful for the senior officer of customs to detain the same, in which case he shall —

(a) give notice in writing to the importer of the detention of such goods, and

(b) within 15 days after the detention of such goods, determine and give notice in writing to the importer either that the value of the goods was correctly declared by the importer and permit the same to be delivered, or that such goods shall be retained for the public use of Brunei Darussalam, in which latter case he shall cause the value at which the goods were declared by the importer, together with an addition of 10 per centum, and the duties already paid to be paid to the importer in full satisfaction of such goods; or he may permit such person to declare the goods according to such value and on such terms as he may direct.

(2) Such goods, if retained, shall be disposed of for the benefit of Brunei Darussalam, and if the proceeds arising therefrom, in case of sale, exceed the sums so paid, and all charges incurred by Brunei Darussalam, such surplus shall be disposed of as the Minister may direct.

123. No person shall in any proceedings before any Court in respect of the seizure of any goods seized in exercise or the purported exercise of any power conferred under this Act, be entitled to the costs of such proceedings or to any damages or other relief other than an order for the return of such goods or the payment of their value unless such seizure was made without reasonable or probable cause.

PART XIV OFFENCES AND PENALTIES

124. (1) Whoever —

(a) makes, orally or in writing, or signs any declaration, certificate or other document required under this Act which is untrue or incorrect in any particular;

(b) makes, orally or in writing, or signs any declaration or document, made for consideration of any officer of customs on any application presented to him, which is untrue or incorrect in any particular;

(c) counterfeits or falsifies, or uses, when counterfeited or falsified, any document which is or may be required under this Act or any document used in the transaction of any business or matter relating to customs;

(d) fraudulently alters any documents, or counterfeits the seal, signature, initials or other mark of, or used by, any officer of customs for the verification of any such document on for the security of any goods or any other purpose in the conduct of business relating to customs;

No costs or damages arising from seizure to be recoverable unless seizure without reasonable or probable cause.

Penalty on making incorrect declarations and on falsifying documents.
Penalty on refusing to answer questions or on giving false information.
Penalty for various smuggling offences.

(e) being required under this Act to make a declaration of dutiable goods imported or exported, fails to make such declaration as required; or

(f) fails or refuses to produce to a proper officer of customs any document required to be produced under the provisions of sections 90, shall be guilty of an offence: Penalty, imprisonment for 12 months and a fine of $40,000.

(2) When any such declaration, whether oral or written, or any such certificate or other document as is referred to in paragraphs *(a)*, *(b)* and *(c)* of subsections (1) has been proved to be untrue or incorrect or counterfeited or falsified in whole or in part, it shall be no defence to allege that such declaration, certificate or other document was made or used inadvertently or without criminal or fraudulent intent, or that the person signing the same, was not aware of, or did not understand the contents of, such document, or where any declaration was made or recorded in English or Malay by interpretation from any other language, that such declaration was misinterpreted or not fully interpreted by any interpreter provided by the declarant.

125. (1) Whoever, being required under this Act to give any information which may reasonably be required by a proper officer of customs and which it is in his power to give, refuses to give such information or furnishes as true information which he knows or has reason to believe to be false, shall be guilty of an offence: Penalty, imprisonment for 6 months and a fine of $8,000.

(2) When any such information is proved to be untrue or incorrect in whole or in part it shall be no defence to allege that such information or any part thereof was furnished inadvertently or without criminal or fraudulent intent, or was misinterpreted or not fully interpreted by an interpreter provided by in the informant.

126. (1) Whoever —

(a) is concerned in importing or exporting any uncustomed goods or any prohibited goods contrary to such prohibition whether such uncustomed or prohibited goods be shipped, unshipped, delivered or not;

(b) ship, unships, delivers or assists or is concerned in the shipping, unshipping or delivery of any uncustomed goods or any prohibited goods contrary to such prohibition;

(c) illegally removes or withdraws or in any way assists or is concerned in the illegal removal or withdrawal of any goods from any control;

(d) knowingly harbours, keeps, conceals, or is in possession of, or permits, suffers, causes or procures to be harboured, kept or concealed, any uncustomed or prohibited goods;

(e) is in any way knowingly concerned in conveying, removing, depositing or dealing with any uncustomed or prohibited goods with intent to defraud the Government of any duties thereon, or to evade any of the provisions of this Act or to evade any prohibition applicable to such goods;

(f) being a passenger or other person, is found to have in his baggage or upon his person or otherwise in his possession, after having denied that he has any dutiable or prohibited goods in his baggage or upon his person or otherwise in his possession, any dutiable or prohibited goods; or

(g) is in any way knowingly concerned in any faudulent evasion or attempt at fraudulent evasion of any customs duty, or in evasion or attempt at evasion of any prohibition of import or export, shall be guilty of an offence: Penalty —

(i) in the case of uncustomed goods, such goods being dutiable goods, be liable for the first offence to a fine of not less than 6 times the amount of the duty or $40,000, whichever is the lesser amount, and of not more than 20 times the amount of duty or $40,000 whichever is the greater amount and for the second or any subsequent offence to imprisonment for a term of 2 years:

Provided that when the amount of duty cannot be ascertained the penalty may amount to a fine of $40,000;

(ii) in the case of uncustomed goods, such goods not being dutiable or prohibited, be liable to a fine of twice the value of the goods or $8,000 whichever is the greater amount:

Provided that where the value cannot be ascertained the penalty may amount to a fine of $8,000;

(iii) in the case of prohibited goods, be liable to a fine of not less than twice the value of the goods or $40,000, whichever is the lesser amount and of not more than 5 times the value of the goods or $40,000 whichever is the greater amount:

Provided that where the value of the goods cannot be ascertained the penalty may amount to a fine of $40,000.

(2) In any prosecution under this section or section 130 any uncustomed or prohibited goods shall be deemed to be uncustomed or prohibited goods, as the case may be, to the knowledge of the defendant unless the contrary be proved by such defendant.

127. Every person who — Penalty for assaulting or obstructing

(a) assaults or obstructs any officer of customs or officers of customs and other public servant or any person acting in his aid or rescuing assistance, or duly employed for the prevention of goods. smuggling, in the execution of his duty or in the due seizing of any goods liable to seizure under this Act;

(b) rescues or endeavours to rescue, or causes to be rescued, any goods which have been duly seized; or

(c) before or after any seizures staves, breaks or otherwise destroys any package or goods to prevent the seizure thereof or the securing of the same, shall be guilty of an offence against this Act:

Penalty —

(i) for a first offence, imprisonment for 9 months and a fine of $16,000; and

(ii) for the second or subsequent office imprisonment for 18 months, and a fine of $40,000.

128. (1) If any officer of customs or other person duly Penalty for offering or employed for the prevention of smuggling — receiving bribes.

(a) makes any collusive seizure or delivers up or makes any agreement to deliver up or not to seize any vessel or aircraft or other means of conveyance, or any goods liable to seizure;

(b) accepts, agrees to accept, or attempts to obtain, any bribe, gratuity, recompense or reward for the neglect or non-performance of his duty; or

(c) conspires or connives with any person to import or export or is in any way concerned in the importation or exportation of any goods liable to customs duties or any goods prohibited to be imported or exported for the purpose of seizing any vessel, aircraft or conveyance or any goods and obtaining any reward for such seizure or otherwise, every such officer so offending shall be guilty of an offence against this Act: Penalty, imprisonment for 3 years and a fine of $40,000, and every person who gives or offers or promises to give or procures to be given any bribe, gratuity, recompense or reward to, or makes any collusive agreement with, any such officer of person as aforesaid to induce him in any way to neglect his duty or to do, conceal or connive at any act whereby any of the provisions of any other law relating to imports or to exports may be evaded, shall be guilty as an abettor and so punishable under this Act.

(2) Any officer of customs who is found when on duty to have in his possession any moneys in contravention of any departmental regulation issued in writing shall be presumed, until the contrary is proved, to have received the same in contravention of paragraph *(b)* of subsection (1).

(3) If an officer of customs has reasonable suspicion that another officer of customs junior in rank to him has in his possession any money received in contravention of paragraph

*(b)*of subsection (1) he may search such other officer.

Every omission or neglect to comply with, and every act done or attempted to be done contrary to, the provisions of this Act, or any breach of the conditions and restrictions subject to, or upon which, any licence or permit is issued under this Act, shall be an offence against this Act and in respect of any such offence for which no penalty is expressly provided the offender shall be liable to a fine of $16,000.

Whoever attempts to commit any offence punishable under this Act, or abets the commission of such offence, shall be punished with the punishment provided for such offence.

(1) Where an offence against this Act or any regulation made hereunder has been committed by a company, firm, society or other body or persons, any person who at the time of the commission of the offence was director, manager, secretary or other similar officer or a partner of the company, firm, society or other body of persons or was purporting to act in such capacity shall be deemed to be guilty of that offence unless he proves that the offence was committed without his consent or connivance and that he exercised all such diligence to prevent the commission of the offence as he ought to have exercised, having regard to the nature of his functions in that capacity and to all the circumstances.

(2) Where any person would be liable under this Act to any punishment, penalty or forfeiture for any act, omission, neglect or default he shall be liable to the same punishment, penalty or

forfeiture for every such act, omission, neglect or default of any clerk, servant or agent, or of the clerk or servant of such agent provided that such act, omission, neglect or default was committed by such clerk, or servant in the course of his employment or by such agent when acting on behalf of such person or by the clerk or servant of such agent when acting in the course of his employment in such circumstances that had such act, omission, neglect or default been committed by the agent his principal would have been liable under this section.

132. The Controller may order such rewards as he may deem Rewards. fit to be paid to any officer or other person for services rendered [S 23/89] or expenses incurred in connection with the detection of cases of smuggling or of offences under this Act, or in connection with any seizures made under this Act.

PART XV GENERAL

133. Minister of Finance with the approval of His Majesty the Power to make Sultan and Yang Di-Pertuan may make regulations to provide for —

(1) the powers and duties to be exercise and performed by officers of customs.

(2) the conditions subject to which goods may be imported under the preferential tariff.

(3) the fees to be paid by the masters or agents of vessels or by pilots of aircraft or agents of aircraft or by the persons in charge of vehicles or by the importers or exporters of goods or their agents in respect of the services of officers of customs rendered on request beyond the ordinary hours prescribed and the conditions under which such services may be rendered.

(4) the amount to be paid as warehouse rent on goods deposited in warehouses other than the Ports Department, customs or licensed warehouses.

(5) the fees, if any, to be paid for permits and licences, other than warehouse licences.

(6) frontier areas and for regulating or prohibiting, either absolutely or conditionally, the movement of goods or persons within such areas for the purposes of this Act.

(7) prohibiting the payment of drawback upon the reexportation of any specified goods or class of goods.

(8) specifying the goods dutiable on import in respect of which drawback may be allowed on re-export as part or ingredient of any goods manufactured in Brunei Darussalam and for fixing the rate of drawback thereon.

(9) compounding offences.

(10) defining any goods for the purposes of this Act.

(11) penalties for any contravention or failure to comply with any of the provisions of any regulation made under this section or with the restrictions or conditions of any licence or permission granted under any such regulations:

Provided that no such penalty shall exceed the penalty prescribed under section 129.

(12) any matter which requires to be prescribed hereunder.

(13) the conduct of all matters relating to the collection of customs duties including the time of payment thereof.

(14) customs ports and legal landing places within those customs ports or at any other places for the landing and shipping of goods imported or exported, and defining the limits of such ports and landing places and prescribing the goods that may be landed or shipped thereat.

(15) places of import and export and the routes to be used for the import and export of goods by land.

(16) customs airports for the import and export of goods by air.

(17) inland customs stations at which customs duties may be collected.

(18) the days and times during which any customs office, or customs or licensed warehouse may be open for business and the times during which any goods may be landed, shipped or loaded at any customs port or customs airport or imported or exported by land at any place of import and export.

(19) the control by officers of customs of traffic carried on in local craft or coasting vessels in the territorial or inland waters of Brunei Darussalam.

(20) the flag to be flown by vessels employed for the prevention of smuggling.

(21) the forms to be used under this Act and may prescribe forms which require by reference to a code or otherwise the classification of —

(a) place of import or export;

(b) country or port of shipment or destination;

(c) country of origin;

(d) goods imported or exported; and the deposit, custody and withdrawal of goods in and from customs and licensed warehouses and warehouses and the management and control of the same.

quantity, value or other details, and the supplying of such particulars as may facilitate the keeping of trade statistics in connection with importation and exportation.

the manner in which dutiable or prohibited goods shall or shall not be packed, and for regulating or prohibiting the inclusion of dutiable or prohibited goods in the same package or receptacle with non-dutiable goods.

standard containers in which dutiable goods shall be exported.

the opening and examination of packages imported, or exported by post for assessment of duty on dutiable goods and detection of attempts to evade the payment of customs duty.

the issue of licences.

the stock books to be kept by licensees and the method of keeping the same.

the method of importing, exporting, transporting or removing any goods under a licence or permit.

the manner in which goods may be transhipped, or goods in transit may be moved.

the manner in which intoxicating liquor shall be denatured in a customs or licensed warehouse.

the conditions under which any goods may be moved in transit through Brunei Darussalam.

permits and other documents to be carried by local craft or barges transporting cargo from or to vessels in a customs port.

(33) the amounts to be paid as wharf dues in respect of Government warehouses other than Ports Department warehouses.

(34) generally for giving effect to the provisions of this Act.

134. Where it is provided in this Act that the decision on any Appeal from Controller.

provided that such decision is at the absolute discretion of the Controller, any person aggrieved by such decision may appeal therefrom to His Majesty in Council whose decision shall be final.

135. The Controller may charge such fee as he may consider Power of the Customs Department which is not required to be done or rendered under this Act and for which no fee is prescribed by any written law.

CUSTOMS (ASEAN PREFERENTIAL TRADING ARRANGEMENT)

SUBSIDIARY LEGISLATION
(section 8)

ORDER, 1988

ARRANGEMENT OF SECTIONS

Rules

[Subsidiary]

SUBSIDIARY LEGISLATION

(section 8)

CUSTOMS (ASEAN PREFERENTIAL TRADING ARRANGEMENT)[S 24/89]
ORDER, 1988

Commencement: 24th December 1988

In exercise of the powers conferred by section 8 of the Customs Act (*Chapter 36*) the Minister of Finance with the approval of His Majesty the Sultan and Yang Di-Pertuan of Brunei Darussalam hereby makes the following Order —

This Order may be cited as the Customs (ASEAN Preferential Short title. Trading Arrangement) Order, 1988.

In this Order — Interpretation.

"ASEAN" means the Association of South East Asian Nations.

"scheduled goods" means goods which have been placed underASEAN Preferential Trading Arrangement (PTA) scheme and theimportation of which shall be eligible for preferential treatment.

"%" means percentage of value.

3. For the purpose of implementing the preferential rates of duty theASEAN scheduled goods must be shown to the satification of the Controller of Preferential Customs to be — Trading

Agreement.

(a) products originated from or manufactured in the exporting member country of ASEAN in accordance with theRules of Origin laid down in the Agreement of ASEANPreferential Trading Arrangement (PTA);

(b) products covered by a certificate of origin issued by theauthorising body in the exporting member country of ASEAN.

4. (1) The rates of import duty on scheduled goods are specified in theRates of fifth column of the First Schedule. Import duty.

(2) Such rates of import duty shall be levied and paid by theimporter in lieu of the full duty where the Controller of Customs is satisifiedthat the provisions of paragraph 3 of this Order have been complied with.

(3) For the purpose of section 8 of the Customs Act, membercountries of ASEAN are hereby specified as prescribed countries.

STRATEGIC INFORMATION FOR BUSINESS

Brunei Darussalam is still very much dependent on revenues from crude oil and natural gas to finance its development programs. Aside from this, Brunei Darussalam also receives income from rents, royalties, corporate tax and dividends. Due to the non-renewable nature of oil and gas, economic diversification has been in Brunei Darussalam's national development agenda. In the current Seventh national Development Plan, 1996-2000, the government has allocated more than $7.2 billion for the implementation of various projects and programs.

Brunei Darussalam is the third largest oil producer in Southeast Asia and it produced 163,000 barrels per day. It is also the fourth largest producer of liquefied natural gas in the world.

Brunei Darussalam is the third largest oil producer in Southeast Asia and it produced 163,000 barrels per day. It is also the fourth largest producer of liquefied natural gas in the world.
National Development Plan 1996 – 2000

Brunei welcomes foreign investment. Foreign investors are invited to actively participate in the current economic diversification programme of the country. The programme hinges on the development of the private sector. The Ministry of Industry and Primary Resources was formed in 1989 with the responsibility of promoting and facilitating industrial development in Brunei Darussalam. Brunei Darussalam offers all investors security, stability, continuity, confidence and competitiveness.

Competitive investment incentives are ready and available for investors throughout the business cycle of start up, growth, maturity and expansion. The Investment Incentive Act which was enacted in 1975 provides tax advantages at start up and ongoing incentives throughout growth and expansion that are comparable if not better than those offered by other countries in the region.

The Investment Incentives Act makes provision for encouraging the establishment and development of industrial and other economic enterprises, for economic expansion and incidental purposes.

Investment incentive benefits vary from one program to other. Amongst the benefits are:

- Exemption from income tax;
- Exemption from taxes on imported duties on machinery, equipment, component parts, accessories or building structures;
- Exemption from taxes on imported raw material not available or produced in Brunei Darussalam intended for the production of the pioneer products;
- Carry forward of losses and allowances.

This Act provides tax relief for a company which is granted pioneer status.

- Companies awarded pioneer status are exempted from corporate tax, tax import of raw materials and capital goods for a period ranging from 2 to 5 years, depending on fixed capital expenditure with possible extension at the discretion of the relevant authorities.

- Enterprises which are given expansion certificates are given tax relief for a period between 3 to 5 years.
- Approved foreign loans can be exempted from paying the 20% withholding tax for interest paid to non-resident lenders.

Brunei Darussalam is flexible towards foreign equity requirements. 100% foreign equity can be considered for export-oriented industries with the exception of industries based on local resources, industries related to national food security and car dealership whereby some level of local participation is required.
Industrial activities are classified into four categories:

- Industries related to national food security
- Industries for local market
- Industries based on local resources
- Industries for export market

Industrial policies including manpower, ownership, government support and facilities remain open and flexible for all categories of industrial activities. Brunei Darussalam maintains a realistic approach where a variety of arrangements are feasible. Policies relating to ownership allow for full foreign ownership, majority foreign ownership and minority foreign ownership, as per the type of industry and situation.
Only activities relating to national food security and those based on local resources require some level of local participation. Industries for the local market not related to national food security and industries for total export can be totally foreign owned. Overall, in Brunei Darussalam, any industrial enterprise will be considered.
The Investment Incentives Order 2001 expanded the tax holidays avaiable to investors. Examples include:

- Corporate tax relief of up to 5 years for companies that invest B$500,000 to B$2.5 million in approved ventures
- 8-years tax relief for investing more than B$2.5 million
- An 11-year tax break if the venture is located in a high-tech industrial park.

Brunei Darussalam is still very much dependent on revenues from crude oil and natural gas to finance its development programs. Aside from this, Brunei Darussalam also receives income from rents, royalties, corporate tax and dividends. Due to the non-renewable nature of oil and gas, economic diversification has been in Brunei Darussalam's national development agenda. In the current Seventh national Development Plan, 1996-2004, the government has allocated more than $7.2 billion for the implementation of various projects and programs.

Brunei Darussalam is the third largest oil producer in Southeast Asia and it produced 163,000 barrels per day. It is also the fourth largest producer of liquefied natural gas in the world.

Brunei Darussalam is the third largest oil producer in Southeast Asia and it produced 163,000 barrels per day. It is also the fourth largest producer of liquefied natural gas in the world.
National Development Plan 1996 – 2004

INVESTMENT AND BUSINESS CLIMATE

Brunei Darussalam has enormous business potential that is yet to be exploited. The country has the advantage of peace and political stability, which is favourable for business activities. Foreign investments are always welcome in Brunei and foreign investors are invited to actively engage in the current economic diversification programme.

The Ministry of Industry and Primary Resources, which was established in 1989, is the main government agency that promotes and facilitates investment, business and trade activities in the country.
Competitive investment incentives are ready and available for investors throughout the business cycle of start up, growth, maturity and expansion.
The Investment Incentive Act enacted in 1975 provides tax advantages at start up and ongoing incentives throughout growth and expansion that are comparable if not better than those offered by other countries in the region.

WHY INVEST IN BRUNEI DARUSSALAM?

¨ Brunei Darussalam is a stable and prosperous country that offers not only excellent infrastructure but also a strategic location within the Asean group of countries.
¨ No personal income tax is imposed in Brunei. Businesses are also not imposed sales tax, payroll, manufacturing and export tax. Approved foreign investors can enjoy a company tax holiday of up to eight years.

¨ The regulations relating to foreign participation in equity are flexible. In many instances there can be 100% foreign ownership.

¨ Approval for foreign workers, ranging from labourers to managers, can be secured.
¨ The cost of utilities is among the lowest in the region.
¨ The local market, while relatively small, is lucrative and most overseas investors will encounter little or no competition.

¨ The living conditions in Brunei Darussalam are among the best and most secure in the region
¨ On top of all, His Majesty's Government genuinely welcomes foreign investment in almost any enterprise and will ensure that you receive speedy, efficient and practical assistance on all your inquiries.

SUPPORTIVE ENVIRONMENT

Brunei Darussalam offers vast land and a variety of facilities throughout all four districts in the country. The majority of the 12 industrial sites presently developed are ready and available for occupation. Large expanses for agroforestry and aquaculture are also available. Rental terms and tenancy agreements are competitive and the sites offer a range of facilities, infrastructure and resources. Brunei Darussalam gives priority to ensuring the stability of the natural environment. As such, all sites are free from pollution and are ecologically well balanced. The government's philosophy is sustainable development. Therefore, all polluting industries are banned and one of the continuing criteria for engaging any industry's participation is the impact on the environment.

INFRASTRUCTURE

The country's infrastructure is well developed and ready to cater for the needs of the new and vigorous economic activities under the current economic diversification programme. The country's two main ports, at Muara and Kuala Belait, offer direct shipping to Hong Kong, Singapore and several other Asian destinations. Muara, the deep-water port situated 29 kilometres from the capital was opened in 1973 and has since been considerably developed. It has 12,542 sq. metres of transit sheds. Container yards have been increased in size and a container freight station handles unstuffing operations. Meanwhile, Pulau Muara Besar is being developed as a centre for dockyard, ship salvaging and for other related industries. The recently expanded Brunei International Airport in Bandar Seri Begawan can now handle 1.5 million passengers and 50,000 tonnes of cargo a year. The 2,000 kilometre road network serving the entire country is being expanded and modernised. A main highway runs the entire length of the country's coastline. It conveniently links Muara, the port of entry at one end, to Belait, the oil producing district at the western end of the state.

ECONOMY

The economy of the country is dominated by the oil and gas and liquefied natural gas industries and Government expenditure patterns. The country's exports consist of three major commodities namely crude oil, petroleum products and liquefied natural gas. Exports are destined mainly for Japan, the United States and Asean countries. The second most important industry is the construction industry.

This is directly the result of increased investment by the Government in development and infrastructure projects within the five-year National Development Plans. Brunei Darussalam has entered a new phase of development in its drive towards economic diversification from dependence on the oil and liquefied natural gas-based economy. Official statistics showed that exports during the 1996 to 2004 period increased from B$3,682.1 million in 1996 to B$6,733.5 million in 2004, while imports declined from B$3,513.6 million to B$1,907.8 million. This trend has increased the balance of trade from B$168.9 million in 1996 to B$3289.0 million in 2004. In the current 8th National Development Plan, which is the last phase of Brunei's 20-year National Development Programme, the government is allocating a total of B$1.1 billion for commerce and industry.

The Brunei International Financial Centre (BIFC) set up in 2004, is another effort undertaken by the government to diversify the country's economy. Brunei Darussalam has the potential to become an international financial centre and has the capability to provide similar facilities as those available in other successful financial centres. Brunei has political stability, modern infrastructure and up-to-date international communications system. Seven bills have been passed to govern the establishment and supervision of BIFC. These include the International Business Companies Order 2004, International Limited Partnership Order 2004, International Banking order 2004, International Trust Order 2004, Registered Agents and Trust Licensing order 2004,

Money Laundering Order 2004 and Criminal Conduct (Recovery of Proceed) Order 2004. The BIFC also plans to establish international Islamic banks in Brunei whose legal framework has been provided under the International Banking Order 2004. The establishment of the international Islamic banks is in line with the national aspirations of encouraging the development of Islamic finance and also of making the Sultanate as a regional and international Islamic financial centre.

INDUSTRIES

Industrial activities are classified into four categories:

1. Industries related to national food security
2. Industries for local market
3. Industries based on local resources
4. Industries for export market

FLEXIBLE POLICIES

Industrial policies including manpower, ownership, government support and facilities remain open and flexible for all categories of industrial activities. Brunei Darussalam maintains a realistic approach where a variety of arrangements are feasible. Policies relating to ownership allow for full foreign ownership, majority foreign ownership and minority foreign ownership, as per type of industry and situation. Only activities relating to national food security and industries for total export can be totally foreign owned. Overall, in Brunei Darussalam, any industrial enterprise will be considered.

FINANCE, BANK AND INSURANCE

Brunei Darussalam has no central bank, but the Ministry of Finance through the Treasury, the Currency Board and the Brunei Investment Agency exercises most of the functions of a central bank. Brunei Darussalam has not established a single monetary authority. All works related to finance are being carried out by three institutions.

· The Brunei Currency Board (BCB) is responsible for the circulation and management of currencies in the country.

· The Financial Institution Division (FID) is tasked with the issuing of licenses and regulations to financial institutions including the enforcement of minimum cash balance in accordance to specified rates for the interest of investors

· The Banks Association of Brunei determines the daily interest rates. However, there is also an indication that a single monetary authority may be established in the future to undertake these functions.

In 2004, it was recorded that there were 85 financial institutions including banks, financial companies, security companies, conventional insurance companies, Takaful companies, remittance companies and moneychangers. The existing nine commercial banks have established many branches from 29 in 1995 to 61 in 2004. The number of finance companies has also increased from three in 1996 to five in 2004. Security companies remain at two and the number of conventional insurance companies decreased from 22 in 1996 to 19 in 2004. This is the result of the merging of the branch and parent companies. The number of Takaful companies have risen from two in 1996 to three in 2004. In 1996 and 1997 there were 20 moneychangers operating in the country. The number increased to 33 in 1998 but has reduced to 24 in 2004. Remittance companies have also experienced the same trend as they increased from 16 in 1996 to 30 in 1998 but have reduced to 23 in 2004. The Brunei dollar is pegged to the Singapore dollar. The Ministry of Finance believes that the Monetary Authority of Singapore exercises sufficient caution and such a link will not have detrimental effects on the economies of either country.

CURRENCY

Currency matters are under the jurisdiction of the Brunei Currency Board (BCB) which manages and distributes currency notes and coins in the country with the main mission of ensuring the integrity of the currency issued to safeguard public interest. In September 2004, the money supply comprising currency in circulation and demand deposits amounted to B$2,295 million compared to B$3,366 million, B$2,430 million, B$2,493 million and B$2,727 million in 1996, 1997, 1998 and 1999 respectively.

FOREIGN EXCHANGE

There is no restriction in foreign exchange. Banks permit non-resident accounts to be maintained and there is no restriction on borrowing by non-residents.

TAXATION

Brunei Darussalam has no personal income tax. Sole proprietorship and partnership businesses are not subject to income tax. Only companies are subject to income tax and it is one of the lowest in the region. Moreover tax advantages at start-up and ongoing incentives throughout growth and expansion offer investors profitable conditions that are comparable if not better than those offered by other countries in the region.

COMPANY TAXATION

Companies are subject to tax on the following types of income: -

¨ Gains of profits from any trade, business or vocation,
¨ Dividends received from companies not previously assessed for tax in Brunei Darussalam
¨ Interest and discounts
¨ Rent, royalties, premiums and any other profits arising from properties.

There is no capital gains tax. However, where the Collector of Income Tax can establish that the gains form part of the normal trading activities, they become taxable as revenue gains.

a. Scope of Income Tax

A resident company in Brunei Darussalam is liable to income tax on its income derived from or accrued in Brunei Darussalam or received from overseas. A non-resident company is only taxed on its income arising in Brunei Darussalam.

b. Concept of Residence

A company, whether incorporated locally or overseas, is considered as resident in Brunei Darussalam for tax purposes if the control and management of its business is exercised in Brunei Darussalam. The control and management of a company is normally regarded as resident in Brunei Darussalam if, among other things, its directors' meetings are held in Brunei Darussalam. The profits of a company are subject to tax at the rate of 30%. Tax concession may be available. The profit or loss of a company as per its account is adjusted for income tax purposes to take into account certain allowable expenses, certain expenses prohibited from deduction, wear and tear allowances and any losses brought forward from previous years, in order to arrive at taxable profits.

TREATMENT OF DIVIDENDS

Dividends accruing in, derived from, or received in Brunei Darussalam by a corporation are included in taxable income, apart from dividends received from a corporation taxable in Brunei

Darussalam which are excluded.No tax is deducted at source on dividends paid by a Brunei Darussalam corporation. Dividends received in Brunei Darussalam from United Kingdom or Commonwealth countries are grossed up in the tax computation and credit is claimed against the Brunei Darussalam tax liability for tax suffered either under the double tax treaty with the United Kingdom or the provision Commonwealth tax relief.
Any other dividends are included net in the tax computation and no foreign tax is available. Brunei Darussalam does not impose any withholding tax on dividends.

ALLOWABLE DEDUCTIONS

All expenses wholly or exclusively incurred in the production of taxable income are allowable as deduction for tax purposes.
These deductions include:
¨ Interest on borrowed money used in acquiring income
¨ Rent on land and buildings used in the trade or business
¨ Costs of repair of premises, plant and machinery
¨ Bad debts and specific doubtful debts, with any subsequent recovery being treated as income when received, and
¨ Employer's contribution to approved pensions or provident funds

DISALLOWABLE DEDUCTIONS

Expenses not allowed as deductions for tax purposes include:
¨ Expenses not wholly or exclusively incurred in acquiring income
¨ Domestic private expenses
¨ Any capital withdrawal or any sum used as capital
¨ Any capital used in improvement apart from replanting of plantation
¨ Any sum recoverable under an insurance or indemnity contract
¨ Rent or repair expenses not incurred in the earning of income
¨ Any income tax paid in Brunei Darussalam or in other countries and
¨ Payments to any unapproved pension or provident funds

Donations are not allowable but claimable if they are made to approved institutions.

ALLOWANCES FOR CAPITAL EXPENDITURE

Depreciation is not an allowable expense and is replaced by capital allowances for qualifying expenditure. The taxpayer is entitled to claim wear and tear allowances calculated as follows:

a. Industrial Buildings
An initial allowance of 10% is given in the year of expenditure, and an annual allowance of 2% of the qualifying expenditure is provided on a straight-line basis until the total expenditure is written off.

b. Machinery and Plant
An initial allowance of 20% of the cost is given in the year of expenditure together with annual allowances calculated on the reducing value of the assets. The rates prescribed by the Collector of Income Tax range from 3% to 25%, depending on the nature of the assets. Balancing allowances or charges are made on disposal of the industrial building machinery or plant. These adjustments cover the shortfall or excess of the tax written down value as compared to the sale proceeds. Any balancing charge is limited to tax allowances previously granted, and any surplus is considered a capital gain and therefore does not become part of chargeable income.

Unabsorbed capital allowances can be carried forward indefinitely but must be set off against income from the same trade.

LOSS CARRYOVERS

Losses incurred by a company can be carried forward for six years for setoff against future income and can be carried back one year. There is no requirement regarding continuity of ownership of the company and also the loss set-off is not restricted to the same trade.

FOREIGN TAX RELIEF

A double taxation agreement exists with the United Kingdom and provides proportionate relief from Brunei Darussalam income tax upon any part of the income which has been or is liable to be charged with United Kingdom income tax.
Tax credits are only available for resident companies. Unilateral relief may be obtained on income arising from Commonwealth countries that provide reciprocal relief. However, the maximum relief cannot exceed half the Brunei Darussalam rate. This relief applies to both resident and non-resident companies.

STAMP DUTY

Stamp duties are levied on a variety of documents. Certain types of documents attract an ad valorem duty, whereas with other documents the duty varies with the nature of the documents.

PETROLEUM TAXES

Special legislation exists in respect of income tax from petroleum operations, which is taxable under the Income Tax (Petroleum) Act 1963 as amended.

WITHHOLDING TAXES

Interest paid to non-resident companies under a charge, debenture or in the respect of a loan, is subject to withholding tax of 20%. There are no other withholding taxes.

ESTATE DUTY

Estate duty is levied on an estate of over $2 million at 3% flat rate for a person who has died on or after 15th December 1988.

IMPORT DUTY

In general, basic foodstuffs and goods for industrial use are exempted from import duties. Electrical equipment and appliances, timber products, photographic materials and equipment, furniture, motor vehicles and spare parts are levied minimum duties, while cosmetics and perfumes are subject to 30% duty. Cigarettes are dutiable items, but the rates are low compared with neighbouring countries.

BUSINESSES AND COMPANIES

Registration and Guidelines
In Brunei Darussalam a business may be set up under any of the following forms:
¨ Sole proprietorship
¨ Partnership
¨ Company (Private or Public Company)
¨ Branch of foreign company

All businesses must be registered with the Registrar of Companies and Business Names. The proposed name of business or companies must first of all be approved by the Registrar of Companies and Business Names. For each name proposed, a fee of $5.00 is imposed.

Sole Proprietorship

¨ Upon arrival, a business name certificate is issued and a fee of $30.00 is imposed
¨ At the moment, it is not subject to corporate tax
¨ Foreigners are not eligible to register

Partnership

¨ May consist of individuals, local companies and/or branches of foreign companies
¨ The maximum permitted number of partners is 20
¨ Upon approval, a business name certificate is issued and a fee of $30.00 is imposed
¨ Application by foreign individuals are subject to prior clearance by the Immigration Department, Economic Planning and Development Unit and the Labour Department before they are registered
¨ At the moment, it is not subject to corporate tax

Private Company

¨ May be limited by shares, guarantee or both by shares and guarantee or unlimited
¨ Must have at least two and not more than 50 shareholders
¨ Shareholders need not be Brunei citizens or residents.
¨ Restrict the right of members to transfer shares and prohibit any invitations to the public to subscribe for shares and debentures
¨ A subsidiary company may hold shares in its parent company
¨ Memorandum and Articles of Association must be filed with the Registrar of Companies and Business Names with other incorporation documents in the prescribed form
¨ Upon arrival, a Certificate of Incorporation will be issued and a fee of $25 is imposed
¨ The registration fees are based on a graduated scale on the authorised share capital of the company
¨ No minimum share capital is required
¨ Private Companies are required to do the following:
1. Appoint auditors who are registered in Brunei Darussalam
2. Prepare a profit and loss account and balance sheet, accompanied by the Director's Report annually
3. Submit accounting data annually to the Economic Development and Planning Department of the Ministry of Finance
4. File annual returns, containing information on directors and shareholders
5. Keep the following records:
a. Minute Book of Members' Meetings
b. Minute Book of Director's Meetings
c. Minute Book of Manager's Meetings
d. Register of Members
e. Register of Directors and Managers
f. Register of Charges
¨ Subject to corporate tax of 30% of the gross yearly profit

PUBLIC COMPANY

¨ May be limited or unlimited
¨ May issue freely transferable shares to the public
¨ Must have at least seven shareholders
¨ Shareholders need not be Brunei citizens or residents
¨ Subsidiary company may hold shares in its parent companies
¨ Half the directors in the company must be either Brunei Citizens or ordinary residents in Brunei

Darussalam.

¨ Memorandum and Articles of Association must be registered with other incorporation documents in the prescribed forms

¨ Upon approval, Registration of Companies Certificate will be issued and a fee of $25.00 is imposed

¨ The registration fees are based on a graduated scale on the authorised share capital of the company.

¨ No minimum share capital is required

¨ Public Companies are required to do the following:

1. Appoint auditors who are registered in Brunei Darussalam
2. Prepare each year's profit and loss account and balance sheet, accompanied by the Director's Report annually.
3. Submit accounting data annually to the Economic Development and Planning Department of the Ministry of Finance
4. File annual returns, containing information on directors and shareholders
5. Keep the following records:

a. Minute Book of Members' Meetings
b. Minute Book of Director's Meetings
c. Minute Book of Manager's Meetings
d. Register of Members
e. Register of Directors and Managers
f. Register of Charges

¨ Subject to corporate tax of 30% of the gross yearly profit.

BRANCH OF FOREIGN COMPANY

The following documents must be filed with the Registrar of Companies and Business Names.

a. A certified copy of the charter, statutes or Memorandum and Articles of Association or other instruments defining the constitution of the foreign company duly authenticated and, when necessary, with English translation.

b. A list of directors together with their particulars and the names and addresses of one or more persons residing in Brunei Darussalam authorised to accept notices on the company's behalf.

¨ Upon approval, a Certificate of Incorporation will be issued and a fee of $25 is imposed

¨ The registration fees are based on a graduated scale on the authorised share capital of the company.

¨ No minimum share capital is required

¨ Branch of foreign company is required to do the following:

1. Appoint auditors who are registered in Brunei Darussalam
2. Prepare each year's profit and loss account and balance sheet, accompanied by the Director's Report annually.
3. Submit accounting data annually to the Economic Development and Planning Department of the Ministry of Finance
4. File annual returns, containing information on directors and shareholders
5. Keep the following records:

a. Minute Book of Members' Meetings
b. Minute Book of Director's Meetings
c. Minute Book of Manager's Meetings
d. Register of Members
e. Register of Directors and Managers
f. Register of Charges

¨ Subject to corporate tax of 30% of the gross yearly profit.

REGISTRATION OF TRADEMARKS AND PATENTS

Trademarks are registrable provided the requirements laid down in the Trademarks Act (Cap 98) are satisfied. Once registered, they are viable for an initial period of seven years and renewable for a further period of 14 years.

Any person who obtains a grant of a patent in the UK or Malaysia or Singapore may apply to the Ministry of Law within three years of the date of issue of such grant to have the grant registered in Brunei Darussalam under the Invention Act (Cap 72). There is no specific legislation for copyright protection, but UK legislation would apply where necessary.

EMPLOYMENT REGULATIONS

All non-Brunei Darussalam citizens require a work permit which are valid for two years. Application must first be made to the Labour Department for a labour license. On the recommendation of the Labour Department, the Immigration Department will give permission for the workers to enter Brunei Darussalam. The Labour Department requires either a cash deposit or a banker's guarantee to cover the cost of a one-way airfare to the home country of an immigrant worker. An approved labour licence cannot be altered for at least six months after issue. Applications will not be accepted until the formation of a local company or branch of a foreign company has been officially approved and registered.

INDUSTRIAL RELATIONS

The Trade Disputes Act (Cap 129) accords to trade unions the customary immunities and protections in respect of facts done in furtherance of trade disputes. It prescribes procedures for conciliation and subject to the consent of the parties, arbitration in disputes where machinery within the industry concerned does not exist or has failed to achieve settlement. Trade unionism of either the employers or workers is extensively practiced in Brunei Darussalam. As has been already observed, the industrial structure consists almost entirely of small scale enterprises. This state of affairs and nature and cultural characteristics of the population are conductive to accommodation and a 'give and take attitude' rather than a confrontational attitude. Except in the oil industry, the system of collective bargaining has not emerged. Relations between employers and employees are generally good. Existing labour laws have adequate provisions such as for termination of employment, medical care, maternity leave and compensation for disablement. Labour disputes are very rare. The Government has recently implemented the Workers' Provident Fund Enactment to cover workers both in the public and private sectors.

INTERNATIONAL RELATION AND TRADE DEVELOPMENT

In the perspectives of economic co-operation with foreign countries at the bilateral and multilateral levels, Brunei Darussalam seeks relevant agencies that can contribute to development and networking.

The areas of concern are:
¨ To facilitate investment into Brunei Darussalam
¨ To facilitate the development of trade
¨ To enhance human resources development and technology transfer, and
¨ To enhance bilateral, regional and multilateral economic cooperation

In pursuing these areas, mechanism for consultations and cooperation have been established through bilateral, regional and multilateral forum such as Association of Southeast Asian Nations (ASEAN), Asia Pacific Economic Cooperation (APEC), Organisation of Islamic Countries (OIC), European Union (EU), the Commonwealth, United Nation (UN) and the Non-Aligned Movement (NAM).

INVESTMENT PROMOTION

In the area of investment, Brunei Darussalam is currently engaged in a programme to improve its investment climate to create and enhance investment opportunities in Brunei Darussalam, both for local and foreign investors. The programme involves the establishment of bilateral trade investment treaties with foreign Government and Memorandums of Understanding (MoUs) between Brunei Darussalam's private sector and private sectors of other countries.

TRADE DEVELOPMENT

In the area of trade development, Brunei Darussalam is facilitating market opportunities to increase market access in the region as well as globally. Brunei Darussalam practices open multilateral trading system which are being pursued through regional and multilateral trading arrangements such as the ASEAN Free Trade Area (AFTA) and General Agreement of Trade and Tariffs (GATT). This open trade policy is consistent with Brunei Darussalam's efforts in pursuing outward looking economic policies that will assist the country in expanding its industrial and primary resource-based industries.

HUMAN RESOURCE DEVELOPMENT AND TECHNOLOGY TRANSFER

In the area of human resource development and technology transfer, there is a need to improve the technological capabilities of existing local industries, which are mainly small and medium scale enterprises. This is in view of the existing shortage of local manpower and thus the need to import foreign workers. The programmes are targeted towards the development of the mid-band occupational structure in which Brunei Darussalam has the advantage in view of cost factors such as the non-existence of income tax. Within the context of general economic cooperation, Brunei Darussalam will continue to enhance economic linkages with other countries in the region as well as outside the region.

THE INVESTMENT & TRADING ARM OF THE GOVERNMENT

Semaun Holdings Sdn Bhd

Semaun Holdings Sendirian Berhad, incorporated on 8th December 1994, is a private limited company that serves as an investment/trading arm of the Government with the purpose of accelerating industrial development in Brunei Darussalam through direct investment. Semaun Holdings is wholly owned by His Majesty's Government and plays an important role in supporting the economic diversification programmes in the country. The Chairman is the Honourable Minister of Industry and Primary Resources, Pehin Orang Kaya Setia Pahlawan Dato Seri Setia Haji Awang Abdul Rahman bin Dato Setia Haji Mohammad Taib, who is also the Chairman to the Industrial and Trade Development Council, a body entrusted with facilitating the industrialisation programme of Brunei Darussalam. The mission of Semaun Holdings is to spearhead industrial and commercial development through direct investment in key industrial sectors. Its primary objectives are:

¨ To accelerate and commercial development in Brunei Darussalam
¨ To generate industrial and commercial opportunities for active participation of citizens

Investment Philosophy

a. Local investment
First priority shall be given to investment in the country. Investment shall be in areas of strategic importance and NOT in direct competition with local companies
b. Overseas Capital

The Holdings may invest overseas in activities which reinforce the position of its local investment, preferably through strategic partnering with suitable local companies

Authorised Capital
BND 500 million (Five hundred million dollars)

Type of Investment
The Holdings shall invest through its
¨ Wholly owned operations
¨ Joint Venture Companies
¨ Equity Participation

Scope of Operation
The Holdings shall invest in business, trading and commercial enterprises including agriculture, fishery, forestry, industry and mining activities in Brunei Darussalam. Participation in investment related activities outside the country are also considered.
For more information please contact:
Semaun Holdings Sdn Bhd,
Office Unit No. 02, Block D,
Complex Yayasan Sultan Haji Hassanal Bolkiah,
Bandar Seri Begawan 2085,
Brunei Darussalam
Telephone no: (673) 223-2957 Fax : (673) 223-2956

BANKS OPERATING IN BRUNEI:

Citibank NA
12-15 Bang Darussalam
Bandar Seri Begawan
Tel: 02-243983 Fax: 02-225704

Hongkong and Shanghai Bank Corp
Main Office:
Jalan Sultan/Jalan Pemancha
General Office: Tel: 02-242305/10, 02-242204 Fax: 02-241316

Baiduri Bank Bhd
145 Jalan Permancha
PO Box 220, Bandar Seri Begawan 1922
Tel: 02-233233 Fax: 02-237575

Islamic Bank of Brunei Bhd
Head Office:
Bangunan IBB Lot 155, Jalan Roberts
PO Box 2725, Bandar Seri Begawan 1927
Tel: 02-220686, 221692, 220676
Fax: 02-221470

Development Bank of Brunei Bhd
1st Floor RBA Plaza, Jalan Sutlan BSB 2085
PO Box 3080 , Bandar Seri Begawan 1930
Tel: 02-233430
Fax: 233429

Malayan Banking Berhad
148 Jalan Permancha
Bandar Seri Begawan 2085
Tel: 02-242494 Telex: BU 2316

Overseas Union Bank Ltd
Unit G5 RBA Plaza, Bandar Seri Begawan
Tel: 02-225477 Fax: 02-240792

Standard Chartered Bank
Main Office:
51-55 Jalan Sultan
General Office: Tel 02-242386 Fax: 02-242390

United Malayan Banking Corporation Berhad
141 Jalan Permancha
Bandar Seri Begawan
Tel: 02-222516 Fax: 02-237487

INSURANCE

Every member of the community in his day to day life is invariably exposed to the possibility of encountering incidents which give rise to misfortunes and tragedies such as injury, death, fire, motor accidents and so on.

A Muslim believes any catastrophe that befalls him as 'Qadha' and 'Qadar' from Allah, and he must face these events of ill luck with strength of faith and patience.

Nevertheless, it is also the duty of every Muslim to find ways and means to legitimately avoid such incidents of misfortunate wherever possible, and to lighten his or her family's burden should such events occur.

A takaful policy is an Islamic form of cover that a Muslim can avail himself of as a means of protection against consequences of catastrophe. Brunei Darussalam now has three takaful operators, namely:
1. Insurans Islam TAIB Sdn Bhd
2. Takaful IBB Berhad and
3. Takaful IDBB Sdn Bhd

INSURANS ISLAM TAIB

Insurans Islam TAIB Sdn Bhd (IITSB) is a wholly owned subsidiary company of Perbadanan Tabung Amanah Islam Brunei (TAIB) and it provides Islamic insurance products in Brunei Darussalam. This company was established on 3rd March 1993 when it was first known as Takaful TAIB Sdn Bhd. On 11th June 1997, Takaful TAIB Sdn Bhd changed its name to Insurans Islam TAIB Sdn Bhd (IITSB).

TAKAFUL IBB SDN BHD

Takaful IBB Berhad, established on 5 May 1993, is one of the Islamic insurance companies in Brunei. It is limited by shares incorporated under the Companies Act, 1957 with an authorised capital of B$20 million and a paid up capital of B$10.2 million. At present, there are already nine branches in service in all districts with Kiarong as its main office.

TAKAFUL IDBB SDN BHD

Takaful IDBB Sdn Bhd is a new subsidiary company of the Islamic Development Bank of Brunei Berhad. It was launched on 1st March 2001 and is intended to further complement the takaful and insurance industry in Brunei with the belief in educating individuals and the community about its services and its ltimate protection plans. Its main branch is situated at the Setia Kenangan Complex in Kiulap.

TYPES OF POLICIES

Essentially these Takaful operators offer two types of policies:
- Savings plan which cover losses against untimely death under family takaful and
- General takaful which covers disasters against fire, theft, etc.

Each takaful operator offers a variety of schemes and plans for individuals, groups and companies. The contributions (premiums) are price-value leaders for the services provided and this has made takaful operators the benchmark in the insurance industry orders.

The participation by Muslims in these takaful policies offered by the takaful operators is in full compliance with the Islamic syariah law where the main concern in takaful is to avoid these three elements:
- AL RIBA - the practice of Al-Riba (or interest) and other related practices in investment activities, which contravene the rules of the syariah
- AL MAISIR - the element of Al-Maisir (or gambling) which arises as a consequence of the presence of Al-Gharar (uncertain factor). An example is a promised profit at a certain period of time
- AL GHARAR - the element of Al-Gharar (unknown or uncertain factor in the operation of a contract) in contracts. According to Ibn Taymiyyah, 'gharar' occurs when one party takes what is due to him but the other does not receive his entitlement. Gharar also pertains to 'deliverability' of the subject matter, that is uncertainty as to:

1. Whether the insured will get the compensation promised
2. How much the insured will get?
3. When the compensation will be paid?

WHY GHARAR IS PROHIBITED

The reason why the Holy Prophet prohibited 'gharar' in any business contract is obviously to ensure that one party does not have unfair advantage over the other. There are numerous verses in the Quran and examples from the sunnah of the Holy prophet to support the fact that Islam seeks to ensure justice, equity and fair play in all business dealings.

Although Muslims are encouraged to do business, they must do so by mutual consent and not to make money by unfair and unlawful means.

WHAT IS THE FUNCTION OF TAKAFUL?

It is one of the many ways to manage risk and is an effective risk transfer/homogenisation mechanism. It functions as a social device where the fortunate may compensate the unfortunate few with a financial solution to a financial problem.

HOW DOES TAKAFUL CONTRIBUTE TO THE SOCIETY?

In view of the necessity to provide cover against misfortunes to Muslims, Muslim jurists conducted a detailed study with a view of designing an alternative form of cover, which strictly conforms to the rules of the syariah. On the basis of this study, the Muslims jurists unanimously agreed that a cover which fits the requirements of the syariah be based on the Islamic concepts of takaful.

Takaful in this context means 'joint guarantee'. It is an act where groups of people reciprocally guarantee each other against losses or damages caused by any catastrophe or disaster whereby the needy will be given financial compensation.

Under this concept, a takaful company will provide takaful plans and schemes for both Family takaful and General takaful for the benefit of any member of the community who wishes to participate in the takaful programme. The contract of takaful is based on the principle of Al-Mudharabah, which is the sharing of profit in business.

HOW IS THE FUND MANAGED IN TAKAFUL?
Al-Mudharabah is derived in an altruistic and benevolent manner with the takaful operators fund managing in the following ways:

The contributions from the participants of General takaful scheme will be pooled into the General takaful Fund. This fund will be invested in any investment approved in accordance to syariah guidelines.

The profits received from the investments will be ploughed back into the fund where it is used to cover all the operational and administrative costs of General takaful , for example claims, retakaful costs and any cost related to it.

If there is a surplus from this fund, the surplus will then be shared between participants and the takaful operators. The ratio of surplus shared (depending on the ratio stipulated by takaful operators) is at the rate of 50:50; i.e. the participants will receive 50% from the surplus and 50% to takaful operators.

MANAGEMENT OF FAMILY TAKAFUL FUND
All installments contributed by the participants participating in the Family takaful Plan will be pooled into the Family takaful Fund. The fund will be divided into two accounts, namely the Participant's Account (PA) and Participant's Special Account (PSA).

This fund will also be invested through investment instruments or Islamic counters approved by syariah principles. The takaful operator and its participants will share profits earned from the investments according to the principles of Al-Mudharabah with the ratio as per agreed. The Al-Mudharabah ratio shaped (depending on the ratio stated by takaful operators) is 30% to the takaful operator and 70% to participants.

CONTRIBUTIONS OF TAKAFUL TO ECONOMY
In many developed countries, the Takaful or insurance industries together with pension fund institutions are major players in the development of the domestic capital market.

The takaful and insurance industry in the ASEAN region was urged to prepare itself to be a major player and be an engine for creating an efficient and liquid capital market.

Above all, aside from contributing to the economy of Brunei Darussalam, it is also the duty of takaful operators to educate the public on the beauty and the importance of takaful in our every day lives.

OTHER INSURANCE IN BRUNEI
In general, insurance policies in Brunei can be broken down into Motor and Non-Motor Insurance.

Motor Insurance covers can be provided for Private Vehicles, Commercial Vehicles and Motorcycles and can be covered by a Third party or Comprehensive Insurance Coverage.

The most common form of Non-Motor Insurance is coverage for fire related damage to property and content followed by Workman Compensation, Public Liability, Personal Accident, Group Personal Accident (for corporate clients), Contractors, Marine Cargo, Marine Hull (boat operators) and Guarantees.

THE GENERAL INSURANCE ASSOCIATION OF BRUNEI
The General Insurance Association of Brunei (GIAB) was formally registered and approved on 23rd of August 1986 with the full endorsement and support from the Ministry of Finance, in particular its Insurance section.

The principal activity of GIAB is to act as a representative body of the general insurance industry in Brunei Darussalam and to promote and protect the interests of all members in connection with the general insurance industry in the Sultanate.

The members of the Association are:-
- AXA Insurance (B) Sdn Bhd
- Borneo Insurance Sdn Bhd
- Cosmic Insurance Corporation Sdn Bhd
- CGU Insurance Bhd
- Liberty Citystate Insurance Pte Ltd
- MBA Insurance Company Sdn Bhd
- Malaysia National Insurance Bhd
- Motor and General Insurance Sdn Bhd
- National Insurance Company Bhd
- Royal & Sun Alliance Insurance (Global) Ltd
- South East Asia Insurance (B) Sdn Bhd
- Standard Insurance Sdn Bhd
- The Asia Insurance Company Ltd
- Winterthur Insurance (Far East) Pte Ltd

CHAMBERS OF COMMERCE

The four chambers of commerce in Brunei play a very important role in the development of SMEs (small medium enterprises) in the country and were set up to promote the interests of the different business groups.

FUNCTIONS
The Brunei Darussalam International Chamber of Commerce and Industry is active in creating dialogue opportunities between its members and Government officials, diplomatic representatives and groups from the private sector.

The Chamber also receives numerous contacts from overseas for business opportunities and distributes contact information to all its members. The chamber also serves as a bridge between local and international businesses, fostering friendly co-existence.

The National Chamber of Commerce and Industry of Brunei Darussalam, Brunei Malay Chamber of Commerce and Industry and the Chinese Chamber of Commerce have more or less the same functions as the Brunei Darussalam International Chamber of Commerce and Industry.

The chambers of commerce in Brunei Darussalam often meet and exchange information and views on matters of common interest. Some of the chambers of commerce organise trade fairs to promote products and business.

HOW TO CONTACT THEM

· The Brunei Darussalam International Chamber of Commerce and Industry
(Dewan Perniagaan dan Perindustrian Antarabangsa Negara Brunei Darussalam)
Address:
Unit 402-403A, 4th Floor, Wisma Jaya
Jalan Pemancha Bandar Seri Begawan 8811
Postal Address: PO Box 2988
BS 8675
Tel: 222-8382, 223-6888
Fax: 222-8389

· Brunei Malay Chamber of Commerce and Industry
(Dewan Perniagaan dan Perusahaan Melayu Brunei)
Address: Unit B1, 2nd Floor
P.O Box B1-3, Lot 44252,
Kg. Kiulap, BE1518
Tel: 223-7113
Fax: 223-7112

· Chinese Chamber of Commerce
(Dewan Perniagaan Tionghua)
Address: 2nd/3rd/4th Floor Chinese Chamber of Commerce Building
72 Jalan Roberts, Bandar Seri Begawan

Postal address: PO Box 281 Bandar Seri Begawan
Tel: 223-5494/5/6
Fax: 222-35492/3

· National Chamber of Commerce and Industry
(Dewan Perniagaan dan Perusahaan Kebangsaan Brunei Darussalam)
Address: Unit 10-14, First Floor
Bangunan Halimatul Saadiah, Jalan Gadong
BE 3519, Bandar Seri Begawan

Postal Address: PO Box 1099 Bandar Seri Begawan BS 8672
Tel: 222-7297
Fax: 222-7298

BRUNEI INTERNATIONAL FINANCIAL CENTRE (BIFC)

In an effort to establish itself in a world capital market, Brunei is slowly but surely catching the eyes of global financial players as one of the emerging bright stars of the world money market.

Since the inception of its International Offshore Financial Centre in June 2004, some 150 international business companies have checked in and set up their operations here. Many more are coming to join the growing community of international financiers, advisors, consultants and other players already in the country.

Brunei, as a new player, has comparatively many advantages that are conducive for a healthy growth of international financial business. Indeed this worries some International Offshore Financial Centres like Hong Kong.

While there are many other, more established, international offshore financial centres in the world such as those in Africa, Asia, Europe, the Western Hemisphere and the United States, Brunei as a newcomer, has sowed good seeds for the growth of international business companies that deal in the world capital market.

THE FIRST INTERNATIONAL SECURITY EXCHANGE IN BRUNEI
The decision by the Royal Bank of Canada to open its branch in the Sultanate last year was a testimony to this. Soon after that, Brunei saw its first international security exchange come into being. The Brunei International Exchange or IBX became the first securities exchange of international stature to win a license to operate in the country.

The establishment of the two entities was indeed historic in the development of the Brunei's fledgling financial services sector.

REASON TO INVEST
There are many factors that attract international companies to Brunei. For example the law of the country is based on the British Legal System with an independent judiciary that has the right of final appeal to the Privy Council.

In addition, there is the zero tax for individual income and the country's political stability. The high ratio of its educated population, its excellent infrastructure with direct connection to most major cities in Asia and Europe and wealth in resources are the additional plus points to investors.

In addition, Brunei's matured banking sector, with foreign banks such as HSBC, and its initiative to adopt the latest sets of offshore laws and regulation that include the provision on money laundering (MLO 2004) are some of the good elements that have lured them to Brunei.

Investors looking for a good halal place to invest are also encouraged by the open door policy adopted by Brunei to develop Islamic services and products. There are 1.3 billion Muslims in the world. The amount of Arab funds looking for syariah-compliant products has been estimated at US$670 billion in 1998 and US$950 billion in 2001.

NEW FRONTIERS
With the establishment of its first securities exchange, Brunei is now in a position to tackle the money markets in Asia, the Middle East and Europe as well as the United States.

His Majesty The Sultan and Yang Di-Pertuan of Brunei in his recent birthday titah highlighted his hope of seeing Brunei play an important role in the global financial market. The setting up of the IBX is one of the vehicles to realise this goal.

With IBX, Brunei will be the virtual hub of the pan-Asian securities market place that will allow trade in a range of financial instruments in multiple markets. Using Brunei as a base, IBX would use Internet and communication technologies to develop a global financial platform to connect to the world's major capital markets called CitiDEXes.

GOALS OF THE IFC
Brunei's motives in establishing the International Offshore Financial Centre are more subtle and

socio-economic in inclination than simply generating an income-stream to supplement tourism. These goals include developing the capacity to:
· Diversify, expand into and grow the value added financial service sector of the economy of Brunei and the Asia Pacific Region (APR)
· Provide a secure, cost-effective, sensibly regulated IFC facility which will offer a safe harbour for the conduct of significant regional and international business for corporate and private clients
· Attract overseas professionals to assist in running the IFC to the highest standards, encourage expatriate professionals to become involved in the training and development of rewarding opportunities for professionally qualified and trained Bruneians in the International Business Sector
· Increase returns for the hospitality, transport and amenity industries, including eco-tourism, culminating in a holistic result for the country's economy
· Position Brunei as an equal partner in the globalisation of financial and commercial activity, thereby generating greater communication with and between other nations

In its efforts to realise this goal, Brunei has deployed its sovereignty, wealth and human resources in a conservative but assertive manner to establish a jurisdictional environment which will be tax-free, and free from over-regulation or "business pollution".

Brunei IFC now offers a range of international legislation carefully crafted to permit flexible, cost effective capabilities which are up-to-date. Such capabilities include the full range of facilities necessary for the efficient conduct of global business.

As a sovereign nation of high repute (capable, for example, of hosting Apec Summit), Brunei is serving notice at the outset that criminal abuses of its financial systems will not be tolerated.

The country is taking these steps voluntarily, rather than under pressure. This reflects responsible economic and social attitudes.

The first tranche of legislation enacted for the IFC regime therefore includes Money-Laundering and Proceeds of (serious) Crime measures implemented to international standards. As for Severe Drug Trafficking, that legislation has been in place for some time along with enforceable regulations on the Trust, Company Administration, Insurance and Banking industries.

The initial legislation consists of anti-crime measures already mentioned and the following:
· International Banking Order, 2004 ('IBO')
· International Business Companies Order, 2004 (IBCO')
· Registered Agents and Trustees Licensing Order, 2004 ('RATLO')
· International Trusts Order, 2004 ('ITO')
· International Limited Partnerships Order, 2004 ('ILPO')
· Insurance, Securities and Mutual fund legislation.

BRUNEI'S NATIONAL VISION AND OPPORTUNITIES

The following is Brunei Darussalam's National Vision or Wawasan as authorised by His Majesty Sultan Haji Hassanal Bolkiah, Sultan and Yang Di-Pertuan of Brunei Darussalam, launched in January 2008.

WAWASAN BRUNEI 2035

By 2035 we wish to see Brunei Darussalam recognised everywhere for:

- the accomplishments of its well-educated and highly skilled people
- the quality of life
- the dynamic, sustainable economy

As we work towards these aims, we will be united in:

- our loyalty to our Sultan and our Country
- our belief in the values of Islam
- our traditional tolerance and social harmony

TOWARDS 2035: CONTINUITY AND CHANGE

Brunei Darussalam today enjoys one of the highest standards of living in Asia.

Its per capita income is one of the highest in Asia and it has already achieved almost all the target of the Millennium Development Goals.

Its standards of education and health are among the highest in the developing world.

This has been largely the result of political stability created by His Majesty's Government's investment of oil and gas revenues in infrastructure and in the development of far-reaching programme of social welfare.

Current prosperity, however, cannot be taken for granted. If the people are to continue to enjoy their high standard of living, planning must take account of a number of emerging social and economic facts.

- Although oil and gas resources have contributed much to the nation's prosperity, economic growth has, on the whole, not kept pace with population growth.
- The public sector that is the main employer of the majority of the citizens and residents can no longer adequately absorb the growing numbers of young people wishing to enter the work force each year.
- There is a widening gap between the expectations and capabilities of the nation's youth and the employment opportunities currently being created.
- The oil and gas sector that makes up about half of the economy and over 90% of export earnings employs less than 3% of the work force.
- The local business community continues to be weak and is unable to create the employment opportunities now required.

In order to offer its people a bright and prosperous future, Brunei Darussalam must, therefore, adapt to change and all that this entails by way of ambition, innovation and bold planning.

The challenge facing the nation lies in finding ways to do this successfully whilst, at the same time, upholding the values upon which the nation has developed and progressed.

OUR VISION FOR 2035

To meet this challenge successfully by 2035 we aspire to excel in the following key areas:

An educated, highly skilled and accomplished people

We will seek to build a first class education system that provides opportunities for every citizen and resident to meet the requirements of our changing economy and encourages life-long learning as well as achievements in sport and the arts.

Our success will be measured by the highest international standards.

Our quality of life

Our people deserve the best home we can give them. We will seek to provide our people with high standards of living and political stability while ensuring proper care of our environment and the vital support needed by all members of our society.

We will measure our quality of life by reference to the United Nations Human Development Index and aim to be among the top 10 nations in the world.

Our dynamic and sustainable economy

A continued high standard of living requires our economic growth to keep pace with our population growth. We will seek to build an economy that provides our people with quality employment in both public and private sectors and also offers great economic opportunities.

We will measure our economy by reference to its capacity to support continuously rising living standards. Our aim is for Brunei Darussalam's per capita income to be within that of the top 10 countries of the world.

ENDURING VALUES

While recognising the need to change, we will continue to uphold vigorously the values that have been the foundation of our political stability, social harmony and prosperity.

In our work we shall be guided at all times by our commitment to the Brunei monarchy and nation, our faith in the values of Islam, based on the *Ahli Sunnah Wal-Jemaah, Mazhaf Shafie* and our tradition of tolerance, compassion and social harmony.

We believe that our ability to adapt and manage change is greatly enhanced by the MIB concept which is inspired by these core values.

ACHIEVING BRUNEI 2035

We will need to develop and implement an integrated and well-coordinated national strategy comprising the following key elements:

- **An education strategy** that will prepare our youth for employment and achievement in a world that is increasingly competitive and knowledge-based.
- **An economic strategy** that will create new employment for our people and expand business opportunities within Brunei Darussalam through the promotion of investment, foreign and domestic, both in downstream industries as well as in economic clusters beyond the oil and gas industry.
- **A security strategy** that will safeguard our political stability and our sovereignty as a nation and that links our defense and diplomatic capabilities and our capacity to respond to threats from disease and natural catastrophe.

- **An institutional development strategy** that will enhance good governance in both the public and private sectors, high quality public services, modern and pragmatic legal and regulatory frameworks and efficient government procedures that entail a minimum of bureaucratic “red tape”.
- **A local business development strategy** that will enhance opportunities for local small and medium sized enterprises (SMEs) as well as enable Brunei Malays to achieve leadership in business and industry by developing greater competitive strength.
- **An infrastructure development strategy** that will ensure continued investment by government and through public-private sector partnerships in developing and maintaining world-class infrastructure with special emphasis placed on education, health and industry.
- **A social security strategy** that ensures that, as the nation prospers, all citizens are properly cared for.
- **An environmental strategy** that ensures the proper conservation of our natural environment and cultural habitat. It will provide health and safety in line with the highest international practices.

To realise our Vision of Brunei 2035, the strategies listed above will need to be developed by both government and private bodies and implemented as a well-coordinated national strategy.

NATIONAL DEVELOPMENT PLAN

th NATIONAL DEVELOPMENT PLAN (2007 - 2012) Total Allocation (B$)	9.5 bil	100%
ALLOCATION BY SECTOR	B$	%
Industry and Commerce	1,024,965,460	10.8
Agriculture	101,771,500	1.1
Forestry	65,368,000	0.7
Fishery	115,839,960	1.2
Industrial Development	404,334,000	4.3
Commerce & Entrepreneurial Development	38,514,000	0.4
Pulau Muara Besar	299,138,000	3.1
Transport and Communication	1,067,038,300	11.2
Roads	568,535,000	6
Civil Aviation	114,527,000	1.2
Marine and Ports	26,753,000	0.3
Telecommunications	116,517,000	1.2
Radio and Television	118,241,300	2.4
Postal Services	12,465,000	0.1
Social Services 'A'	1,294,267,900	13.6
Education	822,468,500	8.7
Medical and Health	149,152,000	1.6
Religious Affairs	27,180,600	0.3
Human Resource Development	295,466,800	3.1
Social Services 'B'	1,761,451,800	18.5
Government Housing	23,281,000	0.2
Public Facilities and Environment	182,500,800	1.9
National Housing	1,555,670,000	16.4

Public Utilities	1,492,717,900	15.7
Electricity	587,904,000	6.2
Sanitation	178,013,000	1.9
Water Supply	524,573,900	5.5
Drainage	202,227,000	2.1
Public Buildings	672,958,800	7.1
Science, Technology and R & D	165,178,400	1.7
ICT	1,145,687,800	12.1
Security	596,789,000	6.3
Royal Brunei Armed Forces	421,286,000	4.4
Police	175,503,000	1.8
Miscellaneous	278,944,640	2.9
Contingency Reserves	244,944,640	2.6
Site Development	15,000,000	0.2
Consultant Fee	15,000,000	0.2
Liabilities for Completed Project	4,000,000	0

COMMUNICATIONS

Airport

The present day Brunei International Airport, located at Berakas about fifteen minutes drive from Bandar Seri Begawan operates 24 hours a day, providing facilities for both regional and international air traffic. It has a 4000-metre runway that can accommodate any type of aircraft currently in service, including the 'Jumbo' 747s. Its passenger and cargo handling facilities can handle 1.5 million passengers and 50,000 tones of cargo a year. Equipped with the latest state-of the-art technology in surveillance and tracking, the airport boasts radar, flight and auxiliary data processing, 2,000-line, high-resolution color raster displays, simulation facilities, voice switching system, voice and data recording and VHF/UHF air-ground transmitters. The national air carrier is Royal Brunei Airlines founded in November 18, 1974.

Another airport, at Anduki near Seria, is used by the Brunei Shell Petroleum Company for its helicopter services.

Ports

The main Port is Muara, which is about 28 kilometers from Bandar Seri Begawan. The port can accommodate ships over 196 meters L.O.A. and take up to 7 or 8 vessels averaging 8,000 Gross Registered Tonnage {GRT} or a single ship of up to 30,000 {GRT} with a draught of not more than 9.5 meters.

Since 1973, the port has undergone extensive improvements. These include extensions to the wharf bringing the total length to 948 meters including 250 meters dedicated container wharf and 87 meters aggregate wharf. The overall storage space in the form of covered storage is 16,950 square meters, long storage warehouses 16,630 square meters and open storage space 5 hectares. Facilities for the dedicated container wharf covers an area of 92,034 square meters including 8,034 square meters covered areas.

Besides Muara Port, there are two smaller ports located one at Bandar Seri Begawan and one at Kuala Belait. The port at Bandar Seri Begawan is utilized by vessels under 93 meters LOA drawing less than 5 meters draught carrying conventional cargoes for direct deliveries and passenger launches plying between Bandar Seri Begawan, Limbang and Temburong. The wharf also accommodates various small government crafts. The port at Kuala Belait can accommodate vessels with draught of 4 meters which carries mainly general cargo for Kuala Belait and the Brunei Petroleum Shell Company.

Road

The road network in Brunei Darussalam is the primary means of movement for people, goods and services on land. It plays a vital role in the overall growth and development of the State. The network has been designed to integrate housing, commercial and industrial development. The Sultanate has constructed a good road network with various types of road throughout the country that includes highways, link roads, flyovers and round-abouts. A major road, which was completed in 1983, is a 28-kilometre highway linking Muara through Berakas and Jerudong to a point in Tutong, where it connects with the existing Bandar Seri Begawan-Tutong-Seria trunk road thus providing an alternative routes to these places.

An 11-km road between Sungai Teraban and Sungai Tujoh, makes the journey from Brunei Darussalam to Sarawak's Fourth Division such as Miri and other parts of Sarawak much easier.

The State had 2,525 kilometers (km) of roads, of which 2,328 km were covered with asphalt, 187 with pebbles, and 10 km with concrete. Of the total 1,514 km were in Brunei/Muara, 481 km in Belait, 400 km in Tutong and 130 km in Temburong district.

PRACTICAL INFORMATION AND REGULATIONS[1]

CUSTOMS PROCEDURES

ENTRY AND EXIT

argo can only be unloaded at prescribed ports of import and export and landing places approved by the Controller of Customs :

By Air
ØBrunei Darussalam International Airport

By Sea
ØMuara Port
ØSerasa Ferry Terminal
ØPutat Control Post
ØBelait Wharf

By Land
ØSungai Tujoh Control Post
ØKuala Lurah Control Post
ØPuni Control Post
ØLabu Control Post

Before any cargo can be unloaded, transshipped or removed on to another vessel, permission must be obtained from a proper Customs Officer.

IMPORET DUTIES

Dutiable goods imported to Brunei Darussalam are subject to Customs Import Duties Order 2007. ASEAN Trade in Goods Agreement (ATIGA) could be given to importer based on qualification given by Ministry of Foreign Affairs and Trade (MoFAT). Most import duties are imposed based on Ad Valorem rate and only some taxes are based on specific rate. Ad Valorem is the percentage, for example, 20% of the price of good, while specific rate is calculated by the amount of weight or quantity such as $60 per kg or $220 per tonne. Determination of classification of imported goods whether dutiable or not are based on Customs Import Duties Order 2007. Since 1973 Brunei did not impose duties on exported goods. It Is intended to promote local enterpreneurship.

CUSTOMS IMPORT DUTY GUIDE

Every person arriving in Negara Brunei Darussalam shall declare all dutiable goods in his possession, either on his person OR in any baggages OR in any vehicles to the proper officer of customs for examination.

If failed to do so, such goods shall be deemed to be uncustomed goods and imprisonment OR fine can be imposed.

Dutiable Goods

[1] Brunei Customs Department Materials

All goods subject to payment of customs duty and on such duty has not yet been paid. According to paragraph 3(3) of customs import duties order 2007 where the total amount of import duty:

- Is less than $1 no import duty shall be charged.
- Exceed $1 and includes a fraction of $ 1, the fraction shall be treated as a complete dollar.

Importer od Dutiable Goods shall:

- Declare his/her goods.
- Produce documents such as invoice, bill and etc.
- Produce customs dutiable import declaration form no 5/C-16. (If necessary)

List of some Dutiable Goods and rate of Customs Import Duty

DUTIABLE GOODS	RATE OF CUSTOMS IMPORT DUTY
Coffee (not roasted)	11 cents/ 1 kg
Coffee (roasted)	22 cents/ 1 kg
Tea	22 cents/ 1 kg
Instant coffee/tea (Extract, essences and concentrates)/ coffee mate	5%
Grease	11 cents/ 1 kg
Lubricants	44 cents/ 1 kg
Carpet and other textile floor covering	5%
Mat and matting	10%
Wood and articles of wood	20%
Footware, slippers and the like	5%
Headgear and parts thereof	10%
Cosmetic, perfumes, toilet waters, soap, hair shampoo and other washing preparations	5%
Other preparations for use on the hair	30%
Electrical goods	5% OR 20%
Auto parts	20%
Articles of apparel and clothing accessories, of leather OR of composition leather	10%
Jewellery including imitation jewellery	5%
Clocks and watches and parts thereof	5%
Musical instruments	10%

- See more at: http://www.mof.gov.bn/index.php/royal-custom-matters/customs-procedures/custom-import-duty#sthash.ilZqIfJE.dpuf

BASIC EXPORT-IMPORT PROCEDURES

Goods To Be Imported & Export

All goods may be imported or exported except for restricted, prohibited and controlled goods under Section 31 of the Customs order, 2006.

Customs Declaration

Every imported & exported goods should be declared to the RCED by a declaration form except for the following goods:
ØPassenger hand baggage's or personal effect on arrival.
ØGoods arriving by post except for dutiable goods.

Declaration should give full and true account of the number of packages, cases description of goods, value, weight, measure or quantity and country of origin of the goods.

Customs Declaration Form must be submitted in triplicate and attached together with the following supporting documents :
ØInvoice or purchase bill.
ØFreight and Insurance Payment Slips.
ØDelivery Order or Air Waybill.
ØPacking List.

Other than the above documents, importer should also provide other documents related to the imported goods required by Customs coinciding with the declaration of goods such as:
ØCertificate of Origin.
ØCertificate of Analysis.
ØA.P (Approval Permit) of the RCED.
ØImport license issued by the relevant Government Department/Agencies.
ØVerification Certificate of a recognized foreign agency.
ØOther relevant documents.
ØPersonal qualified to declare.

The owners:

ØThe owners or importers or exporters are qualified to declare the imported/exported goods to RCED.

Representatives:

ØThe owner may authorize the agents or forwarders as their representatives in declaration.

Conditions of qualification of importer and exporter:

ØTrader or Agent ID registrations;
ØEvery company or agents/forwarder must be registered with the RCED.
ØIndividual registration is not compulsory however customers (traders) are advised to make use of the services of Customs agents (forwarders).

Registration of Company:

ØApplication form available at the Customer Services Unit of RCED Headquaters, Jalan Menteri Besar.
ØThe application will be entered into the computer system of RCED, i.e Computer Control and Information System (CCIS).

Documents for Registration:

ØA copy of the company's registration certificate.

ØA copy of smart identity card.

EXAMINATION

Examination is carried out after the declaration of goods has been accepted and duties have been collected. Goods for examination must be produced by the importer or the importer's agent at prescribed places during the normal working hours. If an importer or the importer's agent request his/her goods to examined outsite the normal working hours, he/she has to pay overtime fees to Customs. Examination is carried out in the presence of the importer or the importer's agent.

He/she will be responsible for opening, weighting, sorting and marking of goods and all other necessary operations as directed by the Customs Officer.
Examination is carried out to the satisfaction of the Customs Officer. He/she may, as his/her duty requires, take samples of any goods or cause such goods to be detained. - See more at: http://www.mof.gov.bn/index.php/royal-custom-matters/customs-procedures/examination-of-goods#sthash.OLFtFmNc.dpuf

PROHIBITIONS AND RESTRICTIONS

Import and Export Prohibition and Restriction

Brunei Darussalam imposed restriction/prohibition and control on several types of goods either for import, re import, export and re export as provided in Customs Order 2006 (Section 31). There are four (4) schedules in the Customs Order (Restriction and prohibition) on import and export.

First Schedule: Prohibition on Import

The following goods are prohibited to be imported or brought into the country:

- Dangerous drugs such as Opium, Heroin, Morphine and Psychotherapy materials such as LSD, DEI, DMT, DOM, Mescaline, Barbiturates and Amobarbital.
- Arms and ammunitions.
- SALK polio vaccine.
- JAVA sparrows (padda oryzivora).
- Local domestic pigs exported from Thailand.
- Fire crackers (known as double bangers).
- Vaccines of Chinese Taipei origin.
- Cigarettes without health warning written on their packages.
- Fabric of tissue consisting of any fibre whatsoever and of any other article whatsoever which fibre or tissue or other article bear the imprint of any currency note, bank note or coin which are, or have at any time been, issued or currently in use in any country whatsoever.

Second Schedule: Restriction on Import

The following goods are prohibited to be imported or brought into the country except with the approval of the Controller of Customs on his behalf:

- Any living plants or materials.
- Live cattle and birds.

- Pin schedule, fruit machines, slot machines and any other schedule or machines of a like nature whether involving an element of change or not.
- Persian glue.
- Poisons and deleterious drugs.
- Rice paddy and the products thereof.
- Separated skimmed or filled milk.
- Poh Ka, Poh Kah or Poh Kau.
- Koyoh or Koyok.
- Liow Ko.
- Ch'ow Ko.
- Sugar, salt and converted timber.
- Used (including reconditioned) motorcars, motorcycle, lorries, omnibuses, including mini buses, tractor and trailers.
- Alcoholic liquors.
- Any radioactive materials.

Third Schedule: Prohibition on Export

The following goods are prohibited to be exported or taken out of the country:

- Prawn refuse and copra cake.
- Stone or gravel.

Fourth Schedule: Restriction on Export

The following goods are restricted to be exported or taken out of the country except with the approval of the Controller of Customs or on his behalf:

- Derris Species (tuba).
- Elaeis Quineesis (oil palm).
- Rice, paddy and products thereof.
- Timber Class 1A, 1B, 1C, Nibong, Rattans.
- Article of an antique or historical nature made or discovered in Brunei Darussalam.
- Kerosene.
- Cigarettes.
- Sugar.
- Premium and Regular Gasoline.
- Diesoline.

- See more at: http://www.mof.gov.bn/index.php/royal-custom-matters/customs-procedures/prohibition-and-restriction#sthash.aUCAreKO.dpuf

EXPORT-IMPORT LICENCES

Licence or Permit

Licence or Permit is a verification or approval given/issued by the relevant Government Department/Agency responsible for the commodities before importation or exportation.

Application of licence/permit

Written application or completed form (subject to the requirement of the Department/Agency) must be submitted to the Government/Agency responsible for such prohibited and controlled commodities.

Additional requirement

There are some prohibited or controlled commodities that require A.P (Approval Permit) issued by the RCED other than the license/permit issued by the relevant Government Agency before being imported or exported.

Types of commodities and issuing Government Department/Agency

Types of Commodities Government/Agency Hotlines/email

Publication Materials/ Royal Brunei Police Force -+673-2459500

Prints, Films, CD, LD -info@police.gov.bn

VCD, DVD, Cassette,
Recital of Al-Quran, Islamic Dakwah Center -+673-2382525
Hadith, Religious books, -info@pusat-dakwah.gov.bn

Talisman commodities
(such as textiles/clothing Internal Security Department -+673-2223225
/etc.), bearing dubious -info@internal-security.gov.bn
Chop/photo

Halal, Fresh, Cold Halal Import Permit -+673-2382525
And Frozen Meat Issuing Board -info@religious-affairs.gov.bn
Health Services Department -+673-2381640
-info@moh.gov.bn

Agriculture Department -+673-2380144
-info@agriculture.gov.bn
Royal Customs and -+673-2382333
Excise department -info@customs.gov.bn

Firearms, Explosives,
Fire Crackers, Royal Brunei Police Force -+673-2459500
Dangerous Weapons, -info@agriculture.gov.bn
Scrap Metal

Plants, Crops, Live
Animals, Vegetables, Agriculture Department -+673-2380144
Fruits, Eggs -info@police.gov.bn

Fishes, Prawns, Shells,
Water Organisms and Fisheries Department -+673-2382068
Fishing equipments etc -info@fisheries.gov.bn

Poison, chemicals and Ministry of Health -+673-2381640
radioactive materials. (Refer to the Food -info@moh.gov.bn

Medicines, Herbal, Quality Control Section.
Health Foods, Soft Health Services
Drinks and Snacks. Department)

(Refer to Medical
Enforcement Section,
Pharmaceutical Services Department

Radio Transmitter Info-Communication -+673-2333780
and Receiver and Technology Industry (AiTi) -aiti@brunet.bn
Communications
Equipment such as
Telephone, Fax
Machines, Walkie-
Talkie, etc.

Used Vehicles such Land -+673-2451979
as Cars, Motorcycles, Transport Department -info@land-transport.gov.bn
Mini Buses, Pickups,
Trucks, Trailers and Royal Customs and -+673-2382333
non-motor vehicles Excise Department -info@customs.gov.bn
such as Bicycles

Timber and Forestry Department -+673-2381013
products thereof -info@forestry.gov.bn

Badges, Banners, Adat Istiadat Department -+673-2244545
Souvenirs comprising -info@adat-istiadat.gov.bn
of Government Flags
and emblems, Royals
Regalias, Government
flags and crests

Historical Antiques made Museums Department -+673-2244545
or found in Brunei -info@museums.gov.bn

Mineral water and Ministry of Industry -+673-2382822
Building Construction and Primary Resources -info@mipr.gov.bn
Materials such as
cements

Rice, Sugar and Salt Information Technology -+673-2382822
and State Store Department -info@itss.gov.bn

Broadcasting
Equipments such as Prime Minister's Office -+673-2242780
Parabola, Decorder, etc. -info@jpm.gov.bn

RULES FOR PASSENGERS

Personal Effect

Section 9, Chapter B Customs Import Duty Order 2007, passengers aged 17 and above who enter this country is allowed to bring personal items of their own with no more than a concession given:

•Items that have been personally used (not new)
•Perfume - 60 mililiters
•Aromatic water - 250 grams

Cigarette / Tobacco

Since 1st November 2010, according to Customs Import Duties (Amendment) Order 2010 and Excise Duties (Amendment) Order 2010, cigarette / tobacco were deleted to be included in Passenger's Concession (Personal Effect). Every cigarette / tobacco enter this country must be declared and duty must be paid at B$0.25 per stick.

Liquor

1.For passengers who are not muslims aged 17 and above who enter this country are allowed to bring in not more than a concession given as follows:

2 bottels of alcoholic beverages (liquor) of about 2 liters (1 liter per bottle)
12 cans of beer (one can x 330ml)

2.Owners are required to declare imported drinks (liquor) to Customs Officers on duty at point where drinks are imported.

3.Special form of liquor is available at every Customs Post Control or Customs Offices and passenger ships.

4.Terms and Conditions for Importing Liquor

•Importers are aged 17 and above, and not muslim.
•Importers entrance to Brunei Darussalam is valid.
•Imported liquor is for personnel used and not to be granted, transferred or sold to others.
•Liquor should be kept and consumed at importers own place of residence.
•Form must be produced on demand by any officer of Customs.
•The total number of declared liquor and liquor kept in saving of not more than two bottles of liquor (a maximum of 2 liters) and 12 cans of beer @ 1 x 330ml

WARNING

It is an offense under Section 138 Customs Act 2006 for anyone who:-

I. Make oral or written, or signed any document that is untrue or incorrect in any matter; or

II. Forges or counterfeits any such documents; or

III. Intentionally alter any documents or counterfeit seal, the signature or short signatures of the Customs officer.
- See more at: http://www.mof.gov.bn/index.php/royal-custom-matters/customs-procedures/passengers-concession#sthash.lhwhfvyb.dpuf

CUSTOMS VALUATION

Customs Valuation (price) for imported goods is based on the agreed WTO Valuation Code. The valuation is made in accordance with the following methods:

•Method 1: Transaction Value
•Method 2: Similar Goods
•Method 3: Identical Goods
•Method 4: Deductive Value
•Method 5: Computed Value
•Method 6: Flexible and Reasonable Method

Customs used rule or method hierarchically and not otherwise, for example, if Method 1 failed to obtain the actual value (price) then Method 2 will be used and so forth.
- See more at: http://www.mof.gov.bn/index.php/royal-custom-matters/customs-procedures/customs-valuation#sthash.HN8scqSI.dpuf

PREFFERED TARIFFS

Import and export procedures of goods under CEPT Scheme.

Document Procedure

Type of declaration

ØFor import - Customs Import Declaration.
ØFor export - Customs Export Declaration.

Processing and approval
Traders are required to submit their application to the Customs at the point of importation or exportation.

Requirement for issuing CEPT form
ØManufactures must first apply to the Ministry of Foreign Affairs and Trade (MoFAT).
ØApplication must be complied with rules of origin of the CEPT Scheme.
ØWith the approved CEPT Form D, the manufacturers or exporters may apply for the Customs Export Declarations.

Customs Export Declarations

The CEPT Form D comprises of 4 copies. The original and triplicate are given to the importer for submission to the Customs authority at the importing country. The duplicate copy is retained by MoFAT and the quadruplicate is retained by the manufacturer or exporter.

Import Procedure

The importer shall produce the cargoes together with Customs Import Declaration, CEPT Form D, invoice, packing list, bill of landing/airway bill and other relevent supporting document to the Customs at the entry point for verification and examination.

CLASSIFICATION

1. Method

Commodities classification carried out by RCED is in accordance with the 1996 version of International Convention Standard on Harmonized Commodity and Coding System.

2. What is the responsibility of importer and exporter in classification?

Importer /exporter or their representatives are responsible to determine the classification of their imported or exported commodities.

3. Where does importer/exporter can obtain classification service?

i) The importer/exporter or their representatives can apply for classification services from Customs Classification Unit, RCED Headquarters, Jalan Menteri Besar.

ii) Phamplets, brochures, sample of commodities, etc should also (if necessary) be submitted.

iii) Classification process will take 3 working days to complete.

4. Pre Entry Classification

This is a method of commodities classification prior to importation.

5. Aim of Pre-Entry Classification

This is to assist and facilitate traders in the determination of correct classification of commodities especially with regards to taxation.

6. Validity of method

This method is valid and adopted for declaration at the Customs counters.

Classification by this method is not valid if the imported commodities are not concordant with the submitted samples.

7. Application for the service

Application forms can be obtained and submitted to the Customs Classification Unit, RCED Headquarters, Jalan Menteri Besar.

The completed forms should be submitted together with phamplets, brochures, commodities samples (if necessary) etc.

8. Charges

Application for pre-entry classification service is free of charge.

9. Application process

Application will be processed in 7 working days.

Incomplete application will be referred back to the applicant with request for any other information, etc.

APPROVAL PERMIT

A.P. is issued by the Royal Customs and Excise Department to enable the Department to take appropriate actions regarding security and control measures for statistical purpose.

Completed A.P. applications should be submitted to the Customs Service and Technique (CST) Division together with the following supporting documents:-

Ø Licence or written approval from the relevant agencies.
Ø Packing list.
Ø Other relevant documents (if any).

Approved A.P. copies should be faxed to the Customs branches where the commodities will be released.

The CST Division will contact the relevant Customs branches to ensure that they received the copies:-

Ø Terms and conditions of general approval permit.
Ø Terms and conditions of used car approval permit.
Ø Terms and conditions of heavy machinery approval permit.
Ø Terms and conditions of import duty exemption for industrial machinery.

RE-IMPORT

Re-import is a facility which enables the dutiable local commodities or products to be exported and then re-imported for the following purpose:-
For improvement/repair process either still under warranty or being damaged.

1. Application for export approval
   Prior to exportation of dutiable commodities, the owner or their representative should submit application to the Customs Department. Failure to do so will cause the good to be charged with full import duties on re-importation.

2. Documentation
   Besides the usual relevant documents the importer should also submit the following documents during commodities declaration:-

   Ø Export declaration form together with the relevant documents.
   Ø Export approval letter from Customs Department.
   Ø Import declaration.
   Ø Other relevant documentation.

3. Re-import duty
   i) Re-import duty will be imposed on the following:-

   Ø Spare parts costs.
   Ø Repair costs.
   Ø Packaging costs.
   Ø Insurance and freight (export or re-export and re-import).
   Ø Other costs related with re-imported commodities.

   ii) Full duty.
   Full duty rates will be charged according to the current value determined by the Customs for the following reasons:-

   Ø If the applicant fail to submit the export declaration form and the relevant documentation during exportation.

Ø If drawbacks for re-imported commodities has been approved after being released.
Ø If there any changes to the original forms, shapes and appearance of commodities.

TEMPORARY IMPORT

Negara Brunei Darussalam has not adopted the A.T.A Carnet Convention yet. How ever we are committed to speed up the flow of temporary importation of commodities with out import duty.

1. Commodities approved for temporary importation

Ø Commodities for demonstration and exhibition.
Ø Commodities for trade samples.

2. Approval or Verification letter

Ø Exhibition or demonstration commodities should get the approval of Ministry of Home Affairs.
Ø Demonstration commodities for government agencies or private companies should obtained the verification of the relevant agencies or companies.
Ø Application for temporary import together with the approval or verification of the relevant agencies or companies should be submitted to the customs department.

3. Duration of approved temporary import

Ø 3 months from the entry date of commodities.
Ø Commodities should be taken out after the approval due date.

4. Extension of duration

Ø Duration may be extended to not more than 6 months from the initial import date subject to the Customs clearance.

5. Failure to export within in the given period

Ø Fill import duty will be imposed on the commodities.

6. Security of financial guarantee

Ø Financial guarantee in the form of cash or bank cheque is required in accordance with the amount of import duty on the temporary imported commodities.

7. Refund of financial guarantee

Ø Financial guarantee will be refund when the commodities has been taken out in compliance with all export terms.

DUTY REFUND

Refund is the return of extra payment to importer. Section 13 of Customs Act authorised the Controller of Customs to refund the extra payment on Customs duty, good on rental or any other payments under this Act.

Drawback is the return of payment about 9/10 of the paid import duty on any commodities imported and then re-exported.

Approved refund and drawback.

Refund and drawback will only be approved if the claim is made within in 12 months from the date of payment if import duty.

Ï Approved category for drawback.

Ø Damaged commodities.
Ø Visitors and business sample commodities.
Ø Imported industrial commodities mixed with any locally produced commodities and then re-exported.

Terms and condition of refund application.

Terms and condition of drawback application.

TIME SCHEDULE

Each application will be approved within the time given if the applicants propose the application with supporting documents needed and comply with the regulation required as an applicant.

No.	Type of Service	Duration (Days)
1.	Application of classification approval. a) Valuation and classification	9 days
	b) Taxation	6 days
	c) Procedure	6 days
2.	Application of exempted. a) Industrial Machines	14 days
	b) Used vehicles	7 days
	c)Used heavy vehicles	7 days
3.	Application of Drawback.	30 days
4.	Application of Refund.	30 days
5.	Application of A.P (Approval Permit). a)New motor vehicle (Personally/Company)	1 day
	b)Used motor vehicles (Personally)	2 days
	c)Heavy vehicles (Company)	7 days
	d)Salt / Sugar / Rice / Alcohol Beverage / Cigarette	2 days
	e)Meat from Chicken / Ox / Bull / Cow	2 days
6.	Process of Drawback / Refund.	30 days
7.	Process of Declaration (Long Room).	1 day

CUSTOMS FORMS

REGISTRATION OF TRADERS AND AGENT

Royal Customs and Excise Department
Ministry of Finance
Jalan Menteri Besar. Bandar Seri Begawan BB 3910
Brunei Darussalam
Tel : 0673- 2382333 Fax : 0673- 2382666

***REGISTRATION TYPE**

- [ ] Registration of Trader
- [ ] Registration As An Agent

PART I	***PARTICULAR OF ESTABLISHMENT**		
Trader Registration no:		Trader's Name:	
Registered Address:		Post Code:	
Postal Address:		Post Code:	
Telephone No:	Other Telephone No:	e-mail	Fax No:

PART II	***COMPANY DIRECTORS**
Director Name 1:	Director Name 2:
Director Name 3:	Director Name 4:
Director Name 5:	Director Name 6:

PART III ***BUSINESS TYPE**

- [ ] Air Cargo Agent
- [ ] Airline
- [ ] Airline Agent
- [ ] Courier Agent
- [ ] Declaring Agent
- [ ] Exporter
- [ ] IForeign Embassy
- [ ] IFreight Forwarder
- [ ] IFreight Forwarding Agent
- [ ] Government Department
- [ ] Importer (dutiable goods)
- [ ] Importer (non-dutiable goods)
- [ ] Foreign Embassy
- [ ] Liquor & Tobacco Law Operator
- [ ] Manufacturer
- [ ] Non Commercial Organisation
- [ ] Ship Owner
- [ ] Shipping Agent
- [ ] Shipping Handler
- [ ] Warehouse Agent
- [ ] Authorised Car Dealers
- [ ] Others (Please specify)

PART IV **** BANK GUARANTEE DETAIL*** *[to be filled by Agent and Traders inwich payment made by Company's Cheque to the Customs)*

Reference No :	Amount :
Bank :	Expire Date :

PART V **** DECLARATION*** *[to be filled by Trader's and Agent's Authorized personal]*

I declare that the information contained in this form is true and correct and I undertake to inform Customs immediately of any change(s) to the particular in this form. [To be signed by the Chairman/Managing Director/ Director/ Proprietor or a partner of the company/ firm. His/ her name should appear in the Registry of Companies & Firm]

Name :	NRIC/ Passport No :
	Date :
Designation :	Signature:

Important: Don't forget to include
1. Photocopies of NRIC/Passport of authorized person 2. A copy of Business Certificate of Registration Sec 16 and Sec 17 3. Copy of each Company Partnership identity Card 4. Any relevent documents to support this application (i.e. Customs Certificates) 4. A copy of Bank Guarantee Detail from authorized Bank

Company/FirmStamp

PART VI **FOR OFFICAL USED ONLY** [CUSTOMS APPROVAL OFFICER]

Approval Ref No :	Cash Receipt No :	
Date Received :	Effective Date :	Expire Date :

Approval Officer's Name :

Designation :

Departmental Stamp

Signature/ Date

TRADER AUTHORISATION FORM

To
The Controller
Royal Customs and Excise Department
Jalan Menteri Besar
Bandar Seri Begawan BB 3910
Negara Brunei Darussalam

Dear Sir,

We ____ (Name)

of ______________________ (Company's name) ____________ (Reference no)

have the honour to inform you that we have authorized the following trader (s):-

(1)	Agent Name :	Trader Registration no:	
		Effective Date :	
		Expiry Date :	
(2)	Agent Name :	Trader Registration no:	
		Effective Date :	
		Expiry Date :	
(3)	Agent Name :	Trader Registration no:	
		Effective Date :	
		Expiry Date :	
(4)	Agent Name :	Trader Registration no:	
		Effective Date :	
		Expiry Date :	

to act as our agent to transact Customs Business

a) to sign or submit online Customs Declarations

b) to handle customs clearance

c) to receive money or grant receipts and

d) to execute bank guarantees

I declare that all information contained in this form is true and correct and I undertake responsibility to inform Customs immediately of any changes to the particulars in this form

Yours faithfully

____

( ) Designation : ________________ Date : __________

TRADE REGULATIONS AND STANDARDS

IMPORT TARIFFS

Brunei generally has very low tariffs. In 2005, the average tariff rate for most favored nations was 2%. The Asia Pacific Economic Cooperation (APEC) online database lists 932 tariff rates for Brunei: http://www.apectariff.org/tdb.cgi/ff3235/apeccgi.cgi?BN .

In general, basic foodstuffs and goods for industrial use are exempted from import duties. As of January 1, 2008, customs import duty on cars is abolished. All cars are levied excise duties at 20%, except for heavy vehicles, which are taxed at 15%. There is no tax on computers and peripherals. Other consumer products such as perfume, cosmetics, clothes, carpets, shoes, jewelry, office equipment, telephones, television sets, lamps, cameras, etc., are taxed at 5 percent. The Association of Southeast Asian Nations (ASEAN) online data on tariff and duty rates for Brunei: http://www.aseansec.org/14270.htm .

TRADE BARRIERS

The World Trade Organization has made available its analysis of Brunei's trade policies online: http://www.wto.org/english/tratop_e/tpr_e/tp165_e.htm

IMPORT REQUIREMENTS AND DOCUMENTATION

The import of all goods into the country is monitored by The Royal Customs and Excise Department. Importers must register with the port of entry. Determination of classification of duty is based in the Customs Import Duty Order (Revised) 2004.

Completed Customs Declaration Forms have to be submitted together with supporting documentation such as invoice, freight and insurance slips, airwaybill and packing list.

Additional documentation that may be required include certificate of origin and analysis, Approval Permit (A.P.), import license and other documentation as deemed necessary by the Customs and Excise Department.

Further information can be obtained from:

Royal Customs & Excise Department

Ministry of Finance

Tel : 673-2382333

Fax : 673-2382666

Website : www.mof.gov.bn/mof/en/departments/rced.

The Department of Health Services under the Ministry of Health ensures food imported and distributed in Brunei is safe for human consumption. Food importers are required to comply with the Public Health Order (Food), 1998, Public Health (Food) (Amendment) Order 2002 and its

Regulations 2000. Food importers are required to comply with the provisions of the said food legislations and import requirements. Importers are required to submit the customs declaration form together with the relevant export health certificates from the countries of origin

Other requirements include provision of Hazard Analysis Critical Control Point (HACCP) certificate, samples of all items to be imported to Brunei, list of all the ingredients and additives used and other valid documentation or certification as determined by the Ministry of Health. Food products imported are mainly „halal', for the consumption of the majority Muslim population. Halal food cannot contain alcohol or derivatives from non-halal animals.

Processed food imports must be registered and must identify additives' origin under Regulation 9, Public Health (Food) Regulation, 2000.

Further information can be obtained from:

Food Safety and Quality Control Division

Department of Health Services

Environmental Health Service

Ministry of Health

Tel : 673-2331100

Fax: 673-2331107

Website : www.moh.gov.bn .

U.S. EXPORT CONTROLS

Companies wanting to export controlled items to Brunei must apply for licenses from the appropriate government agencies in the United States. The Bureau of Industry and Security (BIS) is responsible for implementing and enforcing the Export Administration Regulations (EAR). Certain specialized exports are regulated by other U.S. government

agencies. A list of agencies involved in export controls can be found at www.bis.doc.gov .

TEMPORARY ENTRY

Brunei has not adopted the ATA Carnet Convention but allows temporary entry of commodities for demonstration, exhibition and trade samples for a duration of three months. Instructions are available at the Royal Customs and Excise website: http://www.mof.gov.bn/English/RCE/customservices/Pages/TemporaryImport.aspx .

LABELING AND MARKING REQUIREMENTS

(Under the Public Health Order (Food), 1998, Public Health (Food) (Amendment) Order 2002 and its Regulations 2000, all food imported into the country must bear a label containing information such as list of ingredients, expiry date and details of the local importer, distributor or agent. The print for the expiry dates must not be less than three millimeter in height. Information on food label is required to be labeled in a prominent and conspicuous position on the package.

Importation of food products (25 categories that require date markings) including food supplements are subject to "set requirements" as outlined by the Public Health (Food) Regulation 2000 and are required to registered with the Food Quality and Safety Control Division, Environmental Health Services, Department of Health Services. Health supplements that contain ingredients which can be used therapeutically or contain any medical claims are required to be referred to the Department of Pharmaceutical Services, Ministry of Health for clearance.

Detailed information on the food labeling requirements can be obtained from:

Food Safety and Quality Control Division

Department of Health Services

Environmental Health Service

Ministry of Health

Tel : 673-2331100

Fax : 673-2331107

Website : www.moh.gov.bn .

PROHIBITED AND RESTRICTED IMPORTS

Brunei imposes restrictions / prohibitions on the import of certain goods under the Customs Order 2006 (Section 31). Details of restricted /prohibited goods are available from:

Royal Customs & Excise Department
Ministry of Finance
Tel : 673-2382333
Fax : 673-2382666
Webpage :
http://www.mof.gov.bn/mof/en/departments/rced/customsproc/prohibition+and+restriction/.

Importers for "halal" meat and food products need prior approval from the Ministry of Religious Affairs.. Prior to approval, inspection of the foreign plant facilities will be carried out by two officers from the Religious Affairs Department. Importers have to pay for the trip. Currently only selected approved plants from Australia, Malaysia and India are accredited to supply halal beef.

Brunei imports live cattle from the state owned cattle farm located in Northern Australia for slaughter locally. Brunei claims to be 90% self sufficient for poultry production. Halal certification for poultry is issued on strict compliance with slaughter methods set by the Ministry of Religious Affairs.

Importation of alcoholic beverages has been prohibited since 1991. Pork is consumed only by non-Muslims. There is no production of pork in Brunei. Brunei imports fresh and frozen pork from neighboring Malaysian state of Sarawak.

The Halal Certificate and Halal Label Order 2005 covers the issuance of Halal Certificate and Halal Labels on processed food, separation of food storage and business premises such as restaurants and others.

The contact for Halal issue:

The Secretary

Board for Issuing Halal Import Permits

Ministry of Religious Affairs

Jalan Elizabeth II

Bandar Seri Begawan BS8510

Brunei Darussalam

Tel: 673-2242565 / 6

Fax: 673-2223106

Website: http://www.religious-affairs.gov.bn/index.php?ch=bm_service&pg=bm_service_halhar

CUSTOMS REGULATIONS AND CONTACT INFORMATION

Royal Customs & Excise Department
Ministry of Finance
Jalan Menteri Besar
Bandar Seri Begawan BB3910
Tel : 673-2382333
Fax : 673-2382666
Website : www.mof.gov.bn/mof/en/departments/rced

FREE TRADE ZONE

Brunei has established a Free Trade Zone on Muara Port (Muara Export Zone), and plans another FTZ at Sungai Liang.

The Muara Export Zone (MEZ) was established to develop Brunei as a trade hub for the region. Managed by the Ports Authority, the MEZ offers attractive rates on monthly warehouse rent and container movement and handling, and customs procedures from the MEZ to Muara Port.

Further information on the MEZ can be obtained from:

Director of Ports (Commercial and Marketing Division)

Ports Department

Muara BT1728

Tel : 673-2770222

Fax : 673-2770283 / 2770625

E-mail : ports@brunet.bn

Website : http://www.ports.gov.bn/en/muara_export/index.html

STANDARDS

The construction industry in Brunei uses metric system. Further information on Piawaian (Standards) Brunei Darussalam (PBD) can be obtained from:

Construction Planning and Research Unit Ministry of Development Old Airport Complex, Berakas BB3510 Brunei Darussalam

STANDARDS ORGANIZATIONS

The Ministry of Development prefers ISO 9000 for contracting jobs. A list of ISO 9000 certified companies in Brunei is available at the Ministry of Development's webpage : http://www.mod.gov.bn/index.php?option=com_content&view=article&id=163&Itemid=3 (in local language – Malay) or contact the Ministry of Development at:

Ministry of Development
Old Airport Complex, Berakas BB3510
Brunei Darussalam
Tel: +6732383222 Fax: +6732380298
email:info@mod.gov.bn

NIST NOTIFY U.S. SERVICE

Member countries of the World Trade Organization (WTO) are required under the Agreement on Technical Barriers to Trade (TBT Agreement) to report to the WTO all proposed technical regulations that could affect trade with other Member countries. **Notify U.S.** is a free, web-based e-mail subscription service that offers an opportunity to review and comment on proposed foreign technical regulations that can affect your access to international markets. Register online at Internet URL: http://www.nist.gov/notifyus/

CONFORMITY ASSESSMENT

Conformity Assessment Procedure is available at:

http://www.mod.gov.bn/index.php?option=com_content&view=article&id=163&Itemid=3 (in local language – Malay) or contact the Ministry of Development at:

Ministry of Development

Old Airport Complex, Berakas BB3510
Brunei Darussalam
Tel: +6732383222 Fax: +6732380298
email:info@mod.gov.bn

TRADE AGREEMENTS

Brunei is a member of the ASEAN, APEC, WTO, BIMP-EAGA (Brunei Darussalam, Indonesia, Malaysia & the Philippines-East Asean Growth Area) and the Multilateral Agreement on the Liberalization of International Air Transportation (MALIAT). In addition to trade liberalization regimes under ASEAN, Brunei is party to a multilateral free trade agreement with Singapore, New Zealand and Chile known as Trans-Pacific Strategic Economic Partnership Agreement. In January 2008, the United States announced that it would join in negotiations on the services and investment chapters of the Trans-Pacific Strategic Economic Partnership Agreement as it explores participating in this trade agreement. .

WEB RESOURCES

Ministry of Development: www.mod.gov.bn

Royal Customs and Excise Department: www.mof.gov.bn/mof/en/departments/rced

BUSINESS TRAVEL

BUSINESS CUSTOMS

Introductions and connections are important and necessary in status-conscious Brunei. Relationship building precedes business negotiations and brokering deals can sometimes require several visits. Handshakes are common among male businessmen. Muslim women prefer not to shake hands with men, so don't be offended if a woman does not wish to shake hands.

When invited to dinner, the host will be offended if the guest offers to pay the dinner tab: Shoes should be removed before entering a private home. Avoid passing in front of a seated person or pointing with the index finger; Bruneians point with their thumbs with their hands clenched. Yellow is a royal-designated color and should not be worn in the presence of royalty.

The visitor to Brunei will find restaurants to fit all budgets and tastes. Malaysian, Indian, Chinese, and Western food are all ubiquitous. Tipping is not customary in Brunei. Large hotels and restaurants add a 10 percent service charge to the bill. Alcohol is not available for purchase in Brunei although some restaurants may allow customers to discretely bring in their own wine and beer. Muslims generally will not offer or accept alcoholic beverages.

TRAVEL ADVISORY

Brunei has a warm, humid climate year-round but most places of business are well air-conditioned. The Department of State advises travelers to view its travel advisory site at http://travel.state.gov for latest updates. Brunei Darussalam's official website offers tourism, government, business, and other information, and can be accessed at http://www.jpm.gov.bn/ . Within the sultanate, information center at the airport and downtown can provide maps and tourist services. Travel agencies are located throughout the capital.

VISA REQUIREMENTS

Business visitors and tourists from the United States do not need visas for visits of up to 90 days. Renewals and residency permits are routine and simple.

Brunei citizens are eligible to participate in the U.S. Visa Waiver Program allowing travel to the U.S. without visa for short business trips.

U.S. Companies that require travel of foreign business persons to the United States should be advised that security options are handled via an interagency process. Visa applicants should go to the following links.

State Department Visa Website: http://travel.state.gov/visa/index.html

United States Visas.gov: http://www.unitedstatesvisas.gov/

Embassy website: http://brunei.usembassy.gov

TELECOMMUNICATIONS

Brunei has one of the best telecommunication systems in South-East Asia and has major plans for improving it further. There are three operators providing telecommunications services in Brunei. They are Syarikat Telekom Brunei Berhad (TelBru), DST Communications (DSTCom) and B-mobile Communications Sdn Bhd.

TelBru (www.telbru.com.bn) provides fixed line. DST (www.dst-group.com) provides GSM and 3-G. B-mobile (www.bmobile.com.bn) provides 3G. Internet Service Providers are TelBru and DST. TelBru is called BruNet (www.brunet.bn) and DST is known as SimpurNet (http://www.simpur.net.bn/).

TRANSPORTATION

The international airport is a fifteen-minute drive from downtown Bandar Seri Begawan, the capital (a B$25 taxi ride). Additionally, taxi and bus services serves the capital and the outskirts although the bus has limited hours of operation. Air-conditioned buses frequently travel to Muara, Kuala Belait, Seria and Tutong. Rental cars and drivers can be hired with ease at competitive rates.

LANGUAGE

Most of the population speaks English. English menus and signs are common. Additionally, the bulk of the population speaks Malay, and the Chinese community (15% of the total population) generally speaks Mandarin and the Hokkien dialect.

When in doubt, Sir, Mr., Mrs. and Ms. can be used without fear of insult. Should U.S. businesses wish to follow local custom, Bruneian males can be called Awang, and women, Dayang. These titles roughly correspond to Mr. and Ms.

Additionally, Dato and Pehin are the two principal titles bestowed by the Sultan. Dato is a state honorary medal conferred by the Sultan, and may be bestowed on anyone the Sultan wishes to honor, regardless of nationality. The female equivalent to Dato is Datin, as is the wife of a Dato. Dato is roughly the equivalent to Sir in Britain. Pehin is a conferred honorary title generally associated with an official position within the royal court.

Pengiran refers to a Bruneian of royal descent. A daughter or son of a Pengiran is also a Pengiran. At the highest end of the scale is the title Pengiran Anak, denoting Bruneians closely related to the Sultan's family.

HEALTH

Brunei offers all its citizens free and modern health care. Most doctors speak English, many having studied in the United States and Europe. In the most extreme cases, emergency transportation to Singapore by airplane is possible, though expensive.

LOCAL TIME, BUSINESS HOURS, AND HOLIDAYS

Government offices are open for business from 7:45 am to 12:15 pm and from 1:30 pm to 4:30 pm in the afternoon Monday – Thursday and Saturday and are closed on Fridays and Sundays. Most shopping centers are open daily from 10 am to 10 pm, including Sundays. Private offices generally work from 8 am to 5 pm on weekdays and from 8 am to 12 noon on Saturdays. Banks generally operate on these hours as well. Most have ATM's and can exchange foreign currency. Citibank in Bandar Seri Begawan has two ATM's available 24 hours a day that are connected to the major American ATM networks.

Official Holidays 2010 U.S. Embassy, Bandar Seri Begawan
Date Day Holiday Observance
Jan 01 Fri New Year 2010 American
Jan 18 Mon Martin Luther King's Birthday American
Feb 14 Sun Chinese New Year Bruneian
Feb 15 Mon Washington Birthday American
Feb 23 Tue Brunei National Day Bruneian
Feb 26 Fri Prophet Muhammad's Birthday Bruneian
May 31 Mon Memorial Day American
July 04 Sun Independence Day American
July 10 Sat Israk Me'raj Bruneian**
July 15 Thur HM Sultan's Birthday Bruneian
Aug 11 Wed 1st Day Ramadhan Bruneian**
Aug 27 Fri Nuzul Al-Quran ** Bruneian
Sept 06 Mon Labor Day American
Sept 10 Fri Hari Raya Aidilfitri Bruneian**
Sept 11 Sat Hari Raya Aidilfitri Bruneian**
Oct 11 Mon Columbus Day American
Nov 11 Thur Veterans Day American
Nov 16 Tue Hari Raya Aidiladha Bruneian**
Nov 25 Thur Thanksgiving Day American
Dec 7 Tue 1st Day Hijrah 1432 Bruneian
Dec 25 Sat Christmas Day American
**** Actual Holiday Subject to Sighting of the Moon**

TEMPORARY ENTRY OF MATERIALS AND PERSONAL BELONGINGS

There is no sales tax in Brunei. Arriving passengers over 17 years old are eligible to import 200 cigarettes or 250 grams of tobacco, 60 ml of perfume and 250 ml of toilet water. Non-Muslims at least 17 years old may bring in up to two bottles of liquor or wine and 12 cans of beer for personal consumption, but these goods must be declared to customs upon entry.

A B$12 (US$8) airport departure tax must be paid upon departure.

CONTACTS

GOVERNMENT AGENCIES:

Attorney General Chamber www.agc.gov.bn

MINISTRY OF FOREIGN AFFAIRS AND TRADE WWW.MFA.GOV.BN

Trade Associations/Chamber of Commerce:
Chinese Chamber of Commerce & Industry
Tel: 673-223 5494 Fax: 673-223 5492 E-mail: ccc@brunet.bn

Brunei Malay Chamber of Commerce & Industry
Tel: 673-242 1840 Fax: 673-242 1839 E-mail: mccibd_dppmb@yahoo.com

Brunei Darussalam International Chamber of Commerce & Industry
Tel: 673-222 8382 Fax: 673-222 8389 E-mail: kpmg@brunet.bn

Federation of Brunei Malay Entrepreneurs
Tel: 673-887 6788

IMPORTANT EXPORT-IMPORT REGULATIONS

Examination is carried out after the declaration of goods has been accepted and duties have been collected.
Goods for examination must be produced by the importer or the importer's agent at prescribed places during the normal working hours. If an importer or the importer's agent request his/her goods to examined outsite the normal working hours, he/she has to pay overtime fees to Customs.

- Examination is carried out in the presence of the importer or the importer's agent. He/she will be responsible for opening, weighting, sorting and marking of goods and all other necessary operations as directed by the Customs Officer.
- Examination is carried out to the satisfaction of the Customs Officer. He/she may, as his/her duty requires, take samples of any goods or cause such goods to be detained.

LICENCE OR PERMIT

Licence or Permit is a verification or approval given/issued by the relevant Government Department/Agency responsible for the commodities before importation or exportation.

Application of licence/permit

Written application or completed form (subject to the requirement of the Department/Agency) must be submitted to the Government/Agency responsible for such prohibited and controlled commodities.

Additional requirement

There are some prohibited or controlled commodities that require A.P (Approval Permit) issued by the RCED other than the license/permit issued by the relevant Government Agency before being imported or exported.

Types of commodities and issuing Government Department/Agency

Types of Commodities	Government/Agency	Hotlines/email
Religious Publications/ Prints, Films, CD, LD VCD, DVD, Cassette, Recital of Al-Quran, Hadith, Religious books, Talisman commodities (such as textiles/clothing /etc.), bearing dubious Chop/photo	Royal Brunei Police Force	-+673-2459500 -info@police.gov.bn
	Islamic Dakwah Center	-+673-2382525 -info@pusat-dakwah.gov.bn
	Internal Security Department	-+673-2223225 -info@internal-security.gov.bn
Halal, Fresh, Cold And Frozen Meat	Halal Import Permit Issuing Board	-+673-2382525 -info@religious-affairs.gov.bn

	Health Services Department	-+673-2381640 -info@moh.gov.bn
	Agriculture Department	-+673-2380144 -info@agriculture.gov.bn
	Royal Customs and Excise department	-+673-2382333 -info@customs.gov.bn
Firearms, Explosives, Fire Crackers, Dangerous Weapons, Scrap Metal	Royal Brunei Police Force	-+673-2459500 -info@agriculture.gov.bn
Plants, Crops, Live Animals, Vegetables, Fruits, Eggs	Agriculture Department	-+673-2380144 -info@police.gov.bn
Fishes, Prawns, Shells, Water Organisms and Fishing equipments etc	Fisheries Department	-+673-2382068 -info@fisheries.gov.bn
Poison, chemicals and radioactive materials. Snacks. Department)	Ministry of Health (Refer to the Food Medicines, Herbal, Quality Control Section. Health Foods, Soft Health Services Drinks and (Refer to Medical Enforcement Section, Pharmaceutical Services Department	-+673-2381640 -info@moh.gov.bn
Radio Transmitter and Receiver and Communications Equipment such as Telephone, Fax Machines, Walkie-Talkie, etc.	Info-Communication Technology Industry (AiTi)	-+673-2333780 -aiti@brunet.bn

Used Vehicles such as Cars, Motorcycles, Mini Buses, Pickups, Trucks, Trailers and non-motor vehicles such as Bicycles	Land Transport Department Royal Customs and Excise Department	-+673-2451979 -info@land-transport.gov.bn -+673-2382333 -info@customs.gov.bn
Timber and products thereof	Forestry Department	-+673-2381013 -info@forestry.gov.bn
Badges, Banners, Souvenirs comprising of Government Flags and emblems, Royals Regalias, Government flags and crests	Adat Istiadat Department	-+673-2244545 -info@adat-istiadat.gov.bn
Historical Antiques made 2244545 or found in Brunei	Museums Department	-+673- -info@museums.gov.bn
Mineral water and Building Construction Materials such as cements	Ministry of Industry and Primary Resources	-+673-2382822 -info@mipr.gov.bn
Rice, Sugar and Salt	Information Technology and State Store Department	-+673-2382822 -info@itss.gov.bn
Broadcasting Equipments such as Parabola, Decorder, etc.	Prime Minister's Office	-+673-2242780 -info@jpm.gov.bn

CUSTOM IMPORT DUTY (CUSTOM TAXES)

According to Section 9 Part B of Customs Import Duties Order 1973, passengers aged 17 and above arriving to this country are allowed to bring in their personal effect not exceeding the given concession as follows:-

Personally used goods (not new)

- Perfume - 60 milliliters
- Scented Water - 250 grams
- Cigarettes - 200 sticks or Tobacco - 250 grams
- Alcoholic beverages
  For non-muslim passengers over 17 years of age may be allowed to bring in not more than:-
  - 2 bottles of liquor (approximately 2 liters)
  - 12 cans of beer @ 330ml

- The importer may only import alcoholic liquor not less than 48 hours since the last importation.

- The alcoholic liquor shall be for importer's personal used and not to be given, transferred or sold to another person.

- The alcoholic liquor shall be stored and consumed at the place of residence of importer.

- The owner should declare liquor to Customs Officers in charge.

- Liquor form can be obtained from any Customs Control Posts or Customs Branches of Passenger Ships.

IMPORT AND EXPORT PROCEDURES OF GOODS UNDER CEPT SCHEME. DOCUMENT PROCEDURE

Type of declaration

- For import - Customs Import Declaration.
- For export - Customs Export Declaration.

Processing and approval
Traders are required to submit their application to the Customs at the point of importation or exportation.

Requirement for issuing CEPT form
- Manufactures must first apply to the Ministry of Foreign Affairs and Trade (MoFAT).
- Application must be complied with rules of origin of the CEPT Scheme.
- With the approved CEPT Form D, the manufacturers or exporters may apply for the Customs Export Declarations.

Customs Export Declarations

The CEPT Form D comprises of 4 copies. The original and triplicate are given to the importer for submission to the Customs authority at the importing country. The duplicate copy is retained by MoFAT and the quadruplicate is retained by the manufacturer or exporter.

Import Procedure

The importer shall produce the cargoes together with Customs Import Declaration, CEPT Form D, invoice, packing list, bill of landing/airway bill and other relevent supporting document to the Customs at the entry point for verification and examination.

- Dutiable goods imported to Brunei Darussalam are subject to Customs Import Duties Order 2007. ASEAN Common Effective Preferential Tariff (CEPT) could be given to importer based on qualification given by Ministry of Foreign Affairs and Trade (MoFAT). Most import duties are imposed based on Ad Valorem rate and only some taxes are based on specific rate. Ad Valorem is the percentage, for example, 20% of the price of good, while specific rate is calculated by the amount of weight or quantity such as $60 per kg or $220 per tonne. Determination of classification of imported goods whether dutiable or not are based on Customs Import Duties Order 2007. Since 1973 Brunei did not impose duties on exported goods. It is intended to promote local enterpreneurship.

CUSTOMS IMPORT DUTY GUIDE

Every person arriving in Negara Brunei Darussalam shall declare all dutiable goods in his possession, either on his person OR in any baggages OR in any vehicles to the proper officer of customs for examination.
If failed to do so, such goods shall be deemed to be uncustomed goods and imprisonment OR fine can be imposed.

Dutiable Goods

All goods subject to payment of customs duty and on such duty has not yet been paid.
According to paragraph 3(3) of customs import duties order 2007 where the total amount of import duty:

- Is less than $1 no import duty shall be charged.
- Exceed $1 and includes a fraction of $ 1, the fraction shall be treated as a complete dollar.

Importer of Dutiable Goods shall:

- Declare his/her goods.
- Produce documents such as invoice, bill and etc.
- Produce customs dutiable import declaration form no 5/C-16. (If necessary)

List of some Dutiable Goods and rate of Customs Import Duty

DUTIABLE GOODS	RATE OF CUSTOMS IMPORT DUTY
Coffee (not roasted)	11 cents/ 1 kg
Coffee (roasted)	22 cents/ 1 kg
Tea	22 cents/ 1 kg
Instant coffee/tea (Extract, essences and concentrates)/ coffee mate	5%
Grease	11 cents/ 1 kg
Lubricants	44 cents/ 1 kg
Carpet and other textile floor covering	5%
Mat and matting	10%
Wood and articles of wood	20%
Footware, slippers and the like	5%
Headgear and parts thereof	10%
Cosmetic, perfumes, toilet waters, soap, hair shampoo and other washing preparations	5%
Other preparations for use on the hair	30%
Electrical goods	5% OR 20%
Auto parts	20%
Articles of apparel and clothing accessories, of leather OR of composition leather	10%
Jewellery including imitation jewellery	5%
Clocks and watches and parts thereof	5%
Musical instruments	10%

EXPORT-IMPORT PROCEDURES

Goods To Be Imported & Export

All goods may be imported or exported except for restricted, prohibited and controlled goods under Section 31 of the Customs order, 2006.

Customs Declaration

Every imported & exported goods should be declared to the RCED by a declaration form except for the following goods:

- Passenger hand baggage's or personal effect on arrival.
- Goods arriving by post except for dutiable goods.

Declaration should give full and true account of the number of packages, cases description of goods, value, weight, measure or quantity and country of origin of the goods.

Customs Declaration Form must be submitted in triplicate and attached together with the following supporting documents :

- Invoice or purchase bill.
- Freight and Insurance Payment Slips.
- Delivery Order or Air Waybill.
- Packing List.

Other than the above documents, importer should also provide other documents related to the imported goods required by Customs coinciding with the declaration of goods such as:

- Certificate of Origin.
- Certificate of Analysis.
- A.P (Approval Permit) of the RCED.
- Import license issued by the relevant Government Department/Agencies.
- Verification Certificate of a recognized foreign agency.
- Other relevant documents.
- Personal qualified to declare.

The owners:

- The owners or importers or exporters are qualified to declare the imported/exported goods to RCED.

Representatives:

- The owner may authorize the agents or forwarders as their representatives in declaration.

Conditions of qualification of importer and exporter:

- Trader or Agent ID registrations;
- Every company or agents/forwarder must be registered with the RCED.
- Individual registration is not compulsory however customers (traders) are advised to make use of the services of Customs agents (forwarders).

Registration of Company:

- Application form available at the Customer Services Unit of RCED Headquaters, Jalan Menteri Besar.
- The application will be entered into the computer system of RCED, i.e Computer Control and Information System (CCIS).

Documents for Registration:

- A copy of the company's registration certificate.

- A copy of smart identity card.

TRAVEL TO BRUNEI

US STATE DEPARTMENT SUGGESTIONS

COUNTRY DESCRIPTION: Brunei (known formally as the State of Brunei Darussalam) is a small Islamic Sultanate on the north coast of the island of Borneo. The capital, Bandar Seri Begawan, is the only major city. Tourist facilities are good, and generally available.

ENTRY REQUIREMENTS: For information about entry requirements, travelers may consult the Consular Section of the Embassy of the State of Brunei Darussalam, Suite 300, 2600 Virginia Ave., N.W. Washington, D.C. 20037; tel. (202) 342-0159.

MEDICAL FACILITIES: Adequate public and private hospitals and medical services are available in Brunei. Medical care clinics do not require deposits usually, but insist upon payment in full at time of treatment, and may require proof of ability to pay prior to treating or discharging a foreigner. U.S. medical insurance is not always valid outside the United States, and may not be accepted by health providers in Brunei. Travelers may wish to check with their health insurance providers regarding whether their U.S. policy applies overseas. The Medicare/ Medicaid program does not provide payment of medical services outside the United States. Supplemental medical insurance with specific overseas coverage, including provision for medical evacuation may be useful. Travel agents or insurance providers often have information about such programs. Useful information on medical emergencies abroad is provided in the Department of State, Bureau of Consular Affairs' brochure *Medical Information for Americans Traveling Abroad*, available via our home page and autofax service. For additional health information, the international travelers hotline of the Centers for Disease Control and Prevention may be reached at 1-877-FYI-TRIP (1-877-394-8747), via the CDC autofax service at 1-888-CDC-FAXX (1-888-232-3299), or via the CDC home page on the Internet: http://www.cdc.gov.

INFORMATION ON CRIME: The crime rate in Brunei is low, and violent crime is rare. The loss or theft abroad of a U.S. passport should be reported immediately to the local police and to the U.S. Embassy. Useful information on guarding valuables and protecting personal security while traveling abroad is provided in the Department of State pamphlet, *A Safe Trip Abroad*. It is available from the Superintendent of Documents, U.S. Government Printing Office, Washington, D.C. 20402 or via the Internet at http://www.access.gpo.gov /su_docs.

CRIMINAL PENALTIES: While in a foreign country, a U.S. citizen is subject to that country's laws and regulations, which sometimes differ significantly from those in the United States and do not afford the protections available to the individual under U.S. law. Penalties for breaking the law can be more severe than in the United States for similar offenses. Persons violating the law, even unknowingly, may be expelled, arrested or imprisoned. The trafficking in and the illegal importation of controlled drugs are very serious offenses in Brunei. Brunei has a mandatory death penalty for many narcotics offenses. Under the current law, possession of heroin and morphine derivatives of more than 15 grams, and cannabis of more than 20 grams, carries the death sentence. Possession of lesser amounts carries a minimum twenty-year jail term and caning.

AVIATION OVERSIGHT: The U.S. Federal Aviation Administration (FAA) has assessed the Government of Brunei's Civil Aviation Authority as Category 1 - in compliance with international aviation safety standards for oversight of Brunei's air carrier operations. For further information, travelers may contact the Department of Transportation within the U.S. at 1-800-322-7873, or visit the FAA's Internet website at http://www.faa.gov/avr/iasa/index.htm. The U.S. Department of Defense (DOD) separately assesses some foreign air carriers for suitability as official providers of air services. For information regarding the DOD policy on specific carriers, travelers may contact DOD at 618-256-4801.

ROAD SAFETY: Roads are generally good and most vehicles are new and well-maintained. However, vehicular accidents are now one of the leading causes of death in Brunei. Possibly due to excessive speed, tropical torrential rains, or driver carelessness, Brunei suffers a very high traffic accident rate.

CUSTOMS INFORMATION: More detailed information concerning regulations and procedures governing items that may be brought into Brunei is available from the Embassy of the State of Brunei Darussalam in the United States.

Registration/Embassy Location: U.S. citizens living in or visiting Brunei are encouraged to register in person or via telephone with the U.S. Embassy in Bandar Seri Begawan and to obtain updated information on travel and security within the country. The U.S Embassy is located on the third floor, Teck Guan Plaza, Jalan Sultan, in the capital city of Bandar Seri Begawan. The mailing address is American Embassy PSC 470 (BSB), FPO AP, 96534; the telephone number is (673)(2) 229-670; the fax number is (673) (2) 225-293.

Brunei-Muara

On her state visit to Brunei in September of 1998, Her Majesty Queen Elizabeth II of Britain made a tour of the Kampung Ayer in the capital a part of her busy itinerary. Made up of numerous communities, and home to some 30,000 people, the Kampung Ayer ("Villages on Water") is certainly the most well-known of all attractions in the country.

Kampung Ayer has been around for a very long time. When Antonio Pigafetta visited the country in the mid-16th century; Kampung Ayer was already a well-established, "home to some 25,000 families," according to Pigafetta. It was the hub for governance, business and social life in Brunei at that time.

The Kampung Ayer of today retains many of its old-world features described by Pigafetta. Only now, its daily well being is overlooked by the chiefs of the many villages in the area. The Kampung has almost all the amenities available in other communities, such as schools, shops and mosques. The houses there are usually well equipped with the latest in modern technology.

For as low as $1, boatmen will ferry passengers along the breadth and length of the Brunei river.

River cruises aboard ferryboats can start at both ends of the Brunei river, one at the Muara side, at the Queen Elizabeth jetty (named after the reigning British queen after her first Brunei visit in 1972), and others at the various river boat taxi stations in the heart of town.

The journey from the other end of the river starts at Kota Batu, the 16th century capital. The upstream journey during the 10 miles per hour cruise passes an ancient landmark, the tomb of Brunei's fifth ruler, Sultan Bolkiah, the Singing Captain, under whose reign Brunei was a dominant power in the 15th century.

On one bank of the Brunei river is a newer relic, a British warship used dur-ing World War II, sheltered from the elements.

The ferry moves on to Kampong Ayer, the Venice of the East. During the 18th century, here lived the fisher-men, blacksmiths, kris (native sword) makers, brass artisans, nipa palm mat makers, pearl and oyster collectors, traders and goldsmiths.

A new Kampong Ayer has risen, settlements of concrete houses with glass windowpanes, and connected by cement bridges instead of the rickety, wooden catwalks.

Overlooking the old Kampong Ayer is the House of Twelve Roofs (Bum-bungan Dua Belas), built in 1906 and formerly the official home of the British resident. In the Kota Batu area on Jalan Residency is the Arts and Handicrafts Centre, where traditional arts and crafts have been revived.

But Kampung Ayer is only one of the many charms of Brunei that intrigue visitors to the country.

The Sultan Omar Ali Saifuddien Mosque in the heart of Bandar Seri Begawan continues to attract visitors fascinated by its majestic presence, and its role in the spiritual development of the Muslim citizens of the country. The mosque is practically synonymous with Brunei in general, and with the capital in particular.

Situated very close to the mosque is the public library with its attractive mural depicting Brunei's lifestyles in the 60s. The mural was done by one of Brunei's foremost artist, Pg Dato Hj Asmalee, formerly the director of Welfare, Youth and Sports, but now the country's ambassador to a neighbour-ing country.

Another landmark of the capital is the Yayasan Sultan Hj Hassanal Bolkiah commercial complex, across the road from the Sultan Omar Ah Saifuddien mosque. The newly estab-lished complex is the prime shopping centre in Brunei - four storeys of some of the premier big-name retailers in the region! There're outlets bran-dishing branded clothing, fast food, video games, books and many more. There's a supermarket in the Yayasan's west wing, and a food court on the east.

The Royal Regalia Building is a new addition to the attractions found in the capital. Within easy walking distance of all the hotels in the capital centre, the Royal Regalia Building houses artifacts used in royal cere-monies in the country. Foremost among the displays are the Royal Chariot, the gold and silver ceremonial armoury and the jewel-encrusted crowns used in coronation ceremonies.

Entrance is free, and visitors are expected to take off their shoes before entering. Opening hours are from 8.3Oam to 5.00pm daily except for Fridays, the Building opens from 9.00am until II.30am, and in the afternoon, from 2.30pm till 5.00pm.

Located next to the Royal Regalia Building is the Brunei History Centre. Drop by the centre and learn all about the genealogy and history of the sultans of Brunei, and members of the royal family. There is an exhibition area open to the public from 7.45 am to 12.l5pm, and l.30pm to 4.3Opm daily except for Fridays.

Across the road from the Brunei Hotel, is what is known throughout Borneo as the 'tamu.' A 'tamu' is a congregation of vendors selling farm produce and general items. If you are lucky, you can find valuable bargains among the potpourri of metalware and handicraft hawked by some peddlers.

The main Chinese temple in the country lies within sight of the 'tamu.' Its elaborately designed roof and loud red color of its outer walls make the temple stand out from among the more staid schemes of nearby buildings.

A visit during one of the many festivals that is observed at this sanctum of Taoist beliefs would be a celebration of colors, spectacle and smell. Another place of worship that should not be missed by visitors to Brunei is the Church of St Andrew's. The church, possibly the oldest in Brunei, is designed like an English country parish, complete with bells in the let fry. It lies within walking distance of the Royal Regalia Building.

If you are staying in a hotel or Bandar Seri Begawan, why not pay the nightly foodstalls a visit? The stalls are located at a site in front of Sheraton Hotel, and serve a wide variety of hawker fare cheap! A dollar worth of the fried noodles is enough to fill you up.

Check out the local burgers. They're as delicious as those you'll find in established fast food outlets. Or try out 'Roti John'-the Malay version of the Big Mac. Ask for 'goreng pisang' (banana fritters), 'begedil' (potato balls), or 'popiah' (meat rolls), in your jaunts to the sweetmeat stalls.

Outside the capital center, a worthwhile place to visit is the Jame' Asr Hassanil Bolkiah Mosque in Kiarong, about six kilometers away. This is a beautiful sanctuary for communication with God, a personal bequest from His Majesty the Sultan of Brunei himself for the people of the country.

More than just a place of worship, the Jame' Asr is also a center for learning. Classes teaching Islamic religious principles and practices are held there regularly, as do religious lectures. And every Friday morning, the lobbies of its vast edifice are filled with children studying the Quran.

A visit to the mosque is usually part of the itinerary of package tours to Brunei, but if not, visitors can make the necessary arrangement with local tour operators. Visitors wishing to come inside the mosque need to report to the officers on duty, at the security counter on the ground floor.

Further on, you will find the Jerudong Park Playground. Situated some 20 kms to the west of the capital, JP as it is popularly called, is a must-go place for visitors to the country. It has been described as "Brunei's first high-tech wonderland for people of all ages."

There are many amusement rides at the Jerudong Park Playground to cater to everyone's need.

For those who like to live life on the edge, you would be pleased to know that JP has THREE (that's right, three) roller coasters, each with different degrees of thrills (or insanity factors if you want).

'Pusing Lagi' takes riders up a crest almost six storeys high, and then takes them down a steep incline, before twisting and turning at breakneck speed, so much so you will regret the 'Roti John' you just had.

'Boomerang' is for people who would rather go for diabolical twists and turns, while 'Pony Express' is a ride for those newly-initiated to roller-coasters.

Other popular rides include the 'Condor', a very fast merry-go-round that takes you up some five stores high, the 'Aladdin' (a mechanical 'flying carpet'), 'Flashdance' (no dancing experience required), and the wildly swinging 'Pirate Ship'.

There is also a bumper car arena, only for children and youngsters though, a video arcade and tracks for skateboarding and carting. For those who prefer something more sedate, also available are a 'Merry-Go-Round', certainly the most beautiful this side of London, and the 'Simulator Tour' (virtual reality rides into the fantastic and the exotic). Try the up-tower rides, where you are taken up a tower 15 stores high, and given a superb view of the park, and the surrounding area.

Situated next to the playground is the 20-acre Jerudong Park Gardens, which is well-known for its concert class auditorium. This was where Michael Jackson had his performances some years back, drawing a record 60,000 people to a colorful extravaganza the first time he performed.

Whitney Houston was another megastar who has had performed here, as well as Stevie ("I Just Called To Say I Love You) Wonder and the wonderful Seal ("Kissed By A Rose").

And if all that running and riding gives you an appetite, there's good food to be found in the eating area next to the parking lot. Almost anything you could crave for is available, ranging from the local hawker spreads to international fast food fare. If you're not doing anything on a Friday morning or late afternoon, take the no.55 purple bus to the end of its line at Jerudong Beach. Jerudong Beach on Fridays, especially around 9.00-10.00am, is a hive of activity as fishermen start landing their catch and customers rush to avail themselves of the freshest fish possible. The people you'll get to meet there are among the friendliest in the country, easy with the smile and always ready for the idle chatter.

But the place is more than just an informal fish market. Local fruits hang prominently from many of the stalls, and food stalls sell take-outs to cater to hungry visitors. Swim in the calm, waveless waters of the man-made cove, or try your luck fishing, if that is what you want to do. Just go around people watching.

And if you need to go back to town, just board the purple bus to make the return journey.

The Bukit Shabbandar Forest Park is just the place to put those hiking legs to use. About ten minutes drive from the Jerudong Park Playground, the park is hectares upon hectares of greenery, dissected by tracks and paths for hiking, jogging and biking. While hiking, you can partake the wonders of the local forests - the rich diversity of its plant life, the exquisite charms and colors of the insects and reptiles that live within, and the symphony in the singing of the birds. Bukit Shahbandar Forest Park is just one of the 11 forest reserves in the country. To the east of Bandar Seri Begawan, about 6 kms into the Kota Batu area, visitors will find the Brunei Museum exhibits artifacts that archive the history of Negara Brunei Darussalam, both ancient and the relatively recent.

Well made cannons and kettles with their dragon motifs and elaborate patterns recall the glory days of the country -when Brunei was an important political and mercantile power in the region with territories that stretched that stretched all the way from Luzon Island in the Philippines to the whole western Borneo island.

There are exhibits which depict the traditional lifestyles of the various communities in the country, plus displays on the local flora and fauna. The exhibit by the local petroleum company Brunei Shell, illustrates the history on the discovery of oil in the country, and the commodity's significant role in economy of Brunei.

The Museum is open every day except Mondays from 9.00am till 5.00pm. On Fridays however, there is a scheduled prayer break from 11.30am until 2.30pm.

And situated downhill of the Brunei Museum is the Malay Technology Museum, which, as its name implies, houses the technological tools utilised by the Malays in ancient times.

A government booklet describes it as offering the "the visitor an intriguing insight into the lifestyle of the people of Brunei in by-gone eras". The Technology Museum is open daily, except Tuesdays, from 9.00 am till 5.00 pm. with a 3-hour midday prayer break on Fridays. Entrance is free.

There is an "Asean Square" in Persiaran Damuan which is located on a stretch between Jalan Tutong and the bank of the Brunei River about 4.5km from the capital. The "Asean Square" has on permanent display the work of a chosen sculptor themed Harmony in Diversity from each of the Asean member countries.

HOLIDAYS

Brunei Darussalam's vision is to promote the country as a unique tourist destination and gateway to tourism excellence in South East Asia. The objectives are to create international awareness of Brunei Darussalam as a holiday destination; to maximize earings of foreign exchange and make tourism as one of the main contributor to GDP. In addition, it will create employment opportunities.

The country offers a wide variety of attractive places to be visited and experienced. The rainforest and National Parks are rich in flora and fauna. Its most magnificent mosques, water village (traditional and historic houses on stilts), rich culture and Jerudong Theme Park are among the uniqueness of Brunei Darussalam.

The government is now actively promoting tourism as an important part of its economic diversification. It would like to see a target of 1 million-visitor arrival by the year 2000. From January to August 1999, the statistic recorded 405,532 visitors visited Brunei Darussalam.

National Day Celebration

The nation celebrates this joyous occasion on the 23rd of February and the people usually prepare themselves two months beforehand. Schoolchildren, private sector representatives and civil servants work hand-in-hand rehearsing their part in flash card displays and other colourful crowd formations. In addition mass prayers and reading of Surah Yaasin are held at mosques throughout the country.

Fasting Month (Ramadhan)

Ramadhan is a holy month for all Muslims. This marks the beginning of the period of fasting - abstinence from food, drink and other material comforts from dawn to dusk. During this month, religious activities are held at mosques and *suraus* throughout the country

Hari Raya Aidilfitri

Hari Raya is a time for celebration after the end of the fasting month of Ramadhan. In the early part of the first day, prayers are held at every mosque in the country. Families get together to seek forgiveness from the elders and loved ones. You will see Bruneians decked-out in their traditional garb visiting relatives and friends.

Special festive dishes are made especially for Hari Raya including satay (beef, chicken or mutton kebabs), ketupat or lontong (rice cakes in coconut or banana leaves), rendang (spicy marinated beef) and other tantalizing cuisines. In these auspicious occassion Istana Nurul Iman was open to the public as well as to visitors for 3 days. This provides the nation and other visitors the opportunity to meet His Majesty and other members of the Royal Family, in order to wish them a Selamat Hari Raya Aidilfitri.

Royal Brunei Armed Forces Day

31st of May marks the commemoration of the Royal Brunei Armed Forces formation day. The occassion is celebrated with military parades, artillery displays, parachuting and exhibitions.

Hari Raya Aidiladha

This is also known as Hari Raya Korban. Sacrifices of goats and cows are practiced to commemorate the Islamic historical event of Prophet Ibrahim S.A.W. The meat is then distributed among relatives, friends and the less fortunates.

His Majesty the Sultan's Birthday

This is one of the most important events in the national calendar with activities and festivities taking place nationwide. Celebrated on 15th July, this event begins with mass prayer throughout the country. On this occassion, His Majesty the Sultan delivers a 'titah' or royal address followed by investiture ceremony held at the Istana Nurul Iman. The event is also marked with gatherings at the four districts where His Majesty meets and gets together with his subjects.

Birthday of the Prophet Muhammad

In Brunei Darussalam, this occasion is known as the Mauludin Nabi S.A.W. Muslims throughout the country honour this event. Readings from the Holy Koran - the Muslim Holy Book, and an address on Islam from officials of the Ministry of Religious Affairs marks the beginning of this auspicious occasion. His Majesty the Sultan also gives a royal address and with other members of the Royal family, leads a procession on foot through the main streets of Bandar Seri Begawan. Religious functions, lectures and other activities are also held to celebrate this important occasion nationwide.

Chinese New Year

Celebrated by the Chinese community, this festival lasts for two weeks. It begins with a reunion dinner on the eve of the Lunar New Year to encourage closer rapport between family members. For the next two week, families visit one another bringing with them oranges to symbolize longevity and good fortune. Traditional cookies and food are aplenty during this festivity. Unmarried young people and children will receive 'angpow' or little red packets with money inside, a symbolic gesture of good luck, wealth and health.

Christmas Day

Throughout the world, 25th of December marks Christmas day, a significant day for all Christians. Christmas is nevertheless a joyous and colourful celebration enjoyed by Christians throughout the country.

Teachers' Day

Teachers' Day is celebrated on every 23rd September in recognition of the good deeds of the teachers to the community, religion and the country. It is celebrated in commemoration of the birthday of the late Sultan Haji Omar 'Ali Saifuddien Saadul Khairi Waddien, the 28th Sultan of Brunei for his contribution in the field of education including religious education. On this occassion, three awards are given away namely, Meritorious Teacher's Award, Outstanding Teacher's Award and *"Guru Tua"* Award.

Public Service Day

The date 29th September is observed as the Public Service Day with the objective to uphold the aspiration of the Government of His Majesty the Sultan and Yang Di-Pertuan of Brunei Darussalam towards creating an efficient, clean, sincere and honest public service. The Public Service Day commemorates the promulgation of the first written Constitution in Brunei Darussalam. The Public Service Day is celebrated with the presentation of the meritorious service award to Ministries and Government Departments.

PUBLIC HOLIDAYS

1 January	New Year's Day
8 January	* Hari Raya Aidilfitri
5 February	Chinese New Year
23 February	National Day
16 Mac	* Hari Raya Aidiladha
6 April	Muslim Holy Month of Hijiriah
31 May	Royal Brunei Armed Forces Day
15 Jun	The Birthday of Prophet Muhammad S.A.W.
15 July	The Birthday of His Majesty Sultan Haji Hassanal Bolkiah Mu'izzaddin Waddaulah, Sultan and Yang Di-Pertuan of Brunei Darussalam
25 October	* Israk Mikraj
27 November	* First Day of Ramadhan (Muslim fasting month)
13 December	Anniversary of The Revelation of the Quran
25 December	Christmas
27 December	* Hari Raya Aidilfitri

BUSINESS CUSTOMS

Customs & Traditions:	Brunei Darussalam possess a long heritage of traditions and customs, behavioural traits and forms of address. Muslims observe religious rites and rituals, which is woven into the lifestyle of Bruneian Malays. Breach of Malay conduct can be liable to prosecution in Islamic courts.
Social Protocol for non-Muslims:	It is customary for Bruneians to eat with their fingers rather than use forks and spoons. Always use the right hand when eating. It is polite to accept even just a little food and drink when offered. When refusing anything that is being offered, it is polite to touch the plate lightly with the right hand . As the left hand is considered unclean, one should use one's right hand to

	give and receive things. Bruneians sit on the floor, especially when there's a fairly large gathering of people. It is considered feminine to sit on the floor with a woman's legs tucked to one side, and equally polite for men to sit with folded legs crossed at the ankles. It's rude for anyone to sit on the floor with the legs stretched out in front, especially if someone is sitting in front. It is considered impolite to eat or drink while walking about in public except at picnics or fairs. During the Islamic fasting (Puasa) month, Muslims do not take any food from sunrise to sundown. It would be inconsiderate to eat and drink in their presence during this period. It is not customary for Muslims to shake hands with members of the opposite sex. Public display of affection such as kissing and hugging are seen to be in bad taste. Casual physical contact with the opposite sex will make Muslims feel uncomfortable. In the relationship between sexes, Islam enforces strict legislation. If a non-Muslim is found in the company of a Muslim of the opposite sex in a secluded place rather than where there are a lot of people, he/she could be persecuted. If you are found committing 'khalwat' that is seen in a compromising position with a person of the opposite sex who is a Muslim, you could be deported. When walking in front of people, especially the elderly and those senior in rank or position, it is a gesture of courtesy and respect for one to bend down slightly, as if one is bowing, except this time side way to the person or persons in front of whom one is passing. One of the arms should be positioned straight downwards along the side of the body. Leaning on a table with someone seated on it especially if he/she is an official or colleague in an office is considered rude. Resting one's feet on the table or chair is seen as overbearing. So is sitting on the table while speaking to another person who is seated behind it. To touch or pat someone, including children, on the head is regarded as extremely disrespectful. The polite way of beckoning at someone is by using all four fingers of the right hand with the palm down and motioning them towards yourself. It is considered extremely impolite to beckon at someone with the index finger.

SUPPLEMENTS

IMPORTANT LAWS OF BRUNEI

ACT / ORDER	CHAPTER / NOTIFICATION NO.	DATE OF COMMENCEMENT	STATUS
ADMIRALTY JURISDICTION ACT [2000 Ed.]	CAP. 179	01-10-1996	
ADOPTION OF CHILDREN ORDER 2001	S 16/2001	26-03-2001	
AGRICULTURAL PESTS AND NOXIOUS PLANTS ACT [1984 Ed.]	CAP. 43	01-08-1971	
AIR NAVIGATION ACT [1984 Ed., Amended by S 21/97, S 41/00, S 42/00, Repealed by S 63/06 - Civil Aviation Order]	CAP. 113	01-03-1978	REPEALED w.e.f. 20-05-06
AIRPORT PASSENGER SERVICE CHARGE ACT [2000 Ed.]	CAP. 188	01-05-1999	
ANTI-TERRORISM (FINANCIAL AND OTHER MEASURES) ACT [2008 Ed.]	CAP. 197	14-06-2002	
ANTIQUITIES AND TREASURE TROVE ACT [2002 Ed.]	CAP. 31	01-01-1967	
APPLICATION OF LAWS ACT [2009 Ed.]	CAP. 2	25-04-1951	
ARBITRATION ACT [1999 Ed.]	CAP. 173	24-04-1994	
ARBITRATION ORDER, 2009	S 34/2009		not yet in force
ARMS AND EXPLOSIVES ACT [2002 Ed.]	CAP. 58	08-04-1927	
ASIAN DEVELOPMENT BANK ACT [2009 Ed.]	CAP. 201	25-04-2006	
AUDIT ACT [1986 Ed., Amended by S 39/03]	CAP. 152	01-01-1960	
AUTHORITY FOR INFO-COMMUNICATIONS TECHNOLOGY INDUSTRY OF BRUNEI DARUSSALAM ORDER 2001 [Amended by S 13/03, S 35/03]	S 39/2001	01-01-2003	
BANISHMENT ACT [1984 Ed.]	CAP. 20	31-12-1918	
BANKERS' BOOKS (EVIDENCE) ACT [1984 Ed., Amended by S 29/93, Repealed by S 13/06]	CAP. 107	17-04-1939	REPEALED w.e.f. 12-02-06
BANKING ACT [2002 Ed., Repealed by S 45/06 - Banking Order]	CAP. 95	01-01-1957	REPEALED w.e.f. 04-03-06
BANKING ORDER, 2006	S 45/2006	04-03-2006	
BANKRUPTCY ACT [1984 Ed., Amended by S 12/96, S 52/00]	CAP. 67	01-01-1957	
BILLS OF EXCHANGE ACT [1999 Ed.]	CAP. 172	03-05-1994	
BILLS OF SALE ACT [1984 Ed.]	CAP. 70	16-01-1958	
BIOLOGICAL WEAPONS ACT [1984 Ed.]	CAP. 87	11-04-1975	
BIRTHS AND DEATHS REGISTRATION ACT [1984 Ed.]	CAP. 79	01-01-1923	

BISHOP OF BORNEO (INCORPORATION) ACT [1984 Ed.]	CAP. 88	25-04-1951	
BRETTON WOODS AGREEMENT ACT [2000 Ed.]	CAP. 176	30-09-1995	
BROADCASTING ACT [2000 Ed., Corrigendum S 41/07]	CAP. 180	15-03-1997	
BRUNEI ECONOMIC DEVELOPMENT BOARD ACT [2003 Ed., Amended by S 11/03]	CAP. 104	11-04-1975	
BRUNEI FISHERY LIMITS ACT [1984 Ed., Amended by S 25/09]	CAP. 130	01-01-1983	
BRUNEI INVESTMENT AGENCY ACT [2002 Ed., Amended by S 14/03, S 64/04, S 15/08, S 78/08]	CAP. 137	01-07-1983	
BRUNEI MALAY SILVERSMITHS GUILD (INCORPORATION) ACT [1984 Ed.]	CAP. 115	15-07-1959	
BRUNEI NATIONAL ARCHIVES ACT [1984 Ed.]	CAP. 116	01-08-1981	
BRUNEI NATIONAL PETROLEUM COMPANY SENDIRIAN BERHAD ORDER 2002 [Amended by S 6/2003, S 12/2003]	S 6/2002	05-01-2002	
BRUNEI NATIONALITY ACT [2002 Ed., Amended by S 55/2002]	CAP. 15	01-01-1962	
BUFFALOES ACT [1984 Ed.]	CAP. 59	01-01-1909	
BURIAL GROUNDS ACT [1984 Ed.]	CAP. 49	01-01-1932	
BUSINESS NAMES ACT [1984 Ed., Amended by S 30/88]	CAP. 92	01-03-1958	
CENSORSHIP OF FILMS AND PUBLIC ENTERTAINMENTS ACT [2002 Ed.]	CAP. 69	21-08-1962	
CENSUS ACT [2003 Ed.]	CAP. 78	07-06-1947	
CENTRE FOR STRATEGIC AND POLICY STUDIES ORDER, 2006	S 64/2006	01-07-2006	
CHILD CARE CENTRES ORDER 2006	S 37/06	04-03-2006	
CHILDREN AND YOUNG PERSONS ORDER, 2006 [Corrigendum S 24/06, Amended by S 60/08]	S 9/2006		not yet in force
CHILDREN ORDER 2000 [Amended by S 84/00, S 48/03]	S 64/2000	01-09-2000	
CHINESE MARRIAGE ACT [1984 Ed., Amended by S 44/89]	CAP. 126	31-07-1955	
CIVIL AVIATION ORDER, 2006	S 63/2006	20-05-2006	
COIN (IMPORT AND EXPORT) ACT [1984 Ed.]	CAP. 33	01-01-1909	
COMMISSIONS OF ENQUIRY ACT [1984 Ed., Amended by S 35/05]]	CAP. 9	28-04-1962	
COMMISSIONERS FOR OATHS ACT [1999 Ed.]	CAP. 169	26-08-1993	
COMMON GAMING HOUSES ACT [2002 Ed., Amended by S 20/08]	CAP. 28	01-01-1921	
COMPANIES ACT [1984 Ed., Amended by S 26/98, S 23/99, S 69/01, S 10/03, S 45/06, S	CAP. 39	01-01-1957	

96/08]			
COMPULSORY EDUCATION ORDER, 2007	S 56/2007	24-11-2007	
COMPUTER MISUSE ACT [2007 Ed.]	CAP. 194	21-06-2000	
CONSTITUTION OF BRUNEI DARUSSALAM [2004 Ed., Amended by S 14/06] Article 8A, 9(2), 9(4), 9(5) - suspended by S 15/06 w.e.f. 21/02/06	CONST. I	29-09-1959	
CONSTITUTION [FINANCIAL PROCEDURE] ORDER [2004 Ed., Amended by S 14/08, S 36/08]	CONST. III	01-01-1960	
CONSULAR RELATIONS ACT [1984 Ed.]	CAP. 118	01-01-1984	
CONTINENTAL SHELF PROCLAMATION [1984 Ed.]	SUP. II		
CONTRACTS ACT [1984 Ed., Amended by S 60/02]	CAP. 106	17-04-1939	
CO-OPERATIVE SOCIETIES ACT [1984 Ed.]	CAP. 84	01-07-1975	
COPYRIGHT ORDER 1999	S 14/2000	01-05-2000	
CRIMINAL CONDUCT (RECOVERY OF PROCEEDS) ORDER 2000 [Amended by S 30/07]	S 52/2000	01-07-2000	
CRIMINAL LAW (PREVENTIVE DETENTION) ACT [2008 Ed.]	CAP. 150	26-11-1984	
CRIMINAL PROCEDURE CODE [2001 Ed., Amended by S 63/02, GN 273/02, S 62/04, S 32/05, S 6/06, S 9/06, S 4/07]	CAP. 7	01-05-1952	S 6/06 & S 9/06 not yet in force
CRIMINALS REGISTRATION ORDER, 2008	S 42/2008	01-04-2008	
CURRENCY ACT [1984 Ed., Repealed by S 16/04 - Currency and Monetary Order]	CAP. 32	Please refer Act	REPEALED w.e.f. 01-02-04
CURRENCY AND MONETARY ORDER 2004 [Corrigendum S 71/04; Amended by S 59/05, S 39/07]	S 16/2004	01-02-2004	
CUSTOMS ACT [1984 Ed., Amended by S 23/89, S 82/00, S 52/01, S 39/06, Repealed by S 39/06 - Customs Order]	CAP. 36	01-01-1955	REPEALED w.e.f. 04-03-06
CUSTOMS ORDER, 2006 [Amended by S 98/08]	S 39/06	04-03-2006	
DANA PENGIRAN MUDA MAHKOTA AL-MUHTADEE BILLAH FOR ORPHANS ACT [2000 Ed.]	CAP. 185	25-08-1998	
DEBTORS ACT [2008 Ed.]	CAP. 195	16-10-2000	
DEFAMATION ACT [2000 Ed.]	CAP. 192	17-08-1999	
DESCRIPTION OF LAND (SURVEY PLANS) ACT [1984 Ed.]	CAP. 101	03-09-1962	
DEVELOPMENT FUND ACT [1984 Ed.]	CAP. 136	01-01-1960	
DIPLOMATIC PRIVILEGES (EXTENSION) ACT [1984 Ed.]	CAP. 85	02-12-1949	

DIPLOMATIC PRIVILEGES (VIENNA CONVENTION) ACT [1984 Ed.]	CAP. 117	01-09-1982	
DISAFFECTED AND DANGEROUS PERSONS ACT [1984 Ed.]	CAP. 111	29-07-1953	
DISASTER MANAGEMENT ORDER 2006	S 26/06	01-08-2006	
DISSOLUTION OF MARRIAGE ACT [1999 Ed.]	CAP. 165	29-04-1992	
DISTRESS ACT [2009 Ed.]	CAP. 199	16-10-2000	
DOGS ACT [1984 Ed., Amended by S 14/90]	CAP. 60	17-04-1939	
DRUG TRAFFICKING (RECOVERY OF PROCEEDS) ACT [2000 Ed., Amended by S 29/07]	CAP. 178	30-03-1996	
EDUCATION ORDER 2003 [Amended by S 86/06]	S 59/2003	20-12-2003	
EDUCATION (BRUNEI BOARD OF EXAMINATIONS) ACT [1984 Ed.]	CAP. 56	01-01-1975	
EDUCATION (NON-GOVERNMENT SCHOOLS) ACT [1984 Ed., Repealed by S 59/03 - Education Order]	CAP. 55	01-01-1953	REPEALED w.e.f. 20-12-03
ELECTION OFFENCES ACT [1984 Ed.]	CAP. 26	28-04-1962	
ELECTRICITY ACT [2003 Ed. Amended by S 68/05]	CAP. 71	05-03-1973	
ELECTRONIC TRANSACTION ACT [2008 Ed.]	CAP. 196	01-05-2001	except Part X
EMBLEMS AND NAMES (PREVENTION OF IMPROPER USE) ACT [1984 Ed.]	CAP. 94	18-01-1968	
EMERGENCY REGULATIONS ACT [1984 Ed.]	CAP. 21	21-02-1933	
EMPLOYMENT AGENCIES ORDER, 2004	S 84/2004	20-12-2004	
EMPLOYMENT INFORMATION ACT [1984 Ed.]	CAP. 99	15-05-1974	
EVIDENCE ACT [2002 Ed., Amended by S 1/06, S 13/06]	CAP. 108	17-04-1939	
EXCHANGE CONTROL ACT [1984 Ed., Repealed by S 70/00]	CAP. 141	01-01-1957	REPEALED w.e.f. 01-07-00
EXCISE ACT [1984 Ed., Repealed by S 40/06 - Excise Order]	CAP. 37	01-01-1925	REPEALED w.e.f. 04-03-06
EXCISE ORDER 2006	S 40/06	04-03-2006	
EXCLUSIVE ECONOMIC ZONE, Proclamation of	S 4/94	20-07-1993	
EXTRADITION (MALAYSIA AND SINGAPORE) ACT [1999 Ed.]	CAP. 154	19-05-84 [S] 01-11-83 [M]	
EXTRADITION ACT [1984 Ed., Repealed by S 10/06 - Extradition Order]	CAP. 8	09-12-1915	REPEALED w.e.f. 07-02-06
EXTRADITION ORDER 2006	S 10/06	07-02-2006	
FATAL ACCIDENTS AND PERSONAL INJURIES ACT [1999 Ed.]	CAP. 160	01-02-1991	

FINANCE COMPANIES ACT [2003 Ed., Amended by S 41/06]	CAP. 89	01-08-1973	
FINGERPRINTS ENACTMENT [Repealed by S 42/08 - Criminals Registration Order, 2008]	17 of 1956	01-01-1957	REPEALED w.e.f. 01-04-08
FIRE SERVICES ACT [2002 Ed., Amended by S 79/06] now become FIRE AND RESCUE w.e.f. 1/8/2006	CAP. 82	04-08-1966	
FISHERIES ACT [1984 Ed., Amended by S 20/02, Repealed by S 25/09 - Fisheries Order, 2009]	CAP. 61	05-03-1973	REPEALED w.e.f. 30-05-09
FISHERIES ORDER, 2009	S 25/2009	30-05-2009	
FOREST ACT [2002 Ed., Amended by S 47/07]	CAP. 46	30-10-1934	
GENEVA AND RED CROSS ACT [1984 Ed.]	CAP. 86	12-12-1938	
GENEVA CONVENTION ORDER, 2005	S 40/2005		not yet in force
GUARDIANSHIP OF INFANTS ACT [2000 Ed.]	CAP. 191	01-08-1999	
GURKHA RESERVE UNIT ACT [1984 Ed.]	CAP. 135	09-05-1981	
HALAL CERTIFICATE AND HALAL LABEL ORDER, 2005 [Amended by S 75/08]	S 39/2005	01-08-2008	
HALAL MEAT ACT [2000 Ed., Amended by GN 274/02]	CAP. 183	17-04-1999	
HIJACKING AND PROTECTION OF AIRCRAFT ORDER 2000	S 41/2000	24-05-2000	
HIRE PURCHASE ORDER, 2006	S 44/06	04-03-2006	
IMMIGRATION ACT [2006 Ed., Amended by S 34/07]	CAP. 17	01-07-1958	
INCOME TAX ACT [2003 Ed., Amended by S 51/08, S 52/08, S 13/09]	CAP. 35	31-12-1949	
INCOME TAX (PETROLEUM) ACT [2004 Ed.]	CAP. 119	18-12-1963	
INDUSTRIAL CO-ORDINATION ORDER 2001	S 44/2001	01-06-2001	
INDUSTRIAL DESIGNS ORDER 1999	S 7/2000	01-05-2000	
INFECTIOUS DISEASES ORDER 2003 [Amended by S 27/06]	S 34/2003	08-05-2003	
INSURANCE ORDER, 2006 [Amended by S 88/06, S 28/07, S 54/07]	S 48/2006	04-03-2006	
INTERMEDIATE COURTS ACT [1999 Ed., Amended by S 57/04, S 74/04, S 80/06]	CAP. 162	01-07-1991	
INTERNAL SECURITY ACT [2008 Ed.]	CAP. 133	01-04-1983	
INTERNATIONAL ARBITRATION ORDER, 2009	S 35/2009		not yet in force
INTERNATIONAL BANKING ORDER 2000 [Amended by S 9/01]	S 53/2000	01-07-2000	
INTERNATIONAL BUSINESS COMPANIES ORDER 2000 [Amended by S 37/03]	S 56/2000	01-07-2000	

INTERNATIONAL INSURANCE AND TAKAFUL ORDER 2002	S 43/2002	01-07-2002	
INTERNATIONAL LIMITED PARTNERSHIP ORDER 2000 [Amended by S 7/01]	S 45/2000	01-07-2000	
INTERNATIONAL TRUSTS ORDER 2000	S 55/2000	01-07-2000	
INTERNATIONALLY PROTECTED PERSONS ACT [1984 Ed.]	CAP. 16	08-07-1995	
INTERPRETATION AND GENERAL CLAUSES ACT [2006 Ed.]	CAP. 4	29-09-1959	
INTOXICATING SUBSTANCES ACT [1999 Ed., Amended by S 58/07]	CAP. 161	01-05-1992	
INVENTIONS ACT [1984 Ed., Amended by S 28/97]	CAP. 72	01-03-1952	
INVESTMENT INCENTIVES ACT [1984 Ed., Repealed by S 48/01 - Investment Incentives Order]	CAP. 97	01-05-1975	REPEALED w.e.f. 01-06-01
INVESTMENT INCENTIVES ORDER 2001	S 48/2001	01-06-2001	
ISLAMIC ADOPTION OF CHILDREN ORDER 2001	S 14/2001	26-03-2001	except section 3
ISLAMIC BANKING ACT [1999 Ed., Repealed by S 96/08 - Islamic Banking Order, 2008]	CAP. 168	02-12-1992	REPEALED w.e.f. 30-09-08
ISLAMIC BANKING ORDER, 2008	S 96/2008	30-09-2008	
ISLAMIC FAMILY LAW ORDER 1999 [Corrigenda S 42/04, Amended by S 17/05]	S 12/2000	26-03-2001	except section 3
KIDNAPPING ACT [1999 Ed.]	CAP. 164	22-02-1992	
KOLEJ UNIVERSITI PERGURUAN UGAMA SERI BEGAWAN ORDER, 2008	S 84/2008	30-08-2008	
LABOUR ACT [2002 Ed., Amended by GN 274/02, S 84/04]	CAP. 93	01-02-1955	
LAND ACQUISITION ACT [1984 Ed.]	CAP. 41	03-01-1949	
LAND CODE [1984 Ed., Amended by S 29/09]	CAP. 40	06-09-1909	
LAND CODE (STRATA) ACT [2000 Ed., Amended by S 28/09]	CAP. 189	01-07-2009	
LAW REFORM (CONTRIBUTORY NEGLIGENCE) ACT [1984 Ed., Repealed by S 4/91]	CAP. 53	25-04-1951	REPEALED w.e.f. 01-02-91
LAW REFORM (PERSONAL INJURIES) ACT [1984 Ed., Repealed by S 4/91]	CAP. 10	25-04-1951	REPEALED w.e.f. 01-02-91
LAW REVISION ACT [2001 Ed., Amended by S 93/00]	CAP. 1	01-01-1984	
LAYOUT DESIGNS ORDER 1999	S 8/2000	01-05-2000	
LEGAL PROFESSION ACT [2006 Ed.]	CAP. 132	01-01-1987	

LEGISLATIVE COUNCIL AND COUNCIL OF MINISTERS ACT (REMUNERATION AND PRIVILEGES) [1984 Ed., Amended by S 46/05, S 12/06]	CAP. 134	30-01-1965	
LEGITIMACY ORDER 2001	S 33/2001	21-04-2001	
LICENSED LAND SURVEYORS ACT [1984 Ed.]	CAP. 100	01-07-1980	
LIMITATION ACT [2000 Ed.]	CAP. 14	01-09-1991	
LUNACY ACT [1984 Ed.]	CAP. 48	09-07-1929	
MAINTENANCE ORDERS RECIPROCAL ENFORCEMENT ACT [2000 Ed.]	CAP. 175	25-02-1998	
MARITIME OFFENCES (SHIPS AND FIXED PLATFORMS) ORDER, 2007	S 61/2007	17-12-2007	
MARRIAGE ACT [1984 Ed., Amended by S 42/05]	CAP. 76	03-08-1948	
MARRIED WOMEN ACT [2000 Ed.]	CAP. 190	01-08-1999	
MEDICAL PRACTITIONERS AND DENTISTS ACT [1984 Ed., Amended by GN 273/02]	CAP. 112	29-07-1953	
MEDICINES ORDER, 2007	S 79/2007	01-01-2008	sec.1(2)(a) only
MERCHANDISE MARKS ACT [1984 Ed.]	CAP. 96	07-10-1953	
MERCHANT SHIPPING ACT [1984 Ed., Repealed by S 27/02 - Merchant Shipping Order]	CAP. 145	01-09-1984	REPEALED w.e.f. 16-05-02
MERCHANT SHIPPING ORDER, 2002 [Amended by S 23/09]	S 27/2002	16-05-2002	
MERCHANT SHIPPING (CIVIL LIABILITY AND COMPENSATION FOR OIL POLLUTION) ORDER, 2008	S 54/2008	17-04-2008	
MIDWIVES ACT [1984 Ed., Amended by S 47/02]	CAP. 139	01-01-1959	
MINING ACT [1984 Ed.]	CAP. 42	04-03-1920	
MINOR OFFENCES ACT [1984 Ed., Amended by S 26/90, S 43/98, S 89/06, S 82/08]	CAP. 30	29-07-1929	
MISCELLANEOUS LICENCES ACT [1984 Ed., Amended by S 43/08, S 85/08]	CAP. 127	01-01-1983	
MISUSE OF DRUGS ACT [2001 Ed., Amended by S 7/2002, GN 273/02, S 59/07, S 5/08]	CAP. 27	01-07-1978	
MONEY CHANGING AND REMITTANCE BUSINESS ACT [1999 Ed.]	CAP. 174	01-01-1995	
MONEY LAUNDERING ORDER 2000	S 44/2000	01-07-2000	
MONEYLENDERS ACT [1984 Ed., Amended by S 53/00, S 45/06]	CAP. 62	01-01-1922	
MONOPOLIES ACT [2003 Ed.]	CAP. 73	13-12-1932	
MOTOR VEHICLES INSURANCE (THIRD PARTY RISKS) ACT [1984 Ed., Amended by S 28/98, S 48/08 (corrig)]	CAP. 90	28-02-1950	

MUNICIPAL BOARDS ACT [1984 Ed.]	CAP. 57	01-01-1921	
MUTUAL ASSISTANCE IN CRIMINAL MATTERS ORDER, 2005	S 7/2005	01-01-2006	
MUTUAL FUNDS ORDER 2001	S 18/2001	01-01-2001	
NATIONAL BANK OF BRUNEI BERHAD; NATIONAL FINANCE SENDIRIAN BERHAD ACT [1999 Ed.]	CAP. 156	19-11-1986	
NATIONAL REGISTRATION ACT [2002 Ed.]	CAP. 19	01-03-1965	
NEWSPAPERS ACT [2002 Ed., Amended by S 36/05, S 86/08]	CAP. 105	01-01-1959	
NORTH BORNEO (DEFINITION BOUNDARIES) ORDER IN COUNCIL 1958 [1984 Ed.]	Sup. III		
NURSES REGISTRATION ACT [1984 Ed.]	CAP. 140	01-01-1968	
OATHS AND AFFIRMATIONS ACT [2001 Ed.]	CAP. 3	08-09-1958	
OFFENDERS (PROBATION AND COMMUNITY SERVICE) ORDER, 2006 [Amended by S 80/08]	S 6/2006		not yet in force
OFFICIAL SECRETS ACT [1988 Ed., Amended by S 52/05]	CAP. 153	02-01-1940	
OLD AGE AND DISABILITY PENSIONS ACT [1984 Ed., Amended by GN 273/02, GN 649/03, S 38/08]	CAP. 18	01-01-1955	
PASSPORTS ACT [1984 Ed., Amended by S 6/86, S 2/00, S 44/03, S 24/04, S 54/05, S 33/07]	CAP. 146	14-12-1983	
PATENTS ORDER, 1999	S 42/99		not yet in force
PAWNBROKERS ACT [1984 Ed., Repealed by S 41/05 - Pawnbrokers Order]	CAP. 63	01-01-1920	REPEALED w.e.f. 01-08-05
PAWNBROKERS ORDER 2002 [Amended by S 41/05]	S 60/2002	01-08-2005	
PENAL CODE [2001 Ed.]	CAP. 22	01-05-1952	
PENSIONS ACT [1984 Ed., Amended S 23/87, S 37/08]	CAP. 38	01-03-1959	
PERBADANAN TABUNG AMANAH ISLAM BRUNEI ACT [1999 Ed., Amended by S 15/03, S 29/04]	CAP. 163	29-09-1991	
PERSATUAN BULAN SABIT MERAH NEGARA BRUNEI DARUSSALAM (INCORPORATION) ACT [1999 Ed., Amended by S 40/05]	CAP. 159	28-11-1999	S 40/05 not yet in force
PETROLEUM MINING ACT [2002 Ed.]	CAP. 44	18-11-1963	
PETROLEUM (PIPE-LINES) ACT [1984 Ed.]	CAP. 45	04-03-1920	
PHARMACISTS REGISTRATION ORDER 2001	S 21/2001	01-07-2001	
POISONS ACT [1984 Ed., Amended by S 16/96, S 28/01]	CAP. 114	01-07-1957	
PORTS ACT [1984 Ed., Amended by S 17/88, S 26/02, S 18/05]	CAP. 144	01-01-1986	

POST OFFICE ACT [1984 Ed., Amended by S 17/97]	CAP. 52	01-05-1988	
POWERS OF ATTORNEY ACT [2002 Ed.]	CAP. 13	01-01-1922	
PRESERVATION OF BOOKS ACT [1984 Ed.]	CAP. 125	18-01-1967	
PREVENTION OF CORRUPTION ACT [2002 Ed.]	CAP. 131	01-01-1982	
PREVENTION OF POLLUTION OF THE SEA ORDER, 2005	S 18/2005	28-03-2005	
PRICE CONTROL ACT [2002 Ed.]	CAP. 142	13-03-1974	
PRIME MINISTER'S INCORPORATION ORDER 1984 [Amended the Constitution (Mentri Besar Incorporation) Order 1960 (S 55/60)]	S 5/84	01-01-1984	
PRISONS ACT [1984 Ed., Amended by S 12/89]	CAP. 51	01-07-1979	
PROBATE AND ADMINISTRATION ACT [1984 Ed.]	CAP. 11	01-02-1956	
PROTECTED AREAS AND PROTECTED PLACES ACT [1984 Ed.]	CAP. 147	01-12-1983	
PUBLIC ENTERTAINMENT ACT [2000 Ed.]	CAP. 181	01-06-1997	
PUBLIC HEALTH (FOOD) ACT [2000 Ed., Amended by S 73/00, S 64/02]	CAP. 182	01-01-2001	
PUBLIC OFFICERS (LIABILITIES) ACT [1984 Ed., Repealed by S 40/00]	CAP. 80	25-02-1929	REPEALED w.e.f. 24-05-00
PUBLIC ORDER ACT [2002 Ed., Amended by S 33/05]	CAP. 148	01-11-1983	
PUBLIC SERVICE COMMISSION ACT [1984 Ed.]	CAP. 83	01-01-1983	
QUARANTINE AND PREVENTION OF DISEASE ACT [1984 Ed., Repealed by S 34/03 - Infectious Diseases Order]	CAP. 47	09-08-1934	REPEALED w.e.f. 08-05-03
RECIPROCAL ENFORCEMENT OF FOREIGN JUDGMENTS ACT [2000 Ed.]	CAP. 177	27-03-1996	
REGISTERED AGENTS AND TRUSTEES LICENSING ORDER 2000	S 54/2000	01-07-2000	
REGISTRATION OF ADOPTIONS ACT [1984 Ed., Amended by S 15/01]	CAP. 123	01-01-1962	
REGISTRATION OF GUESTS ACT [1984 Ed.]	CAP. 122	01-07-1974	
REGISTRATION OF MARRIAGES ACT [2002 Ed.]	CAP. 124	01-01-1962	
RELIGIOUS COUNCIL AND KADIS COURTS ACT [1984 Ed., Amended by S 1/88, S 31/90, S 37/98, S 12/00, S 24/03, S 17/05, S 26/05]	CAP. 77	01-02-1956	
ROAD TRAFFIC ACT [2007 Ed., Amended by S 39/04, S 59/08]	CAP. 68	01-01-1956	S 39/04 not yet in force
ROYAL BRUNEI ARMED FORCES ACT [1984 Ed., Amended by S 2/06]	CAP. 149	01-01-1984	
ROYAL BRUNEI POLICE FORCE ACT [1984 Ed.]	CAP. 50	31-12-1983	

ROYAL ORDERS AND DECORATIONS [1984 Ed.]	Sup. V		
RUBBER DEALERS ACT [1984 Ed.]	CAP. 64	01-01-1921	
SALE OF GOODS ACT [1999 Ed.]	CAP. 170	03-05-1994	
SARAWAK (DEFINITION OF BOUNDARIES) ORDER IN COUNCIL 1958 [1984 Ed.]	Sup. IV		
SEAMEN'S UNEMPLOYMENT INDEMNITY ACT [1984 Ed.]	CAP. 75	02-10-1939	
SECOND-HAND DEALERS ACT [1984 Ed.]	CAP. 65	01-01-1934	
SECURITIES ORDER 2001 [Amended by S 33/02, S 43/05]	S 31/2001	01-03-2001	
SECURITY AGENCIES ACT [2000 Ed.]	CAP. 187	01-06-2000	
SEDITION ACT [1984 Ed., Amended by S 34/05]	CAP. 24	06-04-1948	
SMALL CLAIMS TRIBUNALS ORDER, 2006	S 81/2006		not yet in force
SOCIETIES ACT [1984 Ed., Repealed by S 1/05 - Societies Order]	CAP. 66	04-10-1948	REPEALED w.e.f. 04-01-05
SOCIETIES ORDER, 2005	S 1/2005	04-01-2005	
SPECIFIC RELIEF ACT [1984 Ed., Amended by S 59/04]	CAP. 109	17-04-1939	
STAMP ACT [2003 Ed.]	CAP. 34	01-01-1909	
STATISTICS ACT [1984 Ed.]	CAP. 81	01-08-1977	
STATUTORY DECLARATION ACT [1984 Ed.]	CAP. 12	11-01-1951	
STATUTORY FUNDS APPROPRIATION ENACTMENT 1959 [Amended by S 63/63, 7 of 1966, 19 of 1967, 4 of 1975, S 50/76, S 49/76, S 110/79, S 12/82, S 13/82, S 42/84, S 13/86, S 22/93, S 22/03, S 39/08]	9 of 1959	01-01-1960	
SUBORDINATE COURTS ACT [2001 Ed., Amended by S 56/04, S 73/04, S 9/06, S 60/08]	CAP. 6	01-01-1983	S 9/06 and S60/08 not yet in force
SUBSCRIPTION CONTROL ACT [1984 Ed.]	CAP. 91	15-12-1953	
SUCCESSION AND REGENCY PROCLAMATION 1959 [2004 Ed., Amended by S 16/06, S 78/06]	CONST. II	29-09-1959	
SUMMONSES AND WARRANTS (SPECIAL PROVISIONS) ACT [1999 Ed.]	CAP. 155	19-05-84 [S] 01-11-83 [M]	
SUNGAI LIANG AUTHORITY ACT [2009 Ed.]	CAP. 200	06-04-2007	
SUPREME COURT ACT [2001 Ed., Amended by S 55/04, S 61/04, S 72/04]	CAP. 5	16-09-1963	
SUPREME COURT (APPEALS TO PRIVY COUNCIL) ACT [1999 Ed., Amended by S 45/05]	CAP. 158	01-02-1990	
SUSTAINABILITY FUND ORDER, 2008	S 36/2008	11-03-2008	

SYARIAH COURTS ACT [2000 Ed., Amended by S 17/05]	CAP. 184	26-03-2001	
SYARIAH COURTS CIVIL PROCEDURE ORDER, 2005 [available in Malay text only] - PERINTAH ACARA MAL MAHKAMAH-MAHKAMAH SYARIAH, 2005	S 26/2005	06-04-2005	
SYARIAH COURTS EVIDENCE ORDER, 2001	S 63/2001	15-10-2001 except s.5	
SYARIAH FINANCIAL SUPERVISORY BOARD ORDER, 2006 [Amended by S 65/07]	S 5/2006	17-01-2006	
TABUNG AMANAH PEKERJA ACT [1999 Ed., Amended by S 9/99, S 9/00, S 16/03, S 2/07]	CAP. 167	01-01-1993	
TAKAFUL ORDER, 2008	S 100/2008	30-09-2008	
TELECOMMUNICATIONS ACT [1984 Ed. Repealed by S 38/01 - Telecommunication Order]	CAP. 54	01-12-1974	REPEALED w.e.f. 01-04-06
TELECOMMUNICATIONS ORDER 2001	S 38/2001	01-04-2006	
TELECOMMUNICATION SUCCESSOR COMPANY ORDER 2001 [Corrigendum S 25/06]	S 37/2001	01-04-2006	
TERRITORIAL WATERS OF BRUNEI ACT [2002 Ed.]	CAP. 138	10-02-1983	
TOBACCO ORDER 2005	S 49/2005	01-06-2008	
TOKYO CONVENTION ACT [2008 Ed.]	CAP. 198	24-05-2000	
TOWN AND COUNTRY PLANNING (DEVELOPMENT CONTROL) ACT [1984 Ed.]	CAP. 143	19-09-1972	
TRADE DISPUTES ACT [1984 Ed.]	CAP. 129	21-01-1962	
TRADE MARKS ACT [2000 Ed.]	CAP. 98	01-06-2000	
TRADE UNIONS ACT [1984 Ed.]	CAP. 128	20-01-1962	
TRAFFICKING AND SMUGGLING OF PERSONS ORDER, 2004	S 82/2004	20-12-2004	
TRANSFER OF FUNCTIONS OF THE MINISTER OF LAW ACT [2000 Ed.]	CAP. 186	16-09-1998	
TRAVEL AGENTS ACT [1984 Ed.]	CAP. 103	01-01-1982	
TREATY OF FRIENDSHIP AND CO-OPERATION [1984 Ed.]	SUP. I		
TRESPASS ON ROYAL PROPERTY ACT [1984 Ed.]	CAP. 23	01-01-1918	
UNDESIRABLE PUBLICATIONS ACT [1984 Ed., Amended by S 60/07]	CAP. 25	01-12-1986	
UNFAIR CONTRACTS TERMS ACT [1999 Ed.]	CAP. 171	18-06-1994	
UNIVERSITI BRUNEI DARUSSALAM ACT [1999 Ed., Amended by S 22/00, S 17/03, S 84/06]	CAP. 157	01-07-1988	

UNIVERSITI ISLAM SULTAN SHARIF ALI ORDER, 2008	S 71/2008	14-08-2008	
UNLAWFUL CARNAL KNOWLEDGE ACT [1984 Ed.]	CAP. 29	15-01-1938	
VALUERS AND ESTATE AGENTS ORDER, 2009	S 30/2009	01-07-2009	
VETERINARY SURGEONS ORDER, 2005	S 30/2005	02-06-2008	
VICAR APOSTOLIC OF KUCHING (INCORPORATION) ACT [1984 Ed.]	CAP. 110	11-08-1973	
WATER SUPPLY ACT [1984 Ed.]	CAP. 121	01-01-1968	
WEIGHTS AND MEASURES ACT [1986 Ed.]	CAP. 151	01-01-1987	
WILD FAUNA AND FLORA ORDER, 2007	S 77/2007	31-12-2007	
WILD LIFE PROTECTION ACT [1984 Ed.]	CAP. 102	01-08-1981	
WILLS ACT [2000 Ed.]	CAP. 193	21-10-1999	
WOMEN AND GIRLS PROTECTION ACT [1984 Ed., Amended by GN 649/03]	CAP. 120	19-04-1973	
WORKMEN'S COMPENSATION ACT [1984 Ed., Amended by GN 273/02]	CAP. 74	01-04-1957	
YAYASAN SULTAN HAJI HASSANAL BOLKIAH ACT [2008 Ed.]	CAP. 166	05-10-1992	

STRATEGIC GOVERNMENT CONTACT IN BRUNEY

Prime Minister's Office
E-Mail: PRO@jpm.gov.bn
Telephone: 673 - 2 - 229988
Fax: 673 - 2 - 241717
Telex: BU2727
Address:
Prime Minister's Office
Istana Nurul Iman
Bandar Seri Begawan BA1000

Audit Department
Prime Minister's Office
Jalan Menteri Besar
Bandar Seri Begawan BB 39 10
Brunei Darussalam
Telephone: (02) 380576
Facsimile: (02) 380679
E-mail: jabaudbd@brunet.bn

Information Department
Prime Minister's Office
Berakas Old Airport
Bandar Seri Begawan
BB 3510
Brunei Darussalam.
E-mail:- pelita@brunet.bn
Fax: 673 2 381004
Tel: 673 2 380527

Narcotics Control Bureau
Prime Minister's Office
Jalan Tungku Gadong
Bandar Seri Begawan BE 2110
Tel No: 02-448877 / 422479 / 422480 / 422481
Fax No: 02-422477
E-mail: ncb@brunet.bn

One-Stop Agency
The Ministry of Industry and Primary Resources
Bandar Seri Begawan 1220
Brunei Darussalam

Telefax: (02) 244811
Telex: MIPRS BU 2111
Cable: MIPRS BRUNEI

Head Policy and Administration Division
Ministry of Industry and Primary Resources
Jalan Menteri Besar, Bandar Seri Begawan

1220
Brunei Darussalam
Tel: (02) 382822

Secretary of Public Service Commission
Old Airport
Bandar Seri Begawan BB 3510
Tel No: 02-381961
E-mail: bplspa@brunet.bn

Semaun Holdings Sdn Bhd
Unit 2.02, Block D, 2nd Floor
Yayasan Sultan Haji Hassanal Bolkiah Complex
Jalan Pretty
Bandar Seri Begawan BS8711
Brunei Darussalam
E-mail address: semaun@brunet.bn

Department of Agriculture
Ministry of Industry & Primary Resources
BB3510
Brunei Darussalam
Telephone: + 673 2 380144
Fax: + 673 2 382226
Telex: PERT BU 2456

Land Transport Department
KM 6, Jalan Gadong,
Beribi BE1110,
Brunei Darussalam.
Tel : (673-2) 451979
Fax : (673-2) 424775
Email : latis@brunet.bn

FOREIGN MISSIONS

AUSTRALIA

Australian High Commission
(His Excellency Mr. Neal Patrick Davis - High Commissioner)
4th flr Teck Guan Plaza, Jln Sultan
Bandar Seri Begawan BS8811
Brunei Darussalam
or
P.O. Box 2990
Bandar Seri Begawan, BS8675
Brunei Darussalam
Tel: 673 2 229435/6
Fax: 673 2 221652

AUSTRIA

Austrian Consulate General
No. 5 Taman Jubli, Spg 75,
Jalan Subok,
Bandar Seri Begawan BD2717
Brunei Darussalam
or
P.O. Box 1303,
Bandar Seri Begawan, BS8672
Brunei Darussalam
Tel : 673 2 261083
Email: austroko@brunet.bn

BANGLADESH

High Commission of People's Republic of Bangladesh
(His Excellency Mr. Muhammad Mumtaz Hussain - High Commissioner)
AAR Villa, House No. 5,
Simpang 308, Jalan Lambak Kanan,
Berakas, BB1714
Brunei Darussalam
Tel: 673 2 394716
Fax: 673 2 394715

BELGIUM

Consulate of Belgium
2nd Floor, 146 Jln Pemancha
Bandar Seri Begawan BS8711
Brunei Darussalam
or
P.O.Box 65,
Bandar Seri Begawan, BS8670
Brunei Darussalam
Tel: 673 2 222298
Fax: 673 2 220895

BRITAIN

British High Commission
(His Excellency Mr. Stuart Laing - High Commissioner)
Unit 2.01, Block D of Yayasan Sultan Hassanal Bolkiah
Bandar Seri Begawan BS8711
Brunei Darussalam
or
P.O.Box 2197
Bandar Seri Begawan, BS8674

Brunei Darussalam
Tel: 673 2 222231
Fax: 673 2 226001

CAMBODIA

Royal Embassy of Cambodia
(His Highness Prince Sisowath Phandaravong - Ambassador)
No. 8, Simpang 845
Kampong Tasek Meradun, Jalan Tutong, BF1520
Brunei Darussalam
Tel: 673 2 650046
Fax: 673 2 650646

CANADA

High Commission of Canada
(His Excellency Mr. Neil Reeder - High Commissioner)
Suite 51 - 52, Britannia House, Jalan Cator
Bandar Seri Begawan, BS8811
Brunei Darussalam
Tel: 673 2 220043
Fax: 673 2 220040

CHINA

Embassy of People's Republic of China
(His Excellency Mr. Wang Jianli - Ambassador)
No. 1, 3 & 5, Simpang 462
Kampong Sungai Hanching,
Jln Muara, BC2115
Brunei Darussalam
or
P.O.Box 121
M.P.C, Berakas BB3577
Brunei Darussalam
Tel: 673 2 339609
Fax: 673 2 339612

DENMARK

Consulate of Denmark
Unit 6, Bangunan Hj Tahir,
Spg 103, Jln Gadong
Bandar Seri Begawan
Brunei Darussalam
or
P.O.Box 140
Bandar Seri Begawan, BS8670
Brunei Darussalam
Tel: 673 2 422050, 427525, 447559
Fax: 673 2 427526

FINLAND

Consulate of Finland
Bee Seng Shipping Company
No.7 1st Floor Sufri Complex
KM 2, Jalan Tutong
Bandar Seri Begawan, BA2111
Brunei Darussalam
or
P.O.Box 1777
Bandar Seri Begawan, BS8673
Brunei Darusslaam
Tel: 673 2 243847
Fax: 673 2 224495

FRANCE

Embassy of the Republic of France
(His Excelleny Mr. Jean Pierre Lafosse - Ambassador)
#306-310 Kompleks Jln Sultan,
3rd Floor, 51-55 Jln Sultan
Bandar Seri Begawan BS8811
Brunei Darussalam
or
P.O.Box 3027
Bandar Seri Begawan, BS8675
Brunei Darussalam
Tel: 673 2 220960 / 1
Fax: 673 2 243373

GERMANY

Embassy of the Federal Republic of Germany
(His Excellency Klaus-Peter Brandes - Ambassador)
6th flr, Wisma Raya Building
Lot 49-50, Jln Sultan
Bandar Seri Begawan, BS8811
Brunei Darussalam
or
P.O.Box 3050
Bandar Seri Begawan, BS8675
Brunei Darussalam
Tel: 673 2 225547 / 74
Fax: 673 2 225583

INDIA

High Commission of India
(His Excellency Mr. Dinesh K. Jain - High Commissioner)
Lot 14034, Spg 337,
Kampong Manggis, Jln Muara, BC3515
Brunei Darussalam
Tel: 673 2 339947 / 339751
Fax: 673 2 339783
Email: hicomind@brunet.bn

INDONESIA

Embassy of the Republic of Indonesia
(His Excellency Mr. Rahardjo Djojonegoro - Ambassador)
Lot 4498, Spg 528
Sungai Hanching Baru, Jln Muara, BC3013
Brunei Darussalam
or
P.O.Box 3013
Bandar Seri Begawan, BS8675
Brunei Darussalam
Tel: 673 2 330180 / 445
Fax: 673 2 330646

IRAN

Embassy of the Islamic Republic of Iran
No. 2, Lot 14570, Spg 13
Kampong Serusop, Jalan Berakas, BB2313
Brunei Darussalam
Tel: 673 2 330021 / 29
Fax: 673 2 331744

JAPAN

Embassy of Japan
(His Excellency Mr. Hajime Tsujimoto - Ambassador)
No 1 & 3, Jalan Jawatan Dalam
Kampong Mabohai
Bandar Seri Begawan, BA1111
Brunei Darussalam
or
P.O.Box 3001
Bandar Seri Begawan, BS8675
Brunei Darussalam
Tel: 673 2 229265 / 229592, 237112 - 5
Fax: 673 2 229481

KOREA

Embassy of the Republic of Korea
(His Excellency Kim Ho-tae - Ambassador)
No.9, Lot 21652
Kg Beribi, Jln Gadong, BE1118
Brunei Darussalam
Tel: 673 2 650471 / 300, 652190
Fax: 673 2 650299

LAOS

Embassy of the Lao People's Democratic Republic
(His Excellency Mr. Ammone Singhavong - Ambassador)
Lot. No. 19824, House No. 11
Simpang 480, Jalan Kebangsaan Lama
Off Jalan Muara, BC4115
Brunei Darussalam
or
P.O.Box 2826
Bandar Seri Begawan, BS8675
Brunei Darussalam
Tel: 673 2 345666
Fax: 673 2 345888

MALAYSIA

Malaysian High Commission
(His Excellency Wan Yusof Embong - High Commissioner)
No.27 & 29, Simpang 396-39
Kampong Sungai Akar
Jalan Kebangsaan, BC4115
Brunei Darussalam
or
P.O.Box 2826
Bandar Seri Begawan, BS8675
Brunei Darussalam
Tel: 673 2 345652
Fax: 673 2 345654

MYANMAR

Embassy of the Union of Myanmar
(His Excellency U Than Tun - Ambassador)
No. 14, Lot 2185 / 46292
Simpang 212, Kampong Rimba, Gadong
BE3119
Brunei Darussalam

Tel: 673 2 450506 / 7
Fax: 673 2 451008

NETHERLANDS

Netherlands Consulate
c/o Brunei Shell Petroleum Co. Sdn Bhd
Seria KB3534
Brunei Darussalam
Tel: 673 3 372005, 373045

NEW ZEALAND

New Zealand Consulate
36A Seri Lambak Complex,
Jalan Berakas, BB1714
Brunei Darussalam
or
P.O.Box 2720
Bandar Seri Begawan, BS8675
Brunei Darusslam
Tel: 673 2 331612, 331010
Fax: 673 2 331612

NORWAY

Royal Norwegian Consulate
Unit No. 407A - 410A
4th Floor, Wisma Jaya
Jalan Pemancha
Bandar Seri Begawan, BS8811
Brunei Darussalam
Tel: 673 2 239091 / 2 / 3 / 4
Fax: 673 2 239095/6

OMAN

Embassy of the Sultanate of Oman
(His Excellency Mr. Ahmad Moh,d Masoud Al-Riyami - Ambassador)
No.35 Simpang 100,
Jalan Tungku Link
Kampong Pengkalan, Gadong BE3719
Brunei Darussalam
or
P.O.Box 2875
Bandar Seri Begawan, BS8675
Brunei Darussalam
Tel: 673 2 446953 / 4 / 7 / 8
Fax: 673 2 449646

PAKISTAN

Pakistan High Commission
(His Excellency Major General (Rtd) Irshad Ullah Tarar - High Commission)
No.5 Kampong Sungai Akar
Jalan Kebangsaan, BC4115
Brunei Darussalam
Tel: 673 2 6334989, 339797
Fax: 673 2 334990

PHILIPPINES

Embassy of the Republic of Philippines
His Excellency Mr. Enrique A. Zaldivar - Ambassador)
Rm 1 & 2, 4th & 5th floor
Badiah Building, Mile 1 1/2 Jln Tutong
Brunei Darussalam, BA2111
or
P.O.Box 3025
Bandar Seri Begawan, BS8675
Brunei Darussalam
Tel: 673 2 241465 / 6
Fax: 673 2 237707

SAUDI ARABIA

Royal Embassy of Kingdom of Saudi Arabia
No. 1, Simpang 570
Kampong Salar
Jalan Muara, BU1429
Brunei Darusslam
Tel: 673 2 792821 / 2 / 3
Fax: 673 2 792826 / 7

SINGAPORE

Singapore High Commission
(His Excellency Tee Tua Ba - High Commissioner)
No. 8, Simpang, 74,
Jalan Subok, BD1717
Brunei Darussalam
or
P.O.Box 2159
Bandar Seri Begawan, BS8674
Brunei Darussalam
Tel: 673 2 227583 / 4 / 5
Fax: 673 2 220957

SWEDEN

Consulate of Sweden
Blk A, Unit 1, 2nd Floor
Abdul Razak Plaza,
Jalan Gadong,
Bandar Seri Begawan, BE3919
Brunei Darussalam
Tel: 673 2 448423, 444326
Fax: 673 2 448419

THAILAND

Royal Thai Embassy
(His Excellency Thinakorn Kanasuta - Ambassador
No. 2, Simpang 682,
Kampong Bunut, Jalan Tutong, BF1320
Brunei Darussalam
Tel: 673 2 653108 / 9
Fax: 673 2 262752

UNITED STATE OF AMERICA

Embassy of the United States of America
3rd Flr, Teck Guan Plaza,
Jalan Sultan
Bandar Seri Begawan BS8811
Brunei Darussalam
Tel: 673 2 229670
Fax: (02) 225293

VIETNAM

Embassy of the Socialist Republic of Vietnam
(His Excellency Tran Tien Vinh - Ambassador)
No. 10, Simpang 485
Kampong Sungai Hanching
Jalan Muara,BC2115
Brunei Darussalam
Tel: 673 2 343167 / 8
Fax: 673 2 343169

BRUNEI'S MISSIONS IN ASEAN, CHINA, JAPAN AND KOREA

CAMBODIA
Embassy of Brunei Darussalam
No : 237, Pasteur St. 51
Sangkat Boeung Keng Kang I
Khan Chamkar Mon
Phnom Penh
Kingdom of Cambodia
Tel : (855) 23211 457 & 23211 458
Fax : (855) 23211 456
E-Mail : Brunei@bigpond.com.kh

CHINA
Embassy of Brunei Darussalam
No. 3 Villa, Qijiayuan Diplomatic Compound
Chaoyang District
Beijing 100600
People's Republic of China 1000600
Tel : 86 (10) 6532 4093 - 6
Fax : 86 (10) 6532 4097
E-Mail : bdb@public.bta.net.cn

INDONESIA
Embassy of Brunei Darussalam
Wisma GKBI
(Gabungan Koperasi Batik Indonesia)
Suite 1901, Jl. Jend. Sudirman No. 28
Jakarta 10210
Indonesia
Tel : 62 (21) 574 1437 - 39 / 574 1470 - 72
Fax : 62 (21) 574 1463

JAPAN
Embassy of Brunei Darussalam
5-2 Kitashinagawa 6-Chome
Shinagawa-ku
Tokyo 141
Japan
Tel : 81 (3) 3447 7997 / 9260
Fax : 81 (3) 344 79260

REPUBLIC OF KOREA
Embassy of Brunei Darussalam
7th Floor, Kwanghwamoon Building
211, Sejong-ro, Chongro-Ku
Seoul
Republic of Korea.
Tel : 82 (2) 399 3707 / 3708
Fax : 82 (2) 399 3709
E-Mail : kbrunei@chollian.net

LAOS
Embassy of Brunei Darussalam
No. 333 Unit 25 Ban Phonxay
Xaysettha District
Lanexang Avenue
Vientiane
Laos People's Democratic Republic
Tel : (856) 2141 6114 / 2141 4169

Fax : (856) 2141 6115
E-Mail : kbnbd@laonet.net

MALAYSIA
High Commission of Brunei Darussalam
Tingkat 8 Wisma Sin Heap Lee (SHL)
Jalan Tun Razak
50400 Kuala Lumpur
Malaysia.
Tel : 60 (3) 261 2828
Fax : 60 (3) 263 1302
E-Mail : Sjtnbdkl@tm.net.my

THE UNIION OF MYANMAR
Embassy of Brunei Darussalam
No : 51 Golden Valley
Bahan Township
Yangon
The Union of Myanmar.
Tel: 95 (1) 510 422
Fax: 95 (1) 512 854

PHILIPPINES
Embassy of Brunei Darussalam
11th Floor BPI Building
Ayala Avenue, Corner Paseo De Roxas
Makati City, Metro Manila
Philippines
Tel : 63 (2) 816 2836 - 8
Fax : 63 (2) 816 2876
E-Mail : kbnbdmnl@skynet.net

SINGAPORE
High Commission of Brunei Darussalam
325 Tanglin Road
Singapore 247955
Tel : (65) 733 9055
Fax : (65) 737 5275
E-Mail : comstbs@singnet.com.sg

THAILAND
Embassy of Brunei Darussalam
No. 132 Sukhumvit 23 Road
Watana District
Bangkok 10110
Thailand
Tel : 66 (2) 204 1476 - 9
Fax : 66 (2) 204 1486

VIETNAM
Embassy of Brunei Darussalam
No. 4 Thien Quang Street
Hai Ba Trung District
Hanoi
Vietnam
Tel : (84) 4 826 4816 / 4817 / 4818
Fax : (84) 4 822 2092
E-Mail : bruemviet@hotmail.com

FOOD AND RESTAURANTS

Brunei restaurants, including western style fast food centres, cater to a wide range of tastes and palates.
Visitors can also sample authentic local food offered at the tamu night market in the capital.
The market, along the Kianggeh river, is actually open from early morning. It takes on a special atmosphere at night when crowds throng its alleys to shop and eat at the lowest prices in town.
Tropical fruits like watermelon, papaya, mango and banana are also available.
Locals are fond of the Malay-style satay, bits of beef or chicken in a stick, cooked over low fire and dipped in a tangy peanut sauce.

Brunei's first Chinese halal restaurant is Emperor's Court, owned by Royal Brunei Catering, which caters to Cantonese and Western tastebuds.

A list of restaurants in the capital and Seria-Kuala Belait areas follows:
Bandar Seri Begawan
Aumrin Restaurant, 1 Bangunan Hasbullah, 4 Jalan Gadong
Airport Restaurant, Brunei International Airport
Coffee Tree, Unit 3, top floor ,Mabohai Shopping Complex
Emperor's Court, 1st Floor, Wisma Haji Mohd Taha, Jalan Gadong
Excellent Taste, G5 Gadong Properties Centre, Jalan Gadong
Express Fast Food, 22/23 Jalan Sultan
Ghawar Restaurant, 3 Ground Floor Bang Hasbullah 4

Jade Garden Chinese Restaurant, Riverview Inn, Km 1 Jalan Gadong
Jolibee Family Restaurant, Utama Bowling Centre, Km 11/2 Jalan Tutong
Kentucky Fried Chicken (B) Sdn Bhd, G15-G16 Plaza Athirah
Lucky Restaurant, Umi Kalthum Building, Jalan Tutong
McDonald's Restaurant, 10-12 Block H, Abdul Razak Complex, Simpang 137, Gadong
Phongmun Restaurant, Nos. 56-60, 2nd Floor Teck Guan Plaza
Pizza Hut, Block J, Unit 2 & 3 Abdul Razak Complex
Pondok Sari Wangi, 12 Blk A, Abdul Razak Complex, Jalan Gadong
Popular Restaurant, 5, Ground floor, PAP Hajjah Norain Building
QR Restaurant, Blk C, Abdul Razak Complex, Jalan Gadong
Rainbow Restaurant, 110 Jalan Batu Bersurat, Gadong
Rasa Sayang Restaurant, 607 Bangunan Guru-Guru Melayu
Rose Garden Restaurant, 8 Blk C, Abdul Razak Complex, Jalan Gadong
Season's Restaurant, Gadong Centrepoint
SD Cafe, 6-7 Bangunan Hj Othman, Simpang 105, Jalan Gadong
Seri Kamayan Restaurant, 4 & 5 Bangunan Hj Tahir ,Simpang 103, Jalan Gadong
Seri Maradum Baru, Block C6, Abdul Razak Complex
Sugar Bun Fast Food, Lot 16397 Mabohai Complex, Jalan Kebangsaan
Schezuan's Dynasty Restaurant, Gadong Centrepoint
Swensen's Ice Cream and Fine Food Restaurant, 17-18 Ground Floor Bagunan Halimatul Sa'adiah, Gadong
Tenaga Restaurant, 6 1st Floor Bangunan Hasbollah 4
The Stadium Restaurant, Stadium Negara Hassanal Bolkiah
Tropicana Seafood Restaurant, Block 1 Ground Floor, Pang's Building,Muara
Kuala Belait/Seria
Belait Restaurant, Jalan Bunga Raya
Buccaneer Steak House, Lot 94 Jalan McKerron
Cottage Restaurant, 38 Jalan Pretty
Jolene Restaurant, 83,1st Jalan Bunga Raya
New China Restaurant, 39/40 3rd Floor, Ang's Building, Jalan Sultan Omar Ali, Seria
New Cheng Wah Restaurant, 14 Jalan Sultan Omar Ali, Seria
Orchid Room, B5, 1st Floor, Jalan Bunga Raya
Red Wing Restaurant, 12 Jalan Sultan Omar Ali, Seria
Tasty Cake Shop/Pretty Inn, 26 Jalan Sultan Omar Ali, Seria
Tasconi's Pizza, Simpang 19, Jalan Sungai Pandan

WHERE TO SHOP

For many travellers one of the pleasures of visiting another country is finding something of interest and value for one's self, family or friends. There are many shops in Brunei offering a wide variety of goods at competitive prices. These range from modern department stores to small market stalls where bargaining is still commonly practised.

Modern department stores are found in the major towns of Bandar Seri Begawan, Tutong, Kuala Belait and Seria. In addition to these departmental stores there is a wide variety of old-fashioned shophouses as well as more modern air-conditioned shops.

Most items ranging from the latest electronic goods and imported luxury goods to common household items and groceries can be conveniently found in these shops.

Traditional items that reflect the culture of Brunei like the brass cannon, kris and kain songket, better known as "jong sarat" are excellent souvenirs to bring home from a visit to the country.

These can be purchased at the Arts and Handicrafts Centre which is located off Kota Batu, and also at the airport.

Before leaving Brunei make sure you stop by the Duty Free shops at the airport. These offer a wide range of luxury goods, garments, jewellery, writing instruments, perfumes, handicrafts, Brunei souvenirs, books and chocolates at very reasonable prices.

SHOPPING CENTRES

Hua Ho Department Store, Jln Gadong, Bandar Seri Begawan

Kota Mutiara Department Store, Bangunan Darussalam, Bandar Seri Begawan

Lai Lai Department Store, Mile 1 Jln Tutong, Bandar Seri Begawan

Millimewah Department Store (BSB), Bangunan Darussalam, Bandar Seri Begawan

Millimewah Department Store (Tutong),Tutong

Millimewah Department Store (Seria), Seria

Princess Inn Department Store, Mile 1 Jln Tutong , Bandar Seri Begawan

Tiong Hin Superstore,Jln Muara, Bandar Seri Begawan

Megamart,Jln Gadong, Bandar Seri Begawan

Wisma Jaya Complex, Jln Pemancha, Bandar Seri Begawan

First Emporium & Supermarket, Mohammad Yussof Complex, Jln Kubah Makam DiRaja, Bandar Seri Begawan

Seria Plaza, Seria

Seaview Department Store, Jln Maulana, Kuala Belait

TRAVEL AGENTS

BANDAR SERI BEGAWAN

Antara Travel & Tours Sdn Bhd 02-448805/808
Anthony Tours & Travel Sdn Bhd 02-228668
Borneo Leisure Travel Sdn Bhd 02-223420
Brunei Travel Services Sdn Bhd 02-236006
Century Travel Centre Sdn Bhd 02-227296
Churiah Travel Service 02-224422
Darat Dan Laut 02-426321
Freme Travel Services Sdn Bhd 02-234277
Halim Tours & Travel Sdn Bhd 02-226688
Intan Travel & Trading Agencies 02-427340
Jasra Harrisons (B) Sdn Bhd 02-236675

JB Travel & Insurance Agencies 02-239132
JJ Tour Service (B) Sdn Bhd 02-224761
Ken Travel & Trading Sdn Bhd 02-223127
Mahasiswa Travel Service 02-243452
Oriental Travel Services 02-226464
Overseas Travel Services Sdn Bhd 02-445322
Sarawak Travel Service Sdn Bhd 02-223361
Seri Islamic Tours & Travel Sdn Bhd 02-243341
Straits Central Agencies (B) Sdn Bhd 02-229356
Sunshine Borneo Tours & Travel Sdn Bhd 02-441791
SMAS 02-234741
Travel Centre (B) Sdn Bhd 02-229601
Travel Trade Agencies Sdn Bhd 02-229601/228439
Tai Wah Travel Service Sdn Bhd 02-224015
Tenega Travel Agency Sdn Bhd 02-422974
Titian Travel & Tours Sdn Bhd 02-448742
Twelve Roofs / Perusahaan Hj. Asmakhan 02-340395
Wing On Travel & Trading Agencies 02-220536
Zizen Travel Agency Sdn Bhd 02-236991
Zura Travel Service Sdn Bhd 02-234738

KUALA BELAIT

Freme Travel Services Sdn Bhd 03-335025
Jasra Harrisons Sdn Bhd 03-335391
JJ Tour Service Sdn Bhd 03-334069
Limbang Travel Service Sdn Bhd 03-335275
Overseas Travel Service Sdn Bhd 03-222090
Southern Cross Travel Agencies Sdn Bhd 03-334642
Straits Central Agencies Sdn Bhd 03-334589
Usaha Royako Travel Agency 03-334768

SELECTED COMPANIES

- Advance Computer Supplier and Services
- AJYAD Publishing
- Akitek SAA Home Page
- Amalgamated Electronic Sdn. Bhd.
- Anthony Tours & Travel Agency
- Baharuddin & Associates Consulting Engineers
- Beseller Sdn Bhd Homepage
- BIT Computer Services
- BruDirect Business Centre
- Brunei Hotel
- Brupost
- CfBT Homepage
- Compunet Computer & Office Systems
- Dalplus Technologies, Brunei
- DN Private Investigation and Security Consultant
- DP Happy Video House
- Elite Computer Systems Sdn. Bhd.
- Fabrica Interior Furnishing Co
- Glamour Homepage

- HSBC
- HSE Engineering Sdn. Bhd.
- Indah Sejahtera Development & Services
- Insurans Islam Taib
- Interhouse Marketing Sdn. Bhd.
- International School Brunei
- IP and Company
- ISS Thomas Cowan Sdn. Bhd.
- Jerudong Park Medical Centre
- Kristal
- L & M Prestressing Sdn. Bhd.
- Megamas Training Company Sdn. Bhd.
- Mekar General Enterprise Homepage
- Micronet Computer School
- National Insurance Company Berhad
- Paotools Supplies & Services Co.
- Petar Perunding Sdn. Bhd.
- Petrel Jaya Sdn Bhd
- Phongmun Restaurant Homepage
- Poh Lee Trading Company
- Q-Carrier
- Sabli Group of Companies - Brunei Darussalam
- Scanmark Design Sdn Bhd
- SDS System (B) Sdn. Bhd.
- SEAMEO VOCTECH Homepage
- Singapore Airlines
- Sistem Komputer Alif Sdn Bhd
- SPCastro And Associates Sdn Bhd
- Sunshine Borneo Tour & Travel Sdn.Bhd.
- Survey Service Consultants
- Syabas Publishers
- Syarikat Suraya Insan
- Syarikat Intellisense Technology
- Tabung Amanah Islam Brunei
- Tang Sung Lee Sdn. Bhd.
- The Lodge Resort (In Brunei)
- Trinkets Enterprise
- Twelve Roofs / Perusahaan Hj. Asmakhan
- Unicraft Enterprises
- Utama Komunikasi

BASIC TITLES ON BRUNEI

IMPORTANT!

All publications are updated annually!

Please contact IBP, Inc. at ibpusa3@gmail.com for the latest ISBNs and additional information

TITLE
Brunei A "Spy" Guide - Strategic Information and Developments
Brunei A Spy" Guide"
Brunei Air Force Handbook

TITLE
Brunei Air Force Handbook
Brunei Business and Investment Opportunities Yearbook
Brunei Business and Investment Opportunities Yearbook
Brunei Business and Investment Opportunities Yearbook Volume 1 Strategic Information and Opportunities
Brunei Business and Investment Opportunities Yearbook Volume 2 Leading Export-Import, Business, Investment Opportunities and Projects
Brunei Business Intelligence Report - Practical Information, Opportunities, Contacts
Brunei Business Intelligence Report - Practical Information, Opportunities, Contacts
Brunei Business Law Handbook - Strategic Information and Basic Laws
Brunei Business Law Handbook - Strategic Information and Basic Laws
Brunei Business Law Handbook - Strategic Information and Basic Laws
Brunei Business Law Handbook - Strategic Information and Basic Laws
Brunei Business Law Handbook Volume 1 Srategic Information and Basic Laws
Brunei Business Success Guide - Basic Practical Information and Contacts
Brunei Company Laws and Regulations Handbook
Brunei Constitution and Citizenship Laws Handbook - Strategic Information and Basic Laws
Brunei Country Study Guide - Strategic Information and Developments
Brunei Country Study Guide - Strategic Information and Developments
Brunei Country Study Guide - Strategic Information and Developments Volume 1 Strategic Information and Developments
Brunei Criminal Laws, Regulations and Procedures Handbook - Strategic Information, Regulations, Procedures
Brunei Customs, Export-Import Regulations, Incentives and Procedures Handbook - Strategic, Practical Information, Regulations
Brunei Customs, Trade Regulations and Procedures Handbook
Brunei Customs, Trade Regulations and Procedures Handbook
Brunei Darussalam Investment, Trade Strategy and Agreements Handbook - Strategic Information and Basic Agreements
Brunei Diplomatic Handbook - Strategic Information and Developments
Brunei Diplomatic Handbook - Strategic Information and Developments
Brunei Ecology & Nature Protection Handbook
Brunei Ecology & Nature Protection Handbook
Brunei Ecology & Nature Protection Laws and Regulation Handbook
Brunei Electoral, Political Parties Laws and Regulations Handbook - Strategic Information, Regulations, Procedures
Brunei Energy Policy, Laws and Regulation Handbook
Brunei Energy Policy, Laws and Regulations Handbook
Brunei Energy Policy, Laws and Regulations Handbook
Brunei Energy Policy, Laws and Regulations Handbook - Strategic Information, Policy, Regulations
Brunei Export-Import Trade and Business Directory
Brunei Export-Import Trade and Business Directory
Brunei Foreign Policy and Government Guide
Brunei Foreign Policy and Government Guide

TITLE
Brunei Immigration Laws and Regulations Handbook - Strategic Information and Basic Laws
Brunei Industrial and Business Directory
Brunei Industrial and Business Directory
Brunei Investment and Business Guide - Strategic and Practical Information
Brunei Investment and Business Guide - Strategic and Practical Information
Brunei Investment and Business Guide - Strategic and Practical Information
Brunei Investment and Business Guide - Strategic and Practical Information
Brunei Investment and Business Guide Volume 2 Business, Investment Opportunities and Incentives
Brunei Investment and Business Profile - Basic Information and Contacts for Succesful investment and Business Activity
Brunei Investment and Trade Laws and Regulations Handbook
Brunei Labor Laws and Regulations Handbook - Strategic Information and Basic Laws
Brunei Land Ownership and Agriculture Laws Handbook
Brunei Mineral & Mining Sector Investment and Business Guide - Strategic and Practical Information
Brunei Mineral & Mining Sector Investment and Business Guide - Strategic and Practical Information
Brunei Mineral, Mining Sector Investment and Business Guide - Strategic Information and Regulations
Brunei Mining Laws and Regulations Handbook
Brunei Oil & Gas Sector Business & Investment Opportunities Yearbook
Brunei Oil & Gas Sector Business & Investment Opportunities Yearbook
Brunei Oil and Gas Exploration Laws and Regulation Handbook
Brunei Recent Economic and Political Developments Yearbook
Brunei Recent Economic and Political Developments Yearbook
Brunei Recent Economic and Political Developments Yearbook
Brunei Starting Business (Incorporating) in....Guide
Brunei Sultan Haji Hassanal Bolkiah Mu'izzaddin Waddaulah Handbook
Brunei Sultan Haji Hassanal Bolkiah Mu'izzaddin Waddaulah Handbook
Brunei Tax Guide
Brunei Tax Guide
Brunei Tax Guide Volume 1 Strategic Information and Basic Regulations
Brunei Taxation Laws and Regulations Handbook
Brunei Telecommunication Industry Business Opportunities Handbook
Brunei Telecommunication Industry Business Opportunities Handbook
Brunei: Doing Business and Investing in ... Guide Volume 1 Strategic, Practical Information, Regulations, Contacts
Brunei: How to Invest, Start and Run Profitable Business in Brunei Guide - Practical Information, Opportunities, Contacts

BASIC LAWS AND REGULATIONS AFFECTING BUSINESS AND TRADE

COUTRY	LAW TITLE

Brunei	Admiralty Jurisdiction Act
Brunei	Advocates and Solicitors (Practice and Etiquette) Rules
Brunei	Advocates and Solicitors Rules
Brunei	Agricultural Pests and Noxious Plants
Brunei	Air Navigation Act
Brunei	Airport Passenger Service Charge Act
Brunei	Anti Terrorism (Financial and other Measure) Act
Brunei	Antiquities and Treasure Trove Act
Brunei	Application of Laws
Brunei	Arbitration Act
Brunei	Arms and Explosive Act
Brunei	Arms and Explosives Rules
Brunei	Asian Development Bank Act 2009
Brunei	Audit Act
Brunei	Banishment Act
Brunei	Banker's Book Act
Brunei	Banking Act
Brunei	Bankruptcy Act
Brunei	Bill of Sale Act
Brunei	Bills of Exchange Act
Brunei	Biological Weapons Act
Brunei	Bishop of Borneo Act
Brunei	Bretton Woods Agreement Act
Brunei	Broadcasting Act
Brunei	Brunei Board of Examination Act Brunei Economic Development Board Act
Brunei	Brunei Fishery Limits Act
Brunei	Brunei Investment Agency Act
Brunei	Brunei Malay Silversmiths Guild (Incorporation) Act
Brunei	Brunei National Archives Act
Brunei	Brunei Nationality Act
Brunei	Brunei Nationality Act Designation of Areas under Regulation 9
Brunei	Buffaloes Act
Brunei	Burial Grounds Act
Brunei	Business Name Act
Brunei	Censorship of Films and Public Entertainments Act
Brunei	Census Act
Brunei	Chinese Marriage Act
Brunei	Coin (Import and Export) Act
Brunei	Commission of Inquiry Act
Brunei	Commissioner for Oaths Act
Brunei	Common Gaming Houses Act
Brunei	Companies Act
Brunei	Computer Misuse Act
Brunei	Computer Misuse Order
Brunei	Constitution of Brunei

Brunei	Consular Relations Act
Brunei	Contract Act
Brunei	Cooperative Societies Act
Brunei	Criminal Appeal Rules
Brunei	Criminal Law Act
Brunei	Criminal Procedure Code
Brunei	Criminals Registration Act 2009
Brunei	Currency Act
Brunei	Customs Act
Brunei	Debtors Act
Brunei	Defamation Act
Brunei	Description of Land Act
Brunei	Diplomatic Privilege Act
Brunei	Disaffected and Dangerous Persons Act
Brunei	Dissolution of Marriage Act
Brunei	Dogs Act
Brunei	Education (Non-Government Schools) Act
Brunei	Election Offences Act
Brunei	Electricity Act
Brunei	Electronic Transaction Order
Brunei	Electronic Transactions Act
Brunei	Emblems and Names Act
Brunei	Emergency Regulations Act
Brunei	Employment Information Act
Brunei	Evidence Act
Brunei	Exchange Control Act
Brunei	Excise Act
Brunei	Extradition (Malaysia and Singapore) Act
Brunei	Extradition Act
Brunei	Fatal Accident and Personal Injuries Act
Brunei	Finance Companies Act
Brunei	Fire Service Act
Brunei	Fisheries Act
Brunei	Forest Act 2002
Brunei	Geneva and Red Cross Act
Brunei	Guardianship of Infants
Brunei	Immigration Act
Brunei	Income tax Act
Brunei	Intermediate Courts
Brunei	Internal Security Act
Brunei	Internationally Protected Persons Act
Brunei	Interpretation and General Clauses Act
Brunei	Intoxicating Substances Act
Brunei	Inventions Act
Brunei	Investments Incentives Act

Brunei	Islamic Banking Act
Brunei	Kidnapping Act
Brunei	Labor Act
Brunei	Land Acquisition Act
Brunei	Land Code Act
Brunei	Law Reform (Contributory Negligence) Act
Brunei	Law Revision Act
Brunei	Legal Profession (Practicing Certificate) Rules
Brunei	Legal Profession Act
Brunei	Licensed Land Surveyors Act
Brunei	Limitation Act
Brunei	Local Newspaper Act Official Secrets Act
Brunei	Marriage Act
Brunei	Married Women Act
Brunei	Medical Practitioners Dentists Act
Brunei	Merchandise Marks Act
Brunei	Mining Act
Brunei	Minor Offences Act
Brunei	Miscellaneous Licenses Act
Brunei	Misuse of Drugs Act
Brunei	Money-Changing and Remittance Businesses Act
Brunei	Moneylenders Act
Brunei	Monopolies Act
Brunei	Municipal Board Act
Brunei	National Bank of Brunei Act
Brunei	National Registration Regulations
Brunei	Nationality Registration Act
Brunei	Oaths and Affirmations
Brunei	Old Age and Disability Pensions Act
Brunei	Passport Act
Brunei	Pawnbrokers Act
Brunei	Penal Code
Brunei	Pensions Act
Brunei	Petroleum (Pipe-Lines) Act
Brunei	Petroleum Mining Act
Brunei	Petroleum Mining Act
Brunei	Poisons Act
Brunei	Post Office Act
Brunei	Powers of Attorney Act
Brunei	Preservation of Books Act
Brunei	Prevention of Corruption Act
Brunei	Price Control Act
Brunei	Prisons Act
Brunei	Probate and Administration Act
Brunei	Public Entertainment Act

Brunei	Public Health (Food)
Brunei	Public Officers (liability) Act
Brunei	Public Order Act
Brunei	Public Service Commission Act
Brunei	Quarantine and Prevention of Disease Act
Brunei	Reciprocal Enforcement of Foreign Judgments
Brunei	Registration of Adoptions Act
Brunei	Registration of Guests Act
Brunei	Registration of Marriages Act
Brunei	Religious Council and Kadis Court Act
Brunei	Road Traffic Act
Brunei	Royal Brunei Police Force Act
Brunei	Rubber Dealers Act
Brunei	Sale of Goods Act
Brunei	Second-Hand Dealers Act
Brunei	Security Agencies Act
Brunei	Sedition Act
Brunei	Societies Act
Brunei	Specific relief Act
Brunei	Stamp Act
Brunei	Statistics Act
Brunei	Statutory Declarations Act
Brunei	Subordinate Courts Act
Brunei	Subscriptions Control Act
Brunei	Summonses and Warrants (Special Provision) Act
Brunei	Supreme Court (Appeals to Privy Council) Act
Brunei	Supreme Court Act
Brunei	Syariah Courts
Brunei	Telecommunications Act
Brunei	Territorial Waters of Brunei Act
Brunei	Tokyo Convention
Brunei	Trade Disputes Act
Brunei	Trade Marks Act
Brunei	Trade Union Act
Brunei	Transfer of the Functions of the Minister of Law Act
Brunei	Travel Agents Act
Brunei	Trespass on Royal Property Act
Brunei	Undesirable Publications Act
Brunei	Unfair Contact Terms Act
Brunei	University Brunei Darussalam Act
Brunei	Unlawful Carnal Knowledge Act
Brunei	Vicar Apostolic of Kuching Act
Brunei	Water Supply Act
Brunei	Weights and Measure Act
Brunei	Wild Life Protection Act

Brunei	Wills Act
Brunei	Women and Girls Protection Act
Brunei	Workmen's Compensation Act
Brunei	Workmen's Unemployment Indemnity Act

WORLD CUSTOMS, EXPORT-IMPORT REGULATIONS, INCENTIVES AND PROCEDURES HANDBOOK - STRATEGIC, PRACTICAL INFORMATION, REGULATIONS LIBRARY

Belize Customs, Export-Import Regulations, Incentives and Procedures Handbook - Strategic, Practical Information, Regulations
Benin Customs, Export-Import Regulations, Incentives and Procedures Handbook - Strategic, Practical Information, Regulations
Bermuda Customs, Export-Import Regulations, Incentives and Procedures Handbook - Strategic, Practical Information, Regulations
Bhutan Customs, Export-Import Regulations, Incentives and Procedures Handbook - Strategic, Practical Information, Regulations
Bolivia Customs, Export-Import Regulations, Incentives and Procedures Handbook - Strategic, Practical Information, Regulations
Bosnia and Herzegovina Customs, Export-Import Regulations, Incentives and Procedures Handbook - Strategic, Practical Information, Regulations
Botswana Customs, Export-Import Regulations, Incentives and Procedures Handbook - Strategic, Practical Information, Regulations
Brazil Customs, Export-Import Regulations, Incentives and Procedures Handbook - Strategic, Practical Information, Regulations
Brunei Customs, Export-Import Regulations, Incentives and Procedures Handbook - Strategic, Practical Information, Regulations
Bulgaria Customs, Export-Import Regulations, Incentives and Procedures Handbook - Strategic, Practical Information, Regulations
Burkina Faso Customs, Export-Import Regulations, Incentives and Procedures Handbook - Strategic, Practical Information, Regulations
Burundi Customs, Export-Import Regulations, Incentives and Procedures Handbook - Strategic, Practical Information, Regulations
Cambodia Customs, Export-Import Regulations, Incentives and Procedures Handbook - Strategic, Practical Information, Regulations
Cameroon Customs, Export-Import Regulations, Incentives and Procedures Handbook - Strategic, Practical Information, Regulations
Canada Customs, Export-Import Regulations, Incentives and Procedures Handbook - Strategic, Practical Information, Regulations
Cape Verde Customs, Export-Import Regulations, Incentives and Procedures Handbook - Strategic, Practical Information, Regulations
Cayman Islands Customs, Export-Import Regulations, Incentives and Procedures Handbook - Strategic, Practical Information, Regulations
Central African Republic Customs, Export-Import Regulations, Incentives and Procedures Handbook - Strategic, Practical Information, Regulations
Chad Customs, Export-Import Regulations, Incentives and Procedures Handbook - Strategic, Practical Information, Regulations
Chile Customs, Export-Import Regulations, Incentives and Procedures Handbook - Strategic, Practical Information, Regulations
China Customs, Export-Import Regulations, Incentives and Procedures Handbook - Strategic, Practical Information, Regulations
Colombia Customs, Export-Import Regulations, Incentives and Procedures Handbook - Strategic, Practical Information, Regulations
Comoros Customs, Export-Import Regulations, Incentives and Procedures Handbook - Strategic, Practical Information, Regulations
Congo Customs, Export-Import Regulations, Incentives and Procedures Handbook - Strategic, Practical Information, Regulations
Congo, Democratic Republic Customs, Export-Import Regulations, Incentives and Procedures Handbook - Strategic, Practical Information, Regulations
Cook Islands Customs, Export-Import Regulations, Incentives and Procedures Handbook - Strategic, Practical Information, Regulations
Costa Rica Customs, Export-Import Regulations, Incentives and Procedures Handbook - Strategic, Practical Information, Regulations
Cote d'Ivoire Customs, Export-Import Regulations, Incentives and Procedures Handbook - Strategic, Practical Information, Regulations
Croatia Customs, Export-Import Regulations, Incentives and Procedures Handbook - Strategic, Practical Information, Regulations
Cuba Customs, Export-Import Regulations, Incentives and Procedures Handbook - Strategic, Practical Information, Regulations
Cyprus Customs, Export-Import Regulations, Incentives and Procedures Handbook - Strategic, Practical Information,

Regulations
Czech Republic Customs, Export-Import Regulations, Incentives and Procedures Handbook - Strategic, Practical Information, Regulations
Denmark Customs, Export-Import Regulations, Incentives and Procedures Handbook - Strategic, Practical Information, Regulations
Djibouti Customs, Export-Import Regulations, Incentives and Procedures Handbook - Strategic, Practical Information, Regulations
Dominica Customs, Export-Import Regulations, Incentives and Procedures Handbook - Strategic, Practical Information, Regulations
Dominican Republic Customs, Export-Import Regulations, Incentives and Procedures Handbook - Strategic, Practical Information, Regulations
Ecuador Customs, Export-Import Regulations, Incentives and Procedures Handbook - Strategic, Practical Information, Regulations
Egypt Customs, Export-Import Regulations, Incentives and Procedures Handbook - Strategic, Practical Information, Regulations
El Salvador Customs, Export-Import Regulations, Incentives and Procedures Handbook - Strategic, Practical Information, Regulations
Equatorial Guinea Customs, Export-Import Regulations, Incentives and Procedures Handbook - Strategic, Practical Information, Regulations
Eritrea Customs, Export-Import Regulations, Incentives and Procedures Handbook - Strategic, Practical Information, Regulations
Estonia Customs, Export-Import Regulations, Incentives and Procedures Handbook - Strategic, Practical Information, Regulations
Ethiopia Customs, Export-Import Regulations, Incentives and Procedures Handbook - Strategic, Practical Information, Regulations
Fiji Customs, Export-Import Regulations, Incentives and Procedures Handbook - Strategic, Practical Information, Regulations
Finland Customs, Export-Import Regulations, Incentives and Procedures Handbook - Strategic, Practical Information, Regulations
France Customs, Export-Import Regulations, Incentives and Procedures Handbook - Strategic, Practical Information, Regulations
Gabon Customs, Export-Import Regulations, Incentives and Procedures Handbook - Strategic, Practical Information, Regulations
Gambia Customs, Export-Import Regulations, Incentives and Procedures Handbook - Strategic, Practical Information, Regulations
Georgia Republic Customs, Export-Import Regulations, Incentives and Procedures Handbook - Strategic, Practical Information, Regulations
Germany Customs, Export-Import Regulations, Incentives and Procedures Handbook - Strategic, Practical Information, Regulations
Ghana Customs, Export-Import Regulations, Incentives and Procedures Handbook - Strategic, Practical Information, Regulations
Gibraltar Customs, Export-Import Regulations, Incentives and Procedures Handbook - Strategic, Practical Information, Regulations
Greece Customs, Export-Import Regulations, Incentives and Procedures Handbook - Strategic, Practical Information, Regulations
Greenland Customs, Export-Import Regulations, Incentives and Procedures Handbook - Strategic, Practical Information, Regulations
Grenada Customs, Export-Import Regulations, Incentives and Procedures Handbook - Strategic, Practical Information, Regulations
Guatemala Customs, Export-Import Regulations, Incentives and Procedures Handbook - Strategic, Practical Information, Regulations
Guernsey Customs, Export-Import Regulations, Incentives and Procedures Handbook - Strategic, Practical Information, Regulations
Guinea Customs, Export-Import Regulations, Incentives and Procedures Handbook - Strategic, Practical Information, Regulations
Guinea-Bissau Customs, Export-Import Regulations, Incentives and Procedures Handbook - Strategic, Practical Information, Regulations
Guyana Customs, Export-Import Regulations, Incentives and Procedures Handbook - Strategic, Practical Information, Regulations
Haiti Customs, Export-Import Regulations, Incentives and Procedures Handbook - Strategic, Practical Information, Regulations

Honduras Customs, Export-Import Regulations, Incentives and Procedures Handbook - Strategic, Practical Information, Regulations
Hungary Customs, Export-Import Regulations, Incentives and Procedures Handbook - Strategic, Practical Information, Regulations
Iceland Customs, Export-Import Regulations, Incentives and Procedures Handbook - Strategic, Practical Information, Regulations
India Customs, Export-Import Regulations, Incentives and Procedures Handbook - Strategic, Practical Information, Regulations
Indonesia Customs, Export-Import Regulations, Incentives and Procedures Handbook - Strategic, Practical Information, Regulations
Iran Customs, Export-Import Regulations, Incentives and Procedures Handbook - Strategic, Practical Information, Regulations
Iraq Customs, Export-Import Regulations, Incentives and Procedures Handbook - Strategic, Practical Information, Regulations
Ireland Customs, Export-Import Regulations, Incentives and Procedures Handbook - Strategic, Practical Information, Regulations
Isle of Man Customs, Export-Import Regulations, Incentives and Procedures Handbook - Strategic, Practical Information, Regulations
Israel Customs, Export-Import Regulations, Incentives and Procedures Handbook - Strategic, Practical Information, Regulations
Italy Customs, Export-Import Regulations, Incentives and Procedures Handbook - Strategic, Practical Information, Regulations
Jamaica Customs, Export-Import Regulations, Incentives and Procedures Handbook - Strategic, Practical Information, Regulations
Japan Customs, Export-Import Regulations, Incentives and Procedures Handbook - Strategic, Practical Information, Regulations
Jordan Customs, Export-Import Regulations, Incentives and Procedures Handbook - Strategic, Practical Information, Regulations
Kazakhstan Customs, Export-Import Regulations, Incentives and Procedures Handbook - Strategic, Practical Information, Regulations
Kenya Customs, Export-Import Regulations, Incentives and Procedures Handbook - Strategic, Practical Information, Regulations
Kiribati Customs, Export-Import Regulations, Incentives and Procedures Handbook - Strategic, Practical Information, Regulations
Korea, North Customs, Export-Import Regulations, Incentives and Procedures Handbook - Strategic, Practical Information, Regulations
Korea, South Customs, Export-Import Regulations, Incentives and Procedures Handbook - Strategic, Practical Information, Regulations
Kosovo Customs, Export-Import Regulations, Incentives and Procedures Handbook - Strategic, Practical Information, Regulations
Kuwait Customs, Export-Import Regulations, Incentives and Procedures Handbook - Strategic, Practical Information, Regulations
Kyrgyzstan Customs, Export-Import Regulations, Incentives and Procedures Handbook - Strategic, Practical Information, Regulations
Laos Customs, Export-Import Regulations, Incentives and Procedures Handbook - Strategic, Practical Information, Regulations
Latvia Customs, Export-Import Regulations, Incentives and Procedures Handbook - Strategic, Practical Information, Regulations
Lebanon Customs, Export-Import Regulations, Incentives and Procedures Handbook - Strategic, Practical Information, Regulations
Lesotho Customs, Export-Import Regulations, Incentives and Procedures Handbook - Strategic, Practical Information, Regulations
Liberia Customs, Export-Import Regulations, Incentives and Procedures Handbook - Strategic, Practical Information, Regulations
Libya Customs, Export-Import Regulations, Incentives and Procedures Handbook - Strategic, Practical Information, Regulations
Lithuania Customs, Export-Import Regulations, Incentives and Procedures Handbook - Strategic, Practical Information, Regulations
Macao Customs, Export-Import Regulations, Incentives and Procedures Handbook - Strategic, Practical Information, Regulations
Macedonia Customs, Export-Import Regulations, Incentives and Procedures Handbook - Strategic, Practical Information,

Regulations
Madagascar Customs, Export-Import Regulations, Incentives and Procedures Handbook - Strategic, Practical Information, Regulations
Madeira Customs, Export-Import Regulations, Incentives and Procedures Handbook - Strategic, Practical Information, Regulations
Malawi Customs, Export-Import Regulations, Incentives and Procedures Handbook - Strategic, Practical Information, Regulations
Malaysia Customs, Export-Import Regulations, Incentives and Procedures Handbook - Strategic, Practical Information, Regulations
Maldives Customs, Export-Import Regulations, Incentives and Procedures Handbook - Strategic, Practical Information, Regulations
Mali Customs, Export-Import Regulations, Incentives and Procedures Handbook - Strategic, Practical Information, Regulations
Malta Customs, Export-Import Regulations, Incentives and Procedures Handbook - Strategic, Practical Information, Regulations
Marshall Islands Customs, Export-Import Regulations, Incentives and Procedures Handbook - Strategic, Practical Information, Regulations
Mauritania Customs, Export-Import Regulations, Incentives and Procedures Handbook - Strategic, Practical Information, Regulations
Mauritius Customs, Export-Import Regulations, Incentives and Procedures Handbook - Strategic, Practical Information, Regulations
Mexico Customs, Export-Import Regulations, Incentives and Procedures Handbook - Strategic, Practical Information, Regulations
Micronesia Customs, Export-Import Regulations, Incentives and Procedures Handbook - Strategic, Practical Information, Regulations
Moldova Customs, Export-Import Regulations, Incentives and Procedures Handbook - Strategic, Practical Information, Regulations
Monaco Customs, Export-Import Regulations, Incentives and Procedures Handbook - Strategic, Practical Information, Regulations
Mongolia Customs, Export-Import Regulations, Incentives and Procedures Handbook - Strategic, Practical Information, Regulations
Morocco Customs, Export-Import Regulations, Incentives and Procedures Handbook - Strategic, Practical Information, Regulations
Mozambique Customs, Export-Import Regulations, Incentives and Procedures Handbook - Strategic, Practical Information, Regulations
Myanmar Customs, Export-Import Regulations, Incentives and Procedures Handbook - Strategic, Practical Information, Regulations
Namibia Customs, Export-Import Regulations, Incentives and Procedures Handbook - Strategic, Practical Information, Regulations
Nauru Customs, Export-Import Regulations, Incentives and Procedures Handbook - Strategic, Practical Information, Regulations
Nepal Customs, Export-Import Regulations, Incentives and Procedures Handbook - Strategic, Practical Information, Regulations
Netherlands Customs, Export-Import Regulations, Incentives and Procedures Handbook - Strategic, Practical Information, Regulations
New Caledonia Customs, Export-Import Regulations, Incentives and Procedures Handbook - Strategic, Practical Information, Regulations
New Zealand Customs, Export-Import Regulations, Incentives and Procedures Handbook - Strategic, Practical Information, Regulations
Nicaragua Customs, Export-Import Regulations, Incentives and Procedures Handbook - Strategic, Practical Information, Regulations
Niger Customs, Export-Import Regulations, Incentives and Procedures Handbook - Strategic, Practical Information, Regulations
Nigeria Customs, Export-Import Regulations, Incentives and Procedures Handbook - Strategic, Practical Information, Regulations
Northern Mariana Islands Customs, Export-Import Regulations, Incentives and Procedures Handbook - Strategic, Practical Information, Regulations
Norway Customs, Export-Import Regulations, Incentives and Procedures Handbook - Strategic, Practical Information, Regulations
Oman Customs, Export-Import Regulations, Incentives and Procedures Handbook - Strategic, Practical Information, Regulations

Pakistan Customs, Export-Import Regulations, Incentives and Procedures Handbook - Strategic, Practical Information, Regulations
Palau Customs, Export-Import Regulations, Incentives and Procedures Handbook - Strategic, Practical Information, Regulations
Palestine Customs, Export-Import Regulations, Incentives and Procedures Handbook - Strategic, Practical Information, Regulations
Panama Customs, Export-Import Regulations, Incentives and Procedures Handbook - Strategic, Practical Information, Regulations
Papua New Guinea Customs, Export-Import Regulations, Incentives and Procedures Handbook - Strategic, Practical Information, Regulations
Paraguay Customs, Export-Import Regulations, Incentives and Procedures Handbook - Strategic, Practical Information, Regulations
Peru Customs, Export-Import Regulations, Incentives and Procedures Handbook - Strategic, Practical Information, Regulations
Philippines Customs, Export-Import Regulations, Incentives and Procedures Handbook - Strategic, Practical Information, Regulations
Pitcairn Islands Customs, Export-Import Regulations, Incentives and Procedures Handbook - Strategic, Practical Information, Regulations
Poland Customs, Export-Import Regulations, Incentives and Procedures Handbook - Strategic, Practical Information, Regulations
Polynesia French Customs, Export-Import Regulations, Incentives and Procedures Handbook - Strategic, Practical Information, Regulations
Portugal Customs, Export-Import Regulations, Incentives and Procedures Handbook - Strategic, Practical Information, Regulations
Qatar Customs, Export-Import Regulations, Incentives and Procedures Handbook - Strategic, Practical Information, Regulations
Romania Customs, Export-Import Regulations, Incentives and Procedures Handbook - Strategic, Practical Information, Regulations
Russia Customs, Export-Import Regulations, Incentives and Procedures Handbook - Strategic, Practical Information, Regulations
Rwanda Customs, Export-Import Regulations, Incentives and Procedures Handbook - Strategic, Practical Information, Regulations
Saint Kitts and Nevis Customs, Export-Import Regulations, Incentives and Procedures Handbook - Strategic, Practical Information, Regulations
Saint Lucia Customs, Export-Import Regulations, Incentives and Procedures Handbook - Strategic, Practical Information, Regulations
Saint Vincent and The Grenadines Customs, Export-Import Regulations, Incentives and Procedures Handbook - Strategic, Practical Information, Regulations
Samoa (American) Customs, Export-Import Regulations, Incentives and Procedures Handbook - Strategic, Practical Information, Regulations
Samoa (Western) Customs, Export-Import Regulations, Incentives and Procedures Handbook - Strategic, Practical Information, Regulations
San Marino Customs, Export-Import Regulations, Incentives and Procedures Handbook - Strategic, Practical Information, Regulations
Sao Tome and Principe Customs, Export-Import Regulations, Incentives and Procedures Handbook - Strategic, Practical Information, Regulations
Saudi Arabia Customs, Export-Import Regulations, Incentives and Procedures Handbook - Strategic, Practical Information, Regulations
Scotland Customs, Export-Import Regulations, Incentives and Procedures Handbook - Strategic, Practical Information, Regulations
Senegal Customs, Export-Import Regulations, Incentives and Procedures Handbook - Strategic, Practical Information, Regulations
Serbia Customs, Export-Import Regulations, Incentives and Procedures Handbook - Strategic, Practical Information, Regulations
Seychelles Customs, Export-Import Regulations, Incentives and Procedures Handbook - Strategic, Practical Information, Regulations
Sierra Leone Customs, Export-Import Regulations, Incentives and Procedures Handbook - Strategic, Practical Information, Regulations
Singapore Customs, Export-Import Regulations, Incentives and Procedures Handbook - Strategic, Practical Information, Regulations
Slovakia Customs, Export-Import Regulations, Incentives and Procedures Handbook - Strategic, Practical Information,

Regulations
Slovenia Customs, Export-Import Regulations, Incentives and Procedures Handbook - Strategic, Practical Information, Regulations
Solomon Islands Customs, Export-Import Regulations, Incentives and Procedures Handbook - Strategic, Practical Information, Regulations
Somalia Customs, Export-Import Regulations, Incentives and Procedures Handbook - Strategic, Practical Information, Regulations
South Africa Customs, Export-Import Regulations, Incentives and Procedures Handbook - Strategic, Practical Information, Regulations
Spain Customs, Export-Import Regulations, Incentives and Procedures Handbook - Strategic, Practical Information, Regulations
Sri Lanka Customs, Export-Import Regulations, Incentives and Procedures Handbook - Strategic, Practical Information, Regulations
St. Helena Customs, Export-Import Regulations, Incentives and Procedures Handbook - Strategic, Practical Information, Regulations
St. Pierre & Miquelon Customs, Export-Import Regulations, Incentives and Procedures Handbook - Strategic, Practical Information, Regulations
Sudan Customs, Export-Import Regulations, Incentives and Procedures Handbook - Strategic, Practical Information, Regulations
Sudan South Customs, Export-Import Regulations, Incentives and Procedures Handbook - Strategic, Practical Information, Regulations
Suriname Customs, Export-Import Regulations, Incentives and Procedures Handbook - Strategic, Practical Information, Regulations
Swaziland Customs, Export-Import Regulations, Incentives and Procedures Handbook - Strategic, Practical Information, Regulations
Sweden Customs, Export-Import Regulations, Incentives and Procedures Handbook - Strategic, Practical Information, Regulations
Switzerland Customs, Export-Import Regulations, Incentives and Procedures Handbook - Strategic, Practical Information, Regulations
Syria Customs, Export-Import Regulations, Incentives and Procedures Handbook - Strategic, Practical Information, Regulations
Taiwan Customs, Export-Import Regulations, Incentives and Procedures Handbook - Strategic, Practical Information, Regulations
Tajikistan Customs, Export-Import Regulations, Incentives and Procedures Handbook - Strategic, Practical Information, Regulations
Tanzania Customs, Export-Import Regulations, Incentives and Procedures Handbook - Strategic, Practical Information, Regulations
Thailand Customs, Export-Import Regulations, Incentives and Procedures Handbook - Strategic, Practical Information, Regulations
Togo Customs, Export-Import Regulations, Incentives and Procedures Handbook - Strategic, Practical Information, Regulations
Tonga Customs, Export-Import Regulations, Incentives and Procedures Handbook - Strategic, Practical Information, Regulations
Trinidad and Tobago Customs, Export-Import Regulations, Incentives and Procedures Handbook - Strategic, Practical Information, Regulations
Tunisia Customs, Export-Import Regulations, Incentives and Procedures Handbook - Strategic, Practical Information, Regulations
Turkey Customs, Export-Import Regulations, Incentives and Procedures Handbook - Strategic, Practical Information, Regulations
Turkmenistan Customs, Export-Import Regulations, Incentives and Procedures Handbook - Strategic, Practical Information, Regulations
Turks & Caicos Customs, Export-Import Regulations, Incentives and Procedures Handbook - Strategic, Practical Information, Regulations
Tuvalu Customs, Export-Import Regulations, Incentives and Procedures Handbook - Strategic, Practical Information, Regulations
Uganda Customs, Export-Import Regulations, Incentives and Procedures Handbook - Strategic, Practical Information, Regulations
Ukraine Customs, Export-Import Regulations, Incentives and Procedures Handbook - Strategic, Practical Information, Regulations
United Arab Emirates Customs, Export-Import Regulations, Incentives and Procedures Handbook - Strategic, Practical Information, Regulations

United Kingdom Customs, Export-Import Regulations, Incentives and Procedures Handbook - Strategic, Practical Information, Regulations
United States Customs, Export-Import Regulations, Incentives and Procedures Handbook - Strategic, Practical Information, Regulations
Uruguay Customs, Export-Import Regulations, Incentives and Procedures Handbook - Strategic, Practical Information, Regulations
Uzbekistan Customs, Export-Import Regulations, Incentives and Procedures Handbook - Strategic, Practical Information, Regulations
Vanuatu Customs, Export-Import Regulations, Incentives and Procedures Handbook - Strategic, Practical Information, Regulations
Vatican City Customs, Export-Import Regulations, Incentives and Procedures Handbook - Strategic, Practical Information, Regulations
Venezuela Customs, Export-Import Regulations, Incentives and Procedures Handbook - Strategic, Practical Information, Regulations
Vietnam Customs, Export-Import Regulations, Incentives and Procedures Handbook - Strategic, Practical Information, Regulations
Virgin Islands, British Customs, Export-Import Regulations, Incentives and Procedures Handbook - Strategic, Practical Information, Regulations
Wake Atoll Customs, Export-Import Regulations, Incentives and Procedures Handbook - Strategic, Practical Information, Regulations
Yemen Customs, Export-Import Regulations, Incentives and Procedures Handbook - Strategic, Practical Information, Regulations
Zambia Customs, Export-Import Regulations, Incentives and Procedures Handbook - Strategic, Practical Information, Regulations
Zimbabwe Customs, Export-Import Regulations, Incentives and Procedures Handbook - Strategic, Practical Information, Regulations